Hawkwin

Sonic Assassins

Ian Abrahams

Lumoni Press

First Published in 2004
By SAF Publishing Ltd

This Revised and Updated Edition Published in 2017
(In eBook in 2016)
By Lumoni Press through CreateSpace

lumonipress.blogspot.co.uk
lumonipress@gmail.com

ISBN 978-1542379038

Cover Image of Dave Brock by Oz Hardwick

Dedication

For the members of the Redruth Comprehensive School lunchtime record
club, circa 1978:

Robert Bennetts
Mark Vinson
Simon Coley
Tim Stevens
David Pascoe
William Rudd (RIP)

Also Available by Ian Abrahams:

Strange Boat: Mike Scott & The Waterboys

Lumoni Press (eBook)
Gonzo Multimedia (Print)

Also Available by Ian Abrahams & Bridget Wishart:

Festivalized: Music, Politics & Alternative Culture

Lumoni Press (eBook)
Gonzo Multimedia (Print)

Table of Contents

Introduction and Acknowledgements

Over the years since the original edition of this book was published by SAF Publishing I've had many emails enquiring about a second edition. Sometimes I've been enthusiastic about producing an updated volume and sometimes simply wanted to move on from it, but it does seem to be the case that many readers enjoyed the first edition and I'm both touched and amazed by the requests for a new version.

Over that time, I never lost my ingrained passion for the work of Hawkwind and the myriad musicians that have passed through the ranks of the band, "adding their bits" as Dave Brock would say. Indeed, through my *Spacerock Reviews* blog I've had the pleasure of reviewing material by the band and its former members and by the many musicians across the world that have been influenced and informed by their music and ethos. But I've looked back on the book with mixed emotions. In one way, I'm very proud of what I achieved – the first commercially available biography of a band whose reach has spread through multiple musical genres. In another, I'm frustrated by the errors that the original contained and as a now more experienced writer, by some of the phrasing and assumptions made in the first edition's text. This new edition is an opportunity to address some of those issues.

I approached the new edition as a complete top to bottom rewrite of the text and through that saw the original lacking in two particular ways. Firstly, many reviewers noted the dispassionate way I assembled my interview and research material, letting the protagonists tell the story without injecting my voice, as the author and as a fan. On revisiting the book, I found it somewhat clinical and cold for that very reason and so this new version finds its author being more objective about his own feelings on albums and events and I hope from that perspective it's a more thoughtful read this time around, even if readers don't agree with my own assessment of the Hawkwind canon's highs and lows. Secondly, and more importantly, I found that each era's stories were largely told from the point of view of the membership of the day and the overarching 'voice' of Dave Brock himself became lost a few times. I've tried to address this as best I can this time around.

Since the first edition arrived, I've written extensively on Hawkwind and associated musicians not only on my blog but for the music press as well. Among these, I produced two substantial features for *Record Collector* magazine on Hawkwind and spacerock (issues 339 and 360) as well as a feature on the free festival bands of the 1980s (issue 404), all of which are still available from the publisher [recordcollectormag.com]. For these features, I variously re-interviewed some members whom I'd spoken to previously and talked to their long-time but now former manager Douglas Smith. Where I've included quotes sourced from these interviews to add to the text here, I've noted doing so. I also interviewed more recently, Dave Brock, Marion Lloyd-Langton and Dick Taylor for a feature on the eponymous first Hawkwind album, which appeared in a special edition of *Shindig!*, entitled *Interstellar Overdrive*. Though of course that interview informed my revision of the relevant chapter here, with one minor exception I've not quoted from this feature as its publication is contemporary with the release of this second edition and to 'double-dip' from that would be unfair and wrong. I whole heartedly commend this publication, edited with passion and skill by Austin Matthews, to anyone interested in spacerock, and at the time of writing it is available to purchase from the publishers [shindig-magazine.com].

Following on from *Sonic Assassins*, SAF published my book on Mike Scott and The Waterboys, *Strange Boat*, which appeared in 2007, and commissioned a book about the free festivals by myself and Bridget Wishart, *Festivalized – Music, Politics, Alternative Culture*. This book eventually appeared in 2015 through Gonzo Multimedia in print and via my own eBook imprint, Lumoni Press. Of course, in compiling the interviews for that book, material was gathered that was also suitable for use here. Some of the interview quotes from 90s Hawkwind member Jerry Richards hail from this source, and from another interview conducted for a speculative feature that didn't see the light of day in print, alongside new interview material for this book, and quotes from, among others, Adrian Shaw [who also kindly gave time to the original text], and the late Mick Farren also hail from this source.

Mick Farren wasn't the only person quoted here at length to be sadly no longer with us. I never met Jason Stuart, who joined the band after the original book was written, and has since passed away, and so regretfully he doesn't appear in this text. But I did interview Huw Lloyd-Langton for the original edition and was very sad when this great musician lost his battle with cancer in December 2012. I was privileged to write an account of his life for *The Independent* newspaper which appeared in their Obituaries of 12th December and which can still be found, at the time of writing, online [http://tinyurl.com/belevw2]. And I must mention the sad passing also of photographer Roger Hutchinson, who kindly provided wonderful pictures of the Stonehenge and Windsor free festivals, and Val Richardson who, along with her husband Rik, provided some of the terrific later-era pictures in the original edition.

I must repeat my thanks to the people who contributed either to the original edition or this one: Dave Anderson, Steve Bagley, Harvey Bainbridge, Jello Biafra, Tim Blake, Dave and Kris Brock, Michael Butterworth, Richard Chadwick, John Cowell, Thomas Crimble, Alan and Sarah Davey, Del Dettmar, Mr. Dibs, Phil Franks, David Gates, Frenchy Gloder, Tommy Grenas, Oz Hardwick, Scott Heller, Niall Hone, Sophie Knight, Jim Lascko, Huw Lloyd-Langton, Marion Lloyd-Langton, Michael Moorcock, Roger Neville-Neil, P!KN!K, Peter Pavli, Alan Powell, Peter Pracownik, Steve Pond, Paul Rudolph, Mick Slattery, Marc Sperhauk, Phil Reeves, Jerry Richards, Adrian Shaw, Steve Swindells, Scott Telles, Ron Tree, Nik Turner, Kingsley Ward, Bridget Wishart, and Matthew Wright. Other people expressed interest in contributing, and where I didn't, through time constraints, take up their generous offers, I apologise and appreciate their kind interest.

For their advice, encouragement, support and, not least, for commissioning the original edition of this book, and so getting me properly started as an author and journalist, I again thank Dave Hallbery and Mick Fish of SAF Publishing.

Regarding that first edition, I must echo my thanks to Keith Kniveton for his kind assistance, encyclopaedic knowledge and thoughtful insights at many stages in the original text. For their support and help back then, I again thank Colin J. Allen and, from Jello Biafra's office, Allison McBride. My appreciation also goes, then and now, to Fee Mercury Moon for her generosity in arranging and conducting the interview with Ron Tree for the original text. For the information on the background to the *Top of the Pops* broadcast of 'Silver Machine' I am indebted to contributors on the excellent Missing Episodes discussion forum, notably Laurence Piper. Thanks to "gwshark" for permission to quote from his extensive Festivals website, *The Archive*; to Jerry Kranitz for the use of text from *Aural Innovations*, Steve Youles for *Starfarer*, and David Law for the *Hawkwind Museum*. I appreciate the support of Jez Dacombe, who kindly made available his extensive cuttings archive. In addition, the work of Jon Price and Derek Whitaker in making historic music press articles available on their websites proved invaluable, and I thank them both for their help in prioritising the upload of specific cuttings on request. I also thank Paul Bagley, Andy Hemingway and Harry Ripley for their help in finding press clippings and fanzine articles. I am indebted, now and then, to the generosity of Jonathon Green for access to, and permission to quote from, the extensive research compiled for his seminal book *Days in the Life: Voices from the English Underground, 1961-1971*. Quotes from Douglas Smith, unless otherwise noted, derived from this source, other extracts are as noted in the text.

Over the years, the task of committing the story of Hawkwind to the printed page has fallen on the shoulders of dedicated fanzine editors such as Brian Tawn, Trevor Hughes and Adrian Parr. I wanted to write my own account of Hawkwind, and so I avoided contacting these luminaries back then, though I've made the acquaintance of both Trevor and Brian since, and only researched from specific articles as noted in the text. Their work in developing an archive of writings about the band cannot be underestimated. At the same time, I read and absorbed many contemporary music press articles, and whilst again I have noted these in the book, I would in particular acknowledge the writings of Andrew Means, Nick Kent, Paul Morley, David Tibet, Geoff Barton, Allan Jones, Malcolm Dome and Martin Hayman. While I worked on the original edition, the great music journalist Carol Clerk was compiling her work on the band, *The Saga of Hawkwind* [Omnibus Press]. Carol contacted me during the writing of her book and after our volumes were both published and was very kind to this writer who was starting out in music journalism. I often say that my main journalistic claim to fame was enjoying a boozy liquid lunch in a Soho pub with Carol, who made me feel like a proper writer when she could have dismissed me as an enthusiastic amateur. Carol is no longer with us, and music writing is much poorer for that.

I must again take this opportunity to thank the various people who over the years have been a part of my interest in Hawkwind, including Scott Abraham, Simon Coley, Andrew Dunn, Arin Komins, Nick Lee, Stephe Lindas, Phil McConnetty, Stuart Miller, Richard Pascoe, Bernhard Pospiech, Rob Pullan, Chris Purdon, Les Ratcliffe, Alan Taylor, Filip ("I've got 241 versions of 'Silver Machine'") Vanhuyse, and Rich Warren among them. A grateful nod goes to the assembled members of the BOC-L and Yahoo Hawkwind discussion groups, in particular the postings of Keith Henderson, Mike Holmes, Alisa Coral, Bob Lennon, Darrin McKeehan, Doug Pearson, Jon Jarrett, Jill Strobridge and the much-missed Larry Boyd. Any errors in the text are mine and mine alone. During the writing of the first edition, I also appreciated the kind support and encouragement of Alan Linsley, who was another 'beyond the call of duty' friend, Kerren Davcy, Ben Fagin, and Alan Taylor, while one of my oldest friends, Keith Topping, was instrumental in supporting and guiding the bashing into shape of my unwieldy and novice-like original manuscript.

Ian Abrahams
Redruth, Cornwall
Autumn 2016

1

Tent '67 and The Famous Cure

**Dave Brock, with banjo
(Collection of Dave Brock)**

That Dave Brock always enjoyed a catholic taste in music seems undeniable from his pre-Hawkwind days. That this eclecticism would develop into an enthusiasm for experimental electronica is harder to discern from the traditional jazz and blues that he performed in his early career. Born on 20th August, 1941 he spent his childhood in Feltham, Middlesex, attending Longfield Secondary Modern School, in Tatchbrook Road. For Britain, these were grey, austere years, the depravations of the Second World War lingering into the 1950s. Though his parents were not musical, Brock found a mentor within his immediate family circle, his Uncle Maurice: "He was my dad's brother; a pianist in a band in Buckinghamshire and a choirmaster. He was a major influence on me. He gave my dad a banjo, which I started to play when I was around twelve or thirteen." Brock's parents responded to this interest and bought him a guitar.

"My art teacher, Mr. Dyson, was a banjo player in a traditional jazz band. Me and my mate, Alan, were very keen on jazz and blues and Mr. Dyson was pleased to show us the chords, he used to write them down for us – 'off you go!'." At the same time, Brock was furthering his musical education with the records of the day. "I had an old wind-up record player and bought the odd 78rpm out of my pocket money." The first disc he purchased was 'African Queen' by Sandy Brown's Jazz Band, only to find, in enduring parental style, his mother demanding to know why he was buying that "awful music?"

"My first musical influences were Fats Domino, 'Bad Penny Blues' by Humphrey Lyttleton, on Parlophone Records, which I saved up to buy, and 'The Man with the Golden Arm' by the Billy May Orchestra." These recordings started Brock's life-long passion for jazz and blues, "they spurred me on." He started taking guitar lessons, playing until "I got sore fingers."

Dave left school in 1959, having stayed an extra year to get his GCSE qualifications. He took a few odd-jobs, "picked potatoes... for a day" before settling into his first regular position, with Minimax, a factory that made fire extinguishers. He was employed as an apprentice capstan-setter, "an awful, boring job." At that time "if you got a good apprenticeship you were made for life – you'd be there sixty years and get your gold watch!" he notes, wryly. For anybody with a creative aspect to their personality, this was not the way to spend their days. "I used to sit on this bloody machine, capstans going back and forward, drilling these little brass things out. I was forever graunching the tools – off in a daydream." He persevered with this job for a year before leaving to work at Larkin Studios, an animation company, in Mayfair, London.

Founded by Bill Larkin in 1949, his studio had an atmosphere much more in line with Brock's aspirations, "all very bohemian – a wonderful place to work." It was regarded as an innovative studio, where the stated intention was to combine the American comic-strip with Modern Art. Brock had, at that point, no specific intention toward a musical career, but for a few months in 1959 played in a band, the Gravier Street Stompers. This ensemble played a New Orleans style of jazz; seen as the vanguard of the 'purist' approach to jazz playing. More 'modernist' enthusiasts congregated at Ronnie Scott's in Gerrard Street.

He was by now regularly travelling to the dark and dingy basement jazz clubs of London, some of the fifteen hundred small clubs which thrived around Britain at the end of the 50s. "I used to go to Cy Laurie's, in Windmill Street, a seedy venue." This disturbed his parents. "If they found out they'd be asking me 'why are you going down to those horrible clubs', because I was only about sixteen, and you had to be eighteen to get in."

In his biography of Rolling Stone legend Keith Richards, Victor Bockris surveyed the musical scene at the end of the decade: "British jazz, always something of a dubious notion anyway, was dying. The pop field was weak. Folk was strong, but not showing signs of growth." The time was ripe for change, fermented by the emerging strands of the 1960s. Bockris goes on to describe how "people began gathering into groups, centring on the ban-the-bomb movement, but splitting into smaller factions such as the folk movement, the trad-jazz movement, and the poetry movement." Thomas Crimble, a future Hawkwind member, notes that "The nuclear bombs are still all out there, just as likely to go bang today as they were in the 1960s or 70s – but [then] it was very much in everyone's minds; we'd just had the Cuban missile crisis, so that end-of-the-world scenario was very real." Crimble sees that as contributing significantly to the forthcoming peace-and-love generation. "When people started talking about unity and love, and getting on with our neighbours, I was right into that."

12

Dave Bock leads an early jam session
(Collection of Dave Brock)

By the time he had moved on from The Gravier Street Stompers, Brock had turned to busking and had cultivated a friendship with a young musician by the name of Eric Clapton. Their musical interests coincided and they formed a duo, playing around Twickenham and Richmond. As was common, both Clapton and Brock explored other musical line-ups; Clapton with future Rolling Stones Charlie Watts and Bill Wyman, Brock with another blues musician, Jeff Watson.

"We were great friends," Brock says of Clapton. "Eric lived in Cobham and we used to hang-out in Richmond, which was quite an arty area. It had the Crawdaddy Club, which was a big rhythm and blues place, the L'auberge Coffee Bar, where all the beatniks used to be, and there was Twickenham next door, with Eel Pie Island." It was an area that was growing as an important gathering ground in the development of British rock music. The owner of the Crawdaddy Club, Giorgio Gomelsky, gave an early version of the Rolling Stones a residency that led to their first record contract. And, talking to Nick Kent in 1974, Jimmy Page described the impact the area had on his career: "I was involved in those old Richmond and Eel Pie Island sets. It was a good scene… everybody had this same upbringing and had been locked away with their records. It just exploded from there."

Other musicians prominent in the area included Keith Relf, whom Brock met at the L'auberge. "I used to sit with Keith on the riverbank at Richmond," he says, "playing guitar and harmonica. Same with Eric Clapton; though he didn't have a guitar and used to borrow mine. One day we all got drunk at Eel Pie Island

13

and Eric fell over and broke it, actually crushed it, and was really upset. Well, it was a nice guitar!"

With no specific musical affiliations developing, there was a period in the early 60s when this loose collection of blues inspired musicians would work together on an ad-hoc basis. "Keith, his mate Roger who was a guitarist, and me used to play Django Reindhardt stuff back then – it was a close-knit circle of people," says Brock. Clapton's musical successes meant that he soon left the club scene far behind. By October 1963 he was well on his way to iconic guitar hero status, initially, with Relf, as a member of The Yardbirds. "They were playing rhythm and blues at the Crawdaddy Club," says Brock. "I was still at Eel Pie Island playing authentic blues."

If there is one venue that Brock most refers to with special affection, it is Eel Pie Island. No more than 600 square feet in total, this island in the River Thames was home to the Eel Pie Hotel, which at the instigation of Kingston junkyard owner Arthur Chisnall, had been hosting traditional jazz nights since 1957. So popular were these performances that turnstiles were installed to regulate the influx of enthusiasts, a far cry from its 1920s heyday, when the famous maple sprung flooring hosted more genteel tea dances. The hotel's jazz nights featured the biggest names of the day; George Melly, Kenny Ball and his Jazzmen, and Ken Colyer. However, the times were changing. Mick Slattery, another friend of Brock from as far back as 1961/62, recalls that "Trad-jazz was quite popular at the time, but there was also a big interest in blues. After a while they started having a blues night on a Wednesday. People like Alexis Korner used to play, and Long John Baldry."

Interviewed for the Sunday Times, island resident Trevor Baylis recalled the moment when their cosy world of traditional jazz changed forever: "It all went downhill after Acker Bilk played here. We were jazz purists you see. I remember coming over the bridge one night in 1962. I heard this electric music and thought, 'Jesus, what the hell is that?' I turned on my heels. I didn't know it, but it was the first gig by the Rolling Stones." Mick Slattery laughs. "A lot of people did run away!"

After the first wave of British rock moved on, the hotel hosted The Crazy World of Arthur Brown (performing 'Fire', Brown managed not only to set light to his crown but also to the stage curtain), and John Mayall's Blues Breakers. Eventually, even a motley collection of hippie dropouts would appear there, under the name Hawkwind. Quite aside from its musical appeal, Eel Pie Island was famous for its cheap cider and easy sex; eventually leading to the Hotel losing its licence and becoming, by the end of the decade, a commune for the hippie generation. It briefly reopened under the title 'Colonel Barefoot's Rock Garden', and then in 1971 was scheduled for demolition, but burned down before it could be demolished.

Brock continued to perform with Jeff Watson into 1964, but the partnership dissolved and Watson left the music business altogether. From anecdotal evidence collected by Hawkwind historian Brian Tawn (for a feature in his fanzine *Hawkfan*), it seems likely that Brock was the driving force in their partnership, seeking out which venues to play and negotiating with promoters. Other associations were ad-hoc, Slattery noting that "I used to go busking a lot with Dave, go around to his house and play guitar for hours on end. I learned loads from him, because I was a few years younger than he was. We were all just having fun. Clapton and Rod Stewart were more single-minded, but Dave was more ambitious than me."

Dave had also formed an association which saw him playing with pianist Mike King and Luke Francis on harmonica. "Mike learned to play from a guy called Pete Johnson, a famous boogie piano player. Mike lived in Canada, and he went to this bar, and Pete Johnson was playing there. Pete used to show him these fantastic things, laying the rhythm down with your left hand…." At Eel Pie Island, the three backed some notable American blues musicians including Memphis Slim and Champion Jack Dupree, and formed a trio, The Dharma Blues Band. 'We were playing jug band music, like the Mound City Blue Blowers, these wonderful characters who played combs with paper on them. No electric music, we couldn't afford it!" Along with singer Terry Yorath, they played the traditional outer London circuit: the Half Moon in Putney, the Red Lion in Fulham. This alliance was successful enough to enter the studios and record a few songs, two of which saw the light of day on vinyl: 'Dealing with the Devil' and 'Roll 'em Pete'. Although the band would go on to record a full album in 1967, by that time Brock had already departed from the line-up.

Whilst he was mixing with the principle faces of the Richmond scene, Dave also had his parallel life at Larkin Studios, having worked his way up to the position of Despatch Manager, "a well-paid job." But the time had come to take a financial risk and concentrate exclusively on his musical career. Years later, for his song '25 Years', he would write 'I got the sack/my work was slack'. Actually, when he handed in his resignation, "they were shocked and horrified to think I'd leave such a wonderful place; but I wanted to go busking." A compromise was reached where Brock would take a few months off and Larkin Studios would keep his job open for him. He never returned.

Instead, he busked around Europe. It was not the glamorous lifestyle that many of his contemporaries were now enjoying: "I ended up sleeping in horrible old parks when I was busking in Paris." He also spent six months travelling with harmonica player, Pete Judd, driving across Holland in Judd's Mercedes. Together with guitarist John Illingworth, Brock and Judd returned to Holland in spring 1967, this time as The Famous Cure. The group was named after Sonny Terry and Brownie McGhee's Dr Brownie's Famous Cure, though the title was also a nod in the direction of the contemporary American West Coast rock scene's penchant for anachronistic sounding names, Quicksilver Messenger Service to name but one. The Famous Cure created a favourable impression, generating some local press coverage which played on Brock's previous association with Eric Clapton and going so far as to claim that Dave was "an exceptionally good guitarist who played with the Yardbirds six years ago." This created a lingering misconception. Brock was never a Yardbird, despite his friendship with Relf and Clapton. From these dates came the chance for The Famous Cure to record some songs for a possible single. Produced by Evert Wilbrink, the band cut 'Mean Mistreater', 'Dealing with the Devil' (a Sonny Boy Williamson blues classic), 'Sweet Mary' and 'Dust My Broom'. The last of these was the Elmore James and Robert Johnson number that was, coincidentally, adapted by The Yardbirds as 'Dust My Blues'. The session was soon halted when the record company, Negram-Delta, withdrew funding.

Pete Judd summed up his approach to live performances in an interview for the Dutch press. "The audience can see how you really are. There are no technical tricks to help you out, it is really important that the sound on stage is [equal to] the sound on record." How different this was to the style that Brock subsequently championed in Hawkwind, wherein members would be actively encouraged to find new ways of playing established numbers.

The Famous Cure recorded some material for DJ John Peel; presumably for his pirate Radio London show *The Perfumed Garden*. They also appeared at London's Roundhouse Theatre, supporting The Pretty Things, who were then developing their psychedelic masterpiece *SF Sorrow*. Around the same time, Brock's group played bottom of the bill at one of the foremost underground venues, The Middle Earth. The club had a seminal influence on Brock as it often featured Arthur Brown, who would be repeatedly referenced by Brock as having achieved the multimedia presentation he himself would strive for with Hawkwind.

"I'd seen Arthur at the Windsor Festival when I'd taken some LSD," says Brock of one performance that particularly impressed him. "He was on fire and I thought he was lowered from a helicopter, I heard a whirring noise." Years later Brock enthused about this to Brown himself, "but Arthur said he descended from a ladder!"

The Middle Earth, in Covent Garden, was an important venue for anybody interested in the burgeoning underground culture, Captain Beefheart and The Byrds having played there on occasion, though it had to relocate to the greater capacity of the Roundhouse when hosting The Doors and Jefferson Airplane. Towards the end of its existence, Tyrannosaurus Rex was the resident band.

By September 1967 The Famous Cure had been established as a contractual partnership, under the management of Robert Neal and David Butler. Pete Judd, however, had departed the line-up, and had been replaced by Brock's old friend, Mick Slattery. During the mid-60s Slattery had enjoyed a small taste of success with his folk-rock band The Compromise who "had a couple of singles out… and a residency at the Marquee."

The Famous Cure rehearsed at a church hall in Putney, with a new drummer; "another Mick," says Brock, "who went off to work as an actor." The three remaining members embarked again for Holland. "We travelled by train, transporting all this gear, having to carry it bit-by-bit across the platform." This trip culminated in the release of their single, 'Sweet Mary' (b/w 'Mean Mistreater'). During this visit the band secured a support act at 'Tent '67', a rock 'n' roll circus. One of the event's roadies, slightly older than Brock, was renowned for his appalling ability to break wind. To reflect this less than desirable attribute, he claims he became known as 'Hawkwind', though his real name was Nik Turner.

In many ways, Nik Turner (born 26th August 1940) was the antithesis of Dave Brock. Brock had a structure of sorts to his musical career, with each new partnership or band being a progression from what had gone before. Turner had merely drifted from job to job until finally entering the music business as a roadie. Brock appears to have been financially organised from the outset (Brian Tawn describes him, kindly meant, as a "hustler"), Turner eschews this approach in favour of what might best be described as 'ducking and diving'. Originally though, Turner did not perceive Brock as being business-like. "Retrospectively, he's shown himself to be very single-minded. But at the time people weren't aware of that." Turner conversely, "never saw music as a career, never thought I was going to be in a successful band, that wasn't really my goal. My early musical education was jazz: modern jazz, trad-jazz… but I was interested in pop music, soul, whatever was current really. I grew up in a town that was dominated by an American air force base, which got me involved with real rock 'n' roll. I'd hang-out with all these American kids and listen to the music they were listening to, Bo Diddley and people like that."

Turner had originally trained as an engineer and, in this capacity, he worked on a passenger ship on an Australian round trip. A life on the open seas failed to appeal to him and on his return to England he joined London Transport as an engineer on their fleet of buses. By the time that Brock encountered Turner, Nik had already befriended two members of England's formative counterculture scene who would become involved in Hawkwind: Robert Calvert, a young poet, and Richard Michael Davies: known as Dik-Mik.

Nik spent his summers in Margate (he met Calvert there) selling that staple of the English seaside resort: 'Kiss Me Quick' hats. Interviewed for the website *Starfarer*, Turner recalled "[driving] the guys to London for all night psychedelic experiences." The underground scene of this era has been described as "teeming with kindred spirits… who had decided to take the dictum 'l'art piur l'art' to a greater or lesser degree literally."

Perhaps Turner and friends saw The Pink Floyd Sound drop its collection of Chuck Berry covers and regenerate into The Pink Floyd, acknowledged house-band of the underground. If they did, it would probably have been at The Spontaneous Underground, the Floyd's Saturday residency at the Marquee. Maybe they were there when the band played at the launch party (in October 1966) for counterculture newspaper *International Times*, at the Roundhouse. Were they, perhaps, among a reported 10,000 people crammed into the Alexandra Palace on 29th April 1967 for the legendary 14 Hour Technicolour Dream? Organised by the creators of the UFO Club, with two stages, psychedelic rock bands, acoustic performers, and 'a very strange assortment of poets', it can be seen as a forefather to the free festival scene of the 1970s. In *Revolution in the Head*, Ian MacDonald describes the event as "the first tribal gathering of the British beautiful people." Here, John Lennon watched Yoko Ono perform, arguably setting The Beatles on the road to disintegration. Other acts, aside from the ubiquitous Floyd, included UFO regular Arthur Brown, The Pretty Things and Soft Machine.

It's most tempting, however, to see Turner and friends in October 1966 driving into a Ladbroke Grove not yet dwarfed in the shadow of the Westway flyover and attending the Floyd's weekly gig at All Saints Church Hall, Notting Hill. If they were there, observing the band's first experiments with projected lightshows (developed by Joel and Toni Brown from Timothy Leary's Millbrook Institute in the USA) then this would surely have been a formative experience.

The delights of hiring deck chairs to day-trippers faded and Turner moved to Europe, enjoying something of a bohemian lifestyle. Though he never studied art, he had discovered an interest in the subject: "Picasso, surrealism, expressionism, pre-war German expressionists and Franz Grass." Art was not his only passion. Influenced by his admiration of saxophonist Charlie Parker he had taken up playing sax and flute. While resident in Amsterdam during the summer of 1967 he was invited to join the rock 'n' roll circus, not as a performer, but "actually putting up the tent and working in the bar."

"I'd always been involved in fringe things," says Turner, "Like [Tent '67], working all around Holland, pitching up the tent every day, taking it down at night when we'd finished the show, jump in the truck… sleep… arrive at the next site. It was awesome, held about three thousand people. There were three Dutch people and myself… they were alcoholics culled from the Salvation Army in Rotterdam, quite bizarre!"

Through the summer of 1967 it is possible to track Dave Brock's growing interest in electronic and psychedelic music. There is the vision of Arthur Brown, self-styled God of Hellfire, there is the consuming of that most vital of sixties drugs, LSD, and there is the support slot with The Pretty Things. Perhaps most importantly there are the Tent '67 shows, of August, September and October 1967. "We took LSD and played against a psychedelic lightshow," says Brock. The Dutch music press commented that "for Tent '67 the band turned in their acoustic guitars for electric ones."

Brock: "I bought an electric guitar and an echo unit and made all sorts of noise, sliding a knife up and down, thinking it would be quite good to do all this live!" Slattery explains the band's progression from being predominately blues-based to embracing psychedelia as due to "listening to a lot of the early psychedelic records, doing acid and trying to reflect that. The acid was a huge part of it, before acid it was The Beatles' *Rubber Soul* and *Revolver*. After acid, it was all these sounds we'd never heard before, or could even imagine. I'd heard 'Third Stone from the Sun' on the first Jimi Hendrix album and thought it was music

18

from another planet." Thomas Crimble, similarly, remembers "getting exciting and waiting, really waiting, for the latest Hendrix single, which had a wow-wow [wah-wah] guitar on it. Nobody had heard of it before. But by the time you'd listened to it in the shop, or rushed home and put it on your little sound-system, it was really *wow-wow*! We had really ground-breaking aural experiences."

Around this time, the Famous Cure supported The Deviants. Led by underground lynchpin Mick Farren, The Deviants had a stated intention to take the peace and love out of psychedelia and inject it with hard-bitten social commentary instead. Styling themselves as an English version of American proto-punks such as The Stooges or the MC5 and noting as influences the beatnik writers Burroughs and Ginsberg, The Deviants had formed in 1967 as The Social Deviants. "We wanted to be incredibly loud and violent, the hippies wanted to be nice and gentle, but our style was the opposite of that," recalled Farren. What he aimed to do was to reflect the issues of the day: "drugs, politics, the Vietnam War."

The Famous Cure lasted throughout '67 but disbanded early in 1968. Brock returned to his roots as a busker appearing at a concert held at the Royal Albert Hall in London. This led to a track by Brock appearing on a spin-off album *The Buskers*. Flushed with this minor success, Brock assembled some musicians, to perform as Dave Brock and Friends. During October 1968, he telephoned the BBC to hustle for a radio session audition. On 21st January 1969, Brock was joined by Mike King, Mike Griggs and Peter Judd to record for John Peel's Radio One show, *Night Ride*. First broadcast on 29th January 1969, the songs played were 'Diamond Ring', 'When I Came Home This Morning', 'Hesitation Shuffle', 'Illusions', 'Ripley's Blues' and 'Roll 'em Pete'. Most significantly, 'Illusions' would emerge the following year as 'Mirror of Illusion' on the first Hawkwind album.

Brock was then contracted by Don Paul to do a 'Busker's Tour' around Britain ("sleeping on London buses – horrible"). He had the opportunity to perform with some "wonderful characters: Meg Aitken, Banjo and Spoons, Happy Wanderers, and Jumping Jack who used to tap dance with bottle tops on his shoes, jitterbugging." The tour was headlined by one-man-band Don Partridge, who, with the success of his single 'Rosie', had temporarily made busking fashionable.

'Some of the finest street entertainers in Europe' proclaimed the poster for the tour's appearance at the Manchester Free Trade Hall, on 21st May 1969. The advertising listed 'Dave Brock & Mike Griggs', indicating that at least one other member of Dave Brock and Friends was still on the scene. At the same time, Turner had moved on from Amsterdam and spent a winter in Berlin mixing with its collection of *avant-garde* artists, free form jazz musicians, and bands that would have a direct influence on Hawkwind's sound and approach. Turner claims that he was just an observer of this scene with no musical involvement, though, given his propensity to jump up on stage and play with anybody, it's hard to believe that the clubs of Berlin did not hear some of Turner's earliest musical performances.

The link between Hawkwind's musical sounds and the exponents of what would come to be labelled as 'Krautrock' has often been cited by rock critics as an essential part of the band's make-up. Follow the line from Pink Floyd's *The Piper at the Gates of Dawn* album or the swirling feedback of the Jimi Hendrix Experience and contrast it with Hawkwind's blues and electronic fusion beginnings. Then survey the principal elements of the Germanic rock scene of the mid-60s, and you'd join-up all the clues to the components of the early tone of Hawkwind.

British psychedelic music can be split into two distinct strands that emerged from the 1967 'Summer of Love'. Typified on the one hand by the very English brand of music hall flavoured whimsy that runs through The Beatles' *Sergeant Pepper's Lonely Hearts Club Band,* and the work of The Kinks and The Small Faces, it must be juxtaposed with the interstellar *The Piper at the Gates of Dawn.* They can be drawn back together by the art school ethos of their principal creators. Syd Barrett was a student at Camberwell College of Art, his collaborators in the first incarnation of The Pink Floyd all polytechnic students. John Lennon, Pete Townshend, Ray Davies, Eric Burdon, Keith Richards, Ronnie Wood, Phil May and Dick Taylor, of The Pretty Things, and Brock's old friend Clapton, were all former art students. As a background, it's a common thread in British rock throughout the 60s and 70s.

There was also an Art School element in the Krautrock scene. Edgar Froese who formed Tangerine Dream was a Berlin-based painter and sculptor more interested in the work of Salvador Dali, Picasso and the 1920s French Surrealists than in forming a rock band. What the continental music scene had first-hand, but which British artists could only adopt as a badge, was a genuine political revolutionary scene. France saw a wave of social and industrial unrest during 1968 that left the country wedged between political disenchantment with the last days of De Gaulle and a very real 'barricades and guillotines' uprising. Germany had not only the Berlin Wall establishing a physical line between the capitalist West Germany and the Soviet-style communism of the (East) German Democratic Republic. It also had its violently philosophical struggle, typified by the terrorist Red Army Faction – The Baader-Meinhof Gang – with its anarchist, anti-USA agenda and its 'Don't Argue, DESTROY' ethos. Against this background, the German rock scene developed its own uniquely counterculture atmosphere. Julian Cope in his book *Krautrocksampler* succinctly delineates this in his description of chiefs of the scene Amon Düül as a commune of musicians committed to creating political art. Amon Düül's espousing of free love and drug taking would resonate throughout the British hippie heartland in Notting Hill Gate and Ladbroke Grove.

Froese was developing Tangerine Dream into an abstract sonic experiment, as exemplified by their 1970 album *Electronic Meditation*, historically and spiritually a contemporary of the first Hawkwind recordings. Amon Düül released their first musical manifesto a year earlier with *Psychedelic Underground*, creating what one observer described as "tribal-like improvs/jams... almost always raw and intense." A collision between jazz and rock would result in that most influential of all German acts, Can, noted as being "the Velvets jamming with Sun Ra" and acclaimed in the 1970s by the likes of John Lydon, David Bowie and Brian Eno. Elsewhere, possibly the foremost exponents of purely electronic music, Kraftwerk, spawned Neu!, whose 15-minute mantras and cosmic synthesisers Brock would cite as an accompanying soundtrack to Hawkwind.

Nik Turner was revelling in the opportunity to fully engage the atmosphere of the Berlin counterculture scene and looking for associations that would allow him full access to its possibilities. "I just got involved on the scene; there were a lot of psychedelic clubs. Edgar Froese would hang-out there, but Tangerine Dream was still a blues band at that point. I saw Amon Düül at a gig in their commune."

Whatever the depth of his involvement and friendships with the aristocracy of Krautrock, the impression that his time in Berlin must have created on Turner could be seen as a significant starting block for both Hawkwind's musical and social agenda. Still Turner's biggest passions were the jazz clubs. He frequented the legendary Blue Note in Berlin, "which is where Eric Dolphy used to play… I was a musician who didn't play; I was a bit of a dilettante. I tried to play the saxophone, but I was too lazy to practice." This love for free-form would manifest itself in Turner's playing with Hawkwind and become a significant part of the band's sound in the first half of the 1970s. "I thought I would like to play free jazz in a rock band. That was what Hawkwind was for me."

**Busking Dave Brock, on the South Bank
(Collection of Dave Brock)**

With Mick Slattery, Brock assembled a new band. "There was a long time when we didn't even have a name," recalls Slattery. "We'd kept a band together with different line-ups, a couple of different drummers and bass players." Slattery doesn't necessarily see The Famous Cure and what would become Hawkwind as two distinctive bands. "They kind of merged into each other, a sort of progression."

The band finally settled on the services of a bass player who Brock had met whilst busking. "I used to do all the cinema queues, the subway at Tottenham Court Road. We had hour-long stints and different characters stopped to listen, which is how I met John Harrison."

Harrison had been the bass player for the Joe Loss Band, though like Brock he was also a keen busker, working the crowds in central London. "Huwey [Huw Lloyd-Langton, future Hawkwind guitarist] also used to walk down there; he was working as a sales assistant in Ivor Mairant's Musicentre." Those three – Brock, Slattery and Harrison - had formed the outline, the bones, of the embryonic Hawkwind, the starting point for what Brock would look back on as the "Hawkwind weirdness." Needing a drummer, they advertised in the *Melody Maker*, settling on Terry Ollis. "Terry came down to do an audition, but I wasn't there," says Slattery. "Dave had another guitarist, so I don't know what was going on. Dave was probably trying-out somebody else. He'd try people out and see what they were like, to get different sounds, which he still does now."

"The band rehearsed in my flat in Putney," recalls Brock. "All the neighbours complained! Mick Slattery had fucking great speaker cabinets, like a wardrobe." This problem was solved by music shop owner Bob Kerr, who had a basement under his premises where the band practised. "We kept this going for about two years," adds Slattery. "At one point we were rehearsing in a school hall near Twickenham, every day for about three weeks. We'd been listening to Cream and Captain Beefheart. Pete Meaden had come along and offered us stuff, which turned out to be a load of bollocks, but force-fed us acid and played all this psychedelic music to us." Meaden, a freelance publicist, was an early manager of The Who, and was instrumental in their development from a rhythm 'n' blues band to the close identification with the Mod movement. Brock recalls taking his first LSD trip at Meaden's home.

Another regular visitor to Brock's Putney home was Nik Turner. "We used Nik, as he had a van," says Brock. Initially hired as a roadie for the new group, the band discovered that he could play the saxophone. "Well, honk a few noises, but it sounded quite good."

"I was going to be the road manager," says Turner. "I got involved in playing with them at a rehearsal. I said, 'I've got my saxophone in the van' and they said, 'bring it in', so I had a play and they really liked it and I was in the band." Installed as saxophonist, Turner brought with him his friend from Margate, Dik-Mik, who would handle 'Audio Generators', a piece of test equipment capable of producing a single frequency anywhere throughout the range of human hearing and beyond. Dik-Mik used one or more through a wah-

wah pedal, fuzz and a Watkins Copycat tape loop echo-machine. He also used a Ring Modulator, producing anything from clanging bell tones to extreme 'take the top of your head off' pulsating screams. Whilst Turner and Brock had received no formal musical training, they could at least claim to be self-taught. Dik-Mik gave himself no such qualifications and styled his lack of musical ability as an attribute: "I've got practically no musical knowledge" he wrote on the sleeve-notes for the first Hawkwind album, "but I figure if you let it become your whole trip, you can do anything you like, and do it well." Slattery merely recalls him "twiddling with his generator," but it is indicative of a neo-punk ethic to musical ability. Others have seen in Dik-Mik an influence from the BBC Radiophonic Workshop, who'd been providing music and sound-effects for *Doctor Who* since the programme's start in November 1963, and whose electronics genius, Delia Derbyshire, had created the programme's uniquely striking theme tune from its composer's basic notations. That's not necessarily the case, Brock insisting that instead he simply thought of Dik-Mik going down to London's Tottenham Court Road, with its collection of shops stocking audio equipment, including items from the war years, and stocking himself with his own instrumentation from there, though clearly Derbyshire and her colleagues were working on a similar template of electronic ideas.

"We'd been rehearsing every day, down at the Royal College of Art, behind the Royal Albert Hall," notes Slattery. "We had the place through the summer holidays. We'd get loads of people come down, friends, students. We even had a wedding reception once. Someone would come along with a lightshow and it would become a little event, with maybe twenty people there."

The band had been unable to decide on a name to perform under, so when they talked their way into a supporting slot at a concert, on the 19th August 1969, in the crypt of the All Saints Church in Notting Hill, they appeared as Group X. Headlining on that night were High Tide and Skin Alley, two bands managed by Douglas Smith as part of his Clearwater Productions stable. Whether Group X had obtained agreement in advance to play that evening, as Slattery claims, or whether they blagged their way onto the bill after a short confrontation as is often reported will probably never been known. The result is traditionally cited as the first public performance by Group X. Brock, however, is adamant that the band, in some form, were playing as early as 1968, and Slattery is clear that they played at least one prior gig, at Chiswick Town Hall. "We were playing [Pink Floyd's] 'Cymbaline', and some of Dave's stuff, but a lot of it was just twenty-minute jams. At the All Saints Hall we played 'The Sunshine Special', which was really just three chords, the beginning of 'Eight Miles High' by The Byrds. We just jammed around that. We only had four or five numbers at the beginning." Slattery recalls that any previous gigs were "much looser affairs, with different musicians as well as Dave, John, Terry and myself."

Douglas Smith professes himself unmoved by the show, but John Peel, now building a reputation for identifying promising new acts, advised him to "Sign them. Big band" as he was leaving the hall. Talking to Doug for *Record*

Collector, he recalled how "Hawkwind turned up one night at All Saints Hall, ''Ere, can we play?' and we thought, 'how on Earth are we going to do this?' But they went on stage and used High Tide's gear, and I think they broke the drum kit. As I was standing at the exit John Peel said to me 'Yeah, I get them. They sound like they're going to be good'."

2

Hurry on Hawkwind

Douglas Smith left the 'first' performance of Group X without any intention of establishing a relationship with the band: "I walked on, didn't think any more about it, then two months later decided to get involved." Through his Clearwater Productions company, he'd built up a stable of London groups, principally located in and around Notting Hill. This enabled him to package bands together when dealing with promoters, producers and record labels. Aside from the future Hawkwind, most of the acts (Cochise, Skin Alley, Mick Softly) have, to lesser or greater degrees, faded from mainstream musical history. At the time of encountering Group X, Clearwater had landed a contract with Apple Publishing for High Tide, whose membership included keyboard and violinist Simon House. High Tide would release their *Sea Shanties* album on Liberty Records in 1969; Liberty would also release the eponymous first Hawkwind LP.

"Douglas had the 'Ultimate Pad' over disused garages in Westmorland Mews," recalls Tim Blake, a member of Smith's team. "This converted attic with a mezzanine, decorated with adverts and other pieces of 'Art' was both Douglas's flat and 'The Office'. Douglas Smith, Wayne Bardell and Richard Thomas were three young budding music entrepreneurs. Each had come together, as managers, with each a band in hand." Smith had responsibility for Trees, Thomas handled Skin Alley, whilst Bardell ("an amazing man, escaped from Apple Publishing," says Blake) dealt with High Tide. They had wide-ranging contacts, being friendly with Andrew Lauder, who was head of A&R at Liberty Records, and with the increasingly influential John Peel.

"Andrew Lauder was on the case," recalls Brock. "The whiz-boy who used to go around looking at different bands; he also had a fantastic collection of sci-fi artwork, and psychedelic art from America. But Doug Smith was *the man*. He was really sympathetic, very astute."

Smith's handling of folk rock group Trees was moderately successful, but although the group achieved, in Blake's view, "a debut album well put together by Clearwater" they were "more interested in alternative management, and that set the scene of the entry of Group X."

"There was a whole school of managers in the music business who were very manipulative, like Don Arden who managed ELO. When musicians would ask to see the accounts, they would say 'do you want to see them before or after I break your fingers?'" observes Turner. Casting such agents as "business people who exploited the situation," Nik contrasts these with Doug Smith's style: "I thought he was pretty cool, I wouldn't have had much to do with him otherwise. He was enthusiastic and liked music; his style was quite positive."

Chatting to Douglas for a feature for *Record Collector*, he recalled the early days of Clearwater and the scene that had sprung up around Ladbroke Grove.

"We started promoting concerts at All Saints Hall. There was Wayne Bardell, Richard Thomas, Kit Van Henkel and a guy called Max Taylor who was the bass player in Skin Alley. The office was one phone and five people trying to answer it when it rang, so it was very much part of the 'peace and love' hippie thing, that whole sort of culture that went around it. Richard Thomas came on board because he'd finished university and was doing Skin Alley because one or two of them were co-graduates with him. Wayne Bardell had been Apple's plugger and was so well connected. We weren't totally from a hippie culture background. I had an act called Trees that were on CBS - though their album never sold more than about twenty - and then Cochise came along who were very West Coast and very musical, and were in fact fantastic musicians and were, more or less, professional. They grew with up the likes of Steve Marriot and that mob, being very much part of that young, London, blues pop bands of the era. Cochise created quite a lot of interest. They were great friends of the Floyd and were always getting gigs. Only Trees and Skin Alley had record deals, both with CBS and then along came Andrew Lauder of Liberty. Andrew was a young guy who'd been spotted by the boss there and made head of A&R at about twenty-six. We met Andrew and tried to hustle our acts onto his label. The one he wanted was Cochise and offered them an album deal and [at the same time] I persuaded him to take a shot with Hawkwind on a singles deal. Singles deals were incredibly common; The Rolling Stones were signed on a singles deal, as The Beatles were. Nobody [in the business] was really interested in Hawkwind even though they drew people, because they were left-field in what they were doing and spent most of the time tripping on stage and being completely over the top."

Prior to Smith's decision to become involved with what had moved-on from being Group X to playing as Hawkwind Zoo, the band cut three demos, organised by Don Paul. Recorded were 'Hurry on Sundown', 'Kiss of the Velvet Whip', and a cover of 'Cymbaline'. "Don Paul was working with EMI, and arranged for us to go into this very small studio with a Revox ten track machine… really, I owe a lot to Don Paul," says Brock.

The adoption of 'Hawkwind' is still held by Turner as an appropriation of his nickname, though as early as 1972, in *Melody Maker*, Brock was distancing himself from this almost certainly apocryphal story. "It started as a joke, because Nik Turner has a prominent proboscis and suffers from indigestion. But it goes a lot deeper than that." Referencing the image of the Hawk in Egyptian mythology and as a pagan symbol, Brock also connected the name with "Hawkmoon, a character devised by fantasy writer Michael Moorcock." In any case, it's a story the truth of which is lost to the mists of time.

The Notting Hill that Hawkwind emerged into was one radically changed from the environment of the 1950s. The atmosphere that had erupted into the race riots and so inspired the Colin MacInnes London novels, notably *City of Spades* and *Absolute Beginners*, had given way to the socially inclusive aura of the counterculture.

Phil Franks, a photographer who worked extensively in the Ladbroke Grove/Portobello Road area, recalls that "It wasn't exclusive, no colour prejudice – and this was London not many years after the days when you could walk around Notting Hill and see rooms to let with 'No Coloureds' or 'No Irish'." Unlike the area today, "there were no trendy restaurants. There was a macrobiotic café, and The Mountain Grill, a 'greasy spoon' café where we'd all eat." Franks characterises the era as a time of genuine community spirit. "We were all pretty sincere about it. There were people, as anywhere, that were looking to make a fast buck, but generally there was that vibe. Apart from the odd skinhead, there wasn't any of the street violence there is in London as we know it now. Anytime, day or night, you could walk up and down the Portobello Road and meet somebody you knew, not just Fridays and Saturdays when the market was on. It was our Haight-Ashbury, really, though not exclusively hippie. The thing about the alternative scene was that it broke down barriers and pre-conceptions. That was part of 'dropping out', operating away from the traditional stuff."

"We'd all broken away from wherever it was we'd come from," says Franks. "In a sense it was no-man's-land, but at the same time, everybody's."

Hawkwind Zoo returned to the All Saints Hall on 26th September 1969. When Smith brought the band under his wing (he would continue this role through much of the 1970s and again at various times over the following two decades) he discussed the name with John Peel: "I said, 'We got the name, John'." Peel, unimpressed, commented "No. Get rid of the 'Zoo'." It's interesting to see Peel, not a supporter of the band as they developed, being instrumental in steering Smith both into the management of the band and determining its final name.

Playing around London through the rest of the year, notably at the Marquee and the Speakeasy but also at Brock's old Twickenham haunt Eel Pie Island, brought the band to more general attention. Most gigs from this period were London shows, but the band was also gigging in the Home Counties and stretching their reach a little further, as Slattery notes. "I can remember playing in Brighton, and one at Oxford University where we all ended up playing each other's instruments. Nik was playing modulators, Dave was playing sax, or whatever, but it sounded okay to me!"

"Suddenly, there were a lot of gigs, new equipment, and things started to take off quickly," recalls Mick. "It was probably Doug Smith getting involved that gave us a kick up the arse!" The sets were still largely freeform improvisations. "We'd get an intro, maybe a verse or two, but then go off and perhaps come back to the beginning or go into something completely different. It was still undisciplined."

Popular myth has Brock busking outside of Hawkwind's first Marquee gig and, though he denies this story, it's clear that the switch from street musician to band member was not proving as financially attractive as might be supposed. Brock nearly left over his insistence on continuing his busking 'career', recalling in *Melody Maker* that "I was busking regularly up until about 1971. Douglas used to tell me that I had to do one or the other." The monetary rewards of playing with Hawkwind were not matching those he could achieve performing solo: "I used to take me guitar down the Portobello Road... earn a few quid." He's never lost that enthusiasm for those busking days, still talking fondly of the times back then when he'd bring out his guitar and play around the streets of London, particularly remembering how he'd busk in the long underpass that leads from South Kensington tube station to the Natural History Museum and the Royal Albert Hall, with its fabulously echoing acoustics. And through the early Hawkwind albums there's acoustic evidence of 'Busking Dave Brock' to be found, not just in the debut LP's sing-along 'Hurry on Sundown', but in 'We Took the Wrong Step Years Ago' on its successor, and then 'Down Through the Night', 'Web Weaver' and 'The Demented Man' on subsequent records.

But Hawkwind's principal agenda was focused on the development of electronic music and the scene was evolving at a quicker pace than the band's income could keep up with. "One of our troubles is money," Brock told Mark Plummer (*Melody Maker*, 5th September 1970). "We want to add a Moog [synthesiser] to our line-up and really give Dik-Mik something to do." Plummer commented that 'half the band is sleeping rough at any one time.'

Nik Turner remembers those days of rather loose accommodation arrangements: "I was living in squats or sleeping in the van, on floors. That's how I lived for quite a long time." Occasionally, Turner or Brock would be found sleeping on the floor of Phil Franks' flat in the Portobello Road. "Nik was a showman, Dave really the quiet rhythm guitarist who wrote great songs. I have nice memories of Dave staying over at my place, just playing his guitar and singing his newest song."

Inherent in the band's ethos was a commitment to the concept of the free gig. Interviewed by Plummer, Dave remembered "playing a lot of free gigs around the 'Gate. And it was really good." By their willingness to play for free they began to build the reputation of being 'The Peoples' Band', evolving a communal sensibility. It's clearly a concept that Brock very much identified with: "We were completely outside of the established order. We were trying to get something together in the community."

The first departure from the group came when Mick Slattery left for his own crack at the 'hippie trail'. "I sold my guitar and amp to go to India, reached Morocco and stayed there for six months. I loved the place, all the Arabic music." No live recordings are known to exist from his gigs with the band, though he did play on the Hawkwind Zoo demo session. "I read an article in Mojo, where Dave said he thought I'd just got bored," says Slattery. "I think that was it really. When it got hard work, I took the easy option. I was a real hippie, and it seemed to me that we were selling out when we signed up with a major record company." Having an itinerant lifestyle for much of the next two decades, Slattery lived variously in Wales (playing in a band at a commune) and then in Ireland in a gypsy caravan.

Peter Pracownik and Nik Turner
Glastonbury Town Hall
(Collection of Peter Pracownik)

Within a week, John Harrison and Dave Brock had recruited one of their Tottenham Court Road busking friends to replace Slattery. Huw Lloyd Langton, born in the North London district of Harlesden on 6th February 1951, had taught himself to play guitar at school and although he also had a love of painting had decided to make his career in music. "My mother, who is Welsh, always liked singing, and dragged me and my sister off to chapel whenever she could," he told Radio Free Saskatoon. Unlike the rest of the band, aside from Terry Ollis, Langton was still in his teens.

Langton was working in one of Denmark Street's famous concentration of music shops when he first encountered Brock, as he told Bruce Stringer. "[Dave] was a professional busker and he used to come in with a pouch full of pennies to buy strings." The addition of Langton into the band may have marked the transition from Hawkwind Zoo to Hawkwind; Langton was at pains to describe himself as a founder member. Despite his youth, he was already an experienced musician, having toured the British Army bases in the then West Germany with Winston G, noted by the Blogspot website *Forgotten Bands* as "a suntanned singer with Indian roots," who "dabbled with psychedelic rock." "He cut his teeth in Germany," Huw's wife, Marion, told me for *Shindig!*. "He didn't like it, because they were playing covers, mainly soul music, but Winston G was a great singer and though each year had a different line-up they were all really good musicians, lovely and solid, and so he really cut his teeth in Germany and, as a lead guitarist, was allowed to go off on tangents. When Dave asked him to come to an audition for Hawkwind, he was just 'Yessss!'." Huw wasn't the only one auditioning for Hawkwind, Marion recalling one musician who rented a room in the same house as she did. "[He] was this young guitarist from Switzerland; I got home and Huw rang and said he'd got the job... but it turned out this guitarist had also gone for the audition and didn't get it. I didn't know he was going for the audition, but he knew that Huw was my boyfriend and he came steaming in, 'God you did it deliberately, didn't you! You found out about the audition! You sent Huw down there!' He'd told me he was going for an audition but not who and where and what, but he went back to Switzerland swearing that I was an absolute bitch to say the least and I'd ruined his life!"

Langton saw John Harrison as particularly important to the musical structure of the group. "Apart from Dave, John was the man who kept the band together; he was a very solid bass player. On stage, though we were all vaguely *avant-garde* as musicians, John would get up there and just lay it down very solidly."

If money was not a fuelling factor for the band, the burgeoning drug scene of Notting Hill was. Ollis recalled in *Record Collector*, "We played loads of gigs with all of us tripping. You'd go so far out and yet you'd all be there." Hawkwind were gaining notoriety for substance consumption that would make their name a byword for tripped-out rock music in perpetuity. It is entirely possible that this image, however encouraged by the band and their management, was rather exaggerated. Dik-Mik confessed in *Record Collector* to being "probably out of my head on [acid] for three years continually," but believed they were "merely a catalyst. The straight press was always trying to put us down, an excess of sex and drugs and rock 'n' roll."

Turner also played down these reported excesses: "[Hawkwind] was part of the drug culture. Everybody was doing it." This aspect of Hawkwind's story must be taken into context; the principal drug favoured throughout the Notting Hill scene was LSD, outlawed only a few years earlier in 1966. "We always used to record under the influence of LSD," claimed Brock. "Back then it was a very pure form, not corrupted by crap."

Langton, who believed that Hawkwind's association with the drug scene has become exaggerated over the years, explained his early indulgences: "I did like the odd toke, but I only started taking hallucinogenic drugs when I joined Hawkwind. There were all sorts of stuff floating around at the time, thankfully not the heavy-duty stuff, like heroin, but there were some very strange substances going about." Langton saw Hawkwind as a substitute for the seemingly ubiquitous mind-expanding chemicals. "The whole point of it was to create a musical, theatrical circumstance that would be a trip in itself; an alternative, where you could ignore the drugs. Of course, because the band was psychedelic it attracted people who were into substances, hence the members of the band, because they were surrounded by people who took substances, started taking them as well."

They ventured across the channel for an appearance at a festival in Paris on the 29th March 1970. This was a chance for Smith to display his range of acts: Cochise, Skin Alley and High Tide were also billed for the same night, though the major draws were Ginger Baker's Airforce, Atomic Rooster, The Pretty Things and Procol Harum. More significantly, Smith had secured a contract with Liberty Records (owned by United Artists), which he described to *Mojo*'s Mick Wall as being "on the back of Cochise... who the label wanted badly." Former Pretty Things guitarist Dick Taylor was engaged as producer for Hawkwind on a 2% royalty deal. It's another example of Smith compounding his dealings, since Taylor had already produced sessions for Cochise and would subsequently work with Skin Alley.

Interviewed by *Record Collector*, Taylor recalled first hearing Hawkwind at All Saints Hall and thinking their sound "A fearsome racket – absolutely brilliant!" It was this improvised energy that he had to somehow contain in the studio environment and convert to both a manageable soundtrack and commercial accessibility. "I don't think I heard the original demos," he recalled to me for *Shindig!* "Mostly I did everything from having listened to the band live, because I went to quite a few gigs, and actually did a few gigs with them as well. And, of course, I went to rehearsals and things like that – I built up a good relationship with everybody."

So Hawkwind entered the studio, *sans* Slattery (who, in his recollection, worked for a couple of days on the first album before leaving) but with the rest of the line-up that had played their first chaotic set still complete. The omens were not good for a successful transition from live performers to studio musicians;

Langton, in particular, showed little fondness for an environment that he dismissed as "sterile and inhuman."

Whilst the music was largely "a mixture of electronic music, heavy beat and simple chords incorporating *avant-garde* jazz sounds," Taylor focused their efforts on a straight-forward number that leaned on Brock's busking background: 'Hurry on Sundown', soon to be the first Hawkwind single. Sandwiched between this opening number and the closing 'Mirror of Illusion' (the reworked 'Illusions' from the *Night Ride* sessions) was some of the densest, most monotone electronic improvisation to emerge outside of the Krautrock scene. "We started off with 'Hurry on Sundown' and that went very well, we recorded in a reasonably conventional manner, layering the tracks, getting a good rhythm track and so on. I took the liberty of doing a guitar solo on that. When we started doing the rest of the album I got slightly bogged down in the sense that recording it, as you would, in the Abbey Road style, didn't really cut it and I was scratching my head. Andrew said, 'Why not record the whole band live, and if you can, bring in their PA and mic it up very carefully.' And that was how most of the rest of the album was recorded. We tweaked it a lot afterwards, but that was how it then transpired. We did one more track without doing that, possibly 'Mirror of Illusion'. So, that was how we did it; all the bits that went vaguely awry we sorted out and I must admit to being very pleased with what we did."

Dave Brock: "Andrew Lauder suggested that as Dick Taylor had left The Pretty Things it would be a good idea to get him as our producer. He actually played with the band a few times and he did aid us. You see, what did he was, he contained us! He instructed us… because we were electronic barbarians! One of his ideas was to use two 12-string guitars on 'Hurry on Sundown' to 'thicken' the sound. He'd teach us all the things that someone who'd been in the business knows about."

'Hurry on Sundown' is best described as deceptively straight-forward, its jolly sing-along busking vibe belying its darker undercurrent, a proper crowd pleasing song that in a different circumstance might have provided Dave Brock his own hit record, though he confirms that he'd never considered keeping it back for himself, thinking of it as just one of many busking songs that he'd written and played. It seems influenced by the folk singers Peter, Paul & Mary, who'd recorded a song entitled 'Hurry Sundown' and released an album that prefigured one of the lines from Brock's song, *See What Tomorrow Brings*. (That album also sees the singers covering 'Tryin' to Win' by Brownie McGee and Sonny Terry, those influences coming around again). 'Mirror of Illusion' meanwhile was another that Brock would describe as one of his "jolly old busking numbers" but it had a lyrical sophistication and 60s relevance, alluding to the 'Doors of Perception', a phrase coined by the poet William Blake but which became associated with the writer Aldous Huxley. 'Hurry on Sundown' is a much-loved song, even though it was dropped from Hawkwind's set early doors, and not revisited until the 21st century by the band, though it has been covered by others, notably Kula Shaker, whose Crispian Mills told me, "it's a great track. I remember hearing from someone that it was Dave Brock's busking tune. Now, I used to busk when I was at college, not really to make any money, but more to just play and face the crowd and that song always worked a treat, with that great harmonica line… get a good busking pitch with some reverberation on your voice in a tunnel somewhere! It's a great tune!"

Douglas Smith: "[Liberty] went with 'Hurry on Sundown' because it wasn't typical Hawkwind, it was much easier. It got some reasonable reaction so they agreed to release the first album."

Separating the two more traditional songs came what started out as 'The Sunshine Special' several months before. "Dave writes the idea for the song," Turner told *Melody Maker*, "then we improvise around that idea, including the words which Dave writes roughly beforehand." This would inevitably lead to numbers being different each time they were played, or as Harrison saw it: "We cut the album in one take. A second take would have been almost a different album."

Taylor remembered "trying to capture the more way-out stuff as professionally as I could," but eventually conceded "the only way to record them was for the band to set up their PA in the studio and just play live." This would prove, in the future, to be a consistent problem for producers: Jeff Green, recording Hawkwind live a couple of years later for the BBC's *In Concert* radio programme was confronted by a band who simply wanted to play their own set in their own time, but who still managed to bring it in exactly on the required 60 minutes. For Dick Taylor, the challenge was to manage and coordinate a group of players with vastly different levels of experience, from the avowed non-musicians in their ranks to those, such as Dave Brock and John Harrison, who had already several years of work already under their belts. "Because of the way we ended up finishing recording it, the disparity between them didn't matter. That was one of the great things, that it was this mish-mash of people, but when they were unleashed… Nik would go off into a completely other place, shall we say, but there was a kind of bedrock there. Terry did very well, he wasn't the great session drummer or anything like that, but he was perfect for what they were doing at that time. That was what I was trying to do, represent them as they were, because they were a disparate bunch."

"The first album was recorded in a live situation, in a studio, and we just recorded the same piece, about 45 minutes long, three or four times," says Nik Turner. "We didn't do that much overdub. It was fairly simple. I thought [the finished record] was quite good, representative of the band at the time. I wasn't that pleased, in a way, with my own performance, because I wasn't used to hearing what I did. But I wasn't terribly critical of it either. I just thought, 'This is what we do and this is what it more or less sounds like, so I can go with that.' I wasn't very discerning about it!"

Langton, somewhat overawed by the presence of Taylor, took a backseat during the three or four days that it took to record 'Hurry on Sundown'. Much of the lead guitar heard on that track was played by the producer himself. During the two days allotted to the rest of the album however, and particularly on 'Mirror of Illusion', Langton's beautifully delicate lead lines cut through the dense sound of the other players and his reputation as one of the most talented musicians to have played on any Hawkwind recordings begins to shine through. "I thought Huw was a much better guitarist than me," considers Slattery, "I felt in a sense that it was right that they got Huw. He could do far more for the band than I could."

The release of the album, though not a chart success, drew favourable comparisons with Pink Floyd and Soft Machine. "The whole exercise has a Floydish feel about it," wrote one critic, "but the group have sufficient individuality to make them a bright force in the music business." The same journalist heard "electronics held tightly under control, merging with guitars, drums and saxophone." Hawkwind's objective of 'using a complex of electronics, lights and environmental experiences' with which to 'levitate people's minds, in a nice way' seemed to have been captured in the studio. At gigs it was another matter, with reports that the playing of 'Paranoia' was causing people to "pass out, freak out or run out screaming."

Gigs at notable London venues such as the Marquee and the Roundhouse aside, the spring and summer of 1970 saw Hawkwind cementing their status as the 'House Band' of the festival circuit. Their rambling freeform improvisation, often little more than one chord played progressively faster and faster, together with a reputation for substance consumption and advocating of free love, made them a mirror for the misty-eyed idealism of the festival audience.

"I was just happy to be enjoying myself playing music with guys who enjoyed themselves playing music to an audience who appeared to be enjoying themselves!" notes Turner of their growing profile. "I felt the success of the band was down to the grass-roots support. I tended to be one of the band members who cultivated this. I considered myself to be a 'man of the people' really." It was this identification with the alternative scene that Turner attributes to his abandoning his embryonic career in engineering. "I found it too establishment and boring. The people that I worked with were not very stimulating and I didn't see myself going that far in it, or being very excited by it."

With Turner's family having a theatrical background ("my parents and grandfather made movies, my uncle's a cameraman, my aunt is in the Royal Shakespeare Company") the creative arts came quite naturally to Nik. "I thought 'this is something very interesting and I seem to be able to cope with it and create quite a lot of excitement in people,' whether it was by me personally or by the band."

An appearance in Port Talbot on 23rd May spawned the earliest known live recording of the band. It captured Hawkwind performing the loose suite of numbers that approximated the intense middle section of the first album: 'Reason Is', 'Be Yourself', 'Paranoia', and 'Seeing it as You Really Are'. The music press, and Clearwater's advertising, had already started to bracket them under the guise of 'spacerock' but there is little to glean from the scratchy recording of this show (or from the first studio recordings) that suggests this was an avenue actively followed. Smith certainly didn't believe there was any intention to create a tone specifically influenced by science fiction: "Hawkwind weren't really spacerock… the reality was that it was a good way to drop acid." At this point it seems more of an attempt to hang a label on the band that would successfully associate their output with the already commercially established style of Pink Floyd or Soft Machine.

Other festival appearances included their second visit to Europe, at Mantorps, near Stockholm, better known as a motor racing circuit, where they reportedly offered to sell the crowd duty-free cigarettes, whisky and contraceptives. The same report also claimed that "[Hawkwind] asked girls in the audience to join them later. Many were ready to accept." Back on home ground, an unbilled appearance at the Bath Festival saw the band organising a collection which, according to Turner, netted them "Money, acid and loads of other things."

Steve Swindells, then a teenage musician, who would himself later join Hawkwind, recalls seeing the group at this time. "They were playing in this empty, hotel squat in Great Pulteney Street [famous for its Georgian architecture]. A bunch of hippie anarchists there organised the 'alternative' Bath Festival and Hawkwind were playing. They were just awesome, really powerful. It was the old hotel lobby they were playing in, and it was packed – it was free. There was the wonderful faded grandeur of the hotel, semi-derelict, but it still had these lovely touches, like pink velvet curtains, so it was very atmospheric."

This wasn't the only appearance. Steve Mann, then working as a publicist for the band, recalled "bashing a tambourine with The Pink Fairies and Hawkwind at Bath. They were putting on an alternative festival off a flatbed truck in the next field." Pink Fairies roadie David Goodman, noted that "We took an Avis Flatbed lorry to a field above the Bath Festival … somebody like Doug Smith came wandering over and said, 'Hey man, we've got this group called Hawkwind, can they use your stuff?' We said, 'Sure!'" This led to a long-term association between the Hawks and the Fairies. Pete Frame, in his seminal Rock Family Trees, described how "when the two bands played regular gigs together, there was invariably a 'Pinkwind' set … a big din session at the end of the evening, bashed out by those still able to stand up!"

The Bath Festival (26th and 27th June, 1970) appears to have marked the final appearance of John Harrison with the band, with Langton recalling how "one day he just wasn't there anymore." He disappeared from the music scene, his fate, for many years, unknown. "John didn't like taking drugs," says Brock. "We went off to Altarnun, in Cornwall, and rented a cottage on the moors where we rehearsed. 'Larry the Mole' had come down with some organic mescaline and was trying to spike everybody up. We all took some, except for John who was off playing golf. Larry eventually spiked him up; I don't know how he managed to do it!"

Brock is quick to acknowledge Harrison's role in the embryonic Hawkwind: "He was a big influence because his bass playing was right there, you know? I regarded him as a great friend of mine, and he vanished, I don't know what happened to him! After 1970 and we'd done the [first] album, he was disenchanted with all the stuff that was going on, the band taking loads of drugs..." Another factor that may have frustrated Harrison's professional approach to music was the free and easy lifestyle of the other members. "All these characters were floating people, they used to travel around a lot; it wasn't very strict. Sometimes I didn't turn up," says Brock.

Turner: "John Harrison was probably somebody who was bored with straight music. I guess he thought, 'This is quite an interesting alternative.' It was probably undemanding musically, as the keys we were playing were pretty simple, uncomplicated chord structures. But this enabled him to be quite creative rather than just reading the dots!" On Harrison's departure, Turner simply reflects that "maybe he just didn't want to go with the band..."

Harrison's whereabouts remained a mystery across the decades, with rumours abounding of a pot of royalty cash locked away for him, should he return. Actually, he'd moved to America where on 26th May 2012, two days before his 70th birthday, he died quietly, surrounded by family and friends, having suffered from Huntingdon's Disease for several years. The great pleasure was that his location had finally become known and in his final months he'd become aware of the importance of his work with the band, and just how much that contribution was still appreciated both by Dave Brock and Hawkwind fans alike.

Thomas Crimble had been a member of Skin Alley prior to joining Hawkwind as Harrison's replacement. Skin Alley had a deal with CBS and featured their brand of jazz-rock on the compilation album, *Fill Your Head with Rock*, alongside Santana, Leonard Cohen, Spirit and Janis Joplin. "Skin Alley got together in 1968," recalls Crimble. "It was a busy, working band, playing mainly the university circuit."

"Things came to a head in Skin Alley because the guys I was playing with didn't want to add anything extra to our shows, but I wanted a lightshow and dancers. Being idealistic I made the decision to leave the band. There was a gig at the Lyceum, Hawkwind were playing as well, and Dave Brock asked if I'd like to join them. That was in May 1970." The timings suggest that it was already apparent that John Harrison was nearing the end of his interest in the band.

Crimble still talks passionately about the spirit inherent in the Notting Hill area of the time. He joined Hawkwind during a period when its co-operative, community ethos was increasingly visible, through free gigs around Ladbroke Grove and at major festivals such as the Isle of Wight. "We did the first gigs 'Under the Arches', where the Westway crosses over the top of Portobello Road," he recalls. "On a Saturday you'd just walk up and down Portobello Road, saying hello to everyone, and somebody said, 'why don't we do a gig,' so we said we'd give it a go. Slung a thirteen-amp cable around the corner to the fish shop, they seemed perfectly happy, and we just made a racket! Loads of people turned up, and went away smiling."

Crimble felt an affinity with the staff of the legendary underground publication *Friends* which was soon to adopt its now better-known title, *Frendz*. "They used to give us copies of their magazines, both *Oz* and *Friends*, and we'd give them out at the end of the gigs." Crimble saw it as an aspect of the counterculture: "We didn't analyse it too deeply, because there were flaws in the basic arguments… but on a positive/negative stance, peace and love was a good thing to be into. These guys were talking about that kind of thing, tinged with a certain element of anarchy. Nature's pretty chaotic, so a bit of chaos I wasn't too fussed about, but total chaos? There's no light at the end of that particular tunnel."

"We tried to do as many free gigs as we could, fund-raising things," Crimble adds. "We'd do one every two weeks or so, though the majority of gigs were clubs and universities paying proper money." In terms of who he saw as being idealistic in this area and the counterpoint of how that idealism could be structured, Thomas considers that "Nik Turner was the more philanthropic, into supporting weird and wonderful causes. Dave Brock seemed to have more of a handle on actually paying the bills at the end of the week. Dave wasn't against playing for no money, but only if we could subsidise it by playing for money at a load of other gigs." On reflection, Crimble wonders "where this free music came from, because nothing is free, everything costs somebody something… a nice idea but totally impractical."

Through their willingness to play benefit gigs, Hawkwind enjoyed a higher profile at the expense of making money for themselves or Smith's management company. "Clearwater needs expenses of about £200 a week to keep going," Brock told journalist Caroline Boucher, "And they get about £140." But there was clearly some method in the madness: the amount of newspaper coverage that such festivals generated would go a long way to generating demand for the band and its imminent record release, even if some of the writers covering the events didn't quite know who they were writing about. "500 turned up [at a gig on Wormwood Scrubs] to hear music from… a group called Hawk Wind [sic]" wrote one such reporter.

"The first free gig Hawkwind ever did was at Wormwood Scrubs," recalled Doug Smith. "There's all these hippies watching the gig and we look down the road and see these QPR skinheads… they're saying, 'Kill the hippies'. The crowd just split, they marched right through the middle, and then it closed again. The skinheads were just looking."

"Back then we did play lots of places for free," Brock says. "I recently found an old diary of all the dates we were playing and we were working every day, for free, loads of places. We had this old yellow parcel van, called the Yellow Wart, which had no heater in it and only two seats, one for the driver and one for his mate, so we used to be in our sleeping bags, travelling around in this ropey old van freezing cold. We found it in Cornwall and drove it back; Glory days!" To that less than glamorous recollection, Marion Lloyd-Langton would add: "Nik would ring and say 'Are you doing the gig' and we'd say 'Yes, where is it?' and it would be Birmingham or somewhere and we'd ask for a lift and he'd say, 'Just get there, mate!' And rather than try and get back we'd ask a student or two if they had room and sleep on their floors!" But their devotion to playing for free would pay its own dividends, and elevate them above their peers and into rock legend over the traditional August Bank Holi-day weekend at the famous Isle of Wight festival… and they weren't even on the bill.

The story of the 1970 Isle of Wight festival has passed into rock music folklore, partly for its huge attendance (reportedly between half a million and six hundred thousand, without a doubt a record for a British festival), but most significantly for the clash of ethos between the 'free festival' culture and the corporate organisations of the future. The promoters (the Foulk brothers) had created a logistical nightmare in the location of the site, being surrounded by hills, which afforded most attendees a free view of proceedings. Set this into the context of an underground ideal still dominated by revolutionary left-wing politics and the widening gulf between the bands of the era and their audience. Mix in the ubiquitous presence of the White Panthers and the usual motley anarchist collectives, and by the end of the festival, on 1st September 1970, Ron Foulk had declaimed "a beautiful dream [that became] a monster."

"The Isle of Wight Festival seemed a practical demonstration of the way the wealth of the underground is distributed," wrote a cynical and disillusioned Mick Farren. "A V.I.P enclosure surrounded by fences and protected by guards."

Over each day of the festival, Hawkwind cemented their reputation as 'The Peoples' Band' by performing for free outside the festival gates. This wasn't any sort of strategy, Crimble recalling simply that "we wanted to go and play at the festival… it was full-up with big names, but that didn't deter us, we just wanted to go and be part of it. We got to the car park, and there was a load of inflatables, one run by a guy called Fred Davis. He had bands playing and we asked if we could… it was this amazing, sausage-shaped tent, run by air… we played several sets in there, and several outside of it."

"It wasn't Hawkwind, as such; most of them were out tripping with the elves! There was Thomas Crimble and myself, and there was a bunch of Brazilian drummers who were marvellous!" contends Langton.

"Terry Ollis, Huw and myself set up on a stage, started playing late evening, when we finished it was eight o'clock in the morning; we'd played for about eight hours. Nik came in, played some sax and flute, then wandered off, as did Dave Brock," notes Crimble of one set. "The audience were simply people wandering in and wandering out again, as were the musicians. I was interested in getting a rhythmic pattern, with the echo chamber going. The music we were playing through our guitar amps was being picked up by the vocal microphones and echoed … we'd build up on that theme in time with the echo and it go into a trance thing, repetitive long music. It was the beginning of dance music as we know it now!" Crimble didn't see this in the Krautrock context, however: "Dave Brock was always on at me to go and listen to some Can, or 'play it like Can', but it was so sparse and regimented that I couldn't see any heart or soul in it." Captured fleetingly on celluloid, for Murray Lerner's documentary *Message to Love – Isle of Wight 1970* was Terry Ollis, stripped to the waist and trashing his drum kit for all it was worth.

Steve Swindells, also at the Isle of Wight, recalls seeing another configuration of the band playing. "No one was there! There was no audience! It was virtually an extension of Dave as a busker, with Nik on flute and Terry on drums. I don't remember Huw there. It was like they were playing to a couple of ants on the grass! I just thought Dave Brock's guitar had such an extraordinarily unique, powerful sound."

Langton remembers being told that Jimi Hendrix had turned up and watched Hawkwind play during one of their performances. "Somebody asked him if he wanted to get up and play. He actually said to them that if he did so, he'd spoil it!" This makes a lot of sense to Crimble, who had played with Hendrix a few weeks earlier at The Revolution Club in London. "He, being man enough and realising a few things, knew that as soon as he started playing, it would change the whole vibe of the thing. As soon as Jimi Hendrix started playing on that stage, the whole circus would begin." At the Revolution Club, Crimble and Skin Alley's drummer Giles Pope had been asked to form the backing band for Hendrix and Stephen Stills. "Stephen Stills played really well, and Hendrix really badly. It opened my eyes because he was all over the place, bum notes, but still got a standing ovation at the end. I saw this two-faced thing... I talked to him after the gig, and he said he couldn't figure out what was good anymore, he only had to blow his nose and he'd get a standing ovation."

Turner had his faced painted silver. "He fell asleep on the main stage when Hendrix was playing... and Hendrix dedicated a number to him: 'This next one is for the cat with the silver face.' Out of it came an article in the *Observer* colour supplement of July 1973 on festivals; there was a photo in it, by Ron Reed, of Hawkwind," notes Crimble.

The mind-twisting effects of Hawkwind's audio generators and strobe lighting were succinctly described by Dave Brock to Jerry Gilbert after the Isle of Wight: "The sounds send out a force field... we were playing a heavy riff for about four hours with strobe lighting going on and off, and it freaked me out so badly I just had to get away. I gave my guitar to the nearest person and walked up to the top of the hill, but I still couldn't get rid of this thing in my head."

However important the Isle of Wight festival was in developing the ethos of Hawkwind for their stand on ticket prices, it ended very badly for Huw Lloyd-Langton. In this respect, it demonstrated that the drug culture that had permeated throughout Ladbroke Grove was in danger of derailing some of Hawkwind's original intentions. Langton unwittingly drank some orange juice which had been spiked with LSD. This wasn't the first occasion that Huw, no more than a casual user of soft drugs, had suffered from being set-up in this way, but it had the most serious consequences.

Langton expressed the effects of the overdose plainly and simply when I talked with him for the first edition of this book: "I'm very lucky to be able to sit here and talk about it. The whole circumstance was quite horrific." Perhaps as a safety valve with which to release the distress of the situation, Langton recalled that the following day, "I walked down to the seas and baptised myself, then got to the gig; stood up and started playing when it was daylight and finished when it became daylight the next day." The impact of this spiking, when Langton had already decided against using LSD again after a similar previous experience, was a primary cause of his departure from Hawkwind following a nervous breakdown. "I went very funny in the mind and I had to walk away from the whole music business." Langton thought he would abandon music as a career, but these feelings lasted only a few months. "[Marion] took me off to the South of France, with a little acoustic guitar, and I started playing again. If you're an artist or a musician, really you have no choice, you do what you do!"

"Huw left within a month or six weeks of the Isle of Wight," explains Crimble (Langton places this as being around the time that Hendrix died, so circa 18th September 1970). "Dave Brock tried some lead guitar, but though he's a brilliant rhythm guitarist, he's not a lead." Crimble recalls that a temporary solution was found by engaging the services of Dick Taylor, who played some gigs with Hawkwind during the autumn. "Brock said, 'We can carry on without Huw,' but I missed him because he was a bloody good guitarist and the whole thing needed his soaring solos over the top of it... it lost something at that point."

Langton maintained contact through the years, eventually returning to the band in 1979, by which time he'd played in numerous ensembles, including Amon Din with Hawkwind's next bassist Dave Anderson and Jawa, alongside a significant figure in Hawkwind history, Simon King. He and Marion also wrote prolifically through the 70s; some of those songs would emerge from their collaborations to become much loved Hawkwind numbers in some instances, others ones that the band would play live or experiment with in the studio. There was 'Rocky Paths', which Marion recalled being written "when we were staying with Dave Anderson in Shepherds Bush. Huw was messing about with new ideas for an Amon Din tour [circa 1971/72]. We never had a set system of collaboration. Huw would play me new ideas and riffs and that inspired me to write lyrics on the spot, or I would write lyrics and hand them to Huw, or we co-wrote." Also intended for Amon Din was an Arthurian fantasy, 'Dragons & Fables', which actually had a more personal tale hidden within. "I suppose the lyrics were meant to convey what it felt like being a free spirit following a nasty period of being imprisoned by a jealous maniac... not Huw, he was a breath of fresh air in comparison!"

Others, particularly 'Mark of Cain' and 'Got Your Number' emphasised the couple's commitment to God. "Occasionally I thought about [the conflict between religion and Hawkwind's 'Chaos' imagery]" said Huw, "but the bottom line is that your internal religious feelings are yours. Anything that Hawkwind does is entertainment. Unless you're a complete idiot you don't take any of it seriously. If you haven't got that mustard seed of belief in you, you can get written off to all spectrums of sci-fi and God knows what…" Of 'Got Your Number', Marion recalled how "The lyrics speak for themselves. Huw was not a bible-bashing Christian but often said 'If that's what they did to Christ…' then we should not be surprised when justice doesn't serve us? That's not to say we shouldn't fight for it!"

Crimble also left Hawkwind near the end of 1970, "invited to leave by Dave Brock," and playing his last gig with the band at the Roundhouse on 13th December. "I was reading *Siddhartha* by Herman Hesse, about someone who goes on a quest and leaves everything behind – it's quite a spiritual book – and it was obviously time to move on, so I didn't kick up a fuss. At the end of the Isle of Wight, I was standing in a sea of Coke cans, looking at the main stage with my girlfriend, Jytte Klamer. She introduced me to some people who thought that these big, commercial, festivals weren't the way forward and that free festivals would be more idealistic and better for everyone. Within a week [of leaving Hawkwind], I was asked to help get Glastonbury Festival together, with Andrew Kerr." Crimble relocated to Somerset and lived at the festival's home, Worthy Farm; his involvement with the festival stretched through until the end of the 1990s.

"I really enjoyed playing [in Hawkwind] …the creation of music. I'm not very big on the repetition of the music, I like creating the songs, that's the buzz I get. A lot of the Hawkwind stuff, there's a beginning and an end, but there is a gap in the middle where anything can happen and when the music takes off, that's an experience you can't buy. Every gig we did, we played nonstop; it wasn't three minutes and stop for the clapping, we played an hour and a half solid, and then at the end the audience went berserk."

3

In Search of Spacerock

During the first eighteen months of their existence, Hawkwind steadily established their reputation in the underground community and particularly within the free festival scene. The promotion of their first album leaned heavily on the concept of 'spacerock' as a convenient label rather than any kind of mission statement, and a refining of what the band would be about was starting to become much needed.

Lurking in the background however, were major catalysts that would develop the band more firmly towards their stated goal of an 'audio-visual thing' and lead them into the areas of performance art and sci-fi theatre. It's hard to pin down exactly when Hawkwind moved from being a promising, if unspectacular, rock band and started to offer a more conceptually rounded presentation of music, spoken word, dance and visual display. Useful reference points could be some 1971 gigs, when Hawkwind were joined on stage by a doyen of the British science fiction community and by a poet whose ambition was to take poetry out of the English garden of verse and transpose it into a mix of street theatre and space opera.

At some point in the spring or summer of 1971, the imposing figure of Michael Moorcock joined Hawkwind on stage to fuse their embryonic spacerock with his own brand of epic sword-and-sorcery fantasy and his edgy, contemporary SF vision. Widely acknowledged as a literary genius, he had come to prominence in British science fiction circles in the early 1960s when he took over the editorship of *New Worlds* magazine from E.J. Carnell. Moorcock used *New Worlds* to grab British SF by the tail and give it a hefty swing into what others would quickly define as the 'new wave'. He unlocked the surrealist imagination of J.G. Ballard, probably the most notable literary SF figure of all, and gave full vent to SF's young chargers, such as Charles Platt (whose story 'The Failures' in issue #158 is an early SF/rock crossover), M. John Harrison, Thomas M. Disch and Roger Zelazny.

Moorcock's professional fiction and editorial work started at the precocious age of seventeen, producing Edgar Rice Burroughs fanzines, leading to the editorship of *Tarzan Adventures* magazine. Aside from this, Moorcock worked as a journalist, and played jazz and blues in the London clubs that had provided the setting for Dave Brock's early musical ventures. "Alexis Korner, Cyril Davies, Skiffle Cellar, Topic Records and the invasion of old black geniuses into London," he recalled to Patrick Hamilton in an interview for *Zone-SF*. Moorcock claimed to have been "around pretty much since the beginning of British rock 'n' roll." There is a resonance with Brock's embryonic career, when Moorcock told *Orbit* fanzine that "everything I learnt was picked up from people playing little clubs, coffee bars where you weren't actually on stage, but a few people just gather round and start playing."

New Worlds established a link between science fiction and what might loosely be described as 'pop culture' that Moorcock would build upon during the 1970s. "People of my generation were attracted to SF and rock 'n' roll because they had no standing with authority. They were in the margins and out of sight," he told *Zone-SF*. His appearance with Hawkwind was not as a musician but as a poet, reading material with a pronounced science fiction theme: perhaps 'Black Corridor', a declamation of the emotional and physical emptiness of space that was actually a straight reading of the opening paragraphs of a novel of the same name officially credited to Moorcock but generally understood to have been written by his then wife, Hilary Bailey, or 'Sonic Attack', a meshing of a nuclear-style three-minute warning with an invocation of a rock music assault on the senses. 'Sonic Attack' seemed to parody the British Government's 'Public Information Film' entitled 'Three Minute Warning' that was itself intended to prefigure a nuclear attack. "I saw 'Sonic Attack' as the distinctly urban sound of the band," Mike recalled.

Moorcock was entrenched in the Notting Hill underground scene, which he firmly marked *New Worlds* as a part of, telling SF historian Colin Greenland in 1994 that "I lived in Ladbroke Grove; everything happened [there] in the sixties and seventies... it all happened around me. You couldn't actually move for bloody rock and roll bands!"

"The first time I saw Hawkwind play was when Bob Calvert and [*Frendz* journalist] Jon Trux took me to meet them," Moorcock recalls. "I seem to remember it was somewhere in Fulham. [*New Worlds* writer] M. John Harrison was also with us." Moorcock's initial impression was "that they were like the mad crew of a long-distance spaceship who had forgotten the purpose of their mission, which had turned to art during the passage of time." Brock and Turner were both enthusiastic about Moorcock's work, and, upon meeting him, did not waste any time in asking him to become involved with the band. At the time, however, Moorcock was aware that Robert Calvert was already starting to work with them: "It didn't feel right somehow to move in as Bob was starting up his career."

Moorcock's influence on the development of Hawkwind's SF pretensions is significant but that would be for a later time. For the moment, the way was clear for Robert Newton Calvert to assume the mantle of resident poet and guiding light. Although Calvert was born in Pretoria, South Africa, on 9th March 1945, both his parents were English and returned home towards the end of the decade. They settled in the seaside town of Margate, and established a newsagent's shop, though they later elected, along with Robert's brother Derek, to return to South Africa. Opposed to the oppression endemic in the sub-continent's minority rule, the seventeen-year-old Calvert refused the opportunity to move with his family. This led to a distance in his relationship with his parents that became even more emotional than it was geographical.

Though the breakdown in communication with his parents became so pronounced that eventually his mother was forced to engage the services of the

Red Cross in an attempt at a reunion, there were factors in Robert's childhood that contributed to this estrangement. His sister, Rosemary, suffered from cerebral palsy, a condition that demanded a great deal of their mother's time, and may have affected the mother-son bonding. Aside from this, in his youth Calvert had been misdiagnosed as schizophrenic. His creative energy characterised him, absorbed him and, at many stages in his life, overtook him. He was prone to extreme mood swings, manic depression and was sectioned (legally removed to mental institutions) more than once.

Calvert remained in Kent, moving along the coast to Ramsgate and then to Broadstairs, making a living during the summer seasons in much the same way as Turner: "a bit of deck chairs, a bit of beach photography." This worked to his advantage, earning him just enough cash in the summer to see him through the winter months and allowing him to develop his interest in writing ("Most of my formative years were spent writing poetry," he told *Melody Maker*). He was enjoying limited success in placing fiction with *Friends* magazine, and working for *International Times* (*IT*) as a gig reviewer.

Bob spent a considerable amount of time planning and discussing with his friends Nik Turner and Dik-Mik the sort of band that they might put together, so it's surprising that "when they went off to form Hawkwind, I went off to form another band with three French musicians." Turner clarifies this: "When I used to go to Holland, Robert was very interested, but he was never able to go. He had a wife and children. He had ties." Aside from these family commitments (Turner notes at that time, Calvert "treated his wife badly, didn't care much for his children, whether it was from his medical condition... he didn't look after himself as he should have done."), his stability was questionable. "It wasn't easy at the time," says Turner, "for Bob to buzz off with me and form a band. He didn't have the freedom that I had."

Journeys to London, either to visit the editors of *Friends* or to check-out the latest bands took up more and more of Calvert's time. Eventually he left Kent and relocated to the capital. Appearances at the Roundhouse, whether solo as a poet, or with his first attempt at getting a band together, followed. Unfortunately, the band quickly fizzled out, his cross-continental effort failing as "they didn't speak much English and I didn't speak any French."

Calvert recalled to Kris Tait, for her book *This is Hawkwind, Do Not Panic*, an appearance as part of an exhibition, again at the Roundhouse, entitled 'A Better Place to Live'. "We were actually a live exhibit, performing a peculiar arrangement of words, sounds and fiction." If it seems pretentious in retrospect, perhaps Calvert had his tongue more firmly in his cheek than his recollections suggested: "I looked on myself as a kind of anti-literacy establishment guerrilla." At other times, he would describe himself as an 'urban poet' or sometimes ironically as a 'suburban poet'.

These appearances at the Roundhouse brought him back into contact with Turner. Calvert was vaguely aware of Hawkwind, and indeed Brock was already an acquaintance having encountered Calvert whilst busking on the

Portobello Road, but he hadn't taken too much interest in them. He felt the name was rather frivolous and anticipated a pub rock band. Turner changed this perception by enthusing about their 'spacerock' theme, which appealed greatly as it "sounded something brand new." This seemed to be a good fit to Calvert's plans. He'd first dreamed about fusing SF and rock in some sort of 'Space Ritual' whilst minding shop for his mother back in Margate.

Calvert already had some material written and ready to perform and so eagerly accepted an opportunity to appear on stage with Hawkwind at the Seven Sisters Club. On 26th May, 1971 he stepped up to the microphone and opened their set with a reading of his poem 'Co-Pilots of Spaceship Earth'.

As Calvert cemented his place within the band, his contributions would increasingly become a focal point, until his recitals gave way to lead singer, and very occasional rhythm guitar player, status. At the outset, however, he was content with exploring the various ways that spoken delivery could be expanded on: "I'm not really a vocalist. I'm a sound poet," he contended, whilst looking forward to a more expansive role in the future. "I haven't got all the equipment yet but I'm doing as much as I can with microphone and voice." It's a candid, if understated, appraisal of his abilities at that stage.

"Bob had a large influence, with his ideas," says Turner. "He became involved in a literary way. He saw an opportunity to take part in an underground thing. Bob was a fan of Mike Moorcock, because Mike was a successful writer and Bob wasn't. When Robert started performing with Hawkwind, Mike became a fan of his!"

Moorcock's occasional appearances with Hawkwind were generally a result of Calvert being unavailable due to having been hospitalised because of his mental state. On the first occasion that Moorcock was asked to deputise, he notes how "I visited Bob to tell him what I was going to do… that as soon as he came out I would step down. From then on that was how I worked, filling in when Bob wasn't available, but always stepping aside for him when he and the band wanted to work together."

The addition of Calvert is a defining moment, a signal away from the freeform anarchy of the early Hawkwind. *IT* commented the following year that, "in the years before Calvert, Hawkwind were your archetypal freak band, permanently broke and perpetually boogyin'… their un-togetherness was legendary." In a roundup of the way the band had developed through Calvert's nervous energy, the writer believed that Robert had "given Hawkwind the kick up the ass they so obviously needed."

Creating an overall cohesion to Hawkwind's identity required more diverse components than the band's music merged with Calvert's SF obsessions. It needed what, ironically, might today be considered corporate branding and that in turn relied upon the graphic design skills of Colin Fulcher, known as 'Barney Bubbles'.

**Bob Calvert shakes a tambourine at the Gods
(Collection of Dave Brock)**

Though he had a passion for music and was a more than passable guitarist, the outlet for his creative skills was in the field of graphic design. He enjoyed early success, having acquired a wealthy patron who employed him on several mainstream commercial ventures. Barney lived around the vicinity of Notting Hill throughout the 1960s, firstly in a block of flats in Addison Crescent, West Kensington, later purchasing 307 Portobello Road where he set-up a design studio and basement rehearsal room.

He was a self-deprecating character, as his friend John Cowell (who first met Barney around 1964/65) describes: "He never thought he was good enough, he refused to sign his name on his paintings; people were not able to persuade him of his abilities. He'd much rather help someone else achieve, than do it for himself."

Barney frequented the Middle Earth, getting involved in producing the house lightshow. Cowell recalls him "driving around in 'The Love Lorry', a painted-up ice-cream van." 307 Portobello Road became an essential hang-out, "a real centre" for artists, musicians and drifters. The interior was used in one of the earliest rock promo-films, for the Ronnie Hawkins single 'Down in the Alley'. "We felt an integral part of the movement, anti-materialistic," says Cowell. "I remember sitting by the window, watching the Notting Hill Carnival go past... three reggae bands on lorries." The free and open atmosphere of the house led to its downfall, with too many unwelcome visitors stealing from the occupants. "Barney was a true hippie. He didn't want to own anything. Possessions really upset him."

Phil Franks, who worked closely with Barney on the imagery for some of the early Hawkwind albums, remembers him as being "a very complex person, somebody who always wanted to give his most. It didn't matter how much people were paying him, or if they paid at all ... he wanted to pass that on to whoever was paying the money in the record shop, buying it and taking it home. Hence, old, cheap, cardboard... but out of old, cheap, cardboard rather than hi-gloss and lots of colours, you could get the money from the budget to do a foldout sleeve, or even a small book. Barney always did it for the end-user, the fan."

Friends magazine eventually rented a part of 307 and Barney became the magazine's art director. Amongst his achievements was recognising the potential of photographer Pennie Smith and publishing much of her early pictures. Her work on record sleeves (notably The Clash's *London Calling*) would become just as iconic as Barney's own. Keith Morris, another photographer that Barney used extensively, recalled his influence as being "brilliantly able to use text and pictures and satisfy [anyone] who was involved. He was the ultimate designer, probably the most original and innovative that has worked in London, bar none." And Doug Smith described how "Barney was, as far as media direction of the youth of this country, probably the most important artist of our generation. His influence on Hawkwind was substantial. His life was really tripping out of his head, and painting."

"I met Barney through *Frendz*," notes Nik Turner. "Hawkwind got involved with the underground scene, not through consciously thinking we'd like to be involved... we just were. We liked to play, and I was organising a lot of concerts for the band at the time. For instance, we'd do a gig in Portobello Road, under the flyover, where *Frendz* magazine was based. Mike Moorcock and Barney were involved in the magazine, and Bob had been writing articles for it... all part of the underground, which we endorsed and which endorsed us. Barney was really inspired by the band; he came to one of our gigs and was completely mind-blown by it."

"Mike Moorcock, Barney Bubbles and Robert Calvert had a profound influence on the band," states Turner. "Moorcock endorsed Hawkwind publicly as being the sort of band that his Jerry Cornelius character would listen to, and so the band appeared in the Jerry Cornelius books. Mike dedicated several of his fantasy novels to members of the band and endorsed it on that level as well."

The gathering together of these disparate figures would propel Hawkwind towards limited singles chart success and enable them to achieve the cult status of a band outside of the music business but drawing on the industry's resources to satisfy their goals. That the band could become one of the biggest live acts in England – two thousand people were turned away from a sell-out show at the Roundhouse in 1972 – but maintain their sense of community would be their biggest challenge, and their most extraordinary achievement in the years ahead.

4

Masters of the Universe?

As Hawkwind had always demonstrated a musical link to Krautrock, it's perhaps little surprise that they replaced Thomas Crimble with Dave Anderson, who had already established himself with Amon Düül II, though he'd initially gone out to Germany with Nick Lowe, who was with a band called Kippington Lodge, which eventually became Brinsley Schwartz. "I got asked to do an audition [for Amon Düül II] and ended up in Munich for the next three and a half years."

"The original Amon Düül community had split into different directions," notes Anderson. "Amon Düül II was the musical side of it. There wasn't much of a German music scene going on at the time, but there were lots of underground things happening. The Paris student riots had happened the year before, and now it was Munich's turn." Krautrock is often characterised as being more than just influenced by the political scene, perhaps dependent upon it would be the more succinct assessment. Anderson might not necessarily agree, considering instead that "I don't think any of us were that [politically] aware, we were just living our lives the way we wanted to – which might have been political – but it was just gaining a bit of freedom." Anderson remembers seeing "Can and Tangerine Dream; the two main bands. Can was on the same label as Amon Düül, so we saw each other regularly. Amon Düül II was successful to a point, but other bands became more successful. There wasn't always continuity within Amon Düül, they didn't like to play that often, so they were limited to the amount of promotion they could get. The type of music they were playing was a bit extreme, and Can and Tangerine Dream took over and sold even more, but Amon Düül were a couple of years ahead of anybody."

Anderson's ambitions led him to want to play in a British band. However important, in an esoteric way, the Krautrock scene was, the natural progression was to break Germany, then Britain, and then the USA. "I wanted to be living where I could speak the language properly, and everybody respected what was going on in England at the time." Returning home, initially still as member of Amon Düül II and commuting back to Germany for tours, Anderson was excited about the social and cultural changes that had developed in his absence. "It was just great; the late 60s, early 70s was the most magical time in British rock history. There were so many different kinds of music, and the audiences weren't blinkered in any way. The government had just put lots of money into universities, so the social side of life was beginning to blossom after the austerity of the post-war years. There were gigs every night, and every town had a band of its own, playing to an audience that was young and had just come into wealth compared to what their parents had been putting up with."

"I don't think people were that aware at the time about politics; perhaps that's why [the counterculture] didn't develop into much more," notes Phil

Franks. "It was the Wilson-era, what got called 'the affluent society', post-war recovery and expansion, jobs for everybody. When I left home and 'dropped out', went to share a flat in the Portobello Road, you could get a job anywhere. You just went out, bought a newspaper and had a look. Or living frugally, you could get by with what you got from the dole. So there was that social, political, economic air around that encouraged the permissive society."

Before joining Hawkwind, Anderson "played in Van Der Graaf Generator, but I was made redundant by Hugh Banton playing bass pedals on the Hammond, which broke my heart." Anderson had encountered the members of Hawkwind at the offices of United Artists, which led to Nik Turner putting Anderson's name forward as a potential bassist for the band. "Dave Brock came over to the house that the members of Brinsley Schwartz were living in at the time. We had a bit of a jam together, and I was asked to join."

"My first impression was that Nik was more important than Dave," observes Anderson. "Nik certainly was the frontman, Dave very much in the background, he wouldn't turn up at gigs, which used to really piss me off, because I had to play guitar, which I didn't like very much." Although it would be wrong to draw too many parallels between Anderson and John Harrison before him, Anderson does describe himself as "the straightest one out of the band. I was asked to deal with all the finances, so I did the business side of things and collected the money [at gigs]." In terms of the influence upon the early Hawkwind, Anderson viewed Krautrock contributing "in as much as it was experimental music. It was improvising, seeing what happened."

On 9th April 1971, the band were joined on stage by the statuesque figure of would-be dancer Stephanie Leach – known as Stacia - whose uninhibited performances would become such an important, if notorious, part of Hawkwind's visual identity. This show, at the Flamingo Club just outside of the town of Redruth in Cornwall is commonly thought to have been on 16th April, though local newspaper advertising places it as being the previous week, and was bizarrely billed as an 'end of term dance in the ballroom'.

"We were halfway through the gig at the Flamingo Club, and I remember thinking 'my God! There's somebody at the front with their shirt off,'" notes Anderson of Stacia's first appearance. "You couldn't see properly, because we played with a lot of strobes, but you could see it was somebody dancing naked. She came back stage after the gig and said, 'That was fantastic! I've always wanted to do that!' We asked her to do it on a regular basis, but she said, 'I can't. I'm a petrol pump attendant!' We told her that we'd book her into a hotel for the night and that she should go off the next day and tell her employers that she was leaving." Anderson recalls that Stacia wouldn't leave her job and join Hawkwind without first working the morning shift!

Stacia's own recollections of that event suggest something a little more organised than the impromptu performance remembered by Dave Anderson. In an interview for *Penthouse* magazine (which breathlessly described her as 42-28-39, a spectacular set of measurements even by *Penthouse* standards) she talked of having been invited to a rehearsal after seeing the band at a show in Exeter. "Then I went with them to a concert in Redruth. We were all bombed out of our heads and I asked if I could dance on stage. We found some greasepaint; I made up and went on."

Her famous trademark of stripping on stage, an enduring recollection, if not to say hugely formative experience, for a misty-eyed generation of men who could claim to be adolescent admirers back in the day, was put down to a response to her innate shyness. "I just covered my whole body in paint," she told Laurie Henshaw for *Melody Maker*. Stacia's original ambition, to be a ballet dancer like her idol Isadora Duncan, was thwarted by her six-foot height, and she had turned her attention towards acting and more freeform styles of dance. Despite a passion for classical music (she professed a love of Delius, Mozart, Verdi, Wagner and Dvorak at age eight), her interests had developed into jazz and then onto The Beatles.

She had already encountered Hawkwind at the Isle of Wight festival and then again "[in] London where they were rehearsing at the Middle Earth." Occasional appearances led to full membership, indiscernible at times due to the band's lighting effects but gradually enjoying a more expansive role. (One music paper reported a 15-minute mime sequence with Nik Turner.) "The face make-up is probably to hide my identity," Stacia told Melody Maker. "Arthur Brown was the first one. When 'Fire' came out, that really blew my mind and I started to muck around with my mother's make-up, psychologically that had something to do with it."

"A lot of *In Search of Space* was written on the road," notes Anderson of Hawkwind's second album. "Improvisations that were really group things, though there were songs like 'Children of the Sun' that Nik and I did, and 'You Shouldn't do That', which probably I wrote if you think about what I'm doing on it."

Hawkwind were making the transition from improvising around the themes that made up the first album, and starting to develop a wider suite of material that would encompass the songs and jam-based numbers of *In Search of Space*. By May 1971, they had cut a session for BBC Radio 1 which included 'Master of the Universe', Hawkwind's first spacerock classic, which Turner recalled writing "as a poem, really, it was what I felt," though he conceded also that "I think Bob came in on it with me, chipped in a few words." There was also the loose and hazily sprawling number 'You Know You're Only Dreaming' which was already in the live set and which recent discoveries of live cuts and a studio demo have revealed to have been a particularly pliable and evolving song, and the agitprop sprawl of 'You Shouldn't do That'. The latter's title may have been inspired by the words from The Velvet Underground's 'Sister Ray' ("Aw, you shouldn't do that…"). From then onwards, live shows appear to have left behind Brock's busker roots of 'Hurry on Sundown' but retained the more sonically unsettling elements of the early gigs, such as 'Paranoia' and 'Seeing it as You Really Are'. It was a clear move to refine the group's ability as individual

50

musicians and develop their available song list. "The initial thing was quite undisciplined, but when you get self-awareness of what you're doing, musically, you tend to become more structured and write songs with lyrics that are relevant to the time and the influences that you're involved with," observes Turner.

Rehearsing for *In Search of Space* was a difficult task for a band with a seven day a week itinerary and therefore sound checks were the most opportune time to experiment. However, in May, Hawkwind travelled to Aviemore, in Scotland, specifically to work through their material, with quite horrific consequences. "We had a terrible car crash, all our equipment got smashed and somebody got killed," recalls Anderson. The accident involved Hawkwind roadie 'John the Bog', who normally travelled to gigs in advance of the band to check on technical requirements, an American driver, and Dik-Mik, along with a couple of other passengers. "John had his arm resting out of the car's window; the crash removed a large part of his elbow. The driver of the car they hit was killed. '[John] was in hospital for months afterwards, having skin grafts. It was the nephew of the landlady where we were staying who was killed – horrible."

The accident led to the temporary departure of Dik-Mik, who was badly affected by the incident and decided that the amount of travelling involved in Hawkwind was too much for him. He was replaced on synthesiser by the band's road manager, Del Dettmar. "I'd got to Aviemore, gone to bed, and an hour later the telephone rang. Our van had been in a head-on accident three hours down the road." Though no charges were brought, the roadie driving the van was not insured, which meant that the band lost a considerable amount of money on what was a new vehicle, which had been financed by a loan that Dettmar had organised from United Artists.

Dettmar started working with Hawkwind early in 1971. "I turned them down, originally. Doug Smith asked me, I said the only way I'd work for them was for more money, and Doug said, 'No Problem!' I'd been working as a road manager since 1969, with The Pretty Things, then Edgar Broughton, Arthur Brown, a couple of gigs for High Tide, Juicy Lucy, and Cochise." Though he had taken some music lessons at the instigation of his parents ("My original teacher told them, 'Save your money'"), Dettmar didn't see his work as a stepping-stone. "It was a job in its own right. I didn't join as a musician, I wasn't one! Terry's drum roadie was on ten quid a week, which nobody could live on, so I gave him some of my money. Gone was the raise and we were both on fifteen pounds."

On Dik-Mik's departure, Dettmar recalls simply that, "I was mixing the band and driving the transit. They just gave me the synthesiser to do as well and at some point I moved from the mixing console to the stage. Nobody really wanted to see Dik-Mik leave, so he was in-and-out for a while." Like Dik-Mik before him Del was essentially creating effects rather than playing keyboard solos. "We had a small WEM mixer, six channels and the reverb. I could either create an effect with the synthesiser or take a line out of one of the instruments and feed it through." Moorcock describes Dettmar "plugging things into the synthesiser apparently at random, like a crazed electronics engineer, but with the steady movement of the ship's progress emphasised by the band's rhythmic music." Around this, Moorcock saw the directing hand of Dave Brock. "I came to realise how much Dave kept the band together. He was like the captain of the ship, his signals mostly coming through the tone he gave to his guitar. He has a great sense of the dramatic and the band surged and subsided at his touch."

There was also a change in management. "We'd left Clearwater Productions," Del explains. "Clearwater was basically four guys; one who put up the money and three who did the work. Out of the three, one person was super-efficient – so eventually you'd end up going to the person who could make something happen, which was Douglas. The other guys wanted to actually do something, so Doug said he'd take a backseat for a while. We took the 'booker' out of the agency, who was Dave Anderson's girlfriend, Angie, and United Artists gave her an office."

The regularity with which Hawkwind were gaining mainstream coverage was significantly raising their profile. "When I joined the band, we still had to pay people to give us a gig," claims Anderson. "When I left, we were on £1,500 a night, seven nights a week. Not making any money as there were so many on the entourage, but in the space of a year we went from being absolutely nowhere to being the hippest thing in town."

During this period Hawkwind played many gigs at unusual venues, at Marazion, in Cornwall, overlooking the former Benedictine Priory on the granite causeway-linked St. Michael's Mount for example, or under the shadow of the Westway in Ladbroke Grove.

"I was asked to appear at a gig under the motorway at Portobello Green," notes Moorcock. "I had helped put the little theatre there together and in fact the murals were done by my friend and regular illustrator, Jim Cawthorn. They were free Saturday afternoon concerns, often fraught with difficulties because residents on the far side of the Green objected to us." Moorcock adds that, "I always suspected they didn't like the look of the audiences, who consisted of locals, hippies, and a lot of black people; a wonderful mix of pretty much everyone in that part of London." For Moorcock's premiere appearance with Hawkwind, he recalls "performing several pieces, one of which was 'Sonic Attack'. They were all metaphorical pieces. I think I did 'Use Your Armour' too, but 'Sonic Attack' was the one which captured everyone's imagination."

For the first Glastonbury Festival (23rd June, 1971), a legendary appearance, mainly through the context of what Glastonbury became in the 80s and beyond, at which Dave Brock was unable to perform due to sickness, Hawkwind were joined on the Pyramid Stage by Thomas Crimble. "There had been about twenty people at Worthy Farm, trying to get the festival together, but it was too many cooks. It got whittled down to a few of us; Andrew Kerr, Jytte Klamer, Mark Irons, Arabella Churchill, and myself, and we organised the free festival. At the festival, I bumped into Hawkwind, and they told me Dave Brock wasn't going to play and would I fill in; Dave Anderson moved onto guitar and I played bass and we swapped over halfway through." In terms of the change in

Hawkwind over the six months since he'd played with the band, Crimble professes himself "amazed to discover that jams, notably 'You Shouldn't do That', which was a bass riff that I used to do at the Isle of Wight, turned into numbers on the second album… that's just the way of it, so I didn't waste any sleep over it."

At the Tregye Hotel, near Truro, Hawkwind played a controversial, among the locals, all-day festival, headlined by Arthur Brown. On the day, though, the gig passed off peacefully, with one retired school teacher noting wistfully in the local newspaper that she had "seen more rebelliousness at the end of term prize-giving ceremonies." Important to the band was their deconstruction of the barrier with the audience, a 'fourth-wall' breaking approach which became the foundation for Turner's later claim that the audience was the 'real Hawkwind'. Anderson saw evidence of such a mind-set during his tenure. "We would actually be sitting in the audience. Come the time for Hawkwind to play, we'd climb up onto the stage. People would be going 'Christ, I was just sharing a spliff with him', or 'he's just given me some incense – and actually he's in Hawkwind.' That was very important; it made it special."

"We got an old lorry canvas from Terry Ollis's dad," recalls Dettmar. "We took it back to my parents, cut it into triangles and sewed it together to make a tepee, with a scaffolding pole to hold up the middle. It could get about fourteen people in it, so we took it around the festivals, to Bickershaw… my mum made it!"

"I remember an amazing gig at a Teacher Training College, somewhere near Southampton," says Dave Anderson. "It was in the days when most Colleges were allowed to have one gig a week, but this one only had one a term and it happened to be Halloween Night. They didn't seem to know what they had booked, so we turned up at this very straight venue. Early in the gig, I noticed for the first time that people were having a definite reaction to my bass. I gave up any hope of playing with the band, and concentrated on just playing for the people who I could see were reacting to me. What I didn't realise was that everybody else was having the same kind of reaction. We were all playing together, but not how we normally did. I was the highest I'd ever been in my life, just playing music, it really freaked me out." Anderson notes that after the show, "nobody could talk to each other for about a week; it was like a religious experience."

If it was a Halloween evening, it indicates that Anderson and his successor Lemmy overlapped their membership, since there is a known gig at Southampton on 31st October 1971, after Lemmy had joined the band. Post-Hawkwind, Anderson, together with Huw Lloyd-Langton, formed Amon Din, and supported Hawkwind at a number of gigs during 71/72 so it's entirely possible that on this occasion Anderson was called upon to provide his services during the main act.

Such events demonstrated the concept of 'freaking people nicely, without drugs', the challenge that Hawkwind had set themselves as part of the first album's agenda. This was a socio-political aspect of the band's intent, though Anderson sees this context only with the passage of time. "We weren't doing what my parents had done, or what I was expected to do by my parents, but I was living in a fairly ordered, civilised way. I'd smoke dope, or take acid but I wasn't that aware of it being very political, it wasn't until much later that I felt that maybe it was."

The ill-fated trip to Aviemore was simply to refine the material that was already in place for the new album, although this wasn't the only occasion that the band took an opportunity to work through songs away from the gig circuit. "When we were working out 'Master of the Universe' we were at Glastonbury," notes Anderson. "We used to go down there to rehearse, have all our gear set out on the lawn."

The recording sessions were slow to get underway; the band spent a week at George Martin's Air Studios in London but ended up with little work achieved. "Some of our friends spiked-up the engineer. He flipped out and didn't show for the rest of the week," recalls Anderson. "We were in the most modern studio in the world, and nobody knew how to 'switch it on'. We didn't get anything done." The only song on *In Search of Space* that derives from the time at Air was 'Master of the Universe'. To wrap up the LP quickly, the sessions were relocated to Olympic Studios, where Anderson says The Rolling Stones were working on *Exile on Main Street* at the same time. As that album was recorded later in 1971, at Keith Richards' home in France, it's likely this amounted to little more than rehearsals. The Hawkwind sessions were engineered by George Chikantz, who also worked with the Small Faces and Led Zeppelin ("a bloody good engineer," considers Anderson).

The first side of the LP, the extended 'You Shouldn't do That' and 'You Know You're Only Dreaming', together with the opening song from side two, 'Master of the Universe', replicated the contemporary Hawkwind live set. Most of the remaining material, Brock's acoustic 'We Took the Wrong Step Years Ago', another instance of him bring his busking sensibilities to the party, again with an 'Eve of Destruction' motif, and the bizarre, experimental 'Adjust Me' fitted in with what Turner described to *Sounds* as the album having "a lot of the things we believe, particularly the ecology thing." Turner saw the LP's structure as representing "people in a space-ship visiting Earth in 1985 ... [finding] ... a total mess of concrete and iron."

Andrew Means identified in *Melody Maker* how the 'Big Picture' analysis of contemporary crisis that runs through *In Search of Space* (the loss of individualism, the threat of ecological disaster and nuclear conflict) echoed the work of early 'Global Thinker', Buckminster Fuller. An early American futurist, Fuller saw the solutions to hunger, poverty and homelessness within the context of large-scale trends: 'Comprehensive Anticipatory Design Science'. In his book, *Operating Manual for Spaceship Earth* (the title surely an influence on Calvert's writings), Fuller implores "co-operate and don't hold back on one another or try to gain at the expense of another. These are synergetic rules that evolution is employing and trying to make clear to us." Fuller looked at the concept of 'space' in much the same way that Calvert and Barney Bubbles were attempting to portray it through poetry and art. "Space is presently non-tuned-in within the physical, sensorial range, because we are not receiving electromagnetic energy or information to our eyes, ears, nose, tongue or skin ... but space is identifiable as a metaphysical system – it is 'out there'." Out there, indeed, man.

Extant demo recordings of *In Search of Space* reveal an instrumental 'Adjust Me' that clock in at three minutes longer than the LP version, and an alternate cut of 'Master of the Universe' with an alternative vocal and no phasing in the middle section. "Dave Brock plays his guitar through an echo unit and a wah-wah pedal," noted Martin Hayman in Sounds. "Nik Turner plays his flute and saxes through the same processors." The two 'electronics experts', Dettmar and Dik-Mik, were heard to be producing a sound "ranging over the entire audible spectrum." In Hayman's view "it produces a very clear, pure sound... [which] ... is exploited well by the group in their search for an appropriately spacey sound on the album."

The only track which existed outside the original concept of the LP was the closing song, 'Children of the Sun'. "We never played that live," comments Anderson. "I got a phone call about one o'clock in the morning from George Chikantz saying that the album was five minutes short and could I get down [to the studio] really quickly." Anderson had by that time officially left the band and wasn't keen to contribute but agreed that if a taxi was sent, he would play. "I got down there and said, 'Okay, I've got this idea, 'Children of the Sun', and this is how it goes...' and we just did it, very quickly, a last-minute thing on the final night of the sessions."

Dave Anderson left because he believed his own musical ambitions would be better served in an alternative way. Unlike the other members of the band, his preference was for the studio environment over live performance. He also felt his colleagues less committed to advancing the band's profile by, for example, touring America, which Anderson claims "was all I really wanted to do." He eventually moved to Wales and opened his own recording studio, Foel, and later a label, Demi-Monde. "I just felt very frustrated. I wanted to set up and do it all for myself, so I didn't have to put up with tantrums and people not turning up." His Foel Studios set-up would go on to become a favourite of spacerock bands in future years. I talked to Martin Litmus, of 21st Century spacerockers Litmus after they'd recorded their *Aurora* album there, and he enthused about the experience: "we love going and working there, it's really the ideal place. You get away from distractions in the middle of nowhere; it's got a great sounding live room, it's got a good mix between recording digitally and analogue, a lovely sounding desk in the control room, a big old British Trident mixing desk. Chris Fielding, the engineer there, played a very big part in getting the sound we want, and Dave Anderson is always very welcoming." And Simon Williams of 80s free festival favourites Mandragora remembered recording their album *Over the Moon* at Foel, where he found that "Dave was really cool. We sat down together at the end of our recording and he had the master tapes of *In Search of Space*, put them on and they were wicked, we loved it."

"I never really got along with Dik-Mik," Anderson adds about his departure from the ranks. "We used to share a flat with two girls, then I went off and got married, left him with the girls, and I think he never forgave me for doing that." It has been suggested that Dik-Mik, a speed-freak, was agitating for fellow speed enthusiast Lemmy to be included in Hawkwind thus making Anderson's membership difficult. "I think that was on the cards," reflects Anderson. "I'd done speed in my Amon Düül days but by this time I wasn't interested in the drug thing all that much."

A material difference in lifestyle had opened-up between Anderson and the others. Hawkwind folklore has Anderson arriving for gigs in his sports car while the rest of the band travelled around in a van. Anderson himself makes no apologies for opting for the more comfortable approach to touring. "All I can say is, the queue to get into my car and get a lift back to London… they'd almost kill each other! We were playing seven nights a week, all over the country, coming back to London nearly every time to save money on hotels, and when you've got about sixteen people to drop-off, it's nearly time to get on the road again. Various people had skin complaints. I just thought, 'I don't want to be involved with that!' We were all on exactly the same money, all living on the same level, but instead of sticking things up my nose, or God knows what, I bought a car." By this point, Anderson notes that the drug consumption within the band was happening, "all the time. I can't believe Terry Ollis is still alive and so much better now than he was then! By the time I'd left, Terry could hardly talk. Mandrax was completely doing his brain in. He was just grunting."

Released in October 1971, *In Search of Space* presented a sharp distillation of the concepts that Moorcock, Calvert and Barney Bubbles had injected into the band's visual and lyrical imagery. Legendary rock critic Lester Bangs, writing for *Rolling Stone*, saw it as a natural extension of the works of Pink Floyd, but also referenced the record's science fiction ethos back to the literary works of Jules Verne and Cyrano de Bergerac. "Pink Floyd still take the sweepstakes in the rock race for space, but hold onto yer Buck Rogers beanies because Hawkwind are coming up fast," wrote Bangs. "This is music for the astral apocalypse." Though he described the album as being rooted in the same monotone 'psyche-overload' of Amon Düül ("if you're glad that stuff is part of the past, you'll probably think this album is a pile of dog shit"), Bangs also relished "the absolute glee of filling your skull with all those squawks and shrieks and backwards tapes."

Richard Williams, reviewing for Melody Maker, viewed the lineage of *In Search of Space* in the same context. "I don't feel they reach the heights of [Amon Düül's] *Dance of the Lemmings* in their instrumental playing, but they yield to no-one in their creative use of electronics." And, while I'll confess to remaining not quite sure what it means, *International Times* described it as "music to get damaged to smasherooney," and that, frankly, sounds about right. Years later, in his seminal punk rock survey *England's Dreaming*, Jon Savage annotated *In Search of Space* as, "A submerged but archetypal vein of Englishness. Their best album."

Israeli 'Urban Guerrilla' 7" Sleeve
(Note *In Search Of Space* line-up pictured)

"I'd say it sounds good, even now," reflects Dave Anderson. "I've got a second-generation copy, as close as you can get to the original master, and when I listen to it in the studio it sounds 'WOW'."

The part of the package that held the most fascination for Lester Bangs, however, was not the music, but the 24-page 'Hawkwind Log' that could be found inside the album's gatefold sleeve. With its declamation of ancient British stone circle folklore, married with the shaman teachings of the Lakota Sioux wise man Black Elk and fused into a space-age technological mysticism, it was the collision of Calvert's classic SF obsessions and Barney Bubbles' eastern influences that gave Hawkwind a cohesive style and direction.

"Barney was my art director, if you put it on that level," notes Phil Franks, who provided the photographs of the band for the sleeve of *In Search of Space*. "He was in total charge of style and conception, but he never gave me any precise direction about any image he wanted me to photograph. What was great was that I would show him everything I'd been doing for myself, photos I'd shot on the street or wherever, and very often he'd use photographs that were nothing to do with the band. The Logbook was a good example. There's a nude female figure with astronomical charts overlaid. That is Giana, the mother of Barney's son Aten, a photo done sometime before as an idea for something for *Friends* magazine. The picture of a guy sitting cross-legged on a tree stump? Well, he was called Colin: Barney and I met him at a Grateful Dead concert. After the gig, we drove off with Colin in his Dormobile and just parked in lanes, in forests, for a couple of days." In terms of the ground-breaking foldout package that enfolded *In Search of Space*, Franks notes that "Barney did all the experimentation in his design work. Nobody then had thought about selling an LP in anything other than a flat sleeve. Barney pushed a lot of envelopes."

"Barney and Bob were responsible for creating the mythology of the band," says Turner, "and the vehicle was *In Search of Space*. They were able to coalesce the thing into an idea and an ideal which we all endorsed. Barney was very influential in the band's imagery, the band's philosophy. He created the stage image, the presentation, the graphic image of the band as seen in the press and on record sleeves. Barney said that what his paintings represented was that 'the hawk has stolen the heart of the lotus'. I thought it was a real honour to have him involved with us."

"Calvert was a deep thinker," adds Dave Anderson, "very intense, but a great lyricist and very quick at doing it. He wrote some great bass lines as well." In terms of the move away from simply a musical presentation to include Calvert's recitals, Anderson considers "That's how it should be, the whole thing a real, proper show." In contrast to Calvert's energy, Anderson viewed Barney Bubbles as "the most peaceful, lovely guy you could ever want to meet, almost like a gnome. His style of artwork really caught the mood of the time, painting all our equipment, coming up with the *In Search of Space* sleeve concept. Barney put a lot into that."

"When the band started," noted Calvert in 1971, "it had a very spacey sound. Now the image has become more concrete, though a lot is implied rather than explicit." He was already turning his attention to a far more ambitious project than a mere booklet insert, a grand space opera that would encompass all the themes that had absorbed him throughout his early years, a 'Space Ritual' for the modern age. "It's not predicting what is going to happen," Calvert told Richard Williams. "It's the mythology of the Space Age, in the way that rocket ships and interplanetary travel are a parallel with the heroic voyages of earlier times."

5

They've Got... A Silver Machine!

Simon King
(Collection of Dave Brock)

The final act in the construction of the classic Hawkwind was the recruitment of Ian 'Lemmy' Kilmister as bass player. Born in Stoke-on-Trent on 24th December 1945, Lemmy (who, legend has it, acquired the name from constantly requiring somebody to "lemme a quid 'til Friday") had played in various bands around Manchester in the early 1960s. Interviewed in 1996, he traced his musical roots back to Little Richard: "I heard 'Good Golly, Miss Molly'." On another occasion, he came back to this number as "the song that brought me in. It made me leave my profitable job, join a band and become broke, really." The records that inspired him were American imports: "Elvis, Carl Perkins, Fats Domino, Buddy Holly... they were excellent."

His first significant role, in 1966, was as guitarist for the Rockin' Vicars, a four-piece that played primarily cover versions such as 'Shake, Rattle & Roll', Neil Sedaka's 'I Go Ape' (which was a single release under the establishment-friendly name Rockin' Vickers) and 'Baby Never Say Goodbye'. "We were modelled on The Who to a large extent," Lemmy observed to Jeremy Cardenas. Though the band had some success in the North of England (and, curiously, played behind the Iron Curtain in Marshall Tito's Yugoslavia), it never made the breakthrough nationally. "I'm just an old rocker with my hair grown long... since me old clothes fell apart I had to buy all this hippie gear," he would later tell *Melody Maker*'s Allan Jones.

In between two stints as a member of the Rockin' Vicars, Lemmy worked as a roadie for Jimi Hendrix ("worth it, because I got to see him every night"). In 2000, Lemmy told *Q* magazine that he had few memories of this period: "There was a lot of acid about. It's a bit difficult trying to remember things when there are dragons coming out of the walls at you... Hendrix brought [acid tabs] back in his suitcase and just handed them round to the crew. I was with him for eight or nine months, just lifting and dragging; nothing that required talent. I was pissed off when he died. I was going to audition for him that day." Following his experiences with Hendrix, Lemmy embraced psychedelia as guitarist for tabla player Sam Gopal's self-titled group.

Sam Gopal recorded one album, *Escalator*, which was heavily biased towards Lemmy's fuzz guitar playing and his rough, menacing voice. Though it contained one cover version, 'Season of the Witch', Lemmy wrote most of the other material, including 'You're Alone Now'. This was later reworked as 'The Watcher' for his debut Hawkwind album *Doremi Fasol Latido*. He later joined Opal Butterfly, this final port-of-call before Hawkwind yielding no studio output during Lemmy's membership. "Neither of them were much of a thing, when I joined Opal Butterfly they were already on the way out."

"I actually saw Hawkwind a few times before I bustled my way into the band," Lemmy told Allan Jones. "I went to the Roundhouse, and the whole audience was having this collective epileptic fit. I remember thinking, 'I'll have to join that band'. They fitted exactly into my philosophy." He associated with the ideals of Hawkwind, the willingness to perform for free, the unstructured chaos of their gigs and embraced the lifestyle. "I got disenchanted with the summer of love in '67... the greatest washout of the sixties."

In *Record Collector* (May 2002) Lemmy asserted: "[Hawkwind] weren't the gentle sub-acid Moodies we were made out to be. We were a black fucking nightmare. A post-apocalypse horror soundtrack. We wanted to make peoples' heads and sphincters explode." Lemmy would complement the barbarians at the gate image of Hawkwind with his swastika fixation and his Hells Angels leathers. Musically, he installed his bass as the lead instrument in Hawkwind's wall-of-sound in a style that ranged from all-out driving assault to a controlled melodic scale. Recordings from this period still have the power to surprise modern-day listeners more used to the punk thrash bass of his most famous group, Motörhead.

"Dik-Mik was Lemmy's drinking buddy in the Duke of York pub on the Portobello Road," Dave Brock recalled to me, for *Vive Le Rock*. "Dik-Mik said, 'I've got a mate of mine who is a really good bass player', though I don't think Lemmy had played bass then, he was a guitar player, he didn't even have a bass. But we were getting dissatisfied with Dave Anderson and Dik was saying, 'I'll bring Lemmy along, you'll have to let him have a go, he's really good.' So he brought him along and we had to go and buy him a second-hand bass and that was it really. He was an eccentric speed-freak, really! He was good fun to play with because he was playing guitar lines on the bass, so it was nice because we played together for a long period, used to share a room as well, and we had a good camaraderie, a good feel for the music."

The recruitment of Lemmy wasn't the only change in the rhythm section. Terry Ollis was becoming increasing incapable of filling the drummer's role. "When Terry couldn't get it together, we would get Viv Prince, of The Pretty Things, in," says Brock. "Terry was taking Mandrax, which is a downer, once he sat on his drum stool and never played his drums, he just couldn't do it. We did a gig in Glasgow when that happened; he fell out of the van and never came back! Dik-Mik went off to look for him and there was a trail of Terry's things, pair of socks, pullover… he'd gone into this toilet and was laid out on the seat." Aside from the assistance of Viv Prince, there were a few gigs (including one at the Kinetic Playground in Birmingham on 6th December, 1971) where former Pink Fairies drummer, Twink, sat in. Ollis was eventually replaced by Opal Butterfly drummer, Simon King. "The final straw was a gig in London which we did with the two drummers [Ollis and King], Terry was going slower and slower, couldn't keep the timing anymore. This guy at the front had taken some acid and just freaked and had to be carried out, strapped to a stretcher… so Terry got sacked by the whole band, we just couldn't tolerate it anymore," notes Brock.

"I just kept on sitting in for Terry and I have been ever since – still waiting for him to come back," King told Steve Peacock for *Sounds* two years later. Conventional wisdom had the 'two drummer' gig, and King's first appearance with the band at a show on 2nd February 1972 at Goldsmith College, New Cross, a couple of days before the band would play an almost career-defining gig at the Roundhouse, and indeed when a long rumoured tape of Hawkwind at Cambridge Corn Exchange on 27th January 1972 materialised and was licenced for release by Easy Action Records in 2012, this author followed the usual wisdom and in writing the accompanying notes placed Terry Ollis at this concert. But when the recording was released, under the title *Leave No Star Unturned*, it added something to Hawk-legend for more than just its fascinating dynamic set, because some fans heard it as an early appearance by Simon King instead, and that simply adds to the mystique of the early weeks of what would become their breakthrough year. If it were King behind the drums that night, then there is no known date earlier in 1972 to slot the 'two drummers' performance into, meaning that King was being drafted in before Ollis had played his final performance. It's a biographer's nightmare to unravel, but a lovely added mystery to surround the comings and goings. And it wraps itself around a quite thrilling show, a landmark being as it was a three-way billing with their agitprop soulmates, The Pink Fairies, and what would be called The Last Minute Put-Together Boogie Band featuring Pink Floyd's elusive Syd Barrett.

Though Hawkwind had always intended their stage shows to become a complete audio visual environment, this wasn't properly achieved until lighting expert John

Smeeton was recruited. Art School student Smeeton had managed the lightshow for the Middle Earth, creating what he described as "psychedelic wallpaper... upon every surface [that could] reflect an image." Smeeton established his reputation working for Traffic, Free, and Mott The Hoople, before providing the two miles of fairy lights at the 1970 Bath Festival.

Peter Erskine, in *Disc*, described the set-up employed for Hawkwind by Smeeton and his team, 'Liquid Len and the Lensmen': "Nine industrial projectors with long-range lenses, fifteen stage lamps and smoke apparatus. They also use a low wattage laser capable of projecting three dimensional images, via a complicated system of mirrors, onto a flat surface onstage."

"Aside from Joe Lights' collaboration with the Grateful Dead," wrote Erskine, "this is the first time that light and sound have fused as a whole, each a part of the other." The sequencing of the lightshow was a scripted affair, with some numbers written to fit with imagery created by Smeeton and others having a specific lighting arrangement designed. "I listen out for what Lemmy or Simon are doing rhythmically," added Smeeton. "One of the nicest bits to 'play' is the electronics number 'Brainstorm'."

"I'd like the band to go on *Top of the Pops*," Brock told *NME*'s James Johnson early in 1971. "It's so ridiculous; we could just go on and turn it into a party. They'd never be able to get us off."

Hawkwind's eventual appearance on the BBC's flagship pop music show, during the 1970s always an essential viewing for the nation's youth, was in the form of a promotional film, recorded at Dunstable Queensway Hall (7th July, 1972) to support the single release of 'Silver Machine'. In support of that unlikely but welcome summer hit, the clip ran on the 13th & 27th July editions of *Top of the Pops*, and again on 10th August. None of those editions of the programme are known to exist today, though the promo film itself survives. 'Programme as Broadcast' documents held by the BBC reveal that the film was a bought-in item, rather than shot directly by the BBC as most fans believe, directed by Tom Taylor for Caravel Films, a company that supplied many early 70s inserts for the programme. This is almost certainly the reason for the sequence remaining archived.

There is a theory that the use of a filmed sequence for *Top of the Pops* was a response to the BBC's requirement for mimed performances. Martin Hayman, for *Sounds*, discussed this with the band and explained it pragmatically. "A group which relies on audience reaction and complicated electronic effects could die the death in the strictly controlled TV studio. They settled on a film taken at a live gig."

'Silver Machine' had been included in the band's setlist since autumn 1971, the earliest known performance being at Potters Bar on 14th October. The song was probably the first co-written by Brock and Calvert, with Calvert taking his inspiration from an article by Alfred Jarry called 'How to Construct a Time Machine'. "I seemed to suss-out immediately that what he was describing was his bicycle," recalled Calvert in *Cheesecake* (April 1981). "There were a lot of songs about space travel… I thought it was time to send all that up. 'Silver Machine' was just to say 'I've got a silver bicycle'." Calvert was probably correct! Jarry was obsessed with the bicycle. His short story 'The Crucifixion Considered as an Uphill Bicycle Race' was the basis for a work by another of Calvert's favourite writers, J. G. Ballard, when Ballard wrote 'The Assassination of John Fitzgerald Kennedy Considered as a Downhill Motor Race'. Jarry had written his essay in 1900, in response to reading H. G. Wells' *The Time Machine*. One biographical account of Jarry's life describes him "stalking the streets of Paris, with his green umbrella, wearing the cyclist's garb and carrying two pistols." Nearly three quarters of a century later, following a European Hawkwind tour, Calvert (clad not as a cyclist but as a commando) would strike a similar pose on those same Parisian streets.

Aside from the now well-worn and familiar notion of the song being about Calvert's silver bicycle, there's an intriguing paraphrasing possibly going on in the song. Invoking the phrase 'the other side of the sky', as the lyrics do, might just allude to a famous sentiment concerning women ("The other half of the sky") expressed by Chinese communist leader Mao Tse-tung (1893-1976) in his manifesto, *The Thoughts Of Chairman Mao*. It has environmental declamations ('it turns everything green') and reinvokes the astral mysticism of *In Search of Space* ('an electric line to your zodiac sign'). All in all, not bad for an otherwise appealingly catchy piece of rock music fluff.

The single version of 'Silver Machine' was reworked at Morgan Studios, from a live recording captured by future Stiff Records co-founder Dave Robinson during the Greasy Truckers charity gig at the Roundhouse, 13th February 1972. The original cut is more rambling and less powerful, lacks definition on the electronic effects (notably the opening section) and most significantly, has a languid, foppish vocal performance by Calvert. During the overdubs, Calvert's contribution was largely exorcised from the track and replaced by Lemmy's sandpaper growl. "They tried everybody else, then reluctantly let me. I did it in three takes," recalled Lemmy on Channel 4's *Top Ten of Progressive Rock*. "I'd only been with them about six months," he related on another instance, to the BBC. "It really pissed them off. There was a picture of me, on my own, on the front of the *NME*. They couldn't stand it!"

"Hawkwind were off their faces and off the planet," recalled Dave Robinson of the legendary Greasy Truckers show, which also featured Man and Brinsley Schwarz. "We discovered 'Silver Machine' when Vic Maile and I were mixing down the recordings. Hawkwind's stuff was completely chaotic, unless you were on the right drugs it didn't sound like anything much. But this one stood out, had a rhythm, a bite, and a bit of feel. I remember telling Dave Brock, 'There's one track here that sounds quite good. You might actually get it on the radio.' It was commercial. I mean, there was no part of Hawkwind that you were going to hear on radio at that time, even John Peel didn't play Hawkwind. They got the multi-track, used it as the basis and added to it, that was how the record was made."

"Lovely sound effects, a straining back beat and 'look out, the Earth is about to collide with Mars' type singing," thought *Melody Maker*. "The vocals are so submerged in the thudding, whirling sound that they are largely irrelevant," noted another review. "The overall effect is that of a thunderous rock band recorded in a wind-tunnel." In comparison, the B-side ('Seven by Seven', from an earlier session at Rockfield Studios, though some versions of the single are backed by the live cut of 'Seven by Seven' from the *Space Ritual* LP) was "thin and unsure of itself." The conclusion was drawn that "their live work is better than their recorded output... much of their energy vanishes in the studio."

The success of 'Silver Machine' took the band by surprise and elevated them, temporarily, into the mainstream pop arena. One music paper revealed, shortly after the single's release, that it was "selling 50,000 copies in the first three days of last week" and that "United Artists have to import 25,000 copies from Germany to keep up with demand." At the time, Brock claimed the song was recognised as a potential hit and released to finance the forthcoming Space Ritual tour, but now concedes, "It was a bit of a fluke. It just happened at the right time. We played loads of benefits and became an in-vogue band, we sold out gigs, had a huge entourage of people: lots of weird characters, artists, just a good collection of interesting personalities. Douglas was steering the ship and with United Artists advertising to up our profile we were able to reach greater heights, but it was luck as well."

Though the high position was unexpected (Simon King recalled he anticipated a high of around number 30), it was consistent with other forays into the singles chart by essentially album-orientated bands of the era. Atomic Rooster and Deep Purple both achieved two Top Ten hits the previous year, Black Sabbath their only Top Five in 1970. 'Silver Machine' was held off the number one spot by Alice Cooper and Terry Dactyl & The Dinosaurs on 19th August, 1972 and again by Cooper (with Rod Stewart at number two) the following week.

"['Silver Machine'] makes Hawkwind an altogether more powerful prospect than they were two years ago," claimed Andrew Means. "Their expanding reputation and financial assets must have boosted the expectations of their friends and followers." In his view, "they regard it as two fingers in the air to the music business that used to write them off... their objectives and activities will remain much the same as before."

By the time 'Silver Machine' was released, Calvert had once again left the band, with Nick Kent noting in *Frendz* that "problems centring around the destabilising effect on both the mind and the ego that [his] transcending from writer to being both writer and pop star entailed forced him into a mental hospital." In his place, Turner was increasingly the front man of the band as well as, alongside Brock, its principal spokesperson. Kent captured Nik's larger-than-life showman character when he described him as being "visually amazing, bedecked in jewellery and trinkets, a touch of make-up, gold braces, blue suede shoes and the studded motorcycle jacket that Barney Bubbles painted for him." At other shows Turner would bound on stage, blasting his saxophone and bedecked in strange garb, often a full-length frog costume.

Turner recalled to Michael Butterworth that, "It had painting all over it that was supposed to be Eternity [from Marvel Comics'] *Dr Strange*. We did a tour… I had the idea of being a frog one night, and the next night I was a prince! I'd got this Saracen outfit, with a big cloak and leather chest piece... a sword and stuff. It looked great… a Pre-Raphaelite Knight! We had UV lights, and I used fluorescent paint a lot. I was interested in visuals to make things exciting." Not pretentious at all then. And that might not have been terribly endearing to his band mates. In a delicious story in his autobiography, *White Line Fever*, Lemmy recalled an occasion when Turner, wearing his Frog suit slipped on a wet stage and fell headlong into a moat, taking Stacia with him. Moments before, Lemmy had made a precognitive suggestion to Brock that, "It's about time somebody pushed that fucking frog into the pond."

A side effect of the strong sales of 'Silver Machine', credited to Calvert and S. MacManus (Sylvia MacManus, Brock's wife) due to contract complications, was that it enabled Dave Brock to move away from his Home County roots. "When we did 'Silver Machine', I got five hundred quid for writing it with Robert, and I put it on a deposit for a house and moved to the country [Devon], which I couldn't have done otherwise. I just got fed-up of living in the city and seeing all the scenes that go on. It was the best thing I ever did."

This relocation away from the natural hunting grounds of the music business had its drawbacks. "Getting backwards and forwards to London was a bit of a drag. If we'd been playing late in London, I'd have to catch the 1am train from Paddington, the mail train which used to go all around the houses. It would turn up in Taunton at five in the morning. There I was, hit single in the charts, hanging around Taunton railway station trying to get a lift! Or I'd take a shortcut across the river Exe, tie my shoes around my neck and wade through it to save a couple of miles walk!"

The long-planned Space Ritual tour finally kicked off in Kings Lynn on 8th November 1972. Andrew Means, previewing for *Melody Maker*, anticipated that the event would be "one of the most creatively ambitious shows ever put together by a rock and roll band."

Looking back with a post-punk perspective, it is tempting to see the extravaganza of Space Ritual as being the classic progressive rock excess. This was Robert Calvert's first full tour as resident poet and occasional singer. Stacia was joined by additional dancer Miss Renee and mime artist Tony Crerar and the full force of Jon Smeeton's lightings were in evidence. Smeeton explained to Peter Erskine (*Disc*, January 1973) how he'd been at work on the Space Opera lighting since May, 1972. "We've reached a point where we can do something to expand the whole scope of lighting… get away from connotations of bits of whirling cardboard and slides of The Pope."

Means identified a "reluctance to get labelled 'pseudo-intellectual', a fear that the group will get less entertaining as their ideas become more sophisticated." That said, Brock had already gone on record as wanting to relay a multimedia presentation to get across the band's ideas. "The opera is intended to reach the audience on a deep level… we'll be giving out information sheets to the audience beforehand. It's not fair to expect them to [understand it] without any help at all. That's where Arthur Brown goes wrong…"

The whole concept was neatly wrapped up in the tour programme, a merging of fictional narrative, lyrics and the graphics of Barney Bubbles. The booklet's acknowledgements are revelatory and explanatory, the New Wave SF of Moorcock, the grand Space Opera of Frank Herbert and Robert Heinlein, the Sword & Sorcery of Lin Carter, and 'Colour Television' which was just becoming established in the UK. "The basic idea is that a team of starfarers are in a coma … and the opera is a presentation of the dreams that they are having in deep space," noted Calvert.

Nick Kent, attending tour rehearsals at the Jubilee Studios on behalf of *NME*, advised his readers not to expect, "a grandiose musical experience… Pink Floyd mating itself with the London Philharmonic," or, "mind-blitzed corpses wrecked by the profound cerebral damage of the spectacle." In summing the general ramshackle nature of Hawkwind, he concluded "don't expect anything. The band doesn't really know how the project is going to shape itself." Years later, writing for *Sounds*, future comic book legend Alan Moore summed up that anarchic anything or nothing which might come from Hawkwind, when he reflected on a gig in Wellingborough, which probably pre-dated Space Ritual by a few months in this delicious reminiscence: "Bundles of joss sticks were passed out. Copies of *Frendz* were passed out. Hepatitis sufferers in greatcoats were passed out. The Day-Glo Hawkwind insignia blazed in the ultra-violet light, bouncing semaphore flashes off the retina. Christ, I had one hell of a time."

Space Ritual opened with Calvert's repetitive drone, borrowed from the BBC World Service ('This is London calling'): 'Earth calling… this is Earth calling' as though imploring the occupants of spaceship Hawkwind back to the mother planet, before the band launched into the driving rhythm of 'Born to Go' with its 'breaking out of our shell' imperative, a possible counterpoint to the Gunter Grass poem 'In The Egg' which Calvert would recite the following year at the Empire Pool, Wembley. Calvert's own poem 'The Awakening' described the occupants landing on an alien vista ('a clear century of space away/from the trauma of his birth'), which Calvert had also entitled 'First Landing On Medusa' and which appeared in Lisa Conesa's anthology of SF poetry *The Purple Hours*, while Moorcock's 'Black Corridor' echoed the distant loneliness of the space traveller, cast adrift in the empty void ('it is dark/it is cold').

Outside of these numbers, the overall cohesion of the original operatic vision was achieved not by its ability to provide a compelling narrative, some outer space version of The Odyssey, but in its declamation and juxtaposition of the classic components of traditional SF. In 'Ten Seconds of Forever', its delivery a launch countdown, and once bizarrely given the accolade of a science fiction '12 Days of Christmas', the random dreams of the comatose astronauts are of the mundane ('the sea, and the white yacht drifting'), the oblique ('the pair of broken shades lying on the tarmac') and pain of separation from all things human ('the long past that had led to now'). The zero gravity acrobatics of 'Upside Down', as far as anyone might tell from its overdubbed in the studio, and almost indecipherable, lyrical delivery, are contrasted by the gritty paranoia of 'Brainstorm' wherein the victim, threatened with the fate of having to be 'turned android' and imploring the listener to 'help me avoid that', concludes in the end 'you'd bet I'd kiss it/kiss this body goodbye'. A contemporary nightmare of nuclear fallout parodied in Moorcock's 'Sonic Attack', and the bleak totalitarianism of Calvert's 'Welcome to the Future', in a strange way sit easily with the mysticism of 'Seven by Seven' ('Is the passport to this world my astral soul?') and 'Lord of Light' ('from the realms beyond the Sun').

But in that way, strangely, it successfully joined up a lot of disparate ideas. 'Seven by Seven' invokes a mystical number in many ancient religions and civilisations, representing the seven heavenly bodies of the solar system that are visible from Earth. 'Lord of Light' has its title taken from a Roger Zelazny novel, itself concerned with the Hindu pantheon. But then there's 'Orgone Accumulator' which has more Earthbound, if hardly down-to-earth connotations, being a device created by Dr William Reich in 1940 to capture orgone energy, though there's no real evidence for the existence of this supposed 'life force', which he believed would improve the flow of energy. The device was subsequently banned and all existing copies destroyed, though the song lauds it, tongue-in-cheek, as being a 'Superman-creator'. Really, that one is an early example of Bob Calvert's skill at melding arcane or cult ideas with his sharp sense of humour.

So, it's a space opera that pushes into fantasy and is a joined-up concept work, even if it doesn't specifically have a strong linear narrative. Perhaps it's not supposed to relate a story but simply explore the themes that the band and its associated creative supporters were putting together. It's certainly one that has stood the test of time. "The missing link between psychedelia and punk rock," said Mark Paytress of the resulting double-LP, in *Mojo*, more than a quarter of a century on from its recording, deciding that the album's "trance-rock throb and woozy analogue noodlings remain in remarkably rude health."

Reviewing a show for *Sounds*, Martin Hayman described the visual assault. "The flashing lights that frame one second the ancient and mysterious shrine of Stonehenge, the next the Hawkwind insignia, disintegrating into sharp geometrical edges and shadows." Hayman, noting the sold-out halls talked of the audience and the band being drawn as one into "the compulsive vortex of the music... the stiffness of everyday sinews being melted by the waves from the stage." Commenting on the inroads into Hawkwind's artistic stature achieved by the

Space Ritual, Andrew Means thought the shows proved "the remarkable effects that can be achieved by using rock in a mixed media context."

Viewing a gig at St. Andrews Hall, Norwich (21st November, 1972), Means elaborated about "the lightshow and film stills, the elaborate gestures of the three dancers, and the heightened effect of ritual. The use of sound in advance of anything Hawkwind have done [before]... more variation and subtlety in the rhythm section...," but thought that "the dancing became the king-stone of the show – the neurotic activity of the male dancer and the more expressive movement of Stacia and her blonde counterpart."

Though much of the Space Ritual concept remained in Hawkwind's set for several years, the shows themselves almost cry out across the years to be viewed in isolation from the rest of the band's canon, a pinnacle moment in time when the concept and the music meshed to create something distinct. When interviewed by Steve Peacock in 1973, Simon King took the opportunity to place the project as being firmly in the past. "It was something the band wanted to do, it took them a long time to get together, we did the album of it and it's all done now."

The tour was documented by one of the acknowledged greatest double albums, *Space Ritual – Alive in London and Liverpool*, selected from gigs at Liverpool Stadium (22nd December, 1972) and Brixton (30th December) and released in May 1973. Melody Maker described the result as "a monstrous four-sided, 88-minute sound journey," even if *Sounds* were less impressed. "To me, these live recordings ... seem not unlike the rock and roll equivalent of a couple of episodes of *Star Trek*, without Dr Spock [sic]" mused their reviewer, before conceding to "feeling little or no involvement with the music."

At the same time as the Space Ritual gigs, Hawkwind released their third studio album, *Doremi Fasol Latido*, a return to the dense sound of their first LP but with a more defined song structure and an increasing lyrical finesse.

"It's not melody and it's not harmony, and it's not really rhythm," wrote Andrew Means returning to his favoured theme of the ambiguity in Hawkwind's make-up. "It's demanding to be faced with so many signs and directions. But that's the challenge. The listener is as much a traveller as the musicians."

Though the record echoed the Space Ritual concept in its graphics and packaging, there was no room for Calvert's vocals. His middle-eight narrative during 'Seven by Seven' on the flip side of 'Silver Machine' remained his only Hawkwind studio contribution at that point. Whilst *Doremi...* like its immediate predecessor, owed much to Bob's SF visions and pretences his more tangible input remained in the province of the live performance.

Musically, the new LP expanded more upon the development of song structure than much of *In Search of Space* had done, less on refining live improvisation in a studio setting, even if Lemmy much latter reflected on it as having been "A good sound, just not very well recorded. It was all thin and tinny ... not as good as *In Search of Space*, but then I wasn't on that." [Interviewed by

Scott Heller, for *Aural Innovations*]. Lyrically, some members of the band were beginning to prove they'd become adept at expressing socially aware ideas. Most surprising was Lemmy's song 'The Watcher', an echoing and atmospheric rumination, with its live version, missing from the studio cut, containing one of the shrewdest pre-punk rants on futility and boredom ('every inch exists in miles'). Commenting specifically, however, on the opening track, 'Brainstorm', *NME*'s Nick Kent noted that "the lyrics are in-distinguishable and it's all down to the riff... it carries on for a good 12 minutes with the electronics sounding like spaceships that pass through the night."

'Brainstorm', though, was a stone-cold Hawkwind classic, credited to Nik Turner alone, though demonstrating just how important to the overall sound the combination of Dave Brock, Simon King and Lemmy had become. It's a defining moment of a musical partnership between Brock and Lemmy that both would come to acknowledge as being almost telepathic in its nature, where the two of them would instinctively mesh together. So, though it's Turner's first solo Hawkwind credit, there's a lot more behind it than that credit suggests. Of the lyrics, Turner described how they came to him while he was indeed 'standing on the runway/waiting to take off.' "I was sitting in an aeroplane, waiting to go to France. You just get these ideas on the spur of the moment and they become songs!" In a counterculture sense, the song travelled outside of the confines of the band; the title was one of the inspirations for the underground *Brainstorm Comix*, published by the 'Alchemy' shop from the Portobello Road and featuring the earliest work of artist Bryan Talbot. Hawkwind advertised in the first issue.

The new album showcased how much tighter Hawkwind had become with the additions of King and Lemmy, with *Sounds* considering the sound, contrary to Lemmy's more recent assertions, was "thicker, fuller, more convincing than before," though, noting Pink Floyd's more spacey offerings, claimed that the band had still not produced anything that added up to one 'Interstellar Overdrive'. But it was undeniable that the rhythm section had transformed into a blistering powerhouse that could drive the band in tone and texture in the direction of what came to be termed, in a diverging sense through the decade, as Heavy Metal. There was also a much greater sense of the other musicians, Turner and Dettmar adding their sonic improvisations to this wall-of-sound to create something unique. Andrew Means thought that though the "space sounds are prominent and perhaps the key to the music, Hawkwind have at last begun to combine them imaginatively with more orthodox qualities." *Sounds* proclaimed that "the bass and drums batter on with unflagging pace. Synthesisers swirl and whistle around the thunderous block riffs. Its effect is totally devastating."

If there is a point in time which came to represent Hawkwind at their most pure, most unadulterated essence then it would be the glory year of 1972. An unlikely hit single, the pulling together of a complex and innovative stage show, and a rising profile that saw 'Full House' boards across the country created a moment to be cherished. That the profits from 'Silver Machine' had made possible the crowning achievement of Space Ritual could be in no doubt. That the band had now to build on the commercial achievements of the year while retaining their original ethos and grassroots following was noted with trepidation in the music press.

"The Floyd were the original hippie band," observed Steve Mann in *Let It Rock* (December 1972). 'They came up through the UFO and the Middle Earth, then ignored the community that spawned them as soon as they could afford to. I'm not suggesting that Hawkwind will go the same way… the concept behind their music is heavy enough, though the band themselves are managing to avoid taking it too seriously. It'll be interesting to see how long they can sustain it." Mann's greatest fear was that Hawkwind might get "further and further away from the untogether freak band that used to play under the motorway in the Grove. Not necessarily a bad thing… but the parallels with Pink Floyd are plain enough."

Nick Kent identified 'Brainstorm' as "a natural single which the band perhaps wisely refuse to release, fearing the label that comes with being a successful singles band." Brock saw this avenue as one to be avoided, telling Steve Peacock for Sounds that Hawkwind wouldn't be releasing another single, "Well, not yet. Not 'till the time is right again." Looking back, Brock adds that, "we weren't the darlings of 'oh, let's all be famous'… we were the underground band."

The failure to capitalise on the chart success of 'Silver Machine' marked a point when they could have travelled down the path of financial success, but hesitated. Turner sums this up, with the hindsight of thirty years: "It didn't really bother me; perhaps it should have. I don't think the band should have been a singles band, it was more an albums band, or a live band." At the time, he told Keith Altham (in *Music Scene*) that "We'll probably never be very rich or successful because we're too easy to rip off… we're still paying off debts for the days when we were struggling."

"There is no instant success, in anything," comments Del Dettmar. "The way we built up the thing… we'd buy a lightshow and then rent it out until it was paid for. There was a large organisation behind us. Some people just weren't aware, like Lemmy wasn't aware, of what was being done on their behalf. I think it could have gone a lot further."

"We were like a commune, in a way," Brock considers. "As we progressed, the money we were making got put back into the band."

"I have a lot of faith in people with the right intentions eventually winning through," said Turner in December 1972. "There is no apparent reason for our success in terms of hype, promotion or publicity. It simply seems that people have been to see us and liked what they saw and heard."

6

Banned by the BBC? You'd Better Believe It

Windsor Great Park Free Festival, 1973
Calvert, Moorcock, King, Lemmy, Brock
(Roger Hutchinson)

Hawkwind's line-up held unusually steady through most of 1972, from the recruitment of Simon King onwards, with only the ad-hoc contributions of Robert Calvert and Dik-Mik's aversion to travelling ("he leaves every week," Doug Smith said) leading to on the night changes.

This continuity began to break down early into 1973 with a European tour in the spring demonstrating problems within the ranks when Lemmy failed to arrive for the gigs. By May, the *NME* reported that Lemmy had left and that the departure of Dik-Mik was believed to be imminent. As for Dave Brock's tenure, *NME* repeated a UA spokesman announcing that "he has taken himself off somewhere and is getting uptight and refusing to play with the band. Plans may be afoot to make his departure a reality, as the group have had to play several gigs without him."

Windsor Great Park Free Festival, 1973
Calvert, Turner, King, Brock, Lemmy
(Roger Hutchinson)

All this inconsistency and doubt put in jeopardy a booking to play Hawkwind's most prestigious gig to date, at Wembley's Empire Pool (later Wembley Arena). When the show took place, on 27th May, 1973, all fears of a membership meltdown had temporarily been resolved, with a full Space Ritual contingent appearing.

Reviewing the show for *Sounds*, Martin Hayman observed Stacia "[interpreting] every move of their trip so poignantly," but also spotted a "gallivanting figure in dark cape and mask, whose prancing's were occasionally at variance with what was required (his Olympic-style torch would not light as dramatically as it should have done, either)." This, of course, was Calvert, his increasing stage presence noted by both Hayman ("an almost Daltrey-like figure") and *Melody Maker*'s Michael Oldfield: "There's a singer behaving like Jagger, shaking the mike-stand." Calvert's transformation from nervous declaimer of poetry to front of stage showman and rock star was near complete; a filmed extract from the era shows him prowling the stage with confidence and presence. Once again, though, this peaking of Calvert's talents was his own downfall. Soon after the Wembley gig, Hayman informed his readers (Sounds, 30th June 1973) that Calvert had hospitalised himself, quoting Doug Smith as saying "He was just going over the top, but he recognised it in time."

The mid-70s saw the heyday of open air festivals in the UK. Hawkwind's ubiquitous appearances at Bickershaw and Trentishoe in 1972 and Windsor from '72 to '74 cemented their reputation as the house band of the festival circuit. At Bickershaw, their gig on the first day was overshadowed by the audience's anticipation for the final day's headliners, The Grateful Dead, and by the some of the most atrocious weather ever experienced at a British festival. Despite this, Stacia was still observed "cavorting nude on the left of stage during 'Silver Machine'."

Windsor was a provocative challenge to the establishment, taking place on Crown land in the shadow of Windsor Castle itself. The annual festival managed a run of three years, a rare continuity. Dismissing Hawkwind's set at the first event Ray Telford (in *Sounds*) thought the group "a teenybopper's answer to Pink Floyd" and their performance "too instant, too contrived." Ray Foxcumming, in *Disc*, however, was impressed: "The stark staging with a sail-like screen for the lightshow looked like some grotesque set piece from Fellini's *Satyricon*. Throughout ['Silver Machine'] rockets lit up the night sky over the river."

Hawkwind's 1973 appearance at Windsor provided an unexpected bonus for the audience when both Moorcock and Calvert took part. "At Windsor, I mostly remember climbing onto the roof of my own car while it was moving and sitting on top, clinging to the roof rack while Dik-Mik took the steering wheel," says Moorcock. "It was a very enjoyable gig, though marred by the Hells Angels, who raped a girl during our set." An audience recording of what is almost certainly this gig reveals the band in improvised mode, with an extended bass jam demonstrating Lemmy's increasing dexterity. Curiously, Moorcock read 'Ode to a Time Flower', a Calvert poem that had been published in *New Worlds Quarterly* #5 (January, 1973). As Moorcock and Calvert were not usually paired at Hawkwind gigs the suggestion is that Moorcock's appearance was planned, Calvert's perhaps a spur of the moment arrival.

For an all-day show at London's Oval cricket ground (16th September 1972), Hawkwind displaced Frank Zappa as the closing act due to their need for darkness to exploit the lightshow. Ironically, the concert was promoted by the Foulk Brothers, whose ticket prices at the Isle of Wight Hawkwind had protested only two years earlier. This more formal association was not a success, Martin Marriot in *Disc* explaining that "[Hawkwind] played continuously for at least 35 minutes… and had gone through 'Born to Go', 'Master of the Universe', and 'Seven by Seven'." Those were followed by an announcement from the ground staff that the power would be turned off in four minutes despite the start of Hawkwind's set having been delayed by over two hours. "Hawkwind finished with 'Silver Machine'," said Marriot. "Stacia frolicked naked about the stage. Naturally, the Oval officials were quickly demanding she cover herself up." That really wasn't cricket, chaps...

"People would get in touch with us and invite us to play, and later there was the whole [Peace] Convoy thing going on." Turner recalls. "There was Isle of Wight and then Glastonbury in 1971 and I got involved in those and they created in me an awareness of what festivals were all about; I didn't fully understand it all but I was keen to know about it. Then there were the Windsor Free Festivals in the Great Park and I think by then there was an awareness of festivals and people had a need for them. Hawkwind played one with Queen down in the West Country, there was Trentishoe which was down by the cliffs and organised by an underground newspaper called the *North Devon Snail*. We were on a festivals circuit with bands like Magic Muscle and The Pink Fairies. If there was a festival going on we'd be there because we supported the idea; there were other Ladbroke Grove bands as well, like Mighty Baby and Help Yourself. We were all mates, all into what this was all about and we weren't all totally out of our heads on drugs! And the people organising the events were all like-minded spirits working in the same cause."

The festivals were a focal point for the band; it would become almost a rite of passage for fans to hear them in the open air, in arguably their definitive environment, something that cemented the idea that Hawkwind equalled Freedom, and that following the band and buying into its ethos was a way of life. It became, particularly in the 80s, as though no counterculture or alternative lifestyle open air event was complete without their obligatory appearance so that they crossed musical boundaries and generation changes and became part of the fabric of the scene, an element of what you metaphorically 'bought-into' as part of the on the road, travelling, free festival lifestyle.

It was almost a year before Hawkwind attempted to follow-up the chart success of 'Silver Machine'. In August, 1973 their single 'Urban Guerrilla' was released, supported by a major UK tour, grazed the Top 40 on 25th August, and was withdrawn from sale in a whirlwind of controversy. Though it featured lyrics and vocals from Robert Calvert, both he and Dik-Mik had again left by the time the single was issued. This may be one reason why despite the regular use of the 'Silver Machine' film on *Top of the Pops*, there was no similar promotion of 'Urban Guerrilla', dispute the existence of a supporting film and some Radio 1 airplay.

Taking its lyrical imagery from the Rolling Stones' 1968 agitprop classic 'Street Fighting Man', 'Urban Guerrilla' features one of rock 'n' roll's sharpest opening lyrical couplets ('I'm an urban guerrilla/I make bombs in my cellar'). The idea of an 'urban guerrilla' had been established by left-wing German terrorist groups, coined to contrast with the long-established idea of 'rural guerrillas' fighting as resistance soldiers in the jungle or mountain regions. Inspired by the development of armed factions on the radical left in the aftermath of the student riots which swept Europe during the summer of 1968 and by the Situationist counterculture movement, lyrical references include the Beatles' 'Why Don't We

74

Do It In The Road' and both the Black and White Panthers ['I'm a two-tone panther']. The former was a militant black pressure group founded in 1966, who espoused armed revolution. The White Panthers' most notable spokesman was John Sinclair, manager of the MC5 and a man whose stated aims included "an assault on the culture by any means necessary, including dope and fucking in the streets." Brock recalled having "MI5 raiding us because we were working with the White Panthers who used to put out all this risqué literature about how to stop the cities… and generally cause confusion."

There was a British wing of The White Panthers, instigated by, among others, Mick Farren, for practical reasons of what Farren described to me as plausible deniability to be employed where the underground met the mainstream. "All [the British and American arms] had in common was the badge and rhetoric borrowed from John Sinclair and adapted for England, because England isn't that… we don't have as many organisations as the Americans, we don't have Elks Lodges or Shiners to the same degree. It took off for a while and was useful if you needed an organisational facade to go and negotiate something. If you were going to stick Hawkwind on at Portobello Green, using the White Panthers as an intermediary meant there was someone who was speaking for Dave Brock who wasn't Dave Brock, so if something went wrong he didn't have to carry the can; it was a functional thing."

On the 29th August, 1973 the IRA commenced a sustained bombing campaign on the British mainland, exploding devices in Warwickshire and Solihull. There was an immediate ban on the playing of 'Urban Guerrilla' by the BBC; subsequently the record was withdrawn by United Artists. "It was a difficult situation, in the sense that there was this terrible IRA campaign going on and here we were writing words that are really true to this day," notes Brock. "I was at BBC Radio Newcastle in 2002 and played an acoustic version of 'Urban Guerrilla'; I said 'the words are still relevant, nothing's changed,' but at the time, to say these things got us banned."

Turner reflects that UA may have withdrawn 'Urban Guerrilla' for a different reason: "It didn't sell. You can say that was because of the subject, because the record company were afraid to promote it. But that's not really true – it just wasn't selling." Brock agrees: "Maybe that's the case too, it's hard to say. It was number 39 [in the charts], but the recording sounds a bit demo-ish." In a week when the charts were headed by Donny Osmond's 'Young Love' and The Carpenters' 'Yesterday Once More', it could be concluded that taking three weeks to creep into the Top 40 was a disappointment to the label, and an opportunist chance to cut their losses, possibly aligned to a judicious oiling of the wheels of publicity, was taken.

Turner found it another problem to be overcome in the increasing politicisation of Hawkwind. "At the time [of 'Urban Guerrilla'] I had the bomb squad around at my house. They tore the floorboards up because I had this Hells Angel staying with me from San Francisco. He was with a guy who'd tried to come into the country with a gun on him that had been used to shoot an FBI officer, apparently. I wasn't there – we were in Holland at the time."

Douglas Smith [interviewed by the author, for *Record Collector*]: "The urban myth is that 'Urban Guerrilla' was withdrawn because of the first IRA bomb in London, at Baker Street. Maybe because the BBC didn't want to play it after the bomb happened, rumours going around the BBC that this wasn't kosher to play; then Nik's flat got turned over, and sales did drop off. The best thing to say seemed to be that with decency to what had happened we were withdrawing the single, and that's what we did. It could have really taken off for them at that particular point, but second [hit] singles in those days were notoriously difficult to get up with the first single."

Despite 'Urban Guerrilla' and the idea of free gigs and support for the counterculture, there wasn't really ever such a concept as 'Political Hawkwind' in the way that many punk bands became allied to specific movements or parties later in the 70s. When Hawkwind's songwriters, particularly Calvert in 'Urban Guerrilla' and later with 'Assassins of Allah', but also Brock in 'Psychedelic Warlords', commented on political issues, it tended to be via metaphor rather than a dogmatic manifesto. Much of Hawkwind's radical stance appears political only with historical context. It would be fairer to view the band's lifestyle, their benefit gigs and some of their lyrics, as a reflection of the counterculture's social-politicisation, as a realpolitik response to things happening around them.

"As far as this revolutionary thing goes," commented Simon King in *Melody Maker*, "all we want to say is look around you at the type of environment you're living in. But we're not out to lead a revolution. We don't want to get mixed up in politics." Brock saw Hawkwind as "city music, trying to relate to what's happening. Too many laws against this and that. We can see the world and the way it's run and we're trying to awaken people to the fact it is wrong."

Playing inside the maximum-security prison at Wandsworth (7th February, 1973) or headlining a benefit gig for Dr Timothy Leary at the University of California (10th March, 1974) were aspects of Hawkwind's support for people outside of mainstream society. But, in terms of their relationship to political ideology, it was best summed up at Essen (8th September, 1972) during a concert organised by a local Communist faction that attracted a violent audience determined to 'bottle off' any band that didn't embrace their left-wing aspirations. Despite Turner and Brock's appeals to the crowd for calm (a recording of the show has Brock claiming "we've got fuck all to do with politics") it was Lemmy's growl that the band had "Nicht Politik" which silenced the agitators and enabled the set to commence.

**Lemmy on the road
(Dave Brock Collection)**

It was also an unwelcome fact that financial realities interfered with the group's ability to maintain some of its intentions. Turner recalled a gig at the Roundhouse, intended as a benefit for 'Radical Alternatives to Prisons', which fell afoul of an incident when, ironically, the band had a large amount of their equipment stolen. "The equipment was found," he told IT, "but that didn't alter the fact in some people's mind that we were in a financial state." Turner explained that though he and Doug Smith had donated their share of the concert to the cause, "the rest were just into it being another gig to help the band get by."

"We were doing politically active things," considers Brock. "It wasn't just 'love and peace', we did lots of benefits for the miners, the firemen, people striking… that's why we were having so much trouble with the police. We were forever being stopped in our van, or our places raided, we were on their blacklist." On one occasion in the more anarchistic atmosphere of France, Brock recalls agitators who "broke into the venue where we were, the police were firing tear gas and the gig had to be abandoned – awful scenes."

Turner reflects that "In hindsight, we were really radical. Bob was politically aware and saw it as a platform, through clever innuendoes, but the rest of us weren't so inclined. Hawkwind was sort of anarchistic in its politics, but not in the way that [Punk band] Crass were, we weren't consciously anything." Bemoaning the use of chic revolutionary ideology by the middle classes (for example the 'Che Guevara' boutique in affluent Knightsbridge) Turner recalls Calvert as having "the idealism without wearing the badge. Bob would use current images, topical things, to express basic universal truths."

Mick Farren: "It's my experience that very few musicians, maybe as little as five or six percent and mostly frontmen, really have political awareness. I mean, a lot of musicians are stoned narcissists but the musician's brain doesn't work in a political discipline. At best, in a band, you get one guy who is well-read and politically aware or astute. Take The Beatles; the only political figure in The Beatles was Lennon. McCartney charmed the record company, George was a Hari Krishna and Ringo got drunk, and that's really how most bands function."

The Timothy Leary benefit show came as part of Hawkwind's second visit to America, having finally played their premiere USA gigs late November, early December 1973. Dave Anderson recalled during his tenure a reluctance to try and break the American market. Brock suggests that when they finally decided to give the USA a try, it was Doug Smith who was the instigator. "There was a big hippie movement [in America], and we were The Grateful Dead of England, the freak movement, and that's why Douglas got us off to America."

For their first American dates, Hawkwind were principally still in Space Ritual mode, indeed the basic structure of the set would continue to rely heavily on the space opera until the middle of 1975. There was a nod in the direction of the more fantasy-orientated outlook of the next studio album, *The Hall of the Mountain Grill*, by the introduction of Turner's 'D-Rider', that utopian fairy tale of dragons and astral planes wherein Turner sings of 'children playing in the sun/a sense of freedom on the run' and describes 'our course determined by the stars' and seems to be taking a metaphorical look at all that was good about the alternative lifestyle.

"We were playing large venues, to big audiences," recalls Brock. "We were picked up at the airport in San Francisco by [Timothy] Leary's buddies, some of the Hells Angels, in an entourage, treated wonderfully well. We got taken out to this Chinese restaurant, for a banquet, a fifteen-course meal. Prior to this, we'd smoked this huge joint of Lebanese hash and got stoned, and we were suffering from jetlag. We had bottles of wine, loads of food… and I fell asleep, conked-out, with my hand resting on the table. Somebody knocked my elbow and I fell off my chair, still holding the tablecloth. All this food fell on the floor and I had to be helped up. I didn't know where I was! I thought I was at home, so I was saying 'I want to go to bed, now' … I'd gone all peculiar and shaky. When we left in the van Stacia was sick out of the window because she eaten so much and got drunk."

The *Melody Maker*, following Hawkwind on tour, explained that the opening gig at Philadelphia's Tower Theatre (23rd November, 1973), though beset with logistical problems and curtailed by half an hour, met with an enthusiastic reception. "The glossy lightshow was superb and in fine sync with the music… a huge screen gave a Cinerama-like effect for the visuals,' whilst 'Master of the Universe' brought the audience to their feet for several minutes of applause." Greg Shaw, reviewing the Detroit show for *Phonograph Record*, was somewhat bewildered by the occasion, but thought that, "It's all been done before, and better in its various elements. But no group has ever gathered it all into such an imposingly solid image." Shaw watched Stacia "her face painted with Day-Glo eagle features and her amply endowed frame clad variously in star-emblazoned capes, flashing robes, stylised loincloths and nothing at all." At a sell-out gig at the New York Academy of Music, "Hawkwind's wall-of-sound and headlong pace drew the crowds to their feet [but] the lightshow was rearranged… less relevant."

"We were living the highlife," says Brock. "We had roadies; a big crew… none of us carried our instruments or suitcases. We'd fly everywhere, stayed in nice hotels. It was like a drug binge; all these dealers would turn up and we'd have bags of grass, of downers and uppers. Lemmy would have a bag of reds. You'd be taking these different things and it would just blur… you'd function on stage, not get too badly out of it… but sometimes we did!"

Following the New York show, *Melody Maker* reported on a reception for the band at the Hayden Planetarium: "over 1,000 guests, including Alice Cooper, Stevie Wonder, Genesis, Argent and Spencer Davis." The highlight for Stacia, however, was meeting the New York Dolls. Morrissey, in his book *New York Dolls*, describes how their bass player, Arthur Kane, "showed unnatural affection for Stacia, an amply proportioned dancer of questionable abilities often found gyrating on stage with Hawkwind but without any clothes." The couple spent Christmas together, a dalliance that appears to have lasted long into the next year; the *NME* of 23rd November 1974 featured Stacia describing Kane as "very tall and always drunk" and claiming "we make a good pair." Though she was noted to be carrying a photograph of Kane, "she's uncertain where the relationship stands now," said her interviewer.

Nik Turner: "Whilst we were on that first American tour, Comet Kohoutek was making an appearance in the skies, apparently it'd last visited the Earth about 150,000 years ago and wouldn't be seen again for another 75,000 years, so we had some people come down from the Hayden Planetarium and actually give a lecture at our New York gig about the comet. Afterwards, the Hayden threw a reception for the band at the Planetarium and about a thousand people turned up, really cool guys like Stevie Wonder and Alice Cooper. Peter Gabriel was there I think. It was a party with disco music, they didn't have any bands playing there, but it was great though, a real celebrity event in its way. The New York Dolls were there, and I hung around with them for a bit, mainly through Stacia who'd struck up a relationship with Arthur 'Killer' Kane. I was later to spend an entire night in New York with Stacia and Arthur, trying to talk Arthur out of committing suicide; it was terrible. He just took too many drugs, loads of downers which got him very depressed, and then he'd get drunk and it was, 'Blimey, this is hard work.'"

The brief incursion into the American market of late 1973 was a testing ground for a more substantial assault during the spring of 1974, despite the first tour receiving what James Johnson described as "horrendously bad reviews." They kicked-off in Los Angeles on 7th March, touring across the USA before wrapping up in Canada five weeks later. Labelled as the '1999 Party', the tour included support from Welsh rockers Man. Long-time fan Marc Sperhauk first saw Hawkwind at the Electric Ballroom, Atlanta (29th March), with Aerosmith as the opening act.

"I imagine the Atlanta show was as close to Space Ritual as I ever witnessed," recalls Sperhauk. "Nik in his frog suit and Stacia staring into my soul. The venue was a warehouse-like place, very dark and with an ample stage. The next one I saw was in New York, at Radio City Music Hall [6th April]. I'll never forget Lemmy swaying on the edge of the stage, roaring out 'The Watcher'. It was a sold-out show, with a huge crowd on the street; quite an event."

"We had a lot of what are now famous bands below us on the bill," notes Brock. "Rush supported us... we got them so stoned one night before going on stage, made this gigantic joint into an aeroplane."

"Lemmy, Simon King and Dave Brock have become a rhythm unit who stand up on any level," reported Mick Farren, covering the tour for *NME*. Despite noting the band as unhappy with much of the early part of the schedule, Farren commented on a Detroit show "packed to its 5,000 capacity" and praised them for "the first time I've seen Hawkwind push their hypnotic thing all the way up to raw power."

The spring tour left Hawkwind with an unwelcome legacy in the USA. During their third visit in twelve months (starting in Detroit on 6th September 1974), the band and their entourage were arrested, and their equipment confiscated by the Inland Revenue Service for alleged tax evasion. "We were staggered," Doug Smith told *Record Mirror*. "Our legal advisors had been consulting with the IRS... [They] assured us that we were not liable for tax payment on our last tour, as we only broke even." Interviewed by *IT*, Turner related how "they arrived at the end of a show and said, 'we want this money [estimated at $10,000] or we'll throw you all in jail.' They wouldn't let us have our equipment back until all the money had been paid off. We had to convince our English record company to put the money up for us." The incident, at Hammond Civic Centre on 21st September, delayed completion of the tour, which didn't resume until 15th October at St. Louis Auditorium.

Though financial problems had dogged Hawkwind for several years, Turner thought that, "we're only in debt over short terms, because in some ways we are too ambitious for our position... we would like to put on really spectacular shows, which require a lot of planning and quite a lot of bread."

Simon House
(Keith Kniveton)

For the '1999 Party', they'd recruited violin and keyboard player Simon House. Classically trained, House had been a member of High Tide, headliners on the night of Hawkwind's first appearance at the All Saints Hall. When High Tide disintegrated, House moved on to the Third Ear Band, playing on the soundtrack to Roman Polanski's *Macbeth*, but then went into musical retirement. In *Sounds*, he described to Bill Henderson how he'd "worked in a boiler-room… I used to take my violin down to practise." Contrasting Simon's experience with the rest of the group, Dettmar notes that "Simon knew not only where the notes were, but in what order to play them in," whereas "other stuff was a jam in some key… when I started I had a keyboard, but I didn't know what notes to press, so I'd tend to hold one note down and just turn the tuning knob, so by the end of the first number, it was basically out of tune."

Lacking a work permit, House travelled to the USA with Hawkwind on an 'observer only' basis, though he did illicitly perform on stage each night. It would seem he had been courted by Brock for some months, Dettmar having made clear his intention to leave Hawkwind as early as the 1973 American dates. Though the 1974 USA gigs marked the start of House's permanent membership of the group, he had appeared with Hawkwind in January at London's Edmonton Sundown on a gig recorded for a potential live release, and again at Leeds University the next month. Two tracks, 'Paradox' and 'You'd Better Believe It', were subsequently heavily overdubbed for use on the band's next album. A third song from the Edmonton, 'It's So Easy', was used for the B-side of the LP's single, 'The Psychedelic Warlords (Disappear in Smoke)'.

There was an overlap period between House arriving and Dettmar finally settling in Canada, where he built himself a log cabin and continued his musical interests with the Melodic Energy Commission. With House onstage, Dettmar returned to playing from the mixing desk, where House described him "hearing the sound properly" and being able to "blend his things in better… I wish I could do the same because on stage I can only hear Dave and the drums." This was a succinct description of the reason for Dettmar's retirement from the stage. "It got too loud for me; I never liked loud music," he explains, acknowledging how unique his position became. "I don't know of anybody else who has ever done that. It was great, this beautiful stereo that I could pan stuff across."

"You listen, and if you can't add to it or enhance it, don't play at that moment," says Dettmar. "I was waiting for my emigration papers, so I knew I wasn't going to be there long, and it seemed quite apt to go back to the sound-desk, where I'd started from. I'd get a bottle of wine, and share it with the audience, and they'd give me who knows what!" Today Dettmar lives in the wilds of British Columbia, which he describes as "avalanche country."

Following the "1999 Party", Hawkwind rehearsed material for *Hall of the Mountain Grill* at Clearwell Castle before recording the LP's studio tracks at Olympic Studios during May 1974. Aside from the two live cuts from the Edmonton Sundown (26th January, 1974) and Turner's 'D-Rider', the album included a song co-written by Lemmy and Mick Farren. Interviewed by Alan Burridge, Farren recalled "[Lemmy] said, 'Hey, you got any lyrics?' and I said yeah, and we wrote 'Lost Johnny'." Farren and Lemmy wrote a handful of other songs together, when Lemmy was assembling his band Motörhead, but the writing partnership "faded away, because Lemmy started writing his own lyrics with great fluidity."

After the first edition of this book was published I asked Farren himself about the song. "It's Lemmy's song. It was written for Lemmy, for Hawkwind. They were doing *Hall of the Mountain Grill* and Lemmy was concerned he wasn't going to get any songs on to it, so I said 'Let's write one'. I had this idea about all these loser characters, of which we knew many, looking for drugs and 'baying at the moon'. I mean, it wasn't Terry Ollis and it wasn't Steve Took, and it wasn't nine other people ... it was a combination of all of them, or seven versions or whatever it was. I put it down on a piece of paper, handed it to Lemmy and he took it away and put the music to it and came back and we changed a few things and that was 'Lost Johnny'. I can't sit down with a guitar, a blank mind and somebody else and come up with a song. I usually have to go away by myself and write the lyrics, and that song was no exception."

Aside from Brock's re-use of material from the Space Ritual tour programme for the opening track, 'The Psychedelic Warlords (Disappear in Smoke)', though sadly not using the bit where the words deliriously declaim the band's 'spaced-out rock 'n' roll', Farren's lyrics for 'Lost Johnny' were the most urban of the album's images. Mike Moorcock once talked about Hawkwind's best work as actually being about the city, chiming with the literary material he'd championed during his editorship of *New Worlds*, and these two tracks, particularly 'Psychedelic Warlords' with its agitprop proto-punk attitude, must be among the very best examples of this. But elsewhere there was a change of textures, typified by the selection of three instrumental numbers, 'Wind of Change', an orchestral, rather progressive arrangement led by the violin of House, though it had originally been conceived prior to him joining the band with an earlier demo of the composition being dominated by Brock's guitar in the same way as the album relies on the violin, Simon's own neo-classical title track and Dettmar's 'Goat Willow'. House described it to *Melody Maker* as being "...a bit of a change, I think. Because of the Mellotron I suppose, it's sounding a bit classical."

At the same time, that changing style moved them out of outer space and into a fantasy world typified by Turner's 'D-Rider' with its pastoral idylls and imagery of dragons. "I had the idea for 'D-Rider' during rehearsals at Clearwater Castle, sitting in the woods meditating amongst the bluebells and playing my oboe," he told me for *Record Collector*. "It seemed a nice idea for a song, people riding around on dragons before the Earth had properly formed. 'My momma knows just where we are', it's fairly ambiguous, is this Mother Earth or our own Mothers? There's a reference to Stonehenge, 'the ring has formed out of the stone' and I'm writing about the Tetragrammaton, which is taken to be the sacred sound of God, the sound of Jesus's name. There's a lot of magic and metaphysics in Hebrew; at the time I was reading a lot of books on magic and incantations – in a positive way."

Dettmar's piece was quoted in the LP's pre-publicity as 'Wild African Piano'. "It was one of those odd things," Del says. "I'd been working with Simon House, but when it came to do it in the studio he seemed more interested in watching colour television. Lemmy said, 'I want to play the piano', Nik wanted to play the flute, and Simon agreed to play the harpsichord. Dave had gone home. It starts off with the African piano, which I put through the pitch-to-voltage converter. Then it was meant to go into a cymbal thing, but Simon King wasn't there so I did that myself and should have played much longer. The African piano was bought by my family when they visited Rhodesia. It consisted of a piece of wood, nine inches by five and slightly scooped out. Tied by copper wire was a piece of iron and over that it had flattened nails. You held it with both hands and had to strike the keys, which were the nails, with your thumb. I don't know if it was the real thing... or the real tourist thing." One reviewer described 'Goat Willow' as "a cracked piece of pastoralism."

Turner saw *Hall of the Mountain Grill* being "complex, more sort of musical," as he told Geoff Barton in *Sounds*. "That's the influence of Simon House, as a musician and in his personality." Charles Shaar Murray, confessing "a sneaking fondness for this album," complained that 'The Psychedelic Warlords' and 'You'd Better Believe It' saw the band "bashing around for several minutes with no appreciable textural variation." However, when held down to shorter lengths, they "do quite well for themselves." And from an American viewpoint, with the band working at establishing themselves across the pond, Alan Niester, for *Rolling Stone*, thought it, "as close to being genuinely listenable as anything done by this band yet, if they keep this trend going they might even start to sell some records in this country."

The variation and complexity in the styles employed on *Hall of the Mountain Grill*, arguably the best of their United Artists albums, reflected a growing trend towards musicality within Hawkwind. House, possessing a full musical education, replacing the self-taught Dettmar, who in turn had come in for Dik-Mik, who made no bones about his own lack of ability. The dynamics were to change again; only a few months after bringing House on-board, a football accident left Simon King with broken ribs and temporarily replaced by another musician with experience beyond that of most Hawkwind members, Alan Powell.

Powell had previously played in the final incarnation of Vinegar Joe, with Robert Palmer and Elkie Brooks, and with Stan Webb in blues band Chicken Shack. "Simon House and I were the first 'proper' musicians in Hawkwind," asserts Powell. 'When I first met Dave Brock, he said to me 'we are not musicians', but I thought he was being modest. When I played my first gig with the band, I realised he was not joking."

Although Powell had been specifically recruited for a set of European dates during the summer of 1974, he was retained after King had recovered, bringing in a dual drummer line-up that lasted for the next two years. "Simon King and I had a good thing going there for a while," says Powell. "Both of us were thin and non-muscular, unlike, say, John Bonham, but together we could put out a powerful rhythm."

Simon King returned to the fold in time for the band's appearances on the summer festivals' circuit. On 28th August, 1974 Hawkwind played at the final Windsor Free Festival, before it was abruptly curtailed by a 600-strong deployment of the Metropolitan Police. It wasn't a one-way confrontation, with the 2,000 attendees having been incited by the some of the organisers to resist the attempts of the police to disperse them. A contemporary report considered that "if the organisers had no right to be mobilising resistance, and the fans no right to start hurling tins of beans, the police had no right to draw truncheons and use force." It remained the most violent end to a festival in Britain until 1985. "My spirit mourned for Windsor; the pathetic and perhaps the last manifestation of peace and love," wrote jazz legend George Melly.

Hawkwind's set was recalled by one attendee as a "monochordic riff with a real and deep understanding of the power of climax," though the same person considered "their vocals and pretentiously declaimed lyrics/poems verge too often on the preposterous." Playing in the early evening prevented effective use of the lightshow, and so "Stacia delicately disrobed and the helicopter, which had been buzzing around at intervals, returned." The viewer dryly thought it "more than a coincidence."

Early in 1975, Hawkwind recorded a single, 'Kings of Speed', a song much more in line with the style of 'Silver Machine' than 'Urban Guerrilla' had been, and with a more radio-friendly hook than 'The Psychedelic Warlords' offered.

The lyrics for 'Kings of Speed' had been written by Michael Moorcock for an album by his band The Deep Fix, entitled *The New Worlds Fair*. "It had a different melody, but I dropped it and added a more bluesy number because I felt we needed something like that on the record. 'Kings of Speed' was given to Dave, who modified the tune."

The New Worlds Fair germinated from a business lunch Moorcock had with Andrew Lauder, then head of A&R at United Artists. "When do you plan to deliver the album to us?" he asked, Moorcock told Crescent Blues. "I didn't know he wanted one." To create a line up for what was effectively an imaginary band Moorcock had called upon the services of most of the current Hawkwind membership. Brian Tawn, in his analysis of Moorcock's musical work, *Dude's Dream*, described the underlying theme of the album as "a huge fairground operating as the world around crumbles." Although Tawn felt *The New Worlds Fair* to be "a truly great album," music press response was diametrically opposed to his view. *Melody Maker*'s Allan Jones decried the LP as "a completely retarded experiment" and cited only Simon House, in his role of musical arranger as well as musician, emerging "with any credit."

On the B-side of 'Kings of Speed' was what transpired to be Lemmy's final song for Hawkwind, 'Motörhead'. Alan Powell recalls the song as being written in the Hyatt Hotel in Los Angeles during a break in the 1974 US tour. "The rest of the band had gone back to the UK for two weeks, so Lemmy and I were there to do publicity... we spent the entire time drunk and stoned, and charged everything to United Artists." 'Fourth-day, five-day marathon', wrote Lemmy in the song's lyrics. Indeed! In his autobiography, he recalled the song being written on the balcony of the Hyatt, on an Ovation acoustic guitar borrowed from Wizzard showman, Roy Wood. Possibly the most notorious hotel in the world, Sunset Boulevard's Hyatt (nicknamed 'The Riot House') was the staging area for the wild and lurid antics of several generations of rock stars from Led Zeppelin, The Rolling Stones and The Who onwards. The Hyatt's colourful past can be glimpsed in Cameron Crowe's seminal film, *Almost Famous* (2000).

The original take of "Motörhead" was recorded by Lemmy, Brock, Powell and Dettmar, "just the basic track, at Olympic Studios – Lemmy had lost his voice," recalls Brock. "I was sleeping on the studio floor, which I did because of living in Devon. Everybody had gone home, so I decided to do the vocals; then Lemmy came back a few days later and did it properly. I saved the original tapes and we released it years later, on the Flicknife label." The coda to this track was once related to me by Flicknife's Marc 'Frenchy' Gloder who described how Dave had told him that he'd seen this track as a possible pointer to how the band could be once again reimagined, that he saw a potential new angle by turning Hawkwind into a three-piece line up with Lemmy and Simon King working alongside himself in this version of the band. It didn't come to pass, though many years on from that time departures from the line up did result in a three-piece Hawkwind that was creatively successful.

'Kings of Speed' was included on Hawkwind's 1975 sword-and-sorcery concept album, *Warrior on the Edge of Time*. Geoff Barton, writing for *Sounds*, had already identified, in November 1974, that "[Hawkwind] seem to be moving away from the science fiction thing and into the realms of science fantasy." Turner explained how they'd been working with Michael Moorcock. "He's devised a very loose framework for a show using some of his poetry; we hope to have Stacia saying some of it."

Moorcock related to *Orbit* fanzine that, "I was doing a lot of my Eternal Champion stuff on stage," and noted the idea of producing a concept album on that subject as being "automatic... because there were so many numbers I could fit in to that." The idea of producing a stage show set around those stories had been rumbling around for some time. Brock suggested to Allan Jones that he wanted Arthur Brown for the title role, an idea that came to nothing.

The LP was recorded at Rockfield Studios in March 1975. It contained three spoken word tracks - two recited by Moorcock and the other by Turner - including 'Standing at the Edge', which had featured in Hawkwind shows as early as December 1971. "I had a fair amount of involvement in *Warrior on the Edge of Time*," says Moorcock. "The title was, of course, mine. I remember working with Barney on that, and I did three or four numbers at the studio. I was supposed to get a session fee [as] I did a half-day's work. I don't think I ever got the fee... eighteen quid. Nik covered one of my readings in the end; I didn't even stay to hear them through. There was a picture on nearby which I wanted to see, so I was in a hurry to complete the job and get to the movies." To *Orbit* fanzine, he described the general starting-point of his Hawkwind contributions. "What Dave tends to do is he says 'do us a concept'. I do it, then Dave has a different idea and the whole thing shifts away. It's a perfectly good way of working – to give Dave a bit of a start."

The title poem itself had been used at Hawkwind gigs since late 1973, but didn't feature on the LP, whilst all the other material produced was new and untested. Brock contributed the opening two segued songs, 'Assault & Battery' and 'Golden Void', a choppy, driving number called 'Magnu' and a lovely acoustic song, 'The Demented Man', complete with obligatory seagull effects. Both 'Assault & Battery' and 'Magnu' borrowed from 19th Century literature; The opening verse of the former being taken from 'The Psalm Of Life', a poem by Henry Wadsworth Longfellow (1807-82), while 'sunbeams are my shafts to kill' from 'Magnu' were taken from 'Hymn to Apollo' (Percy Byshe Shelley, 1792-1822). Shelley was a notable figure in the Romantic Movement and an author of politically radical poetry. 'The Demented Man' is arguably, and sadly, the last appearance of 'Busking' Dave Brock on a Hawkwind LP. Maybe a case of "move along, sir, you're blocking the escalator," but a much-missed facet of Hawkwind albums, really. On 'Opa-Loka', an Alan Powell instrumental, Brock played bass because, as Powell notes, "Lemmy had disappeared off somewhere."

Turner's 'Dying Seas' had a Moorcock gestation; "[Mike] gave me a load of titles, I wrote songs about them. 'Dying Seas' was one of them. There were others, which I'm using now, one called 'Sonic Savages'." And 'Kings of Speed' disjointedly added to the album though sounding quite out of place, also had various Moorcock characters imbedded in it. The Mr C mentioned was a reference to Moorcock's Jerry Cornelius character while also mentioned were Frank (Cornelius) and (Bishop) Beasley. In turn, Hawkwind appeared in a cameo role in the Jerry Cornelius novel *A Cure for Cancer* and briefly in the background during the Cornelius film *The Final Programme*.

Warrior on the Edge of Time is a quite legendary album that doesn't always live up to its reputation, though a re-evaluation took place in 2013 when, after years of being out of print, it returned to availability in a majestic box set that included a modern re-mix makeover by the influential contemporary progressive musician, and Porcupine Tree founder, Steven Wilson. In the first edition of this book, I described the original LP as "a now much over-rated slab of progressive rock, which, though it is held in the highest regard by Hawkwind fans, suffered nearly as bad a bruising in some of the music press as New Worlds Fair had endured." I'll still stand by this assertion, if thinking it perhaps a little harsh, and found it fascinating that, interviewed by the *Oxford Times* for a tour the band did in support of the 2013 reissue, Dave Brock himself described it as being an album he was particularly proud of. "It just marked the end of an era, the start of something else."

I'd argue that the spoken word pieces have dated particularly badly and that the realisation of Moorcock's concepts was underdone to the point that the album drifted too far away from its initial vision. But I'd also celebrate what's great about this record: Brock's haunting and ethereal acoustic delivery of 'The Demented Man', made all the better for being a wonderful moment not attempted in a live arena for many years and so remaining as a delightful little secret on the album. The deceptively complex 'Spiral Galaxy 28948' with Brock's guitar skating atmospherically across the surface of Simon House's instrumental masterpiece, and that opening salvo of 'Assault & Battery' and 'The Golden Void' which, while they sound a little slow and laboured compared to some of the band's other realisations of these songs, most notably the versions played for Channel 4's *Bedrock* programme at the end of the 80s, have a real sense of purpose and drive to them. If the Moorcock concepts had been more properly explored and developed, that leading segued barrage could have set the scene for something very special indeed.

In the end, it's a record where the parts are so much greater than the sum of the whole and it does have an end of era feeling about it. It doesn't move the band forward from *Hall of the Mountain Grill*, and, really, nor does it live up to that album, where everything sounded joined-up and properly conceptualised, and not a note seemed out of place. If anything, it comes across as weary re-treads of similar themes and styles, as if the line-up had grown conceptually tired. "Some of those numbers I dislike," Brock conceded.

Anticipating "a ludicrously grand extension of Moorcock's novels," Allan Jones heard only "Brock mixed so low that his guitar is a virtually subliminal influence" and "King and Powell [thrashing] to their hearts content in an ill-defined limbo." The two-drummer live arrangement was not adopted for the LP, Powell noting that "two drummers do not work well on record; it's a live thing, really." Jones gave a half-hearted nod in the direction of 'The Demented Man' ("all the resonance of a Japanese ukulele") and 'Spiral Galaxy 28948', citing them as preferable to "the cosmic redundancy" of 'Opa-Loka' and the dirge of Turner's 'Dying Seas'. As with the praise he'd received for his contribution to *Hall of the Mountain Grill*, House was identified as contributing to the advance in "technical proficiency," but Lemmy's bass was "monotonous" and Brock's words represented "the overall lack of lyrical imagination." The review in *Melody Maker* (10th May 1975) systematically demolished the content of the LP, mitigated only by being linked to a review of Moorcock's *New Worlds Fair* LP, compared to which, *Warrior on the Edge of Time* was "an unqualified masterpiece."

It would take another decade before Hawkwind could gather a collection of material and a full touring show that would properly do justice to Moorcock's work.

7

Lemmy out! Stacia Out! Calvert Back!

**Paul Rudolph and train enthusiast Dave Brock, US tour 1975
(Dave Brock Collection)**

Hawkwind returned to America in April 1975, on the brink of cracking the most difficult market in rock, with *Warrior on the Edge of Time* about to be released by Atco. However, the omens were not good, with Brock having described to that most regular of Hawkwind chroniclers, Allan Jones, a few months previously the difficulties mounting internally.

"Some nights I've unplugged my guitar and marched across the stage to sort Nik out. He keeps playing his saxophone when I'm singing and I've told him a thousand times not to do that. I had a go at Lemmy the other night because he just couldn't pull himself together, and he threw his bass on the stage."

One of the major differences within the band wasn't musical; it was in the choice of drugs. Reflecting on this, Turner told Santtu Laakso: "I read this article in which Lemmy said 'Hawkwind was not a peace and love band, we were always on speed.' I thought Hawkwind were very much a peace and love band." That difference of outlook on substances would soon become pronounced and public. Following a show in the USA, the band travelled across the Canadian border, bound for a gig in Toronto. Lemmy was in possession of a gram of amphetamine sulphate and some pills that he'd acquired from a female admirer in Detroit. At the border, the tour bus was stopped, Lemmy was searched and the speed he was carrying was misidentified as cocaine. Though he was temporarily jailed, then released on bail posted by the band, the incident signalled the end of his membership despite the charge eventually failing because of its inaccuracy. Arriving in Toronto for Hawkwind's next gig (18th May) just after the band's sound check, Lemmy recalled in his autobiography that "we did the gig to tremendous applause, then at four o'clock in the morning, I was fired."

"Lemmy was fired by a vote we all took in a hotel room in Canada," explains Alan Powell. "Dave decided we would have a vote. Nothing happened in Hawkwind unless Dave Brock approved it."

Turner claims to have been saddled with the onerous task of advising Lemmy that his services were no longer required: "I thought it was the first group decision the band had ever made – but retrospectively I'm seen as the guy who sacked him. I was the guy who had the balls to sack him, actually! We'd made the decision, but everyone was saying 'You tell him' and 'No, I don't want to tell him.'"

A contemporary interview in NME told the story from Lemmy's perspective: "I [was] called to Dave Brock's room," he revealed. "They were all sitting there. I was told I was being sacked. I said, 'Thanks very much' and left the room. I must tell you, I was upset. Tears were seen."

Turner saw the complications caused by Lemmy's arrest as being too much for the band to take. "We had to pay lawyer's fees, we had to get another bass player to replace him, it was the last straw for a bunch of people who'd been working with Lemmy; he wasn't the easiest person to work with. He'd take speed, stay up all week and then take some downers and go to sleep for a week. People who take speed are very difficult to deal with, they're very dogmatic, opinionated about things and they're always right... always right, no question about it!" Turner's aversion to 'speed freaks' came from his experiences in the 1960s: "I met so many down in Margate amongst the Mods and the Rockers and I didn't really want to be involved with people who took it – and Lemmy made a virtue of it."

"I was doing the wrong drugs," claimed Lemmy many years later in Q magazine. "If I'd been busted for acid they would have rallied around. They only got me out of jail 'cos the replacement couldn't make the gig that night." He later reflected, with still bitter irony, that "being fired from Hawkwind for drugs is a bit like being pushed off the Empire State Building for liking heights." Lemmy returned to England and issued his famous quote on his plans for the band that eventually eclipsed Hawkwind, Motörhead: "They'll be the dirtiest rock band in the world. If we moved in next door, your lawn would die."

Brock, with hindsight, saw the dismissal of Lemmy as being part of the reasoning behind the split between Hawkwind and United Artists. *Warrior on the Edge of Time* was released by UA in Britain on a licence from Atco: "We had a five-year period with United Artists, but they look at what goes on, record sales and personalities in the band. Things were going alright; the whole era was very successful. It was only when the contract expired, and we had sacked Lemmy –

that was it." As the original contract with United Artists had expired during 1974, this suggests that there was still a possibility of renewal in 1975.

Despite seeing the dismissal of Lemmy as a collective decision at the time, Turner now claims there were other motivations at work. "Doug Smith told me that Lemmy leaving the band was something that Dave Brock had planned at least six months before – he'd talked to Doug about it." That doesn't square with the idea that one tangent for the band to follow was as a trio comprising Brock, Lemmy and King, and so not surprisingly, Brock has a diametrically opposed view to Nik's: "Nik wanted Lemmy sacked because he wanted Paul Rudolph in the band, who was a mate of Nik's." In *White Line Fever*, Lemmy claims that, "Dave, God help him, actually wanted to bring me back, but the drum empire [King and Powell] wouldn't let him." What has become clear is that one of Brock's genuine regrets is the dismissal of Lemmy, the iconic bridge between the band's hippie roots and their biker following.

Paul Rudolph, known as 'Blackie' and by nature a lead guitarist rather than a bass player, arrived to replace Lemmy for the remaining dates. Rudolph had the obligatory Ladbroke Grove connections, having previously been a member of The Deviants and, subsequently, The Pink Fairies. "I had always done a lot of jamming with Hawkwind, from the Pinkwind days, so consequently knew the entire band reasonably well. I received a phone call from Doug Smith asking me if I was available to fly out to Toronto to meet the band and play bass." As Rudolph was Canadian, this solved the crisis without having additional work permit complications.

A subsequent gig in St. Louis was observed by Marc Sperhauk, who recalls it taking place in "a downtown theatre in what looked like a war zone of half demolished and half constructed buildings." Though he enthuses about how he "wandered in a stage door and watched the sound check," the show itself was an anti-climax. "The performance that night was turgid. Paul Rudolph was not up to snuff. I could see Dave often turning to show him the chords, and with a catch-up bass player, the two drummers seemed to wander. It never took off." Sperhauk did locate the band's hotel. "Somehow, I managed to end up taking Stacia out to the liquor store. When I brought her back to the hotel she invited us up to her room." Describing Stacia as "incredibly sweet and, well, larger than life," Marc's most vivid memory was "sitting on her bed drinking and watching TV. Scorched into my impressionable young mind was when she stood up and announced 'It's hot in here, do you mind if I take my trousers off?' Before we could splutter an incredulous 'why no, ma'am', she'd whipped them off." Marc is adamant: "The story ends there!"

There are no known recordings of either the dates with Lemmy or the following shows with Rudolph on bass to represent this tour. If there were, the early gigs would probably reveal a band much like the one captured on a handful of occasions in England earlier in 1975. Ray Coleman, describing Hawkwind's appearance at the Hammersmith Odeon that February, called their music "good, solid, punk rock… their numbers have a fire and discipline. Hawkwind is one of the biggest concert attractions in the land right now." Though reviewing Hawkwind at La Gare de la Bastille in Paris, post-Lemmy, Allan Jones' comments in the Melody Maker of July 1975 might have equally applied to the music the band were producing before the fateful USA tour: "Simon House is no longer relegated to [a] subordinate role. His violin and keyboard playing has become increasingly more assertive."

The more dominant presence of Simon House in the mix is evident right from the start of 1975, with concert recordings demonstrating a substantial overhaul of the Space Ritual numbers, notably Simon's haunting violin on 'Lord of Light'. This was additionally important as the year progressed and the band's most nuts-and-bolts rock 'n' roll member unceremoniously departed, as it delivered another distinctive sound in the spaces where one had been removed. Jones was happy to add that "Rudolph clings more to the careering rhythm of King and Powell, which means that Dave Brock can ease back a little," and felt that this meant that the sound was "not so dominated by [Brock's] surrogate Sterling Morrison guitar vamps."

"I didn't find it difficult to play with Hawkwind," notes Rudolph of the inherited *Warrior on the Edge of Time* material. "I had heard their numbers a lot and liked that there was lots of room of improvisation on the spot, being able to play new things together spontaneously." Nevertheless, as the year progressed and much of the *Warrior* material was dropped in favour of new numbers there was a marked deviation from the denser textures that had always characterised Hawkwind. "I think the shift away from the wall of sound was simply the result of a mixing of new chemicals in thinking and ideas," says Rudolph. "Hawkwind wasn't the Spice Girls, to be replicated, show after show. I don't know if any one person was instrumental in making the sound change." Rudolph sees the development of any band in the context of "different people, as well as different backgrounds and different instruments. Hawkwind started with a basic synthesiser, and when I joined had a keyboard player with a Mellotron, which changes the possibilities quite a bit."

"When Paul Rudolph joined, I finally had a musical accomplice," comments Powell. "We were able to play things that were impossible up to that point, like playing in time and dynamics."

With Rudolph installed as permanent replacement for Lemmy, Hawkwind continued with a tour of Europe through June of 1975, playing a set still predominately built around *Warrior on the Edge of Time*. English dates in late July and early August were the run up to the band's appearance at the annual Reading Festival, on 22nd August. A strong gathering of festival favourites such as Hawkwind and Caravan mixed it with pub rock bands such Dr Feelgood, and the Kursaal Flyers. The more adaptable heavy rockers, including Judas Priest and UFO met rock dinosaurs such as Yes, whilst Lou Reed was billed but didn't show.

Robert Calvert joined the band, probably for the first time since mid-1974. "He looked like an alien being's idea of a Parisian Left Bank beat with his blue beret and manic staring eyes," noted *Melody Maker*. Calvert read a new work, 'Ode to a Crystal Set', a poignant lamentation for a bygone age of faith in progress and square-jawed heroes. 'You were as futuristic as Colonel Dare' he comments at one point, dreaming 'there were voices among the stars'. He returned to read material from Space Ritual ('The Awakening', 'Sonic Attack') and, in a harkening back to the song's roots, provided vocals on the set closing 'Silver Machine'. "It was seen as a groovy idea to have him at Reading," recalls Nik. "Robert had the idea of getting a sub-machine gun and doing that stuff on stage with the 'Urban Guerrilla' or his Lawrence of Arabia stance, all very theatrical."

Though the pronounced hit of the day was second on the bill Dr Feelgood, Hawkwind's set was also a notable success with *Sounds* previewing the appearance as being by a band now "resembling the well-oiled Starship Enterprise [rather] than the lumbering prototype Fireball XL5." Reviewing for the *Reading Evening Post*, Robin Smith added that "To a continuous background of battering drums they built up a wall of sound... [it] just washes over you, and if you're in an inebriated state so much the better." *Melody Maker* found the set "surprisingly tight and well disciplined... one of their better performances" but, touching on that end of an era feeling that had been lingering around the band for many months, viewed Stacia's act as "becoming a bit of a bore" and claimed that, "she stomped around with all the grace of the Statue of Liberty animated by Ray Harryhausen on an off-day." Despite the more favourable critiques there was a sense that this phase had run its course and that there was a need for a regeneration of musical content and style. "Hawkwind have made few concessions to the sweeter tones of today," said the Reading Festival programme. "Even personnel changes don't seem to have altered their music," added the Reading Evening Post. The next Hawkwind studio work would be so radically different from what had gone before that it would split not only the listeners, but the band itself down the middle.

The day after their appearance at Reading saw Brock, Turner, Powell and Rudolph, along with resident Hawkwind DJ Andy Dunkley on synths, play an ad-hoc and largely improvised set at the Watchfield Free Festival in Oxfordshire. Apart from Hawkwind, the number of name bands who could be relied upon to give their services for free was dwindling (ironically, but not unexpectedly, Free declined), with the only other memorable acts appearing at Watchfield being Gong, and Here & Now, who later became a fixture of the Stonehenge Free Festival.

The Watchfield site, a disused airfield that drew some 5,000 attendees in poor weather conditions, was chosen as a replacement for the traditional Windsor Free Festival which had collapsed. "After the violence that occurred in 1974, there was pressure on the government to supply an alternative site," notes the The Archive, a website dedicated to Britain's Rock Festivals. "['organisers'] Bill Dwyer and Sid Rawle were jailed for contempt when they distributed flyers encouraging people to attend the 1975 [Windsor] Festival. A dozen people did actually turn up – overseen by 350 policemen and a coterie of journalists." The Watchfield gathering, though, boasted support from the unlikely figure of right-wing Conservative MP, and Colditz escapee, Airey Neave, who found himself strangely allied with the organising committee when suggesting that a permanent, self-financing site should be found for pop festivals. "Mr. Neave strolled around the site with his family, watching the bands and chatting to one or two bemused festival goers," The Times advised. "'It is very orderly', he commented."

Watchfield was a gig that Alan Powell, open if lonely in his views that Hawkwind were not a particularly strong live band, identified as a highpoint of his membership. "It was one of those gigs when we got it right... if only there had been more like that."

Though the Reading Festival showed that Calvert was still interested in developing his ideas through the medium of Hawkwind, he wasn't quite ready for a full-time return. Calvert was still working through a set of projects that, while they often involved various members of Hawkwind as session musicians, were not in the same style his former bandmates were producing. Interviewed by NME's Vivien Goldman (September 1975), Bob was still talking about Hawkwind in the past tense. "I remember my time with Hawkwind as an endless succession of flashing gigs," he said. "That really was the high point of the British Underground."

His classic solo album *Captain Lockheed & the Starfighters*, recorded at Island and Olympic Studios, between March 1973 and January 1974, was originally conceived as a theatre play. The LP featured contributions from Arthur Brown, Vivian Stanshall and Brian Eno, Del Dettmar recalling that he obtained a pitch-converter during the making of the record and that he "put Arthur Brown's voice through it." Also featured was Paul Rudolph on lead guitar, prefiguring Rudolph's membership of Hawkwind and leading to what one commentator later described as "a hint towards what Hawkwind might have been like if Paul Rudolph had replaced not Lemmy, but Dave Brock." More interesting, in a general rock mythology context, is the pairing of Calvert with Stanshall, the eccentric genius of the Bonzo Dog Doo Dah Band. Interviewed for a posthumous biography of Stanshall, Arthur Brown recalled his involvement in bringing the two characters together. "[Stanshall] could insult anyone deliciously... Robert was no slouch in this area either. I thought, being artists of a like-temperament, they might understand each other." This introduction led to Stanshall's involvement in *Captain Lockheed* where, during one of the idiosyncratic storytelling dialogue sections, Vivian played the German Air Defence Minister, demanding the "long awaited reawakening of German air supremacy."

Captain Lockheed focused on Calvert's fascination with the West German Air Force's disastrous purchase of Lockheed's Starfighter jet aircraft. As the sleevenotes explained, the adaptations made by the Luftwaffe when turning single seat fighter jets into "heavy duty atom bombers" left them "highly unstable and difficult to control." This led to so many crashes that the jet earned the nickname of the 'Widow Maker'. Calvert, in the *Melody Maker*, August 1973, claimed that "I've grown up with the Starfighter jets, which have accounted for the lives of

94

many young pilots. It's become such a part of me that I've had to write about it, in order to get it out of my system."

Calvert saw *Captain Lockheed* not simply in terms of the LP that bore the name, but as an advancement of his ambitions as a playwright. "When I wrote the *Captain Lockheed* play, I started it by sitting on the old hulk of a boat lying in a cove in Cornwall," he told *Melody Maker*. "It looked like the remains of a crashed aircraft."

His second solo LP, *Lucky Leif & the Longships*, moved Calvert from the near-contemporary context and into the age of the Vikings and their possible early discovery of North America. "It's an experimental album," noted Calvert at the time *Lucky Leif* was released. "Some of it works, some of it doesn't." By the time this album was recorded, Calvert had eschewed the mix of dialogue and music that had made *Captain Lockheed* so distinctive, having been advised by producer Brian Eno that "dialogue and humour don't really work on LP." Instead, there was a melting pot of styles and nods towards specific rock music subgenres, which gave the album an incoherent feel. An example was the Californian surf spoof, 'Lay of Surfers' that parodied The Beach Boys ('I guess you could call us, Barbarians/Barbarians, Bar-Bar, Barbarians') and Jan & Dean, who Calvert acknowledged that he "loved," although he "didn't set out to mimic." Whilst having flashes of inspiration, *Lucky Leif* was essentially stillborn in its attempt to further develop Calvert's flirtations with expanding the range of the rock album, and is consigned in many critics' minds to the indulgent excesses of the mid-70s.

Towards the end of 1975 however, Hawkwind were finally reenergised lyrically by Calvert's return, and visually enhanced by his dual role as lead singer and performance artist. His new role took his involvement in the band away from being an occasional visitor to the stage and made him the central figurehead in a way that enabled Calvert to achieve far more of his theatrical rock ambitions. At the same time, the new material that Brock and Calvert were producing played to Bob's strengths.

'Steppenwolf', which was introduced into the set in early 1976, was a classic example of Calvert's character-driven lyrics setting up an image that could be expounded upon in a live context. Calvert noted that "Harry Haller [in the novel *Steppenwolf*, by Herman Hesse] is a fascinating character… a solitary figure who stays in his room writing poetry and letters… The hero figure is something I am fascinated in mostly sending up." The lyrics were originally written for an album by Calvert's friend, Adrian Wagner: *Distances Between Us*. Calvert reused them when "[Brock] played me this riff he'd written and I immediately thought of using the words… with a bit of expansion." Geoff Barton, reviewing Hawkwind's show at the Birmingham Odeon (16th September, 1976) described Calvert dressed, for this song, "in a very sinister fashion with black coat, black top hat, even – so it appeared – a blacked-out face." Later in the set, during the declamation of Middle-Eastern tradition and politics, which Calvert had co-written with Rudolph, 'Assassins of Allah', Bob was seen "adopting a Lawrence of Arabia pose… waving swords menacingly."

**Robert Calvert, Bracknell Sports Centre, 18/12/76
(Keith Kniveton)**

"We're writing numbers with visual ideas in mind," Calvert told Barton. "We're trying to get the visual side of the band focused on individuals rather than on screen projections." Calvert brought some of his solo material with him to Hawkwind, 'The Right Stuff' (from *Captain Lockheed*) providing a new middle-eight bridge for 'Brainstorm' while *Lucky Leif*'s 'The Making of Midgard' was also briefly included in the live set. But generally Bob was intent on moving Hawkwind away from the Eternal Champion fantasy material and back on to his SF agenda. New material was the order of the day. By the time Hawkwind were availing themselves of Calvert's unique talents on a fulltime basis, the set had gained Rudolph's funked-out instrumental 'The Aubergine that Ate Rangoon' (for which Calvert provided the title), the soaring space odyssey of 'Chronoglide Skyway', and the knowing wink of 'Reefer Madness'.

"Working with Bob Calvert was fantastic, it was great that he re-joined," says Rudolph. "He had great ideas and was very energetic. Some nights were incredible, with the band pumping at a hundred and ten percent, the lightshow totally happening and Calvert and Turner doing their theatrical bits."

Turner; "Bob had always been about, always on the fringes and always hungry... and he was always near to hand because we were all playing on his albums and being involved in his projects. He was always in the wings. When he wasn't in the loony bin, he was in the wings. I knew about his condition from when I knew him back in Margate in the 60s and his mother had confided in me that he had these nervous breakdowns every eighteen months."

Post 'Urban Guerrilla', Calvert had lost none of his song writing fire. In the year that the Clash claimed 'I'm So Bored with the USA', Bob was going for the jugular with his take on America's scientific priorities in 'Uncle Sams on Mars'. In the post-Apollo era, Calvert complained bitterly that 'shoals of dead fish float on the lake,' and identified the problem in, environmentally, nobody knowing how to 'work the brakes'. In the song's depiction of the United States, wide-eyed as a schoolboy, bucket and spade in hand and looking for life in rock pools, Calvert characterised an entire national aspiration as cleanly and accurately as he had delineated the anti-hero of Hesse's *Steppenwolf*. As to the intriguing question of the missing apostrophe in the song's title... who knows? Was it a literary nod to James Joyce and the titular ambiguity of *Finnegans Wake* from this most well-read of song-writers? Were there lots of Uncle Sams, all on Mars? Or, less prosaically, was it just a grammatically incorrect title caused by a typographical error? "I work in an obsessive way," Calvert revealed to Tim Gadd. "I can only write about things that currently obsess my mind."

The new style of Hawkwind's music, cleaner, perhaps thinner, but certainly more refined and varied led them to a deal with Tony Stratton-Smith's label, Charisma Records. Deciding on a logo that modelled the Charisma name in the style of a Victorian Public House sign, later featuring an image of the Mad Hatter from Alice in Wonderland, Stratton-Smith released the company's first single, 'Witchi-Tai-To', in December 1969. By the time that the label had contracted Hawkwind,

Charisma had issued albums by the Nice, Atomic Rooster, and Van Der Graff Generator, and enjoyed substantial success with Genesis and Lindisfarne. 'Strat' had suggested the name 'Charisma' to former Remo Four keyboard player Tony Ashton for Ashton's latest band. Ashton rejected it, eventually deciding on Ashton, Gardner & Dyke. The band included drummer Roy Dyke, who Stacia married the day after the 1975 Reading Festival, signalling the end of her involvement in Hawkwind.

Doug Smith: "The story goes that Stacia was just a chick, another freak watching Hawkwind; she came along, she was the house mother. She got £25 a week. When I said I'd like to give her a pay rise, the whole band freaked and said 'Get rid of her'. She was a predominately important part of the whole image of Hawkwind."

Moorcock's occasional guest appearances with Hawkwind diminished with Calvert's full-time return. "Bob was back and working well. I had little contact with the band during those periods, apart from on a social level. I thought Calvert was much better at performing and doing rock lyrics than I was, and really admired him." Instead, Moorcock allowed the association of his name with a projected series of fantasy novels featuring various members of Hawkwind as fictional characters (Turner, for example, appeared under his 'Thunder Rider' alias, Brock as 'Baron Brock', Powell as 'Astral Al'). The books themselves, starting with *The Time of the Hawklords*, continuing with *Queens of Deliria*, but fizzling-out before the trilogy was completed by the planned *Ledge of Darkness*, were written by Michael Butterworth.

"Mike wrote a few lines of synopsis about Hawkwind rocking in the ruins of London," says Butterworth. "Piers Dudgeon, at Star Books, bit on the idea. Mike and Jim Cawthorn had done a comic strip, *The Sonic Assassins*, for *Frendz*, which laid the ground for the idea of the Music Wars. Then I came along, connected the two things together, threw in the Death Generator and expanded the idea into three books."

For *The Time of the Hawklords*, Butterworth shared a writing credit with Moorcock, but notes that "To fulfil the publisher's contract Mike lent his name to the first book, oversaw what I was doing, sprinkled a bit of sorcerer's dust here and there and generously gave me the books – the titles were initially contracted to him." Years later, Butterworth realised that the Death Generator, "probably came from an unconscious childhood memory of watching *Quatermass and the Pit*, so [Quatermass author] Nigel Kneale should also be accredited."

The Time of the Hawklords was Butterworth's first novel. "I remember finishing it one sunny morning in Kensal Green Cemetery, just around the corner from Ladbroke Grove and Notting Hill Gate. Those old stamping grounds of Hawkwind's and Mike's, where I lived for a year, provided the fantasy topography for much of the book." The unwritten third book, *Ledge of Darkness*, found form in Bob Walker's comic-strip adaptation eighteen years after the first was published. "The first two books encapsulate an era of Hawkwind from their psychedelic folk beginnings to their proto-punk late 70s years," comments Butterworth, "while *Ledge...* is Hawkwind as tribal eco-warrior musicians."

When Hawkwind entered the studios to work on their next album, *Astounding Sounds, Amazing Music*, it was with an entirely new musical agenda. Rudolph was in the ascendancy, driving towards a psychedelic jazz tone at odds with the previous direction of the band. Powell viewed this as a positive step. "I think it's the most 'listenable' album the band made. None of them had a clue how to record properly in a studio. Rudolph made sure that at least the instruments were put direct into the board instead of mic-ing everything live." In Powell's particular, if peculiar, view, "early Hawkwind albums are fucking awful. I can't listen to them." While it became common practice to plug a synthesiser direct into the desk for recording, in 1976 it was a pioneering approach, the same transition that Pink Floyd made on *Wish You Were Here*. Contrastingly, in hindsight, Rudolph thinks he would have "liked to live record a lot of it, because that was what the band was."

Turner also felt that the new album was a step in the right direction. "What was good about *Astounding Sounds* was that everybody in the band had a creative input. Everyone was involved in writing songs when previously Dave had written most of the tracks." Not strictly correct; most previous albums had a reasonable spread of writing credits despite Brock's contributions being the defining vision for the band.

Rudolph: "There was creative involvement with producing. Writing was a sensitive issue as that's where most of the future money comes from, and there were discussions about being able to give everybody a chance at this."

Bob and Dave (Two Drummer Era)
(Collection of Dave Brock)

Two Calvert/Brock epics, the studied gothic atmosphere of 'Steppenwolf' and the tongue in cheek crazed dope paranoia 'Reefer Madness' dominated Astounding Sounds. The latter's title was drawn from *Reefer Madness* (Louis J. Gasnier, 1936, aka *Tell Your Children*), a ludicrous propaganda film warning of the dangers of the 'evil weed', told from the perspective of a high school principal. DRUG-CRAZED ABANDON! screams the movie's tag-line. "A terribly made, sensationalised, preposterous film," noted Danny Peary in *The Guide for the Film Fanatic*. "If you've seen the film.... this is what it's all about," added Brock, wryly, in various introductions to the song.

In Rudolph's groovy jazz-fusion 'The Aubergine that Ate Rangoon', "a whimsical sequence that simply started at home on my EMS AKS synthesiser and everybody added some bits," as Rudolph recalls, the quieter moments that made up Powell's 'City of Lagoons' and the soaring trip-out of Simon House's 'Chronoglide Skyway', the LP found Hawkwind adjusting their wall-of-sound for a more considered, spacious approach. The latter two, which had their correct composing credits transposed accidentally on the LP, were described by the *NME*'s Dick Tracy as "lazy, spacey electronics that work," whilst Rudolph's instrumental was a "nice surprise... tricky drums... a warp4 instrumental." Powell contends that he and Rudolph "purposely led the band off in new directions, in order to inject some new dimension – we were bored to death with the same old crap night after night." Powell does add that this didn't include, "trying to take the band into a psychedelic jazz thing."

"I never thought I was a key person in leading the band in any particular direction," states Rudolph, contrary to popular mythology. "Alan Powell and I did like the funky music, but I never thought Hawkwind should be a funk-type band. I think we always looked to Dave to try and get some balance between the music then and now."

"I think people had a lot more freedom on that album," Turner asserts. "They were composing songs together; people's ideas were respected and recorded. You get so much more of a different musical picture than you do on other albums. You can't say there is a stereotype of what Hawkwind music should be, that it should be spacerock or it should be all about science fiction or magic and sorcery. To me, anything that people want to do, that they feel strongly enough about to present, should be valid as Hawkwind." Brock had a very different view of the record, consistently scornful of it in interviews. "We didn't think Nik's track ['Kadu Flyer'] was particularly strong."

"'Kadu Flyer' was an idea I had," says Turner, "about a guy who was trying to fly a glider off the top of Mount Everest. I got an article out of the newspaper about it and thought it very interesting." Contrary to Brock's view, 'Kadu Flyer' with its jaunty keyboards, swirling sounds that take the listener into the biting cold winds of the Himalayas, and tongue in cheek double-entendre ('I hit the trail from Kathmandu/with a different kind of trip in view' notes the narrator, judiciously warning 'Never fly through a cloud/if there's a mountain in it') was a most successful piece of whimsical psychedelia. The writing credits included "Mandelkau" due to copyright complications. Jamie Madelkau, the former manager of the Pink Fairies and author of a book about the British chapter of the Hells Angels, stood in for Nik Turner in name only and the rights to the song were subsequently reassigned. Turner captured the atmosphere of the song, if not quite the delivery, playing 'Kadu Flyer' with other bands, but it's arguably the greatest Hawkwind song never to have been played live by the Hawks themselves, if something of a departure in its textures and playful humour.

Calvert determined the title for Powell's composition. "We were sitting around the studio listening to a playback and Bob announced, 'This should be called 'City of Lagoons'.' It's actually a demo I made in my flat; the only people on it are Rudolph, House and myself," notes Powell. "It's not Hawkwind. I wanted it to sound like Pink Floyd. But it is one of the best tracks, one of the most competently played, on any Hawkwind album."

It's a record that has been unfavourably demeaned over the years in almost equally proportion to the way its immediate predecessor had been mythologised as a pinnacle of classic Hawkwind. Maybe that's as a direct result of Dave Brock's famous recollection than on first receiving copies of the LP he'd "thrown out of the window like a Frisbee." These sorts of quotes linger around until they become the accepted wisdom of a collective fandom. It's absolutely wrong. Sorry, Dave! Accepting aside that it's such a big departure from anything the band had done before, recognising the conservatism of any fandom, and understanding that its nooks and crannies, its decidedly different textures, delivered an animal that was almost, but not quite, unidentifiable as Hawkwind. With Calvert properly ascendant for the first time it's a terrific work that has gained respect over the years. Engaging, witty and enigmatic by turns, the sweep of 'Chronoglide Skyway', the fog and gaslights of 'Steppenwolf' and the rhythmic addiction of 'The Aubergine That Ate Rangoon' are just marvellous pieces, 'Kadu Flyer' a neglected classic, and only the discordant, out of place, and now dated quite badly 'Kerb Crawler' fails to feel like a vital and fresh part of the band's canon.

And, for a recording that many see as the nadir of 70s Hawkwind output following the alleged classic *Warrior on the Edge of Time*, the music press of the time was surprisingly positive. "On the strength of this album all those who stopped listening after 'Silver Machine' should tune into this wavelength again," noted the *NME* (6 November, 1976). Though Calvert might have stated the plainly obvious when he recalled how "the style of the music changed dramatically on the *Astounding Sounds* album," he'd go on to claim that "there was never a time when any conscious planning was made to determine musical content."

To promote the album, Hawkwind toured (September - October 1976) with one of their most impressive lightshows, 'Atomhenge', which Geoff Barton described in *Sounds* as being "every bit as impressive as Ritchie Blackmore's 'Rainbow', even though it cost £3,000 as opposed to the Rainbow's £40,000... full of multi-coloured light bulbs... it pulses on and off dramatically... when slides are projected onto the screen behind, the 3D effect is startling." The tour programme welcomed the audience to 'Atomhenge – the temple for all Hawklords.'

"Larry Smart made up 'Atomhenge'; he was married to Carol Grimes who used to be a famous singer," says Brock. "It was basically a crystal version of Stonehenge, made out of fibreglass. He was quite a well-known artist, a nice character, who designed various Beatles posters. We later erected Atomhenge at Stonehenge (in 1977) and then it was used in a tour of *The Hitch-Hiker's Guide to the Galaxy* and a couple of theatre productions. It ended up in Doug Smith's garage..."

The band employed Rikki Howard as a dancer, later famous for her role as a Yellow-Coat in the BBC sitcom *Hi-de-Hi*. "She was a beautiful girl, a wonderful dancer, but she really used to get Calvert at it," Brock recalls. "She used to dress up as a prostitute for the song 'Kerb Crawler'. Bob would be singing 'with your high-heels clicking/like a pair of cloven hooves', and she'd go waltzing up to him. But she grabbed his bollocks one day! Bob tried to push her hand away, but she wouldn't let go... we were all laughing, but he went bananas afterwards, nearly hit her! 'How dare you ruin my stage presence... do that again and you're sacked!' But she had a real sense of humour!"

Having parted company with Douglas Smith, Hawkwind had come under the wing of Marc Bolan's manager, Tony Howard, of Wizard Artists. Turner: "He was one of the managers, perhaps a bit nicer than the Don Arden school, who basically get a band and then single out the member who they see as the "key" person. Then dump the rest of the band – like they did with Marc Bolan – and just get session people in to tour, pay people wages and keep the lion's share of the money for the person they've singled out as their management baby." Turner saw this as another drift away from his democratic ideal. "Tony Howard had singled out Dave as the person he should deal with, because Dave was straight ahead more business-like than anybody else." This may have been the case, but it didn't stop some members of the band trying to dismiss the services of Brock at this stage.

"After Lemmy was sacked and we finished the tour, we came back to England and a year later, they sacked me," says Brock. "I wasn't playing very well, going through a bad patch. The reason was that Paul Rudolph was a good lead guitarist, though he was playing bass in the band. Occasionally we would swap over and he'd play guitar and I'd think 'Oh God, he's far better than me,' and I actually lost confidence." Rudolph is pretty low-key about this notion, recalling that he "always enjoyed swapping instruments," and that, "Dave had a great feel [for the music]."

"They had a meeting in Tony Howard's office and decided to sack me," says Brock. "Bob Calvert phoned me up and said 'Look, I've just come from a meeting… they've put forward a motion and you're sacked from the band. I'm not having it!' Bob, Simon King and myself went to Tony Howard and said, 'We're not fucking having this!'" Perhaps the thought of losing his main songwriters concentrated Howard's mind on the internal problems of the band. "Nik Turner only wrote seven songs in five years, and any manager is going to turn round and look at that," says Brock. "Any musician goes through bad patches; it's all about confidence. If you boost people's morale they play well and they look good."

While Brock is withering about *Astounding Sounds*, and about what he perceives as Turner's attempts to remove him from the band, he appears to have no bad feelings about the other members' involvement.

"Alan Powell was a really brilliant drummer, a good guy, a gentleman. Paul Rudolph was a nice character; we would share a room when we were on tour. We used to smoke Lebanese dope together, he was very amiable!"

"It was decided then [to get rid of] Nik Turner, Alan Powell, who had started to play his funky music, and Paul Rudolph," recalls Brock. "Simon King and Alan Powell were buddies; they lived in the same apartment block in Kensington. Simon rang me up and said, 'I don't really agree with all this, I think we should stick together', but Bob had put his foot down, and [their] problem was that Bob and me were doing all the writing. Paul Rudolph, Alan Powell and Nik Turner got a big pay-off from Charisma to go away; I've no idea how much they got, but it must have been quite a substantial amount."

It is a particularly murky period, with conventional wisdom citing pressure on Brock and Calvert to dispense with the services of Turner, who had been such a talismanic focal point for the band visually. Hawkwind were due to record a new single, 'Back on the Streets', and a prompt resolution of Turner's membership was needed. "It's difficult to say in a situation where one is the victim of it, how much a situation is manipulated by individuals or is a group decision," comments Turner. "The band said 'We want you to leave', and I was faced with this decision that either I left or Paul Rudolph and Simon King would leave, or everybody was going to leave if I didn't! I was put in a position where I felt 'Oh, fuck off then'. I don't know if I really wanted to be part of this thing. So I bowed out gracefully."

There was a feeling within Hawkwind that Turner had become increasingly unsympathetic to the musical space of his fellow musicians. "You've got to remember," asserts Brock, "Nik couldn't play the saxophone. We're talking about a band of freaks that used to come on stage, take LSD, loon around... all these weird characters. At the time, it was great, but you progressed onwards and became more musically-minded. Well, Nik didn't. He got voted third-best saxophonist in the world, ahead of all those great jazz players... but it was a joke, a bit of fun, and Nik believed it!" Brock does consider that Turner has since become much more accomplished: "When he rehearsed with us [for a mini-tour in the autumn of 1999], he could really play sax. What I don't understand, when he plays with us, he does not play in tune."

Powell recalls the events differently. "1976 was the 'Year of the Long Knives'. First I was fired for making it blatantly obvious that I'd had it with the band. Calvert was getting on my wick – and I'm sure I was getting on his! So, I had to go, which was fair enough, If I'd been running the band, I would have fired me... then I think Rudolph got the chop because we were mates." Unusually within the musicians dismissed from the band, Powell has no bitterness, but then, his comments certainly indicate a general lack of sympathy in the concept of the band in any case. "I stayed with Hawkwind because they were a great bunch of blokes; we had some big laughs and a lot of fun. When I was finally fired, I was totally okay with it." This wouldn't stop *Sounds* journalist Pete Silverton, covering a Motörhead support slot at a Hawkwind gig in 1977, explaining that although Motörhead had brought along Powell as temporary cover for regular drummer, Phil Taylor, Hawkwind refused to let them perform due to Powell "suing us for stupid amounts of money."

"Rudolph and Powell really shouldn't have been considered members of the band," Calvert told Tim Gadd. "They were session musicians who'd come in to fill a gap that existed." Powell wouldn't disagree. "In 1976 I went to New York to rehearse with Robert Palmer. I'd written a song that was going to be on his next album. When I got back to do the *Astounding Sounds* tour, I realised that I had grown up, musically. Hawkwind was not my scene. It never had been. I was a 'hired gun' who played with anybody that paid me. That's the way it was in London in the 1970s when you had a flat in Kensington and a fondness for smoking dope." Years later, the song 'Life in Detail' by Powell and Robert Palmer was included in the film *Pretty Woman*, the royalties from which enabled Powell to move to San Francisco and buy a yacht.

**Atomhenge under construction at Stonehenge
(Roger Hutchinson)**

While these conflicts and upheavals brought themselves to their messy conclusion, rehearsals started in Wales producing demos of what became the next album, *Quark Strangeness & Charm*. "Some of it was quite nice music, actually," recalls Brock. "Del Dettmar was playing with us, doing synthesisers. Paul Rudolph was doing a funky sort of thing. Nik was playing flute as well as sax, some of it nice stuff; he does play quite well at times." Though Dettmar doesn't recall joining the band for any studio work, he remembers going to a gig in Oxford, and then making a guest appearance at the Hammersmith Odeon. "I played the pickaxe. I borrowed it from my dad's garden shed, put a string down it and a pick-up underneath it and plugged it into the pitch-to-voltage, a monophonic device. I'd been living in an old mining town in Canada. I'd this guitar string and was looking for a lump of wood to stretch it down, and there was this double-bladed axe and I thought, 'Wow, that's got to be the thing'. I only came on for the last fifteen minutes; they didn't seem to be that much different."

Existing demos from the end of this era, without Powell and Turner but with Rudolph still on board, detail a band expanding on the *ASAM* groove and sounding very much as though they felt that there was still somewhere to go creatively with the new vibe their last album had delivered. An elongated jam session, probably entitled 'Dawn', borrows from the bass line used on 'Dream of Isis' (the B-side to 'Back on the Streets') and has a swirling, orchestral keyboard arrangement that prefigures 'The Iron Dream', from the following year's album.

Keyboards from Simon House, married with some of Rudolph's jazz-styled lead guitar, are reminiscent of the instrumental numbers from *Astounding Sounds*.

"Things were not too harmonious at Rockfield," recalls Rudolph. "As I remember, Turner was sacked and then Alan Powell. I think things would have turned out differently if the recording had been done in town. Apparently, some band members felt that my attitude was not 'band-like' and I had the opportunity of apologising for something or leaving. I choose the latter, not fully understanding the situation."

8

Starfarer's Despatch is a Spirit of the Age

**Calvert flies the flag – 'Uncle Sams on Mars' 1977
(Keith Kniveton)**

Adrian Shaw travelled with Hawkwind on the Space Ritual tour as part of support act Magic Muscle. "If I remember correctly we did that tour without any songs at all, we would just improvise and no two sets were remotely the same. We would have a starting-off point and a finishing-off point of cacophonous feedback but certainly in the early days of Muscle we had no songs.

"Magic Muscle had a lot of problems with the police thinking *we* were Hawkwind, I can't tell you how often when we were supporting them that we'd walk into the gig a bit before them to sound check and we'd get jumped on by the local drug squad and searched because they'd assume a bunch of long hairs with guitars must be Hawkwind. We'd get caught up in their mess! We got raided at a gig in Exeter; a couple of people, one from Muscle and one from Hawkwind's entourage did get busted with dope on them. The rest of us were a bit sly, we always had our travelling hash pipe with us because it was integral to our sound. We had it stashed in the cistern of our dressing room toilet. The police arrived, searched everyone, and carted a couple of people off. When they finally arrived back from being charged the gig was already running late and crowd were getting restless. But we couldn't go on stage without getting a hit from our hash pipe and the dressing room was full of police as well as musicians. I thought it was worth a try, so I went over to the guy in charge and said, 'Look, we're going on stage in a moment, can you just give us a couple of minutes to get our heads together by taking your officers out?' To my amazement, he agreed, they filed out; we got the pipe out of the cistern, filled it, smoked it, put it back in the cistern and staggered out spluttering on to the stage. I'm amazed to this day I got away with it; clearly they weren't the sharpest pencils in the box!"

At the end of 1976 he was telephoned by Simon House and asked to join Hawkwind as a replacement for Rudolph. This was not the first time that they'd sought out his services. Back in '72, that fabulous year of peak success, Nik Turner and Dik-Mik had come up to stay at the house Magic Muscle shared. "Lemmy was still a member but had been up to something, blotting his copybook, and they'd had enough," Shaw recalls. Sorely tempted, he turned the offer down "out of loyalty to Muscle." It was, perhaps, not a particularly wise move, since Muscle split up shortly afterwards and though they'd evolve and reform into what gets referred to as 'Magic Muscle II', that would be without Adrian Shaw.

Between first being asked to join Hawkwind and finally taking up his position, Shaw had filled in for an errant Lemmy on some dates in Germany. His arrival as a fulltime member delighted Brock, who enthused in an interview that "[Shaw] was a natural choice, it's a pity he didn't join sooner." A frank and honest chronicler of the psychedelic scene, Shaw had learned to play guitar in the early 1960s, with the aid of Bert Weedon's famous *Play in a Day* book and then moved across to bass playing. Sensing something special in the air, he was drawn into the underground movement by its new music, fashion and drugs. By 1970, he'd joined the hippie migration to the West Country, relocating to Puddletown in Dorset. At first, he managed the lightshow for the Crazy World of Arthur Brown, and was then invited to play bass with them. When that collective fell apart, Shaw formed the excellently, if strangely, named Rustic Hinge and the Provincial Swimmers, before establishing Magic Muscle.

Magic Muscle, adopted by the local chapter of the Hells Angels, shared a house in Bristol. As Shaw told Wilson Neale, they "took acid every day... not to mention all the other pharmaceuticals that were knocking around." Establishing themselves as free festival fixtures, Magic Muscle played regularly on the same bill as Hawkwind and The Pink Fairies. They survived a couple of years before disbanding after their Space Ritual support slots. Shaw moved on, working with Steve Took (Adrian describes this as falling apart due to "Steve's substance abuse" but in typical honesty annotates this with "I can't claim to have done anything other than join in enthusiastically") and again with Arthur Brown. "The Pink Fairies, and Hawkwind, were very much like [Magic Muscle] in their attitudes, which was two fingers to authority and wanting to get on and do our thing. This would sound horribly conceited if not for the caveat that we were nowhere near as good, but our music was more like The Grateful Dead's than The Pink Fairies or Hawkwind, very improvised. We had our little ritual, Rod and I, the rest of the band were into their acid and dope, as were Rod and I, but we also looked for anything else that was going. Our gigging diet used to be a quarter of a tab of acid, and we used to carry this huge hash pipe around with us and take hits on that before going on stage. That would give us a little psychedelic tweak and we'd see what happened musically after that. So, in a way, we were a bit more spacey than Hawkwind or the Fairies."

Shaw's first task for Hawkwind was to complete the bass parts for the *Quark Strangeness & Charm* LP. As much of the album had already been recorded, Shaw received "…the tracks that had been virtually finished without [Rudolph's] bass on and I worked out the rest from there. I arrived at Rockfield and got down to doing overdubs. It was a strange experience, but no odder than many I had already gone through."

The only inclusion on the LP not to have been previously worked through was the title track itself, which was written in the studio with Shaw. "'Spirit of the Age' was virtually complete, plus a lot of the others." From the sessions that included Rudolph on bass (and some lead guitar) there survives a version of 'Spirit of the Age' that is far from the near-finished track that Shaw worked on. The final LP cut, a two-verse song that uses science fiction tropes to explore the nature of individuality, was based on the poem 'Starfarer's Despatch', read by Calvert on some of his earliest appearances with Hawkwind.

The extant demo deviates from this, revealing an alternative first verse with Robert ranting, in a way that suggests he was formulating lyrics more or less on the spot, about 'men in white coats' who are 'holding test tubes to the light' and 'searching for the shape of things to come,' while Brock sings 'It is the spirit of the age' over the top.

The second verse, where Calvert makes his heartfelt plea for individualism ('Oh for the wings of any bird/other than a battery hen'), is almost the same as the finished song, but the backing track plays into the final coda with a Rudolph lead guitar break not replicated on the LP. When the first edition of this book was published, this author had only a murky lo-fi recording from which to understand the genesis of both this classic Hawkwind song and its equally revered album. Happily, since then these recordings have appeared in full clarity as part of the Atomhenge (Cherry Red) series of reissues - of which more later. It's a most fascinating aural recounting of the development of one of the cornerstones of the Hawkwind catalogue, the album that crystallised the 'modern' science fiction element of Hawkwind and, compared to the space opera 'Golden Age' SF of Space Ritual, the moment where, 'Urban Guerrilla' and arguably 'Psychedelic Warlords...' aside, the material coalesced around a vision of contemporary scientific advancement juxtaposed with a dystopian rather than utopian outlook. They'd stopped writing elongated declamations of interstellar travel and got themselves back down to Earth where the lyrics found a new resonance in contemporary concerns, such as cloning, nuclear destruction, and the clash of civilisations as represented by the petrol-dollar conflict. The music became sharp, clean and practically new wave, still bound by electronics and sci-fi effects trickery but fresh and accessible to an audience beyond the stoners and the stoned of the United Artists-era. In that sense, though in commercial terms it was another album that failed to yield a 'Silver Machine', it's as much the foundation upon which future Hawkwind themes would be built as that 7" vinyl albatross and looking backwards, despite forays into Moorcockian fantasy, it's really the spring from which the band has constantly replenished itself ever since.

From his prior associations with Hawkwind, Shaw was well placed to judge any developments in how the band was controlled. Previous incarnations appeared a very even-handed collectivist ensemble with a good spread of writing credits (the first album aside) and each member free to talk about their own agendas in the music press. Towards the end of the seventies though, Hawkwind seemed from the outside to be more a vehicle for Brock and Calvert, with the joint leaders dominating interview time and handling the bulk of the writing. However, as Shaw would observe, Hawkwind was still a genuine group effort: "The song writing was pretty fair back then. If you had something worth considering, it was considered." He particularly praises the Brock/Calvert combination and the balance that it brought. "It seemed a very creative partnership; they worked well together. Calvert added sophistication lyrically that Brock never had on his own and Calvert's lack of musical expertise was helped by working with Brock." For the album releases, final track selections were decided by discussion. "Brock and Calvert were the main creative force in the band," acknowledges Shaw, "but it was full of strong characters and good musicians, genuinely a team effort; probably the last line up this was true of. Brock really wanted control over the band, which he achieved later by a mixture of ruthlessness and luck."

The new line-up made their debut at the Roundhouse on 27th February 1977. During the encore, a cover of Lou Reed's 'Waiting for the Man', Shaw's Rustic Hinge bandmate, Rod Goodway, appeared as 'The Man'. Earlier in the show, for 'Uncle Sams on Mars', Pete Blake, a school friend of Shaw, appeared on stage, dressed as a space monster. The set was freshened by new material that included the Simon House composed hammer on anvil instrumental 'Forge of Vulcan', the Brock/Calvert sci-fi lullaby 'Fable of a Failed Race' and the post-apocalyptic 'Damnation Alley', which mixed the nuclear wasteland of Roger Zelazny's novel (forget about the very poor film version, please) with *Dr Strangelove*, from Stanley Kubrick's first science fiction film. 'Spirit of the Age' had already entered the set during Paul Rudolph's final appearances with the band, December '76, but its place was cemented with the arrival of the new line-up. Like much of what Calvert was writing about, it seemed so relevant to the world we were starting to live in; Louise Brown, the world's first 'test tube baby' was born in 1978, only a couple of years later, while that paean to individualism, paraphrasing Felix Mendelssohn's 'For the Wings of a Dove' aria, had so many connotations for modern existence that the enduring presence of this song, heavily reworked at times, is totally apt.

**Adrian Shaw on the bass
(Keith Kniveton)**

Quark Strangeness & Charm was planned for a summer release (it entered the UK album charts in July 1977 and peaked at a disappointing number 30). Hawkwind played a series of European dates during March and April before decamping to Rockfield to rehearse further material. Their profile, coupled with Charisma's financial investment, was still high enough to register even continental gigs for review. Monty Smith, writing for *NME*, saw their Paris show at Salle Pleyel and thought the new five-piece band "hardly sleek… but more than serviceable." Not all reviewers were quite so entertained. Don Fudge described the show, rather strangely given Calvert's presence, as "lacking a clear visual focus," though he conceded in the title of his review that the gig was very well received by the audience: 'Frogs Go Nuts A Lot'. He went on to ponder the effect on the impending UK tour of the development of punk, which had hijacked Hawkwind's own turf: "the fashionable view of the Westway is far less romantic than the psychedelic dreams from under it that inspired the original Hawkwind."

The setlist still contained 'Wind of Change'. Musically, the wind of change was blowing at hurricane force back in the UK. At Rockfield, the band worked through some new material, 'Fahrenheit 451', 'We Like to be Frightened', and an embryonic song entitled 'Death Car'. Paul Hayles, a keyboardist who'd move within the ranks during the latter part of the band's Charisma association, recalled the origin of 'Death Car' deriving from "[Calvert having had a] a crash whilst trying out a car he was thinking of buying, breaking the neck of a girl we all knew." Only the latter, under the revised title 'Death Trap', would see the light of day as a studio recording by the *QS&C* Hawkwind.

The release of *Quark Strangeness & Charm* drew a positive response from the press. "Hawkwind back on course" considered the predominately punk-fixated *NME* (9th July, 1977), commenting that since the switch of record labels "even the cover artwork has improved." The reviewer enjoyed the "sardonic reappraisal of those halcyon daze in '67" made by 'Days of the Underground' (a song Calvert once noted as explaining why there would never be a revolution in England) and the whimsical title track. "It's a very funny album. Hawkwind reckon they are back on course. They are." In the same week's edition of *Sounds*, Geoff Barton, despite a generally favourable write-up described the production as "naff in parts," though he went on to declaim the music as "definitive Hawkwind." Barton summed up by arguing that it was an extension of their niche and that there was no reason why the band shouldn't go from strength to strength.

Quark... was Hawkwind's most cohesive, integrated exploration of modern SF themes to date; indeed, it arguably still has that distinction thirty years later. Like the SF of Moorcock's *New Worlds* magazine, it retains an awareness of the threats and challenges of modern society in a scientifically advanced age. Calvert summed it up as being "not quite the age we are in now, but one we are heading for. I always try to write about things that haven't quite happened yet, but I'm sure will." Indeed, today its cautionary messages on cloning, the oil-led clash of civilisations and the nuclear weapon debate haven't dated at all. This author remembers Dave Brock introducing 'Assassins of Allah' at Swindon's Wyvern Theatre by recounting how "Bob Calvert wrote this song years ago and nothing's changed; the same old problems." Calvert had written of the petrol-dollar crisis of the 70s, of the Palestinian splinter group Black September, the organisation from within the Palestinian Liberation Organisation that had murdered Israeli athletes at the 1972 Munich Olympic Games. Now it was the 3rd of November 2001; the horrors of 9/11 were less than two months previous. I can still hear the nervous groan of the audience and feel the tension that Bob Calvert, had he lived, could have carved through with the scimitar he'd used as a theatrical prop all those years before. Brock was right; Calvert had achieved his goal back in the day by declaiming an age that was just around the corner, while in this album the band had cut a stone-cold classic that had not only a lyrical relevance but one which in its new wave freshness captured the sonic 'Spirit of the Age' as well. In that sense, it probably has a claim to being the reason the band continued onwards: it has a verve that was contemporary and advertised the band's twisting, changing nature that made them both adaptable and influential.

Hawkwind made only their second UK television appearance in September (recorded late August), performing a version of their latest single, 'Quark Strangeness & Charm', on the Marc Bolan-fronted pop show *Marc*. Although it was, primarily a children's series – going out at 5:15 on ITV – *Marc* was one of the first networked TV shows to acknowledge the existence of punk rock, essentially the reason this abbreviated series is still remembered today. There weren't many other places on national television in the summer of 1977 where one could see bands like The Jam, The Boomtown Rats and Generation X, all of whom featured during the programme's six-week run. This targeted the very record buyer that Hawkwind were failing to attract, but that they still held relevance for. Bolan shared the same management as Hawkwind at the time, so the opportunity to give the band some much needed exposure was seized upon. Is it surprising, then, that in Adrian Shaw's opinion, "Brock tried to sabotage the whole thing," or is it another defeat from the jaws of victory that at times seems to have been a specialism of Hawkwind? Dave Brock failed to arrive at the TV studio where the performance was being filmed leaving the band to appear without him.

For many years after, Dave passed his absence off as being an aversion to miming. However, interviewed in 1998 he became more expansive on the subject, recalling an occasion in the early 1970s when he and some friends gate-crashed one of Bolan's parties. "We heard Marc Bolan clanking around on his guitar… I had this guitar and played some blues and of course Bolan didn't like that, 'cos we were good. We were asked to leave." It seems that Brock had a long memory. "That's why I didn't turn up on his TV show in Manchester. I carried resentment for many a year. I didn't fancy travelling all that way just to mime, anyway."

Shaw notes that the band decided to go ahead, re-recording the backing track at Granada's studios in the morning and miming to it in the afternoon. "As Brock wasn't there I played guitar as well as bass on the recording." Truth be told, it's probably nothing to do with Dave Brock's failure to appear that the track was re-recorded for miming purposes – musician's union agreements during this period made it practically compulsory for this to happen since it was perceived to guarantee income to session musicians and was certainly common practice on programmes such as *Top of the Pops* at that time, making it entirely possible that the same ruling was in force for the *Marc* programmes. Bolan introduced the band as the people "who should have written Star Wars, but didn't," and described them as "my best friends." Shaw again: "The 'best friends' remark was for public consumption only; we didn't know him very well."

Calvert was dressed and made-up as though he was second-guessing the 'New Romantic' twist the music industry would embrace a few years later. Miming vocals and guitar, with a small stuffed bird of prey strapped to his wrist, he looked particularly self-conscious. "Bob Calvert with Kestrel... Hawk I think it's called," noted Bolan to the audience. Adrian Shaw seemed to be relishing a chance to make an impression, but Simon King and Simon House looked bored.

Shaw adds a footnote of what might have been, to the appearance: "After [Bolan] died, I found out that he had been putting a new band together and wanted me to play bass with him. An opportunity that I think I would have taken. At the time T Rex consisted of session men like Herbie Flowers and Tony Newman. Marc wanted a proper band. As he had worked hard to clean up his act and was looking and sounding good it could have been very interesting."

The *Marc* programme failed to counteract Hawkwind's failure to trouble the UK singles chart post 'Urban Guerrilla', a shame, since the single itself was contemporary, radio friendly, witty and accessible and deserved to earn itself a wider audience. Typical of Calvert, it's full of character and characters: Albert Einstein (1879-1955) the German-born physicist and mathematician, noted for his theory of relativity E=MC2. Nicolaus Copernicus (1473-1543), an early advocate of the theory of the rotation of the Earth around the Sun. Galileo Galilei (1564-1642) a founder of modern science, though his views were so heretical to the Catholic Church that the Vatican didn't absolve him until 1992! Geniuses all, though they had no luck whatsoever with the opposite sex. Allegedly.

The biggest problem they faced critically was the dominance of punk and new wave on the music scene, even though the 'Quark, Strangeness & Charm' single should have played well to a new wave audience. The journalists of *NME*, *Melody Maker* and *Sounds* were ready to discard Hawkwind as another ageing rock dinosaur outfit, grouped with ELP, Genesis and Pink Floyd. This was ironic, because there were many prime movers in the punk arena that were ready and willing to acknowledge Hawkwind's collectivist approach and political ethics as a starting point in their own musical education. Importantly, the band could claim John Lydon as a fan.

Brock recalls meeting the then Johnny Rotten backstage after Hawkwind gigs. Shaw also, remembers an instance at the Camden Music Machine when Lydon paid the band an after-show visit. "At the time I wasn't a fan [of the Sex Pistols]" says Shaw, "though when I spotted [Rotten] in the dressing room I thought I'd have a chat. After a while we became aware of someone eavesdropping. I looked up and saw it was Calvert. We carried on, and after a couple of minutes Bob leaned over, tapped Rotten on the shoulder and said (gesturing towards me) 'I don't know why he's talking to you; he thinks you are rubbish'. Rather than get offended Rotten just said, 'Well, he's right, we are rubbish.' Exit one deflated Calvert."

Robert Calvert, Reading Festival, 28/8/77
(Keith Kniveton)

Popular legends had Lydon selling acid outside of the Roundhouse, or working as a roadie on the Space Ritual tour. Lydon, probably the greatest rewriter of his own myths, dismissed these suggestions in the *NME*. Blaming fellow Sex Pistols Paul Cook and Steve Jones for the drug-dealing story, he waved away the roadie rumour as making "no sense and good sense!" He does, though, namecheck Hawkwind throughout both his first and subsequent autobiographies.

Interviewed by Julie Burchill for the *NME*, Calvert took great delight in his friendship with Lydon. Before meeting Calvert, Lydon had taken to heart an article that suggested, incorrectly, that Bob was living at the Dorchester Hotel. "The first time I saw Johnny Rotten he came up and started abusing me for it!" Having corrected this misinformation, Calvert claimed to have "taken him to party at a solicitor's house," where Rotten "got off with a debutante who looked like a horse." Burchill, recruited by the NME as a 'hip young gunslinger' turned in an aggressive interview with Calvert and Brock that had all the familiar hallmarks of her deconstructionist, 'Year Zero', approach to contemporary music. At one point, Calvert accused Burchill of seeing Hawkwind as "some of kind of tax-exiled dinosaur like Yes," to which she merely withered, "In one, Honey."

Although Shaw describes Calvert as particularly influenced by punk, Bob was not afraid to slay sacred cows, dismissing The Clash as "the most orthodox band I've ever heard," and complaining that "They just play three-minute pop songs and throw in a few slogans." The Clash's Joe Strummer supplied an interesting counterpoint. During the sessions that produced their eponymous debut album, Mick Jones had suggested a cover of the reggae classic 'Police & Thieves'. Strummer's first reaction, to "do it like Hawkwind," might sound another of those apocryphal stories until we remember that Strummer hailed from the squatting scene and had played at the free festivals with the 101ers and was someone who'd transitioned to the punk scene from a vibe and a lifestyle that wasn't so far out of place with that of Hawkwind.

For Calvert, agitation was about getting results: "[The Clash] don't actually do anything to help anyone! We were always playing benefits!" Calvert's off-the-cuff comments were a total nonsense; if any band deserved to carry on the epithet of being 'The Peoples' Band' which Hawkwind had worn proudly on their sleeves it was The Clash. Strummer, and Mick Jones, both having been living and performing in and around the shadow of the Westway for much of the 1970s, could arguably have taken an influence from Hawkwind's performances in the locality. Calvert did, however, subscribe to the punk view of much of what had gone before. "Pink Floyd became comfortable and bourgeois and settled and just professional studio musicians," he told *Sniffin' Flowers* fanzine before once again losing something of the plot. "Punks came along to smash apart that sort of complacency, but they are not doing anything creative."

Perhaps the best analysis of the synergy between the punk ethic and Hawkwind is instead made by Michael Moorcock. "The band's main thrust had always been in the same spirit as punk. That's why people like Johnny Rotten were given to making statements about us being the only pre-Pistols band worth listening to. We had a lot of prestige amongst punks, I used to go to punk gigs and be very welcome. I was in my thirties by then and punk girls used to offer to get a chair for me, and fetch me a cup of tea – a sort of grand old man." Moorcock claims that he was "very much into punk, since music with an edge of social anger is what I liked best."

The punk-era's designers have also acknowledged Hawkwind's approach. Malcolm Garret, who provided the graphics for the Manchester band Buzzcocks, described to Jon Savage for *England's Dreaming* why he had taken some of his concepts from Hawkwind: "They were completely divorced from the music industry: this family unit with Barney Bubbles and the dancers and the lights. When you went to see them, you entered this whole experience, even without the drugs."

While Hawkwind's positioning left them outside of the revolution that was boiling up and boiling over in '77 and '78, it's not hard to see where their do-it-yourself ethic and their rallying cries against the corporate man had made an impact on the generation that spawned punk. Let's not forget that parts of that movement came out of the free festival generation, whether we talk about Strummer in the first wave of punk or Penny Rimbaud of Crass in the next. It's essentially a clash of cultures but still with a common enemy and a similar objective. Moorcock talked of Hawkwind's best stuff being of and about the city but their free festival ethos and, Lemmy aside, their choice of drugs, informed a rather different outlook, so that they were more about the open spaces and the festivals when directly compared to the inner-city decay and unemployment of punk rock and its preferences for speed (no wonder the Hawk who did get adopted by punk was Lemmy himself) or eventually heroin.

Although Hawkwind's status in America had diminished since the high-profile tours of the mid-70s, they still had supporters on the US scene, notably Jello Biafra of the seminal punk band Dead Kennedys. "In my own evolution as an artist and as a fan, Hawkwind were second only to the Stooges in importance to me," Biafra notes. "A lot of their work still stands up twenty or thirty years later, where many other things of the period do not. I first found out about them in one of my father's porno mags, *Playboy* or *Penthouse*, a little article on spacerock. I'd never heard the term before. It mostly focused on Amon Düül II, but also mentioned Hawkwind. *Space Ritual* had just come out, but the article didn't give me the slightest clue as to what the band sounded like. I was buying albums based on hunches and instinct, which led me away from Uriah Heep and into MC5 and the Stooges. There was a second-hand record shop two blocks away from my High School, and I had systematically worked through everything in the store to figure out which obscurities I liked. Eventually *In Search of Space* came in, I played that and it didn't really do it for me. But then *Space Ritual* popped up and I was completely blown away, much heavier and more powerful. I took it home and played it over and over again. I understood what was going on and really liked it, my first exposure to something heavy and trippy at the same time. It eventually led to exploring electronic music, and even the darker side of prog."

Biafra never lost his "fondness for Hawkwind, and would consider it a major influence on Dead Kennedys even though the other guys would never give them the time of day. I brought in a pretty regular chainsaw, mid-tempo, punk song called 'Holiday in Cambodia' and the others didn't like it, so I was crushed because it was the first thing I ever brought in that they rejected. Then, as I was stewing and pacing the floor, Klaus started playing this unusual bass-riff that immediately clicked with me, so I plugged the chorus, pre-chorus and bridge that I had into that, a slower tempo, more hypnotic feel and thought 'aha, this could affect people the way a Hawkwind song does,' so I steered it that way. It was an important part of my musical direction and instinct to tap into that pile-driving, hypnotic power from time to time."

It wasn't that contemporary music journalists were unable to identify the connection. Phil Sutcliffe, for *Sounds*, claimed he liked "what [Hawkwind] stand for in terms of freedom and sheer imaginativeness." It was that they didn't see a link with the energy of the three-chord thrash that punk espoused: "There are great acres of space in the set filled by relentless electronic swirling. It doesn't mean a thing to me."

Despite the increasing hostility of the music press, there were some important writers still able to give a nod of approval in Hawkwind's direction, though there is a sense that such journalists saw Calvert as the band's saving grace. Paul Morley, writing for *NME* in October 1977 praised Bob for giving Hawkwind "visible direction, hard, long, pop, mechanical realism" and described himself as "frankly shocked, but delighted." Reviewing the band's gig at Manchester's Palace Theatre (1st October 1977), Morley hit upon the central dichotomy of Calvert's relationship with Hawkwind, defining Bob as "a surprisingly strong pop persona, not convenient to Hawkwind but necessary. His tongue is always in his cheek and that helps ease the occasions when the intensity threatens to overwhelm." Indeed, with Calvert on-board, Hawkwind were fully exploiting all venues of communication: clean sounds, tighter structures in their music, lyrical wit, and sci-fi imagery. They had become the sort of band that Brock had aspired to many years before, when going to the Middle Earth and admiring Arthur Brown's mixture of words, music and visual performance.

Monty Smith, in his *NME* piece earlier in the year also identified Calvert as the dominating focal point ("a strong and coherent vocalist, considering the wall of sound he's fronting"). He described the visual style that Calvert employed as "more sword-wielding Saracen than space warrior... his repertoire of gesticulations and poses are unashamedly borrowed from old RKO serials." During 'Uncle Sams on Mars', Calvert was described as "dramatically unfurling the Stars and Stripes before unceremoniously emasculating said symbol with his sword," a most effective description of Calvert's adoption of stage personas. "It's science fiction, not politics."

The downside, as many collaborators of Calvert's discovered, was the chemical imbalance ("Bi-Polar would be the diagnosis now, I guess," notes Shaw) that caused his mood swings and often highly agitated state. Colleagues came to expect the 4am knock on the hotel door, Calvert with black foam around his mouth, desperate to impart an idea he had for a song. His state of mind on a European tour in autumn 1977 demonstrated the difficulties other musicians had to endure in dealing with Bob's peculiar genius. Shaw recalled an incident at a show in Paris (probably at the Palais des Sportes on 26th October): "As we were sound checking there was some point or other that Bob wanted to get across. He wasn't making much sense at that time. He sort of grabbed me by the neck to emphasise a point. I told him if he ever laid a finger on me again I would deck him!" Worse was to follow. In the dressing room after the Paris show, Calvert went out of his way to insult a prominent French music journalist, describing him as "a faggot" and generally attempting to portray himself as the star of the show. The band had had enough and the tour was cut short.

"We abandoned the last few dates and went home," says Shaw. "Not an occasion that I'm proud of, as no one told [Bob]." Calvert entered the band's hotel lobby only to discover the other members assembled, bags packed and ready to leave. "We told him we were all going and while he went back to his room to get his bag we got in the car and left. Worse still, as we pulled away he appeared and realising what was happening ran up the road after us." The scene became farcical. "We hit a traffic jam and he caught up with us, pleading to be let in the car. No one would look at him, the doors were locked and when the jam cleared we just drove off." Tour manager Jeff Dexter was left with the unhappy task of dealing with him, ending up hitting him with a stick at the airport because Calvert had become so far out of control. Back, then, to Morley's point: "not convenient, but necessary."

Brock followed up the autumn 1977 European tour not by readying the release of the current Hawkwind incarnation's second studio album, *PXR5*, but by setting up a side-project in Devon: Sonic Assassins. He and Calvert had made the acquaintance of a local band, Ark, who had played at a number of West Country festivals and benefit concerts, producing an electronic rock and folk fusion. The line-up included bass player (and by day, special needs schoolteacher), Harvey Bainbridge, who had a vague interest in Hawkwind. "I remember when I was living in Exeter and a friend had bought the first Hawkwind album and I quite liked that, because it was weird. Anything strange or electronic I thought was great, but I wasn't a Hawkwind fan, per se."

Bainbridge: "Dave was very kind to us, he loaned us equipment, lights, amplifiers and things. Ark were doing a gig at an arts centre near Torrington, playing in a barn and invited Dave to bring a synthesiser along. He turned up with this old EMS, stayed for about ten minutes and then ran away again! It was the first time I really met him. He said that he was off to Stonehenge, but that the rest of Hawkwind, apart from Bob, weren't interested and so we all piled down there and some of our band played, though I didn't; it was probably 1975 or 1976." Brock wanted to get a band together to play at free festivals, "because Hawkwind didn't want to do them," recalls Bainbridge.

The issue of whether the other members of Hawkwind perceived this to be the case is curious. Whilst Brock complained in interviews that only he and Calvert wanted to continue playing for free, Shaw dismisses the claim in no uncertain terms. "That is such a load of rubbish. We all liked playing free festivals. I've lost count of the number I did over the years. If anything, Bob was less keen, having not as much of a hippie ethic as the rest of us. Doing Stonehenge with Hawkwind was really good. We had our own generator, which other bands used, so consequently the generator ran out in the middle of our act and while it was getting fixed we were desperately trying to think of something to do. I was trying to get Bob Calvert to do his marvellous Frankie Howerd impersonation [a successful comedian of the day] to keep the crowds amused, which had to be seen to be believed. But the festival was nice and peaceful, full of freaks and, actually, I've still got the twelve-string guitar I bought from a hippie at the festival. This fellow was sitting there gently strumming this guitar and he wanted to sell it, I had enough money to buy it and so we did the deal there and then; I've got it in my studio."

Brock's plan was to create a new band that would run in tandem with Hawkwind. Bainbridge remembers how "[Dave] wanted to call this band the Sonic Assassins. We went up to Wales, at one time. Nik Turner was there, and we built this pyramid stage on the top of a mountain, in the middle of a downpour, so we could play a gig. Dave didn't stop for too long, Bob stayed for a little longer. Although the weather was atrocious, people still watched us play, which was fantastic."

A first appearance for the Sonic Assassins was planned for Christmas Eve 1977 in Barnstaple. Aside from Brock and Bainbridge, Ark's drummer Martin Griffin, and keyboard player Paul Hayles were invited to perform. True to Shaw's observation, Calvert decided the evening before the show not to appear. This led to Bainbridge, keen on the idea of having a frontman improvising around the band's basic space-style jamming, spending a night at Bob's house convincing him to take part. Bainbridge told Keith Henderson, for *Aural Innovations*, that he found Calvert "dressed as a First World War officer in the trenches, sitting in his cottage... he had the leather boots and the uniform, with the holster, the belt and everything." The extreme side of Calvert's personality was in full flow. "He was just so over the edge and he wasn't going to do the gig. I sat and talked to him all night... I was shattered the next day." However, Bainbridge had managed to extract a commitment to appear from Calvert. The show was recorded, has appeared on various compilations and is the definitive live capture of Calvert in full 'Mad Bob' flow. Aside from his mental state, according to Paul Hayles in a letter to Hawkwind fan Bernhard Pospiech, Calvert was "concerned about whether Sonic Assassins were rehearsed enough" and also "very much in two minds about the future of Hawkwind."

The setlist included 'Death Trap', from the then still unreleased *PXR5*, a proto-version of a number which later became 'Angels of Death', and a loose rendition of 'Magnu'. But what the show is most remembered for is a stream of consciousness section of total anarchy and absolute genius that starts with an improvised manic rant on life in the trenches of the Great War, which has become known as 'Over The Top' before launching into 'Death Trap' and finishing with what would become – vastly revised for the future Hawklords LP *25 Years* – a spacey and spacious number called 'Free Fall'.

In 'Free Fall', a Calvert/Bainbridge piece, Bob described a breathless descent, the freedom of falling. For 'Over The Top', he let his imagination and paranoia wander through his personal obsessions after first misinterpreting the start ("which came out of me and Dave getting a synth pattern going," says Hayles) as being 'Master of the Universe'. "When it didn't and the others joined in, he then started a very good vocal adlib. Someone told me he used a poem he had already written; in any case, it was all totally unrehearsed or even planned." Anyone who has heard Julian Cope's similarly wandering, ad-hoc delivery of the Teardrop Explodes' 'Sleeping Gas' from Club Zoo in the early 80s might think that sprawling beast of a live cut another new wave nod in the direction of Robert Calvert. Hayles recalled the gig as being successful: "a sell-out… 700 capacity… a good party. Ark could fill the place by itself so the added Hawks was a big bonus."

Perhaps the Sonic Assassins show prefigured it, perhaps the weariness of maintaining a band for so long occasioned it, but by the time Hawkwind played together again, for a tour of the USA in March 1978, it was apparent that their current incarnation was coming to its end. Before the tour started, Simon House had received an offer from David Bowie to join his backing band. Simon called Adrian Shaw, seeking his advice; "I urged him to do it as it was such a great opportunity." House concurred, so after playing the opening shows in New York he left Hawkwind (officially on sabbatical). House performed live with Bowie, in a line-up described by producer Tony Visconti as possessed with "dazzling musical personality." House also joined Bowie at Mountain Studios in Montreaux, Switzerland for the *Lodger* sessions, playing on most of the LP and the single 'Boys Keep Swinging'.

The USA tour was an unhappy affair. Paul Hayles was drafted in to replace House on keyboards and quickly spotted that "the vibes were really bad between all the different members. I think I was the only one who was on speaking terms with all the others; I hadn't been around long enough to fall out with anyone."

And yet, they were still turning in good shows, as Shaw comments and extant recordings testify. "The core of the band was still there and I think we played well even after Simon's departure." Adrian enjoyed his first USA tour; "I had a great time and really took advantage of everything that was on offer. I was partying hard, though never to the detriment of the band. The problems didn't seem any worse than I had been through before, or since for that matter."

Brock was not enjoying the tour, though Shaw confesses to not paying this much attention. "I do remember having an altercation on stage with Brock about tuning. This was before electronic tuners of course and Brock's tuning was a little wayward at times. We had a bit of heated discussion about who was out of tune. After the show, back at the hotel I was hanging out with Simon King when Brock appeared, didn't say much but was being unusually friendly. After he left Simon said, 'I think that was an apology, at least the closest I've ever seen Dave come to one.'"

Partly, that might have been the dynamics and the challenges of dealing with Bob rearing its head again. Though Calvert had been in manic mode the previous year, it was at least with him in an 'up' frame of mind. What goes up, though, must come down again, and this swing of mood impacted on the US dates. "Bob was on a real downer," says Dave. "The previous year he'd been on a high, like the 'Over the Top' thing, one of his great highs, writing loads of stuff, which was very exciting, but he became very depressive after that and when we went off to America it was very hard going. The tour was alright, but the unfortunate thing was Bob's depression. It was hard going when he was like that; in 1977 when we did the French tour – when we left him behind in Paris – he was on such a high he was fantastic to work with, he couldn't stop talking, was up for days on end. The tour manager was a French lady, her father was a very famous actor, she was really nice, but she bought this pair of headphones and gave them to Bob, 'Shut up! Here's some headphones, here's a tape machine, just listen to music and shut up!' She'd had enough of him talking constantly! She slapped him 'round the face once, saying 'Pull yourself together!' So this was Bob in his high state, but then we were off to America with him in a state of total depression, and when he was like that it really did bring everybody down. This is what it was like working with Bob; when he was high, with all these ideas, he'd kick you into this state and you'd stay up late with him, talking, which was quite exciting in a way because his excitement gets into you. But his depression would bring everyone else down."

The tour had a demanding schedule; with early and late shows back-to-back at New York's Bottom Line (which spawned one of the earliest Hawkwind bootleg LPs) and a four-night residency at the Starwood Club, Los Angeles. The setlist was essentially culled from the line-up's studio output and included three numbers from *PXR5*: 'High-Rise', 'Robot' and 'Uncle Sams On Mars'. Marc Sperhauk and his great friend 'Astro' Bill McKinnon saw the 1978 US dates, unlike their view of the early 1970s American gigs, from a position inside of the Hawkwind camp. "I decided catch the L.A. and San Francisco shows. There were quite positive reviews of the shows on the East Coast, though Simon House had not yet bailed for Bowie." Sperhauk goes on to note: "When I saw Bowie with Simon, there was a huge bunch of us screaming 'Simon' and 'Hawkwind', to the point where he had to go to the microphone and say 'Cool it, it's not my gig.'"

What Sperhauk found on arriving at the Starwood, a "none too large L.A. nightclub" (22nd-25th March 1978) took him by surprise. "The Hawks were an opening act for some crap rock and roll nobodies called Detective who had no musical similarities [with Hawkwind] at all." It was at these gigs that Sperhauk cemented an enduring friendship with Brock: "I had been introduced to a woman, named Polly, who was a Blue Öyster Cult groupie and a really terrific person. Polly's 'expertise' in these matters enabled Astro and me to get backstage, and this is where I first really met Dave, Bob Calvert, Simon King and the wonderful Adrian Shaw."

Marc discovered that "Bob seemed quite agitated but he was friendly and gracious… Simon was the only one that I found a bit unapproachable, more like the imagined rock star, but he really enjoyed telling 'Lemmy and me' stories." Sperhauk recalls the shows as being "blistering, very enjoyable, although much too short. I believe the band was, at this point, trying their best for any L.A. music business people that may have been lurking about – but the environment was not good." Noting the club as a far cry from the three venues he had seen them play in prior years, Sperhauk characterises the band as "really unhappy with some of the places Sire had booked them to play. The St. Louis club they had come from was 'just a bathroom.' There was nothing but bad feeling about that."

From Los Angeles, Hawkwind moved on to San Francisco and another small club, the Old Waldorf. On these shows they were the headline act, but Sperhauk recalls "the first set was short, and I thought weaker than the L.A. shows. It was broadcast on the radio, but the soundboard mix was awful with Bob's vocals much too loud. The second set was awesome. Adrian said later that it was the closest they came to sounding like they did in England. Dave did some of the most astounding guitar work I have ever seen him do." Strangely, given some of the strong performances on the tour, a story has circulated that Jefferson Airplane's Paul Kantner attended the San Francisco shows and described Hawkwind as "a shell of a band."

Also present at the band's San Francisco shows was Jello Biafra. "The band tried to recast themselves as more modern, eighties… I wouldn't go as far as to say new wave band because they still had that sound. It was very thrilling for me to see this, finally, even though there wasn't any lightshow and no Nik in his lizard suit anymore – or Stacia. I went backstage to talk to them, even though I was clearly out of place, '78 punk, spiky hair and spray painted shirt. Calvert looked up at me with these eyes under his cap, so I thought I'd better say something. I asked him where he got the information for the *Captain Lockheed* concept. Of course, there was a huge scandal over Lockheed executives bribing foreign leaders in order to get military contracts. This was not publicly exposed at the time. I realised that Calvert was talking about this a year or two before the Lockheed scandal broke in the mainstream press. He mentioned a magazine called *Flight* and that he kept dossiers on corporate wrongdoers. I'd never heard of such a thing before, reverse surveillance, reading what's out there and making a note of it. I took that to heart and years later began doing that. I'm not sure that would have occurred to me in the same way if Calvert hadn't given me the idea."

Dave Brock – Bracknell Sports Centre 18/12/76
(Keith Kniveton)

The final dates, at the Old Waldorf, (26th-27th March) were the last shows that Hawkwind would perform before disbanding. Eight years after their first performance at the All Saint's Club, and unrecognisable from the original incarnation bar the ever-present Dave Brock, the band appeared to be finished. One of the most popular Hawkwind legends has Brock, frustrated and disillusioned, coming off stage and immediately selling his guitar to Sperhauk. The impression is of someone who couldn't go on any more, walking away from the band he'd created and a music industry that had proved fickle and disinterested.

Sperhauk: "Here are the myth-deflating facts. Polly told me that she had heard Dave wanted to sell his guitar, so I asked him about this, and we made the deal before even leaving for San Francisco. Dave told me he wanted some cash because he planned to travel a couple of weeks in the Western desert land, which he was really fascinated by." The second night at the Old Waldorf had failed to live up to the previous performance. During the first set there was a power failure and Calvert walked off stage. Although Brock thought that he had gone for good Bob returned when power was restored. "After the second set, Dave walked right over from the stage and asked, 'Still want it?' and handed me the guitar. I gave him the cash and that was that." They sat around chatting, with Marc getting an impression that Brock was disenchanted ("I remember him talking about how different it was from playing in the UK"). All too quickly the club's staff threw everybody out into the damp San Francisco night.

There was no big scene, Shaw recalling that he was only informed about the break-up via the band's management. "The decision to split the band was nothing to do with me. Brock had his plan in place to get rid of anyone who had an opinion and replace them with guys from Devon who would work for a wage and do what they were told. A very short-sighted scheme as it worked out. The creative thrust went out of the band and it was never the same again."

Adrian Shaw comes across as being genuinely frustrated that this incarnation of Hawkwind did not have the opportunity to expand upon the direction that they had started. "Bob Calvert was at his peak… and produced some superb lyrics," he told *Aural Innovations* years later. "It's a shame the *Quark* line-up didn't last longer as I think it could have achieved an awful lot more." In many ways, he is probably right. *Quark Strangeness & Charm* is arguably Hawkwind's most successful studio recording if we are looking for a fusion of the themes that Brock and Calvert had been working towards. It's certainly one of the pinnacles and has stood the test of time with its reputation only enhanced. Spacerock bands of today, playing with the elongated possibilities of the CD or the endless, sometimes interminable, possibilities of the download, should listen to the discipline of the vinyl LP and the conciseness of track choice on this record. Not one outstaying its welcome, not a song or an instrumental that doesn't earn its place; a perfect justification of the vinyl album as the ultimate vehicle for a band in a studio.

A total gentleman, one of the nicest and most approachable members of any Hawkwind era, Adrian Shaw, however, wouldn't be the first or last musician to feel that Hawkwind had descended into Dave Brock's backing band with the ending of a specific line-up.

9

The Phoenix Arises

Hawklords Harvey Bainbridge and Bob Calvert, 1978
(Keith Kniveton)

"I remember Dave saying to me [before the 1978 USA tour], 'look, we'd like you lot to come over, but it can't be done,'" recalls Harvey Bainbridge. "It was a very odd little moment."

Perhaps we can read into this that Brock and Calvert had effectively finished with the existing Hawkwind membership even before leaving for America and were casting around for candidates for a new line-up. "What Dave had in mind was Bob Calvert and himself running it, and having a band behind them," Bainbridge believes. "Dave is very much in control of his own mind, he knows what he wants and he'll do it no matter what – which is fair enough, for him."

You'd have to think, though, that this latest realignment was a decision made between Brock and Calvert. The stage presence and word craft of the latter was an intrinsic part of the game plan and that the two collaborators should move forward together must surely have been a key element of the strategy. "Bob was a creative genius," notes Bainbridge, "and as a wordsmith very clever. Words just came out of him. My experience of working with Bob was brilliant, someone who could just spout – maybe rubbish at times – but he would take Dave's lyrics and say, 'Oh no, we can't have any of this', and change them, for the absolute better. That was the glory of working with Bob, but he was on the edge all the time."

Part of Bainbridge's own creative interest has been the concept of 'spouting', verbalising a stream of consciousness as a live performance. He traces that back to his observation of Calvert. "Bob was a big influence, along with Mike Moorcock, real wordsmiths, which is a big thing for anybody who has a notion that they ought to have some words in them. It helped seeing how they went about it. Over the years I've met a lot of poets; when I was a student I thought I might be one myself. But I'm not that good in having confidence to let words flow. What was wonderful with Bob was that he could play music and flow words as well. It's like Jack Kerouac's *On The Road*, where he came across a character [Dean Moriarty, inspired by Beat poet Neal Cassady] who constantly spoke words, the notion being that he could not let a moment go by without letting a word come out; an expression of where you were at the time."

A few months after Hawkwind had fallen apart, Brock and Calvert began pulling together their new project, the Hawklords (Bainbridge recalls this as probably June 1978). "Bob phoned up and said they were recording the Hawklords album and would I play bass," says Bainbridge. "I thought 'why not?'. Martin Griffin and I went over, but it turned out that Simon King was there as well. Simon was most surprised that we were there, because he'd arranged for Adrian Shaw to come and play bass." As Shaw had anticipated at the end of the previous Hawkwind tour, Harvey explains "I was just on the payroll for the album. I took no notice of what was going on [politically]. I didn't want to know."

Simon House, having completed his assignment with Bowie, returned to record some of the album, but although it was planned (and announced in the music press) that he would also play on the promotional tour, it soon became apparent that the Hawklords arrangement was not to Simon's liking. "The band I left at the beginning of the year is completely different from the band now," he told *NME*. "I don't feel a part of it anymore."

In place of House, the band recruited the highly experienced Steve Swindells as their keyboard player. "I'd moved from Bristol to London when I was 21, and got a solo deal with RCA within the year," recalls Swindells. "I did an album, in 1974, called *Messages*, which I recorded with a full orchestra, but it was dreadfully produced. Then I was in various bands, I joined Pilot, just for the money, and spent a year with them, did an album at Abbey Road. We did lots of TV and stuff, then they split; they were a big band and had a number one in the States with 'Magic' but they were reaching the end of their shelf life." Claiming little musical sympathy with Pilot, Swindells describes his own music interests as "a broad taste, really. I was a Pink Floyd fan from the word 'Go' and remember seeing them at the Bath Festival, but I was also into Tamla Motown, Caravan, Led Zeppelin, and I liked The Who a lot."

"Pilot broke-up and left me at a loose end. One of my best friends, Caroline Guinness, of the brewing dynasty, was running Doug Smith's office. She rang me up and said, 'Hawkwind are looking for a keyboard player, because they're doing an album'. They were renting this farm house in Devon, recording in a big barn." Swindells was driven down from London, by one of the band's roadies, to audition. "I got the gig straight away – was told there and then – and went straight into recording the album. I immediately bonded with Bob Calvert, and I was able to get my boyfriend a job as a roadie, which he loved." Swindells characterises Calvert as "a lot of fun. He was married at the time to Pamela Towney who was a quite successful novelist; she wrote romantic novels, airport stuff. Dave was more distant, but Calvert was in a good frame of mind, and he liked me, he found me to be an intelligent sidekick for him. I think I brought out good qualities in him."

Bainbridge contributed to the sessions the piece that he'd been playing in Ark, and which the Sonic Assassins had improvised back in December 1977, 'Free Fall'. "Bob just liked the riff and sang this stuff over the top of it, and it seemed to work. The intro was something that myself and Paul Hayles had worked out, and Steve Swindells, who was a wonderful keyboard player, added to it. I told him what the chord sequence was and it was all done in a couple of takes." Steve also had a particular enthusiasm for the song. "I loved the spacey keyboards, all dreamy."

When Swindells joined "there were some recordings [already laid-down], which I added to, but most of it was done live in the barn on a sixteen-track mobile studio. I had no writing input because I was new, but I did have plenty of arrangement input; that wall of sound keyboards. I was using a Vox-Continental and a Yamaha CS-80, which was an enormous polyphonic synth, one of the first ones; it needed four people to carry it." Hugely expensive, the Yamaha CS-80 quickly became the rich rock star's 'must have', owned by the likes of Stevie Wonder, Peter Gabriel and, famously, Vangelis.

Apart from 'Free Fall', the remainder of the Hawklords album consisted of Brock and Calvert songs, either jointly credited or solo works. Brock had some material he'd been working on, including the space-punk number '25 Years', which Bainbridge recalls as being lyrically revised by Calvert, though it was originally '25 Years of Solar Research' and written by Dave for an aborted solo album on the subject of astronomy. But it did have a little of Calvert's trademark sharp wit, so it's not hard to imagine he'd chipped in a little on this, while elsewhere his love of cultural references was, as on *Quark*... before it, peppered throughout the album. There's the Greek mythology of Icarus and his father Daedalus on 'The Only Ones' who were imprisoned by King Minos. Daedalus constructed wings of wax and feathers to enable them to fly to freedom, but Icarus flew 'too near the sun', which melted the wax and he plunged to his death. On 'The Flying Doctor', an affectionate name for the Australian outback medical service, he mentions their favoured aircraft, the Percival Proctor, while 'Psi Power' talks of the Zener cards used to determine 'telepathic abilities', through 'triangle' and 'waves' aren't part of the set as the song insists, even if the protagonist claims to visualise them 'crystal clear...'.

Although the recording of any Hawkwind album had traditionally been an ad-hoc affair regarding the musicians working on particular tracks, Hawklords, known on its first pressing as *25 Years On*, had one almost full-band track without an appearance by Dave Brock. Bainbridge notes the recording of Calvert's espionage and trench coat 'Only the Dead Dreams of the Cold War Kid'. "Dave was around; we didn't rush off anywhere secret or anything like that! But it was Bob's song, and it was myself and Steve Swindells who sat down and worked it out, and we recorded it. There was no specific reason why Dave didn't play on it."

"I think the stand-out track was 'Psi Power'," says Swindells. "I really liked the keyboards I did on that, the double-handed thing on two keyboards, and I did backing vocals with Robert on that one. I also had a lot of input on 'Age of the Micro-Man', that multi-layered technique."

"I was reminded of Barclay James Harvest on 'The Age of the Micro Man'," observed one reviewer, "which isn't a bad comparison." Andy Gill, in *NME*, on the other hand, thought '25 Years' to be "the best Roxy Music track that Roxy Music never recorded," feeling the album to be "as engaging a mixture of solidity and sardonic futurism as you'll encounter nowadays."

Polydor, releasing the album in America, described the LP's concept in their press release: "The story of Pan Transcendental Industries, a massive corporate organisation dedicated to the unividation of religious thought and modern technology. Pan Transcendental manufactures car doors, then removes the wings of angels and replaces them with the grey metal doors." It was the album, perhaps even more so than *Astounding Sounds...* that demonstrated just how far the band had come from their roots and the United Artists era, having the most clearly defined new wave sensibility, almost reaching into the harder edge of pop. At the same time, it was an art concept record and it's almost as though the marriage of the two was a deliberate attempt to extend the accessibility of the music that *Quark...* had started, so that the message of the lyrics was at the forefront rather than buried in the wall-of-sound. At the same time, *Hawklords* should be viewed in the context of the *Quark Strangeness & Charm* LP's reliance on stock-architecture SF imagery, and against the contemporary science fiction landscape of J.G. Ballard that inspired some of the still unreleased *PXR5*. In this analysis, *Hawklords* gave a wordy and complex examination of the microcosm of paranoia and disconnection of the individual, but offers some optimism for the future of the human race. "A lot of people who live in cities are influenced by what goes on in them," noted Calvert to Mike Davies in *Melody Maker*, "but we're influenced by the cities themselves," itself a very Ballard type of notion.

The Hawklords concept created an opportunity for Barney Bubbles to become involved with Hawkwind again, having recently worked with his old friend Nik Turner, after Turner had travelled to Egypt to record an album of flute music inside the Great Pyramid at Giza. "I asked Barney if he would do the artwork for my album, and he really loved the idea," comments Turner. "Barney said, 'I'll only do the artwork if I can choreograph the show', and I was really pleased to have that. He produced it like a piece of 'concrete art'. We did a big show at the Roundhouse (18th June, 1978), he helped to arrange the whole thing, in conjunction with Andrew Lauder." Billed as 'Nik Turner's Bohemian Love-In' the show featured several bands making their only ever live appearance. "It was the only performance by the Deep Fix, Mike Moorcock's band. It was the only performance by Steve Took's Horns… we also had Blood Donor, John Cooper Clarke, loads of performance artists, friends of Barney."

Through Calvert, with whom he was still on good terms, Barney became involved in the Hawklords project. "He was responsible for the concept of it, together with Bob," says Turner. "He took thousands of pictures which were going to be used in the lightshow, employed all the dancers I'd used on my show; devised and choreographed the whole concept."

"All the strange, arty geometric shapes [were created by Barney]," notes Swindells. Mike Davies noted the similarity between the concepts being employed and the work of American new-wave band Devo. Answering an accusation that the Hawklords were "ripping-off Devo's use of industrial themes and dramatic movements," Davies noted how "Hawkwind have been involved with industrialisation and technology far longer than Devo have been wearing surgical masks." The parallels between the two bands were apparent however. Jon Savage described Devo in *Sounds* (4th March, 1978) in terms that might have equally applied to Hawkwind: "consistent presentation as a total package… music, visuals, image, ideology, language, films, each referring to itself and each other, solidifying the circular links."

"There was some conflict between Dave and Bob about the conceptual nature of the Hawklords, because it was so different," notes Swindells. "Bob was insistent that [the album] was an experimental departure for the band. He was running that, along with Barney Bubbles, though I don't remember Barney being there. It was a concept album, but it was Calvert's. Brock was fighting it quite a lot, as far as I was aware, because it was too arty. I was saying 'Go for it', because I thought Calvert was a bit of a genius."

Through autumn 1978, The Hawklords played a substantial, ambitious and demanding UK tour to promote the album. "The stage set was fantastic," recalls Swindells. "Very *Metropolis*. The post-industrial vibe was quite punky, but also very visual, the lighting was wonderful. Because I had such a huge keyboard set-up, I had a custom-built metal rig, three tiers to accommodate the Vox-Continental, the Yamaha and a monophonic Korg, which was giving the wobbly effect in 'Free Fall'."

At the start of the tour, the band "adopted the uniform look that Barney Bubbles had designed to heighten the industrial tone of the set," recalls Swindells. "We had paint splattered jumpsuits, a la Jackson Pollock, but we soon dumped that. It was just daft. Then I was given an original cut-off leather jacket to wear by the Hells Angels. I thought that was nice and ironic: being gay." Also wiped out from the touring show were most of the dancers that Barney had recruited. "They were quite weird, which you'd expect with Hawkwind, but they didn't fit with the vibe, they were a bit precious. They cost too much, and didn't add to the thing. They were quite unnecessary, to be honest. The show was much better stripped down and with the focus on Calvert."

"[Barney] had a list of songs they were going to perform and he'd synchronised everything to that. Then, at the end of the day when Barney was going to a rehearsal, he heard Dave had changed the whole thing. Sacked half the dancers, rearranged the songs, basically wasted most of Barney's work," claims Turner. In Turner's view, Barney felt that he wasn't "appreciated or respected" and "at that point he decided not to have anything to do with Hawkwind again." The story grew legs as some sort of ruthless night of the long knives, another part of the patchwork mythology of Hawk-history but there's a burden that an overreliance on visual presentation creates and it certainly seems as though the initial presentation for the Hawklords tour had taken that burden too far, whether logistically or creatively, or indeed from both perspectives. It's interesting to hear the view, such as those of Steve Swindells, who also saw some of this material as essentially adding little to what was a strong concept backed by an exciting new suite of songs, and to re-evaluate this part of the mythology.

Dave Brock: "It was very costly; I mean, it was a wonderful idea, because the idea we were trying to get was *Metropolis*, and one of Barney's things was to have all the dancers in grey and having brooms so that they'd come on stage sweeping stuff up, and the whole stage was scaffolding. They were good dancers, and me and Bob had worked hard on that, the concept of what we wanted to do. But we had a big tour bus that everyone travelled in that was quite costly, and then having to pay six dancers' wages... so we had a meeting and decided that for cost effectiveness we'd have to get rid of the three of the dancers, which was a shame as they were all very good and worked together. They were upset about it, but unfortunately... if we'd had a record label that would have put some money into all of this, the concept of what we had..."

"I think [Brock and Calvert] were interested in taking stuff to the extremes of sound, vision and presentation," comments Bainbridge. "This, to me, seemed like a good thing. I thought the Hawklords was quite a happy tour but there was so much money spent on it, which I didn't realise until later. It was big: three articulated lorries and a huge tour bus. It was quite an adventure, jumping in at the top level." Bainbridge thought the audience "a little bit gob-smacked. It was packed houses everywhere we went, but there was an element of strangeness. You'd get the usual 'we want Lemmy' shouts. It was probably a bit too arty, not psychedelic enough."

The sound that the Hawklords generated through the tour further pushed their fresh, contemporary outlook. "That was probably because they got me, Martin and Steve Swindells in," Bainbridge thinks. "We were almost, but not quite, a generation younger, which was why when the 1979 tour came along it became almost a 'punk heavy rock' band."

Swindells: "At Bradford we were staying in some gruesome hotel and the Buzzcocks were there as well. I was a big fan of Buzzcocks, and of Magazine [formed by Howard Devoto after leaving the original Buzzcocks]. You can hear a lot of Magazine-style keyboards in what I played during Hawklords, think of their single 'Shot by Both Sides'. Pete Shelley and I bonded, playing pool and being all masculine just to confuse everyone. Pete said that Hawkwind were a seminal influence, particularly Brock's guitar." In Steve's view, "Brock's guitar is highly influential on what happened with punk, he's actually the first punk guitarist, no-one else played like that. If you listen to Buzzcocks and Magazine, you hear it." Magazine's first album, *Real Life*, charted in June 1978; its influence on Swindells is most evident on Hawkwind's abortive Hawklords MkII Rockfield sessions early the following year. In the years since leaving Hawkwind, Swindells discovered other major music industry figures who felt the same way about Hawkwind's influence. "Jarvis Cocker [of Pulp] is a massive fan, I met him on a few occasions, at parties, and he told me so. His eyes lit up when I told him I'd been in Hawkwind and written 'Shot Down in the Night', he was really impressed."

Calvert's manic nature once again found its true expression as the tour progressed. Attending a show in Folkestone (9th November, 1978), for *NME*, Andy Gill described Calvert in "guerrilla chic: beret, bullet-belt diagonal across torso." Gill compared the imagery to the hit comedy TV show of the day, *Citizen Smith*, and felt that it was "lending an otherwise absent edge to the images of austerity and alienation that make up the stage show." At one of the tour's final concerts, Uxbridge (24th November, 1978), Calvert was found in full stream-of-consciousness mode during '25 Years', delivering a Strummer-like extended rant. "In '25 Years', which is about the small man, the average person's plight, there's a point at which I read what's in the Daily Mirror on the day we're doing it. That's teleprint music," Calvert told Mike Davies.

"I remember Uxbridge," says Swindells. "It was a kind of bleak campus and it certainly wasn't one of the best gigs. Bob was starting to have [mental] problems, though the tour had been so much fun with him."

The contract that Hawkwind had agreed with Charisma was for four albums, which was completed in 1979 with the release of *PXR5*. "Charisma never invested any money in us, we were always scrabbling around," says Brock. "We did a single, 'Psi Power', they sent Bob and me off to a studio in Wardour Street [to re-mix the A-side], they filmed us live at Uxbridge, and then they never promoted us! I thought: what is the point of spending all this money and when you get to the end... because the owner kept racehorses... let the horse fall at the last fence. He should have been saying, 'Okay, there's something good going on here; let's have a go'. It's a gamble you take."

"There were major financial problems after the tour, and there was no record company," notes Swindells. "We found ourselves in this lovely Edwardian house, with the idea being to write and rehearse a new album. But money was a real problem. I had to take on the cooking duties, just rice and vegetables because that was all the budget ran to." Calvert was still on board at this point, and had engineered the return of Simon King, displacing tour drummer Martin Griffin.

132

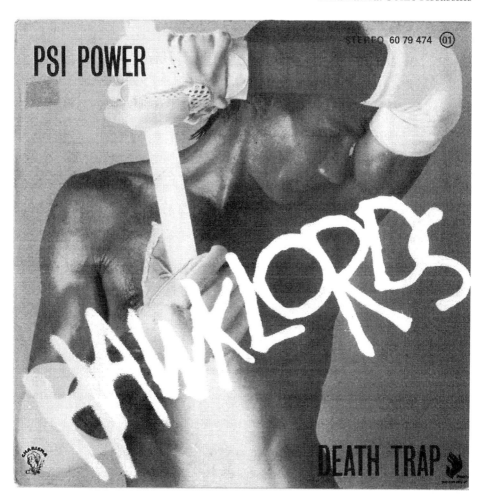

"Simon was a great bloke. A loveable rogue," recalls Swindells. Calvert stayed with the band for only a few weeks before having another breakdown, interlinked with problems in his personal life. The Hawklords concept had been very much a Bob Calvert vision, with Dave dismissing it as "armchair Hawkwind" in one interview. "Bob had a bust-up with Brock, because Brock wanted to resume control of the material, taking it back to a more obvious Hawkwind vibe," Swindells considers. "Brock is not an out-going person; he tends to keep his feelings to himself. He and Bob were chalk-and-cheese."

"It was a shame that Bob and Dave fell out," says Bainbridge. "They were a strong writing partnership. I think Bob had become unmanageable, as far as Dave was concerned, but that was Bob, he would go off the deep end. You just had to be able to talk him back down, like I did before the Sonic Assassins gig." And that's fine, if you have to do it once, or now and again; but for someone running a band that was still a major force, to deal with Calvert's highs and lows must have been an incredible ongoing pressure.

Clearly Calvert felt some form of 'ownership' towards Hawkwind. In his mind, it was something that he'd had played a major part in constructing. "The few appearances Bob made after the Hawklords, it was lovely to see him, but at the same time, he was there in a sense because he felt he ought to be. I think he felt, like a lot of members, that he deserved a bit of acclamation," says Bainbridge. "Dave thought, at one point, every interview Bob gave was selling himself rather than Hawkwind, which there might have been some truth in."

"I think Hawkwind finished at the time of the *Hawklords* album," claimed Calvert in 1982. "I regarded the *Hawklords* album as the last album." This might imply that Calvert viewed Hawkwind as limiting his wider creative ambitions. Swindells disagrees. "I think Hawkwind was perfect for him, because he could be wacky and expressive and wild. He was a fantastic performer, riveting to watch."

The remainder of the band continued working without Calvert. "For that whole period, we were at the Mill House, at Rockfield," says Bainbridge. "There was myself, Dave, Steve and Simon King. It was like, 'let's get some material together'." Amongst Swindells' songs were the ambiguous personal paranoia and wider conspiracy number 'Shot Down in the Night', and another called 'Turn It On, Turn It Off'. Both were recorded at Rockfield featuring Swindells on lead, with Brock contributing backing vocals on the latter. "I've got the first take we did of 'Shot Down in the Night' and it's such classy keyboard playing," says Bainbridge. 'It really is a proper song, Simon fades at the end, he just slows down unfortunately, but otherwise it's solid, heavy and very much of its time when I think of what was going on in 1979. Politically of course, and you had Bruce Springsteen happening in America, that sort of 'grinding' rock sound going on."

"I was asked to take over as lead singer," comments Swindells, "which is why I wrote 'Shot Down in the Night', actually at the Mill House. It's a lot more personal than you'd think. It's about rejection: rejecting, not being rejected. It's also political, about the cultural big brother – and clones, people who just subscribe to something so they'll belong. 'Turn It On, Turn It Off' was very urban, really in the Hawklords vibe. The imagery was that post-industrial wasteland stuff. I declined the opportunity to be the lead singer, because Dave wanted to revert to the sci-fi imagery, which is not me at all. I found it all a bit 'cod'. I enjoyed the ring-modulating and Dave's guitar, but I'd never been interested in sci-fi and found it a bit unpoetic."

There were some other, mainly instrumental, numbers demoed during early 1979 that have since seen the light of day. 'Douglas in the Jungle', a tribute to their manager credited to Bainbridge and Brock, 'Valium Ten' (a heavy trance number signposting a future dance movement that would also cite Hawkwind among its forefathers), and the keyboard dominated 'Time Of' and 'British Tribal Music'. In particular, 'Time Of', a reference to Michael Butterworth's novel, *Time of the Hawklords*, is a pointer to the direction that the Hawklords might have taken if the line-up had stayed together. "Dave recorded lots of our jamming and just put it out, which I'm not very happy about," notes Swindells.

'Douglas in the Jungle' was not appreciated by Doug Smith himself. Brock: "I rang him up, said 'we've just got this number, Douglas, about you…' 'I don't think that's very funny at all' … 'we're on our knees/the chimpanzees'. Harvey would always say, 'We're always on our knees, please Douglas can we have some money?'"

"It was all recorded on a two track, just rehearsing to see what would come out," notes Bainbridge. "Doug Smith was on the end of the phone, panicking because he had no material to sell, which is why 'Shot Down in the Night' was a Godsend, because it was a very powerful song." Other songs that were tried through the sessions included two other numbers that would later be adopted by a new Hawkwind, the brooding wasteland of 'Who's Gonna Win the War' and the grinding but contemporary and smart as hell travelogue, 'Motorway City' ('where you exit on the right'… so not a song about driving in Britain, then!). In the 1980s, 'Motorway City' was accompanied by a visual backdrop of flying dragons, a possible further nod to the writer Roger Zelazny, previously borrowed from for 'Damnation Alley', 'Lord Of Light' and 'Jack Of Shadows'. His lesser-known, but very much worth seeking out, novel *Roadmarks* features a metaphysical highway that has routes off into the past and future, patrolled by just such creatures.

The Rockfield sessions ended up going nowhere, due to the departure of Steve Swindells. This left the band without the musician who was emerging as potentially their major songwriter and spelled the end of the Hawklords concept, if indeed it existed at all post-Calvert. "Steve got offered a lovely deal for his songs," notes Bainbridge, "so he left."

"An Italian Count offered to put me in the studios," Swindells explains with some glee. "Frankly, I seized the opportunity. There was no money [in Hawkwind], and suddenly someone was saying, 'I'll put you in the studio and pay for it'. It all happened quickly. I did some demos in London with Simon King, Huw Lloyd-Langton and Nic Potter and then I was in New York for the first time in my life. I found myself on the 24th floor of the Rockefeller Centre, at Atco Records, with Doug Morris who was Atco's President. We agreed a deal on the spot worth £80,000, a lot of money in 1979." There was, as is almost inevitable in the music business, the cold reality behind the contract. "I never saw any of it because we only made one LP, *Fresh Blood*, and that cost more than the advance."

10

Hawkwind Get Bronze

Harvey Bainbridge, Huw Lloyd-Langton, Dave Brock
Oxford New Theatre, 23/11/79
(Keith Kniveton)

Hawkwind's tenure with Charisma closed in June 1979 with the much-delayed release of *PXR5*. The album courted a degree of controversy, its sleeve showing a picture of an electrical plug incorrectly wired, noting that this could 'damage your health'. This led to a hastily arranged reissue with a non-removable sticker placed over the offending artwork, and a minor amount of press coverage. It's a classic instance of the contents being much better than the whole, a pulled together contract conclusion that has brilliant Calvert new wave ideas, 'High Rise' and 'Death Trap', and exciting pointers to the future, particular in the title track itself, but in no way is it a cohesive album and as such is quite the weakest of the Charisma quartet. As such then, it's a placard demanding change.

"*PXR5* was a bodge-up of bits and pieces," said Brock, "a final flushing of the toilet at Charisma." In true Hawkwind style it contained a mixture of live cuts from the *QS&C* line-up ('High Rise', 'Uncle Sams on Mars' and 'Robot'), a couple of outtakes from an aborted Dave Brock solo album ('Infinity', 'Life Form') and some new studio material ('Death Trap', 'Jack of Shadows', and the title track itself).

Reaching only number 59 in the UK album charts validated Brock's view of *PXR5*, the worst result of any of Hawkwind's major label albums. In addition to being the band's Charisma swansong (though the label subsequently issued a compilation, *Repeat Performance*), the release of *PXR5* drew a line under Robert Calvert's contribution to Hawkwind. Although he was to return as a guest for several concerts in the early 1980s, and despite some of his material being incorporated into future albums, he never again recorded with Hawkwind.

"In a way I do feel as though having stopped any sort of work with Hawkwind at all is kind of coming back to sanity and reality," he asserted in an interview to promote his first novel, *Hype*, a couple of years later. "I just couldn't go on performing 'Silver Machine' over and over again."

Let's not see Hawkwind's tenure on Charisma as being the second string in their existence, the slightly poorer relation to the classic era of their time on United Artists where arguably the big-hitters of the catalogue, *Space Ritual* or *Hall of the Mountain Grill* for instance, benefited from the continued exploitation of that portion of the back catalogue by United Artists successors EMI. With the murkier contract position of *Warrior on the Edge of Time* aside, EMI kept the early Hawkwind LPs in print, transitioning to CD when vinyl became superseded and reinventing the albums with re-masters, expanded editions and associated spin-off collections. That excellent service, spearheaded more recently by Nigel Reeve, maintained a presence on the shelves and racks of record stores for those LPs almost in a consistent unbroken run, keeping them familiar and available and granting them an accessible status in rock history as well as part of the band's history.

Virgin acquired Charisma and released the four Charisma albums as 'vanilla' budget CD editions in the 1980s, then allowed them to drift out print. The used vinyl market aside, these classic albums therefore became the province of the Hawkwind enthusiast rather than the browsing music buyer, and in that way, they became almost caricatures of themselves, most vividly *Astounding Sounds, Amazing Music* which picked up a mythological epithet of being the 'worst' Hawkwind album without many newer converts placing needle onto vinyl and hearing its myriad complexities. In retrospect though the band made some notable twists and turns during its Charisma contract, the four albums released on the Mad Hatter's label contain within them a trio that are genuine peaks of creativity, imagination and almost art-house experimentation... and though *PXR5* it is a totally disjointed record by its very nature, individually the tracks in isolation are certainly not a disappointing part of the canon either.

They have relevance; they bridged the gap between the psychedelic hippiedom of the early albums and the new wave and punk generation at the end of the 70s. Though there were the movers and shakers of that movement that namechecked or otherwise paid homage to Hawkwind, that the band almost effortlessly moved towards them in tone and feel without comprising their ideals and totally abandoning the success of the early 70s kept them refreshed and accessible and, honestly, it didn't matter that Julie Burchill wrote them off as another rock dinosaur outfit, that she and others didn't get them (I'd wonder, deliberately so perhaps). What mattered was that in 'Spirit of the Age' or 'Assassins of Allah', or 'Age of the Micro-Man' or '25 Years', Hawkwind were producing a body of work that said something about the modern condition, that had value, that contributed to debate and which attempted, and largely succeeded, to explain the changing social landscape. And that Calvert's contribution to that was done with a wry sense of humour and a wickedly satirical sharpness is a reason why although the band would take another acute turn after departing Charisma, they kept on going.

But with Calvert vowing, temporarily at least, never to work again "with a band called Hawkwind," and Swindells having moved on, the remaining 'rump' of the Hawklords, Dave Brock and Harvey Bainbridge, were left to pick up the pieces and regroup in the Devonshire countryside.

Dave was enjoying the opportunity to "live a very average life." Asked by Tomm Buzzetta to describe a day in the life of Dave Brock, the response was, "He lives in a vicarage [that] needs a lot of renovation; he's been working on it since last November. There's so much to do. I had to dig the well out today and do some cement work. It's an endless task, but it's going to be good."

A complication to a 'new' Hawkwind emerging phoenix-like from the ashes of Hawklords was, supposedly, the ownership of the name. It's been suggested that this effectively rested with Simon House, who had been contractually on 'sabbatical' and found himself, having finished his session work with David Bowie, as the only remaining member of Hawkwind. Brock and Bainbridge forged ahead with rebuilding the band, and indeed though it's a popular rumour that there were issues with using the name post the US tour of 1978, it seems just another one of those mythological stories with no basis in fact, having come out of the notion that Hawklords was conceived to get around not being able to use the Hawkwind name. "I don't think so," says Brock. "I think we just tried to do something a bit different, to get away from the Hawkwind persona as it were, to do something different."

Synthesiser virtuoso and former member of Gong, Tim Blake, one of the younger veterans of the Ladbroke Grove scene, had just finished a world tour when he received a telephone call from Douglas Smith asking him to join the reformed Hawkwind. The mercurial Blake, who revels in the opportunity to relate his presence at the famous Group X gig at All Saints Hall in 1969, had absorbed the underground culture and from it had come his enthusiasm for electronic music. "I'd left school in 1968, done a short 'apprentice-like' summer in a small recording studio, and then started a year of Drama and Dance school in Central London." Describing his departure from the closed circuit of academic life as being "extraordinarily liberating," he enthusiastically recalls how "in one summer evening I discovered the music of Arthur Brown, the joys of hashish, and sex with a woman!"

When one of his fellow students, Celia Humphries, told him that she was leaving to sing with folk rock band Trees, his interest was piqued, resulting in Blake becoming involved with Douglas Smith and Clearwater Productions, Trees' management. From 1969 to 1970, Blake worked with several the major underground bands: "I was Thomas Crimble's roadie [while Crimble was a member of Skin Alley], then Simon's roadie and sound man [Simon House, then of High Tide]." He moved in the same circles as the embryonic Hawkwind: "I took my first LSD trip with Nik and Dik-Mik" and credited both Dik-Mik and Del Dettmar as catalysts for his own early experimentation with synthesisers.

Blake had been listening to "some contemporary electronic music... Berio, Pierre Henry..." but he really saw his musical future when Clearwater's Wayne Bardell "rolled me a big spliff and played me *Switched-on Bach* by [Walter, later Wendy] Carlos. There was I, a hopeless hippie who played around with echo boxes, guitars and electrical testing equipment. Wayne played me a record that appealed to my excellent musical education." Bardell informed him that the sound of the future was "called the Moog Synthesiser."

With his background and interests perhaps we could be forgiven for wondering why an earlier entry into Hawkwind hadn't occurred. "Only Dik-Mik and Nik seemed to notice any musical potential in me." Dik-Mik appears to have felt his position under threat from Blake's emerging talent though: "When the VCS3 finally arrived in Dik-Mik's hands, he was a little shirty: 'With your musical knowledge, and this machine, I'll be out of a job,' he used to say."

Instead, Blake spent the 1970s exploring a fusion of synthesiser music coupled with extraordinary laser lightshows, both as a member of Gong and its spin-off Paragong, and as a solo musician under his 'Crystal Machine' by-line. "We called it Crystal Machine," he told one interviewer, "because we were swallowing a lot of crystals at the time, also, repetitive music has crystalline qualities."

Andrew Garibaldi, in his analysis of Blake's career, for *Hawkfan*, describes the impact of Crystal Machine as "true theatre," and described "concerts at L'eglise St. Gervais, with Nico; whole events which furthered the use of lasers in conjunction with music." A short British tour resulted in a principally live LP, *Crystal Machine*, which was followed up in 1978 with his first solo studio recording and a classic in its own right, *New Jerusalem*.

I interviewed Tim for *Record Collector* a few years after the first edition of this book, and he described the evolution of *New Jerusalem* in more detail: "Barclay records came in, and offered to release the first live recordings and to help me produce *New Jerusalem*, really my first solo album. I was given the opportunity to build a temporary studio at Ridge Farm, and start recording 'Jerusalem'. The title came to me after a joke from Michael Eavis, 'I hope you'll call the new album Blake's New Jerusalem.' Originally, the album was to have been mainly instrumental, but during the recording, the words 'And here inside these

Valleys/That are so full of Energy' came to me. Barclay lent me their recording studio in Paris so that I could re-record the title track with my new ideas.... and there it was!"

Despite being influential in his chosen field (French composer Jean Michel Jarre cited Blake's mixing of music and lasers as a way-marker in his own artistic direction), Blake struggled to develop his ideas in a business not in tune with his style of music, so the call from Smith had come at precisely the right time: "I was fed up with 'handling' Tim Blake and said to [his girlfriend] Nadege, 'if a properly managed group phones up, right now, I'll accept!'" By one of those instances of serendipity, "it was exactly that moment that Douglas chose to ask if I was available... I left for Rockfield the next day!"

"Douglas has his faults, as we all do," notes Blake, "but when he is handling things, things *are* handled, and personally I appreciate that side of things."

Tim Blake
(Collection of Dave Brock)

With Simon King again brought back to the drummer's stool, there was an opportunity to once again redefine the Hawkwind sound. However, it may have been that in assembling the new line-up, Brock's initial thoughts formed around developing upon the keyboard-led style of the second phase of the Hawklords, with a suggestion that he was keen to install Blake as his lead musician: "It had been Dave's idea to use me as the 'soloist' on the Moog." Blake had less confidence that this would be the right way for the band to go and so he "suggested we had Huw [Lloyd-Langton] as well." No reason to doubt Blake's recollections, but Huw was also suggested as a potential re-recruit by Simon King, who'd been working with him and Nic Potter, once of Van der Graaf Generator, as a three-piece under the name Jawa. King had broached the idea with Dave Brock and was told to bring him along to rehearsals. Jawa had themselves been searching for a record deal but found their situation overshadowed by Hawkwind and disbanded.

Since his departure from the early Hawkwind, Langton had been involved in a diverse range of musical set-ups, from playing as a session musician for Leo Sayer to his membership of minor supergroup Widowmaker alongside Luther Grosvenor, aka Ariel Bender from Mott The Hoople, and Steve Ellis, of Love Affair. He particularly enthused on his time with Batti Madamoiselle, a Trinidad steel band ("I did play the Commonwealth Institute Festival of Black Music with that band, they were very good musicians," he told Sounds). Though Langton had left Hawkwind before the band achieved anything more than underground notoriety, he had enjoyed some commercial success with Widowmaker, as he described to the Music Street Journal. "When I went over [to America] we had Jet Records behind us. We had limos and the like. It was all highly financed and well looked after."

"Although I hadn't been in [Hawkwind] for about ten years it didn't take me long to make up my mind to come back; it was like I never stopped being involved," Huw told Dave Brown. "Brock asked... and I said something remarkably original, like 'why not?'" Langton had maintained "all sorts of contacts" with Hawkwind during the 1970s. He and wife Marion had lived near Portobello Road right through the 70s so Huw regularly bumped into various members and was regular visitor to the nearby Clearwater offices and, given that he'd never fallen out with Hawkwind, he'd kept in touch with them and their management. During the 70s he was occasionally asked to fill in for Brock when Dave had other plans on those dates, either being called by Doug Smith, Nik Turner or even Dik-Mik; when he wasn't working the Langtons often went up to a Portobello Road café and sometimes met up with Dave and others over the intervening years. "I re-joined for three or four gigs which Dave had decided he didn't want to do," he recalled. "One was a gig in Liverpool that Dave had pulled out of." Aside from these intriguing excursions, sadly undocumented in Hawkwind bootleg history, but confirmed very recently by the surfacing, on Facebook, of photographic evidence, Huw had spent the 1970s watching the band's success through its 'Silver Machine' and *Space Ritual* period from the side-lines, feeling "vaguely jealous, as one would!"

"The Hawklords circumstance was woven around the fact that Hawkwind had been disbanded. But it didn't achieve what people wanted it to; it floundered and fell to pieces. I was totally interested in coming back. Simon King and I had been setting up a band, planned to be a three-piece, but it wasn't the right time for that to happen. Simon got involved with Hawkwind again, and I'd been invited to join a soul band, but that didn't go anywhere."

Whilst it is tempting to think of this re-establishment of the Hawkwind name as the moment when the band passed from collective to Brock's ownership, Langton was quick to dismiss the idea that it had ever been anything other than Dave Brock's group. "It was always his band, really. Dave was the initiator of the situation and there were several of us around in those days that he got involved in the band. But it was always Dave's circumstance. Nik reckoned that it was partly down to himself, but he was just a roadie in the early days!"

"Huw Lloyd-Langton impressed me, personally," notes Bainbridge. "I thought he was one of the best guitarists I'd heard, and I've heard quite a few. He played beautifully."

The new line-up created a much harder-edged rock sound than both previous Hawklords and Hawkwind incarnations, and this led to problems gelling in the studio, as Blake recalls. "One great difference was my introduction of clocks into Hawkwind. A lot of 21st Century Hawkwind is clocked and sequenced, but in 1979 it was a lot different, with analogue sequencer." Blake notes that this had ramifications for Simon King, described as being already in "a long-term grumble. The clock thing only made it worse."

Within two weeks of coming together, the regenerated Hawkwind headlined at the Futurama Festival in Leeds (9th September 1979). Organised by John Keenan, it was billed as 'The First Science Fiction Music Festival', being principally a punk or 'post-punk' assembly of bands who might be thought of as having a science fiction influenced element to their work. Joy Division occupied top billing on the first night, another band that had taken inspiration from J.G. Ballard. Siouxsie & The Banshees headlined the final evening.

Only a very poorly recorded audience tape is known to exist of Hawkwind's Futurama appearance, showing the band developing a raw prototype of what would become their 1980s direction. The gig opened with 'Shot Down in the Night', followed by another song from the Hawklords final Rockfield demos, Brock's 'Motorway City'. The latter contained an opening section different from the one that emerged later in the year, filled with Blake's Moog synthesiser where Langton's guitar would later dominate. It did, though, set the scene for one of Hawkwind's great set opening combinations, the two numbers continuing into that autumn's tour as a quite blistering and powerful duo, as demonstrated on the document of the tour, *Live Seventy Nine*.

The rest of the Futurama show consisted of 'old' favourites with 'Sonic Attack' and 'Urban Guerrilla' leading into an extended spacey synthesiser-led jam, while towards the end of the set, the new boys were joined by Nik Turner for 'Brainstorm' and 'Master of the Universe'. As ad-hoc as it perhaps felt, it was a clear indication that once again the dice had been thrown and landed in a different configuration than before, that the new wave style of the Charisma records had given way to something as different again as those LPs were to those that had come before them.

142

The hastily arranged UK tour later in 1979, was unique for Hawkwind in that Blake's contract required him to perform a solo slot within the main set. "I was an exclusive solo artist to France's most celebrated privately-owned record company, Barclay. They had a tough time wondering why their star New Age synth player was running round England playing hard psychedelic rock 'n' roll!" Douglas Smith had convinced Barclay that to include Tim Blake as a member of Hawkwind would be good exposure. "I would get my solo spot and a part of my laser show incorporated into the set." In return, Barclay allowed Blake to perform on Hawkwind recordings.

The setlist for the tour was built on the structure of the Futurama gig, with those striking new opening numbers kicking-off in powerful style before moving into a heavily reworked 'Spirit of the Age' which showcased the deftness of Langton's lead guitar. While there was still room for several Hawkwind standards adapted for a near 'heavy metal' style ('Brainstorm', unusually, contained a Simon King drum solo) the shows were much-changed from the Hawklords tour with 'World of Tiers', 'Dust of Time', 'Who's Gonna Win the War' and 'Levitation' all receiving outings prior to their definitive studio versions being recorded. Partly that was the natural evolution of a wall of sound replacing the concept art-rock of Hawklords and an engagement with the new recruits but it left the Charisma sound firmly in the past, never revisited in quite the same way by any future incarnation.

The Blake solo spot featured 'New Jerusalem', which never really stuck with a Hawkwind audience, but was expanded to include another of his songs: "What surprised me was Dave and Harvey saying 'When you've finished 'New Jerusalem', we'll all play 'Lighthouse'...'. It hadn't occurred to me. Little was I to know how much 'Lighthouse' was to become an integral part of Hawkwind's repertoire." And as it transpired, with its extended 'Captain's Log' intro and studied, evocative imagery of a deep space beacon signalling out across the galaxies, 'Lighthouse' was a perfect mid-set, tempo-lowering mood piece, highly effective against the heavier songs that surrounded it and even, in one future tour, adapted as a striking set opener.

The show at St. Albans City Hall (8th December) was recorded with a view to a potential live album. "It was a bizarre evening," says Bainbridge. "There were as many people outside the gig as inside, and that was packed. I think a lot of speed was being taken, and we ravaged through the set in about eighty minutes! I met Adrian Shaw that night. He'd come along with Rod Goodway, who I knew from my time in Wiltshire."

The tour was generally viewed as a success. There's an audience recording from one date during which somebody is overheard to comment, "It's much better than the fucking Hawklords, innit?" a view which Bainbridge has some sympathy for. "When you think of the Hawklords stuff, and then suddenly you've got 'Shot Down in the Night', and this wonderful rock 'n' roll guitar going on, it's brilliant. It was a little bit more high-tension."

Dave Brock
(Oz Hardwick)

At the time of the tour, however, Hawkwind had no record label, leading to very little advance publicity for the schedule. Their pulling power as a live act was still strong, though. Brock told *Sounds*: "It was a virtual sell-out... very successful, except commercially. The roadies got paid more than the band." What the tour did achieve was a very powerful and contemporary sounding live capture which Douglas Smith could use when negotiating a new contract.

"We went away, not considering the St. Albans recording was going to be any good," recalls Bainbridge. "Then Doug sent us a cassette, saying 'Listen to this!' It was this wonderful rock music. I think Dave had that view too, so we rattled off to Eel Pie Island and did a re-mix. It gave Doug something to work with, and that's where Bronze Records came in." Impressed by the new direction, Bronze, who also had Motörhead under contract, signed them, making them the band's third major label in ten years. There wasn't much over-dubbing of the live

144

tape, although Bainbridge notes that Brock re-recorded his vocals, but the difference between the upfront keyboards of Swindells earlier in the year and Blake's more restrained playing was identified. Bainbridge: "We would go, 'right, let's get the keyboard tracks in,' and there'd be a blip and a blop…"

The tapes spawned Hawkwind's first LP for Bronze. *Live Seventy Nine* featured the best of the new material ('Shot Down in the Night', 'Motorway City'), an extract from Blake's section ('Lighthouse'), some heavily reworked standards ('Brainstorm', 'Master of the Universe', 'Spirit of the Age') and, most famously, a short burst of 'Silver Machine', appended with the qualification 'Requiem'. This deconstruction of their most famous record ended shortly into the song with an explosion of white noise, leaving the listener with the clear impression that Hawkwind had, in no uncertain terms, "blown-up" their most recognisable work.

Although it received a mixed reception from regular Hawkwind followers, some appreciating the return to a heavier, musically dense sound, others bemoaning the loss of the cerebral lyrics and theatrical sense of Bob Calvert, *Live Seventy Nine* was a commercial success. It outperformed all the Charisma releases, reaching number 15 in the UK. Except for a United Artists compilation, *Roadhawks*, this was the highest position reached by any Hawkwind album since *Space Ritual*. There was even a fleeting appearance in the Singles Chart for its accompanying 7", 'Shot Down in the Night'. At the same time, its writer, Steve Swindells, had his solo LP, *Fresh Blood*, released and that too utilised the song as its 7" calling card. "It was real shame," thought Langton who, by a twist of fate, played on both versions, noting how "they sort of clashed heads with each other."

"I think that was rather unnecessary; probably a record company decision," adds Swindells. "The Hawkwind version was good, but mine had more energy and power, more crafted. Dave sang it in a completely different way from me, but it's a bit folksy."

"[Bronze] is a pretty together little company," thought Brock at the time. "And they've proved they can do it with the live album, which shows we can do it if the record company are with us." After his dissatisfaction with Charisma ("I think they were pleased to see the back of us, and us of them"), there was a new sense of optimism. It didn't translate into the sort of rock 'n' roll lifestyle that Hawkwind had enjoyed during their UA era, though. "We had 'Shot Down in the Night' in the charts, we had *Live Seventy Nine* in the top twenty and Douglas had us booked into this seedy hotel round the back of Paddington Station," Brock recalls of one particular London gig.

They played a handful of shows in the early summer of 1980, including the band's annual pilgrimage to Stonehenge (21st June). During one, at Folkestone's Lea Cliff Halls (12th July), 'New Jerusalem' was dropped from Blake's spot in favour of a new song, 'Waiting for Nati', one of a few little gems secreted away in the Hawkwind canon that are known principally through their existence on live recordings. Lyrically it was a most unusual number for Hawkwind, as it concerned Blake's joy on his impending fatherhood, enthusing how 'that little cosmic magic has worked, at last', a song that sparkles with new age brightness and zest.

"Nadege was expecting a child, to be called Nati, so from time to time I dropped that in." This was the only song that Blake had incorporated into the set that wasn't one of his previously released solo numbers; he didn't revisit the composition for a studio recording until his *Magick* album, many years later. A lovely song, 'Waiting for Nati' is one of Hawkwind's great lost numbers.

At Rockfield Studios ("a mythical place," says Blake), late in the summer of 1980, Hawkwind wrote and rehearsed the new material that would form the original *Levitation* sessions.

Blake: "I bought the first sync-able to tape system, in search of a solution [to the clock issue]. Simon's difficulties were personality clash, technical, and I'm told, some personal ones too. As a result, we weren't getting a good rhythm track down, we weren't getting to boogie!"

King finally departed after the first mix for *Levitation* had been completed, at the Roundhouse Studios in Camden. "Dave didn't think Simon was cutting it," recalled Langton. "I went out to get a bag of chips one night and when I got back Simon was walking out practically in tears. I didn't know what the hell was going on. I almost felt like walking after him, because Simon was a real nice bloke." In contrast to Blake's view that King was not able to handle the technical demands of the album, Huw believed that a satisfactory result would have been achieved "with a bit more patience." Brock aside, the last member of the 'classic' *Space Ritual* line-up had now left.

In one of those intriguing quirks of rock music mythology, King was replaced by Ginger Baker, a drummer legendary both for his playing in supergroup Cream and his notorious reputation for being difficult to work with. "Marion was working for Ginger's band," Huw recalled. "We'd been booked into the studios for two weeks and were struck down without a drummer. Ginger's band had fallen to pieces and Marion suggested we got him in to finish the sessions. He'd seen Hawkwind before so he knew what to expect. Ginger came in and did immediately [the work that Simon King had struggled on], but then he's this ancient jazz drummer and can play anything."

Tim Blake: "Hawkwind were not ready to dare the electronic thing, so Ginger saved the day."

The *Levitation* album re-recorded some of the material from the final Hawklords Rockfield sessions, including 'Motorway City' and 'Who's Gonna Win the War'. Though the cover artwork was arguably the least inspired to have graced a Hawkwind LP, the album's production values were far in advance of anything previously committed to vinyl by Hawkwind ('this is a headphones album', stated the back cover). "Bronze informed me that this was the best Hawkwind album EVER," wrote Malcolm Dome. Whilst he considered this somewhat overstated, Dome heard "a return to the style of the early 70s… blistering sci-fi imagery [used] as an angry searchlight.' Particularly praising the "agoraphobic wilderness of

146

'Motorway City',' and "the desolate synthesisers of the J.G. Ballard-esque 'Dust of Time'," Dome rated *Levitation* as "an album of the year."

"I think the final result was quite classy," says Bainbridge, "almost Hawklords-ish. The thing about rock music is that it works on analogue, because there is lots of noise, but when you put it on a digital machine it's so clean that the tones have to be good. In that sense, *Levitation* does well, it's a pioneering album."

There was a substantial UK tour in support of the album. At its outset, the setlist was similar to the previous winter's. Unlike the success of that tour, the new schedule soon proved to be difficult, generating bad feeling and misunderstanding between some members. Tim Blake departed after a gig in Hanley (17th October), reported in *Hawkfan* as down to a domestic dispute which "led to him being in a temper, arguing with the band and walking out." A more detailed version of Blake's departure, from the band's point of view, was related in *This Is Hawkwind, Do Not Panic*. Dave described a breakdown in the band's relationship with Blake, due to Tim spending an inordinate amount of time on the telephone to his girlfriend. In the lobby of their hotel, Blake was repeatedly asked to curtail a phone call and join the band in their car. When he persisted with his conversation the band drove off without him.

Blake: "At the end of recording *Levitation* I informed Hawkwind management that I didn't wish to tour until the baby was born, as I knew Nadege to be having a risky pregnancy. A lot of unjustified pressure was put on me to go on the road." The result was that Blake found himself, quite naturally, in "a strange state of mind and passing a great deal of time on the phone to Nadege." Apparently due to a change of management at the beginning of the tour, nobody had briefed the band about Blake's private life. This might indicate that there had been some level of strain in the relationship between Blake and the rest of the band, since it's difficult to understand why it needed a manager to relay this information between work colleagues. However, it is impossible not to have sympathy with Blake's dilemma and his retelling of the story from his viewpoint distinctly changes another myth of Hawkwind history.

"On the second or third gig, Nadege was taken into hospital and miscarried. While I was talking to her on the phone – in a more than worried state – the band became incredibly impatient to leave for a couple of days off. No one knew why I was stuck in a phone box, and someone suggested they drove off." The result was that Tim Blake "had nothing more to do with Hawkwind or the UK at that point in time... and just went home [to France]." To this day, the name 'Nati' remains engraved in the woodwork on the front of Tim's Minimoog synthesiser.

Hawkwind filled their personnel gap first with a member of the road crew known as 'Twink' (not John 'Twink' Alder who'd played in The Pink Fairies and deputised for Terry Ollis in Hawkwind in the early 70s, but Paul Noble, the former synth player of Here & Now), before bringing in Keith Hale as their latest keyboardist. "Dave heard a tape of Keith's stuff with his group, Blood Donor," Langton told Simon Veness during an interview at the Lewisham Odeon "He particularly liked this track, 'Dangerous Visions', and suggested we have a go at it." Named after a radical collection of new wave SF edited by Harlan Ellison, 'Dangerous Visions' became a curious addition to the Hawkwind setlist. On the one hand, it's a middle of the road soft rock song with a theme about the plight of children in the third world that wears its conscience on its sleeve in a quite awkward manner, and yet strip it out of the context of a Hawkwind set and it has a quite appealing smoothness, enhanced by a restrained guitar lead from Langton, and is by no means unmemorable. Incorporated into the set to fill the gap where 'Lighthouse' previously resided, it's just not a Hawkwind number, really.

Where 'Dangerous Visions' did fit in with the work that was being developed was in the evolving theme to the new material that expanded on some of the more pessimistic imagery of the Charisma albums. 'Who's Gonna Win the War' was a barren coda to the nuclear wasteland of 'Damnation Alley' with its unsettling talk of death lurking in the creeping radiation sickness, while 'Dust of Time' covered a similar ground to 'Spirit of the Age' with its claim 'I am son born of father never related'. Langton saw this as "Dave writing science fiction based on truth... the future doesn't look too bright, does it?" and this bleak view of things to come remained a part of the band's studio recordings for some time. "You can't ignore it unless you're a total dreamer," said Huw. "The music entertains, but I believe in writing about these things."

It wasn't a particularly happy line-up. Ginger Baker had his own aura, his own position in the rock music world that made him a difficult proposition within the narrower context of an established band. "We did a gig up North, and there were lots of people sitting around the dressing room," recalled Huw. "Either Ginger or Harvey brought up a musical comment, something pathetic, but they had a big set-to about it. Harvey was the protagonist, but Ginger stuck to his guns and Harvey to his. Everybody knew that Ginger was right. Even Harvey knew he was wrong, but he wouldn't step down and after that Ginger just blanked him out. Harvey's a lovely bloke, but he's very proud, and so is Ginger."

"I thought we got on well for ages," says Bainbridge of his relationship with Ginger Baker. "There was just one moment when we had a big meeting, midway through the tour, in which Ginger reckoned we could all make a lot more money if we got rid of the lightshow. No-one said anything, so I said, 'I don't think that's a good idea, the lights are as much an integral part of the show as we are; we need them'. Ginger and I argued about it at great length, and from that moment on it seemed as though he didn't like me very much!"

This breakdown within the Hawkwind rhythm section was worsened by Bainbridge's interference in Baker's increasingly elongated drum solos during 'Brainstorm'. "At the Hammersmith Odeon, we'd all come off stage, because he was going on and on. I turned to Dave and said 'watch this.' I was still plugged in, so I went back on and joined in and it really pissed him off, but it actually made him finish sooner."

Ginger Baker, Harvey Bainbridge, Dave Brock
St Austell Cornwall Coliseum 25/10/80
(Oz Hardwick)

After the *Levitation* tour, Hawkwind made an appearance on the German TV show *Lieder und Leute*, opening and closing the programme. The edition also featured Bonnie Tyler ("A nice girl" says Bainbridge, "but she had minders and you couldn't get close to her.") and, most deliciously from a rock history and a personal baggage perspective, Baker's former Cream colleague, Jack Bruce, who was then playing with Alexis Korner.

"Jack and Ginger hadn't spoken since Cream split up," notes Bainbridge. "We played live for the programme, and during the end number Jack Bruce was behind Ginger's drum-kit, lobbing stuff at him. When the show finished and we were off air, Jack walked up to me and said, 'He's a bastard, isn't he?' I just said, 'Yeah!', but Jack said, 'Don't worry, you did OK.' I'll always remember that because he was my hero when I was a teenager; I used to nip off school to go and watch him play. Jack was lovely, because he said a few things that made a lot of stuff very clear. I could understand what he was saying, because Ginger, brilliant drummer though he was, would get up blind alleyways with his rhythm patterns and it would be hard for him to get back sometimes."

The TV Company took the performers off to a tavern after the show. "Alexis Korner, Jack Bruce, Huw and myself were playing pool and having a laugh. Then I went and sat down, and suddenly Jack Bruce's girlfriend was tapping me on the shoulder and asking for a hand. We had to carry Jack back to his hotel. He was pissed... face-down on the pool table! I couldn't believe it. In the meantime, Ginger Baker had met this German woman and taken her back to

149

his hotel room. But Ginger and Jack had managed a few words together and not actually come to blows."

The final split in the unsettled and unhappy *Levitation* tour line-up occurred soon after. "We had a big European tour booked, and we were back in Rockfield rehearsing," explains Bainbridge. "Dave came up to my room one day and said, 'Look, we've got a problem downstairs.' I went down, and it seemed like Ginger and Keith had decided that I was useless and ought to go. Huw just sat there muttering, 'I think it's disgusting,' so I turned to Dave and said, 'What do you think? If I'm useless, I'll go...' Dave didn't commit himself one way or the other."

Bainbridge rang the band's manager, by this time Danny Betesh, and suggested that it might be in Hawkwind's best interests if he left quietly ("I didn't want to fuck it up for everybody else"). Betesh simply advised Bainbridge to make the decision himself. "I had a chat with Dave and said, 'Look, who do you want... me or him?' Huw had stated his position, Keith Hale had made his. Dave had the casting vote, and seemed to take about three days to make it. Eventually he said he'd rather keep me than Ginger, so I had to turn to Ginger and say, 'Look, I'm sorry, but you've got to go.' He didn't take it very nicely."

Baker later informed the music press that "the world's worst bass player has sacked the world's best drummer," but he was clearly neither a drummer in the Hawkwind mould or a musician who in any way subscribed to the band's ethos. "Ginger saw it as making money," observes Bainbridge. "He always thought that Dave was 'The Boy'; he'd say that. If Dave had been canny he could have gone with it, and made loads of money, but I think he would have had problems with Ginger later-on."

11

Sonic Attack in the Church of Hawkwind

"Good show, chaps!" Dave Brock – Hammersmith 1980
(Keith Kniveton)

Hawkwind played a double-header festival weekend on 19th and 20th June, 1981, firstly their annual Stonehenge appearance, then at the resurgent Glastonbury CND Festival. With the dismissal of Ginger Baker, several potential replacements had been auditioned, including Rik Martinez, but in the end Martin Griffin filled the drummer's seat.

They were the Peoples' Band in the early 70s, and through the festival scene of the 1970s, particularly those put on and played at for free, they were still the Peoples' Band. Those moments of turning up and putting on a show and just being part of the wider counterculture was ingrained into Hawkwind DNA and would continue to be for another decade, until the scene that they were synonymous with turned in on itself and on them. "Politically, it was very important that we just made a show," notes Bainbridge. "The notion of anarchy in its true sense is right, the idea that the best government is no government. And so, it's right that people get together, almost at a whim. You've got to maintain that freedom, fight for it. When you're young the energy is there to do it. You hope that you can get other people to come along and continue it."

Those shows were right at the commencement of recording the next studio LP, to be called *Sonic Attack*, and while they were significant for the statements they made about support for the counterculture and the festival scene, as with the Futurama festival back at the start of the Bronze-era they also presented themselves as opportunities for the band to reveal the latest twists and turns in their sound and identity, replacing the clearly defined rock sound of the previous couple of years with something altogether more industrial and grungy. At the same time, to appear on the Pyramid Stage at Glastonbury as the festival started to reinvent itself, in part as a vehicle for CND fundraising, was a major achievement, despite it being an embryonic revival of the festival, far from its massive attendance and corporate ethos of today. Bainbridge: "It was nice to see Dave relaxing [at Stonehenge]. However, the next day we got to Glastonbury and I was absolutely finished. I'd gone over the top by then. But Dave was absolutely brilliant that night. When I think back, I realise he's a canny old wizard." At that point it was the biggest show Bainbridge had ever played. "Twenty thousand people, a big laser show, and on the Pyramid stage ...." It was a cracking performance, full of energy and purpose, setting the scene for the band that would be the latest to emerge under the Hawkwind banner.

The dalliance with Bronze resulted only in *Live Seventy Nine* and *Levitation*, the company's founder, Gerry Bron, recalling in one interview that, "We did quite well with Hawkwind, but they were a bit lazy... they constantly wanted to do live albums, so they wouldn't have to write songs." Adrift once more outside of the music business, the band were next signed by Kingsley Ward's 'Active' label, which was marketed through RCA under the by-line of 'RCA Active'. Ward, who founded Rockfield Studios in the early 1960s with his brother Charles, simply became involved based on a long-term friendship with Brock, and because the band were between labels. "RCA put up the money and called all the shots," explains Ward, "so Hawkwind were effectively signed to RCA."

Dave Brock: "We had a three-year deal with Bronze and both of their albums sold really well, but towards the end they had financial problems and so we then signed a deal with RCA. Kingsley Ward came to the rescue with Active, we had a meeting with him at Rockfield and then with RCA at their Tottenham Court Road offices where Shaun Greenfield signed us up. We'd virtually lived at Rockfield Studios! The place is one of the great loves of our lives!"

The first RCA album, *Sonic Attack*, was an altogether different animal from its recent predecessors. It had a gritty tone, for all the world like an updated and technologically advanced version of *Doremi Fasol Latido*. "It sounds like the band on the road, but it was recorded in a way that makes it work," notes Bainbridge, contrasting it with the *Levitation* LP, which, with its reliance on digital techniques and the opportunities it offered, was quite far away from a studio capture of the live band.

"It may not sound like it now, but when we recorded *Sonic Attack* we did a lot of experimentation during the mixing, to get effects and different things going. Some worked very well," says Bainbridge. But however satisfied Hawkwind felt with the end-product, they became aware that RCA had taken on a band that it didn't understand or have creative sympathy with.

Without the incisive lyrics of Bob Calvert to rely upon, *Levitation* had lacked the bite and vivid imagery of earlier Hawkwind albums. Though across the years he'd written some razor sharp and provocative lyrics, Brock's wordsmith skills weren't in the same league as Bob Calvert by any stretch of the imagination. It didn't stop his latest songs being extremely evocative but, as an example, 'Motorway City' has the dual strengths of Brock's grinding guitar chords playing against Langton's more expressive lead while lyrically it's not particularly strong and those words fade out early into the track. 'Who's Gonna Win the War' reminds us that when he's penned a worthy lyric he's not averse to resurrecting it again, and its most potent anti-war symbols revisited a much earlier song in his canon. Much of the remainder of that album was instrumentally focused.

Sonic Attack overcame the lack of a principal songwriter by leaning on written contributions from Michael Moorcock. "As always with Hawkwind, I was asked by Dave to come back when things weren't working out with Bob," says Moorcock. But it wasn't just his use of language that Moorcock brought to *Sonic Attack*, but his imposing vocal ability as well.

At Rockfield, Moorcock cut a version of the title track, which was eventually rejected by Brock in favour of a take with Bainbridge providing the vocals. Moorcock did lend his idiosyncratic Johnny Rotten meets Opera voice to 'Coded Languages'. "Michael arrived with a batch of lyrics for us to use; we kind of fiddled around with them," says Bainbridge. "If you think of it being like 'British Tribal Music' going one step further, then it's quite good to have someone like that say 'Ah, that'll fit this…', which is how 'Coded Languages' happened. Michael heard me going around with this sequence, and said 'I've got something…' I asked him if he would sing the song, but he didn't want to at first. But when he did record the vocal track it was great." Out of this collaboration came much that was interesting on Sonic Attack and some lyrics that were used for a later RCA album, *Choose Your Masques*.

"I'd already done some performances 'up north', when I was living in Yorkshire," recalls Moorcock, "and came down to do those recordings." Some of it was reworking existing material; a track that later surfaced on the odds-and-sods LP *Zones*, a number entitled 'Running Through the Back Brain', featuring the earlier line-up that included Ginger Baker and Keith Hale, was a live instrumental cut given voice in this manner, perhaps overdubbed during the *Sonic Attack* sessions. "'Choose Your Masks' [Moorcock notes this as his original spelling] was done around that time, too. We did a version of it using my melody, but then Dave changed it. There's a recording where you can tell nobody had remembered to tell me the song had changed and I begin to sound totally at odds with what's being played."

Recorded between June and August 1981, Sonic Attack captured the essence of the cold-war paranoia that inhabited post 'winter of discontent', early Thatcher administration in its industrial, concrete greyness and downbeat imagery.

The title track, given added menace with its thumping, marching electronic drone suggestive of a nuclear attack let loose and unstoppable, marked out the LP to be played loud and taken seriously. On the babbling, speaking-in-tongues 'Psychosonia' the listener is extorted to listen to the words they are being given. The whole purpose of 'Living on a Knife Edge' is Brock's call to his audience to wake up to the realities of city life and the grinding away of individual liberty where faceless people watch the population on closed-circuit cameras. In this tottering on the brink of apocalypse view of the here and now, 'Angels of Death' walk the city streets, 'Lost Chances' abound and the 'Streets of Fear' are filled with hate. Even for a band that had made performance art into a medium for the danger signs of modern life it was a powerfully constructed message. 'Future generations are relying on us,' warned Brock.

But it also looks back, in the sonic unease that it creates in the listener, to earlier Hawkwind ideas, back to that original notion of freaking people "in a nice way, without drugs." It has an urgent, unsettling manner about it, distilled into 'Sonic Attack' and 'Psychosonia' most particularly. "…this new album has a lot of weird sound effects on it," Brock told *Kerrang!*. "Listen to it on cans and there are lots of subsonic frequencies which will make you jump out of your chair… I guarantee it will make your eyes water. But we don't try to make people ill."

An officially released collection of demo material that Brock had assembled for *Sonic Attack* reveals how much work on the album was predefined before the full band reached the studio, even aside from 'Disintegration', which went all the way back to the era of 'Busking' Dave Brock, an unreleased acoustic song from the early 70s. "One thing that Hawkwind was very good at," comments Bainbridge, "was having its recording sessions complete before you started recording. 'I've done it, here's the song.' Dave turned up with his eight-track, dumped what he had onto the multi-track and the rest of us had to somehow play around with it, which is working the wrong way. Even if we suggested that it would be easier to just play the songs again, it would be 'No, I've done my bit.' That was how some of the tracks were worked out. Thankfully they came out okay." Bainbridge does acknowledge that it was possible for other members to bring in contributions, however. "That was one of Dave's things, 'Oh, I'm fed-up with doing everything', but then again, when someone else did something, it could be changed."

The selection of the single from *Sonic Attack* revealed how much at odds RCA were with Hawkwind, in the eyes of Bainbridge. "I remember the A&R man coming to Rockfield whilst we were recording *Sonic Attack*. He listened to the tracks and asked, 'Have you not got another 'Silver Machine' then?' I said, 'Nope! All you want is three minutes of commercial pap, isn't it?' and he said, 'Yep'." But it wasn't just that the label and the band were at odds; so, it seems, were the members. "In my opinion on *Sonic Attack*, Huw's song ['Rocky Paths'] was the perfect commercial heavy rock record. It's basically a three-minute song, but with nice electronics going on. It had everything, guitar hero stuff, big heavy rock, synthesisers, decent singing. But Dave wanted to put out 'Angels of Death', which really wasn't the same thing."

Whilst clearly proud of the achievements made recording *Sonic Attack*, Bainbridge was less impressed with the supporting tour. "I think there was a very powerful thing going on but I always felt there was something missing at the time." *Sounds*, reviewing Hawkwind's gig at the Hammersmith Odeon (21st October 1981) noted that "They are a heavier band than before, and their softer classics have disappeared," which is perhaps why the critic observed the guest appearance of Robert Calvert to read 'Sonic Attack' with a wistful, "I felt he'd left the temple for too long."

At a legendary show at the Rainbow, (18th December), Hawkwind were joined by Turner, Calvert and Moorcock. The outcome was fictionalised by Moorcock in his 'London' novel, *King of the City*. "Bob wasn't expected to be there," notes Turner. "He and I decided to go and gate-crashed the event. I didn't want to be there particularly, but we sort of encouraged each other." Moorcock was amid divorce proceedings from his wife, Jill Riches, who had started a relationship with Calvert.

"Bob wanted things to be 'alright' between us," explains Moorcock. "That was fine, except that he was trying to get emotional stuff out of me when I was exhausted. I told Dave I'd only do the Rainbow gig if Bob wasn't there. Once my name was on the bill and we were in the dressing room waiting to go on, Nik turned up with Bob and Jill in tow." Mike recited some of his poetry, 'Standing on the Edge', 'Use Your Armour', 'Great Sun Jester', 'The Time Ship' and 'Sonic Attack'. "In the wings, Bob kept hassling me. Every time I went off stage, he'd be trying to get a reaction." Already worn-out from attending the funeral of a close friend that day, Moorcock "more in sorrow than in anger," threatened to punch Calvert. "Bob had a stick with him. I raised my fist to punch him. Bob raised his stick… Jill screamed and stepped between us. Dave could see the tussle from where he stood on stage. I left the tussle on cue for my next number. I didn't even hit Bob in the end. I just wanted him to stop hassling me."

Recorded during an enforced break in the *Sonic Attack* sessions, due to Griffin contracting German measles, was *Church of Hawkwind*, an additional, unplanned, album. A much different animal than the bleak tone of *Sonic Attack*, this was a predominately electronic affair, dominated by Brock and Bainbridge. Though it has its enthusiasts, it's an oddball entry into the canon that doesn't please all and is possibly most intriguing not for its music per se, but because it shows Dave Brock once again thinking of ways in which the configuration of the band could be played around with and changed.

Bainbridge: "Dave reckoned that we could in fact play the guitars and the synthesisers [simultaneously], which I was a bit dubious about. But we began working out ways of doing that, linking them all together and having them triggered, with lots of experimentation going on. We had stuff that we wouldn't have put on *Sonic Attack* or *Choose Your Masques* because RCA wouldn't have thought them commercial enough, so we put them on another album, *Church of Hawkwind*. Dave tried to make it his own album, but it was essentially the third album for RCA; they are not all Dave's ideas." Brock himself went on to describe it as pretty much a solo album, but as to its realisation, Bainbridge reflected that "I quite like it, because it was getting into another area."

But on that notion of it being a Dave Brock solo record, most of the material that made it onto the LP came from a collection of synth jams he'd recorded at home and brought to Rockfield to work on during the *Sonic Attack* hiatus. 'Nuclear Drive', originally the demo for a Bronze-era B-side called 'Nuclear Toy', a track called 'Water Music' that became 'Light Specific Data' and 'Satellite', a number Hawkwind had played on the Winter 1979 tour which was reworked into 'The Phenomenon of Luminosity'. For 'Star Cannibal', almost a full band song with Langton and Griffin playing, Dave recorded his own bass line on a synthesiser. "That came from a science fiction book called *The Nets of Space* [Emil Petaja, 1969], about these creatures that go around to different worlds and eat all the human forms; they're like lobsters with big claws, and they stick them in fondue - 'flesh fondue/main course stew' - 'very tasty, that human' - and I thought that would make a fantastic song. These things give you a good idea for a song, putting music to the storylines."

Bainbridge insists the contributions from Langton and himself made *Church of Hawkwind* part of the Hawkwind canon, which of course it is. However, it has a tone that stands it aside from the style that the band had been playing in post-Hawklords and so it rather makes most sense to listen to it almost in the context of being a Dave Brock solo album, albeit with other band members input; his *Captain Lockheed*, perhaps. That said, the LP was also a staging-post for Bainbridge's own interest in electronica, providing a more inventive outlet for his synthesiser work, removed from the grungy live Hawkwind sound.

Included on *Church of Hawkwind* was a contributor's credit for Marc Sperhauk, for a bass part on 'Some People Never Die', from a Brock demo, 'Assassination'. "I was unaware that I was going to be on the record," comments Sperhauk. "After meeting Dave on the ill-fated US tour, we began trading cassettes; there wasn't any agreement or even verbal communication about it, aside from an enthusiastic postcard from Dave that said: 'Sounds across the sea. Great Stuff!' It was a boost that he was at all interested in my work. The highest compliment I ever received was asking him what he thought about one of my tapes and he replied, 'Sounds like Hawkwind.' I'll never forget the day I stopped into my favourite independent record store and discovered *Church*... had come in via import. I was reading the back cover, excited to have a new Hawk record, when I actually noticed the credit for the first time. I can't describe the feeling."

There are some songs, particularly 'Nuclear Drive' and 'Looking in the Future', which would have sounded at home in the Hawkwind live shows of the era. Others, such as the schlock-fest 'Star Cannibal' (Dave's rhyming of 'flesh fondue' with 'main course stew' is, let's be honest, far from one of his more successful couplets) would have been exorcised from a more typical Hawkwind

156

album. In the more electronically experimental numbers, 'Joker at the Gate', or 'Experiment with Destiny' for example, Hawkwind's Germanic influences had moved on to the more abstract electronica of Kraftwerk or Tangerine Dream.

Despite there being several benefit shows and festivals played by the band around the time that *Church of Hawkwind* saw the light of day, the material generated by this album remained crystallised within the LP's experimental sideshow. Apart from 'Experiment with Destiny', simply an alternative take of *Sonic Attack*'s 'Virgin of the World', nothing from *Church of Hawkwind* crossed-over to Hawkwind's contemporary live set. Fan Paul Bagley was at the band's headline appearance at the Monmore Rock Festival, Wolverhampton, on 2nd May, 1982. The festival, staged on an unusually cold May Bank Holiday, ran extremely late. "Some two hours after the festival was due to finish, we were greeted by a spray of dry ice and effects as the Hawks took to the stage. A flurry of keyboard and synthesiser effects rose to a crescendo, and then the smoke cleared to the intro of 'Shot Down in the Night'. A great start to the gig." What Bagley found unexpected was an unheralded additional to band during 'Urban Guerrilla'. "A mad, Mohican-haired, leopard-skin-clad figure who I at first thought it must be Bob Calvert, being thrown by the bizarre appearance, yet as he produced his saxophone and sung along to the chant of 'Gotta Stay Cool', I realised that it was Nik Turner."

Turner played at a few Hawkwind shows during the summer of 1982, including Stonehenge on 20th June and a disastrous set at the Donington Monsters of Rock festival on 21st August. Inappropriately shoehorned into a line-up that included Saxon, Uriah Heep and Status Quo, Hawkwind took a battering from both audience and critics alike. One radio commentator complained of their "outdated 'Dancers on the Edge of Time' routine." Huw noted to Steve Keaton, in Sounds, that "gigs like Donington are a waste of time. You can't play because you're too busy dodging plastic containers and mud bombs."

"I disliked Donington intensely," Brock revealed to Malcolm Dome, before falling uncharacteristically into standard rock lingo. "It was a terrible day. The kids were really fleeced." Interviewed on the Festival's radio station, he passed off Hawkwind's negative audience reaction on technical difficulties. "I was a bit deafened by the monitors. All I could hear were vocals and synthesisers; it's like fighting a lost cause. We've only got a hundred-watt stack, but you could have three or four hundred watts and they had the monitors up to that level." He saved his fiercest criticism for others on the bill. "Bands lose touch with their audiences. Saxon wouldn't go and play a free gig; we do three or four every year, CND things… That's what they should do, they take a lot but they don't give much!"

The failure of the band to establish themselves with the heavy metal audience at Donington was symptomatic of Hawkwind's association with a musical genre with which they were perceived to be playing in by promoters and casual music fans, but which they had little in common with. Bainbridge: "Where it probably fell apart, in terms of commercial success was that it didn't lie in the heavy metal category completely. You had Iron Maiden becoming huge in places like America, because they fitted neatly into that style, whereas Hawkwind never did. I've never thought of Hawkwind as being a heavy metal band. I always thought we were a bit cleverer than that." The return of Nik Turner, who'd enthusiastically embraced the punk ethos across the late 70s and into the start of the 1980s, gave them a new impetus and a different direction that promised to reconnect them with their roots and join them up with newer musical styles. Disaster, of course, loomed…

12

Turner Turning Point

Dave Brock, Harvey Bainbridge
(Oz Hardwick)

Nik Turner returned on what, from the outside, looked to be a fulltime basis, during the summer of 1982, though this time around his input, through circumstance perhaps as much as anything else, was as a live performer, as an exaggerated frontman and focal point. Although he had made a handful of guest appearances with the band since being ejected in 1976, and had also worked as a solo artist, his focus had been on Inner City Unit, a really great hippie-punk mash-up with a political edge rounded-off by a judicious sense of humour and with some cartoon sci-fi thrown into the mix. Although the line-up was fluid, ICU's mainstays, apart from Turner, were 'Judge' Trevor Thoms and Philip 'Dead Fred' Reeves, who, in the early 1970s, had played together in the Steve Gibbons Band. "Fast forward to 1978/79," says Reeves. "Trev and Nik had talked about setting up some kind of 'urban guerrilla' music festival, finalising as the 'Under the Westway' concerts. I had just finished a tour supporting Steel Pulse and so brought some skanking and dub to these very 70s rock-heads."

Reeves recalls these gigs as being "a big hit with the mixed-race audience" and goes on to describe playing 'The Guns of Navarone', an old ska instrumental originally by The Skatellites, to great effect. What the band lacked in finesse was more than compensated for by its high-energy levels. This seminal line-up, featuring Turner, Reeves and Thoms, plus Baz Magneto and Dave Dog, "with various tambourine shakers and dancers," and known as Kunst Blitz, was later to metamorphose into Inner City Unit."

ICU released a number of singles and an album, *Passout*, on their own Riddle Records label. Following appearances at Stonehenge in 1980, and supporting Hawkwind at the Lyceum, ICU decamped to Turner's Cadillac Ranch, in Wales, to work on a second LP, *The Maximum Effect*. By then, the band's membership had seen many upheavals, and the consumption of hard drugs had brought the continued viability of the band into question. "I became involved in Hawkwind again when ICU was foundering," says Turner. "Heroin was involved. I just couldn't cope with it and broke the band up. Dave invited me back into Hawkwind, and it was convenient at the time."

Earlier in the year, Langton had filled in as a temporary member of ICU. While, therefore, it is tempting to see Langton in the role of the go-between, bringing the two early day members of Hawkwind together again, just as Simon King did with Langton while they worked together in Jawa, Huw was adamant that the decision was Dave's alone. "The bottom line is, whoever re-joined or was invited into the Hawkwind association was down to Dave, nothing to do with any suggestion of mine." Bainbridge saw it as a potential need for a frontman. "Dave's very wary of everyone getting bored because nobody is doing anything... when everyone was just spaced out anyway, looking at the lightshow and getting bombarded sonically. Dave likes taking the lead... but from behind a pillar!"

Only Brock remained to provide continuity with Turner's last incarnation of Hawkwind. This provided an opportunity for Turner to gauge how much of the original Hawkwind ethos remained. "Well, they were still doing my songs! 'Master of the Universe' was probably the most popular song the band ever did." The use of his most well-known numbers ('Brainstorm' was also a linchpin of the live set) aside, Turner saw little of the group he'd left in 1976. "It was completely different, but I saw it as a vehicle for me to perform, be theatrical and do something I thought would be interesting creatively. I believed it would be in keeping with what the band should be about. Whether other people agreed with me is something else." That would be the rub of the problem.

As to whether the original spirit of Hawkwind was still alive, Turner is ambivalent: "I don't know, I think I had that spirit... I got people involved with the band, like Andy Anderson (a temporary Hawkwind drummer, who also played with The Cure), and Dead Fred on violin. People followed the band because they liked that spirit the band had. I'm not sure whether the band embodied it then, but I tried to in everything I did."

Turner enjoyed a guest credit on *Choose Your Masques*, Hawkwind's final RCA album but doesn't recall any contribution to the record, and the 1996 CD reissue deleted any mention of him. "I don't think he did contribute much," notes Bainbridge, whose main number of the album, 'Dream Worker', was adopted by Turner as one of the focal points of his live appearances with the group.

"I was in the studio, just playing with the synthesisers," says Bainbridge. "I started at home, with a backwash of stuff. I had a bass guitar riff that I wanted to use over this, a sort of ambient sound. I played it, we recorded it... and I didn't like the result. So out of interest, I said could we see what it sounded like backwards, and the riff sounded much better, so we used that." The number was included in most Hawkwind sets throughout the 1980s, constantly changing and evolving. "I thought it had just got to the right feel, when we got to 1989... though when I listened to the *Choose Your Masques* version, played to me recently on a brilliant hi-fi system, it sounded very exciting."

Reflecting on the changes made to the title track since its conception, Moorcock thought it "an improvement... the best version." The album also contained his lyrics for 'Arrival in Utopia', and made use of Calvert's 'Fahrenheit 451', which the *Quark* line-up had tried out at Rockfield several years previously. "We had hoped [Moorcock and Calvert] would be on Choose Your Masques," Brock told *Kerrang!*'s Malcolm Dome, "but time was very tight and Mike couldn't make it, whilst Bob had booked himself into a sanatorium."

There were plans to reinstate Simon King on drums for the subsequent tour. King was requested to audition, possibly because of the problems encountered during the Levitation sessions. Turner: "Simon came down and played with the band and Dave rejected him, so there was quite a bit of bad feeling created by that."

This was King's last involvement of any sort with Hawkwind. Within a couple of years, he had left the music business forever. "I've attempted to find his whereabouts,' Huw, who was a close friend, told me at the time of this book's first edition. 'I heard he was working in one of the antique shops in the Portobello Road. I'd love to know where he is..." He'd started working for Hounslow Council, managing their refuse recycling services, and more recently did show his face at a Hawkwind spin-off show fronted by Nik Turner, though as a guest not a musician, but to all intents and purposes he'd walked away from the music business, never to return.

With Martin Griffin again contracted instead, Hawkwind toured *Choose Your Masques* as a five piece, plus dancers Kris Tait and Jane Isaac, through October and November 1982. At Birmingham (27th October), Malcolm Dome, noted that the "capacity crowd lapped up the use of two exotic dancers with gold-painted faces and a succession of costumes, plus a stage set akin to a psychedelic McDonalds and a battery of backdrop TV screens displaying an amalgam of disturbing/relaxing animated sequences."

Dome also noted that Spanish support act, Baron Rojo "successfully negotiated this gig without receiving the abuse Hawkwind fans usually hurl unfairly at support bands." Marc Sperhauk had travelled to the UK for the tour, commenting: "I noticed Nik would go out to play with Baron Rojo. It just seemed natural to Nik to show some support for these guys, who had a pretty thankless task." Regarding Turner's return, Sperhauk adds, "I never saw any friction related to past events. Once Dave talked to me about how he was concerned about Nik being viewed as a 'frontman', and that he didn't think that was appropriate for Hawkwind, but I never saw any personal animosity."

Sperhauk, meeting most of the current Hawkwind line-up for the first time, had an opportunity to assess the individual personalities. "Nik was probably the most gregarious, Harvey quiet and friendly, Huw always looking out for me, and Martin was very much a character, always talkative. They were open to fans, staying long after shows to sign albums and meet with people who waited afterwards. On more than one occasion it was announced that 'this is Marc Sperhauk who played on *Church of Hawkwind*' and autograph seekers would be sent off in my direction." He contrasts this with stories about Ginger Baker whose approach was at odds with Hawkwind's ethics. "They described this picture of the band in one room, talking to fans and hanging out, and Ginger in another by himself, with this vicious dog he travelled with that was ready to bite anyone that disturbed him."

The shows started with a tape loop of the opening sequence from the classic television series *The Outer Limits*, "We are controlling transmission...," which Sperhauk recalls as "an idea that came from a tape I had sent to Dave." The main set was heavily derived from the RCA albums with some numbers adapted to include the addition of Turner. 'Solitary Mind Games', an atmospheric and thoughtful Langton song, particularly benefited from a reworking with an emphasis on Nik's flute-playing that changed the tone dramatically and eliminated much of the harshness of the studio version.

At Folkestone, the band were joined by Calvert, singing on some numbers ("he was expected because he lived near there," notes Sperhauk) and by Moorcock on the first of two nights at the Hammersmith Odeon. Before the Folkestone show, Turner (oddly, considering the British winters) went for a night swim. "He appeared in the dressing room quite wet and excitedly claimed he was caught in a rip tide," adds Sperhauk. Though the Hammersmith gigs were the usual triumphant return to London, the tour wrapped up in a lesser style at the Chippenham Gold Diggers (15th November, 1982). Sperhauk describes it as a "dark cold club and an odd place to end the tour," whilst Kris Tait notes the strategy employed by the record business in scheduling tours in this way. "It was on the *Choose Your Masques* tour that I noticed it. We'd do two nights at Hammersmith, a night at Bristol's Colston Hall, all these big venues, all sold-out. But for the last gig, a seedy little club, where to get to the dressing room from the stage you'd have to come out of the fire exit, go 'round the car park, and in November, when it was freezing..."

"This was done deliberately, to lower the morale of the band so you don't get above yourselves," considers Brock. "You'd go home feeling worthless."

Choose Your Masques proved the last time that Hawkwind released new studio recordings on a major label for many years. Though it was evident in the music press that the relationship between RCA and the band was breaking down (Brock noting in a *Sounds* interview that "they don't seem to know who we are"), it seems that the band would have at least looked at a contract renewal if it had been on the table, though it's certainly clear that their anonymity to RCA management was a frustration to Dave Brock. A story related by Alan Moore in his *Sounds* interview with Brock and Langton that concerned Dave failing to gain entry to RCA's offices, not once but twice, was not the apocryphal tale it might have seemed, but an actual event. But any thought of a fresh deal with the label failed, according to Langton, though opinions on this vary, because of an increasing amount of archive material that was beginning to see the light of day outside of the band's association with RCA.

The Flicknife label had commenced association with Dave Brock that saw the release of the original Hawkwind Zoo demos from 1969 ('Hurry on Sundown' and 'Sweet Mistress Of Pain') and outtakes from the final Hawklords session. Flicknife also established a compilation series, *Friends and Relations*, featuring a side of live cuts from various eras and a studio side of solo work from band members and associated musicians. The first volume was a strong affair, using live versions of 'Robot', 'Golden Void' and 'Who's Gonna Win the War', backed with good studio material from ICU and Michael Moorcock. The second release was poorer in its selections and by the third volume diminishing returns took hold, with only a live version of 'Flying Doctor' (under the alternative title 'Cabinet Key') being of real interest. Flicknife also issued a 12" EP culled from the December 1977 Sonic Assassins concert and a single and 12" version of 'Motörhead' from the Lemmy-era but with Brock's vocals. They'd go on to service fans very well indeed, by releasing some successful 'bits and pieces' LPs in *Zones* and *In & Out Take*, as well as *This is Hawkwind, Do Not Panic*, a live LP + 12" promoted with Stonehenge festival imagery but largely culled from a 1980 gig at the Lewisham Odeon and the studio album *The Chronicle of the Black Sword*.

Other records released during these years starkly symbolised a lack of control over the destiny of their recordings. Following the split from RCA, Brock authorised the release of a double album, *The Text of Festival*, by Illuminated, an independent label, which contained low-grade recordings of Hawkwind's BBC Radio sessions circa 1970 and 1971. A few years later, Turner raided his collection, allowing former bandmate Dave Anderson to release, via his Demi-Monde label, the show from the Wembley Empire Pool (27th May, 1973) under the title *Bring Me the Head of Yuri Gagarin*. It was a poor-quality capture of the Space Ritual era Hawkwind and over time has become synonymous with the repetitious glut of unofficial Hawkwind albums that have since been issued. Brock, who supplied some of the tracks on *Text of Festival*, was horrified by the release of *Yuri Gagarin* and supplied Anderson with superior tapes from the Space Ritual tour, which were released under the uninspired title, *Space Ritual Volume Two*. There's no way of specifically drawing a line that links these releases to the decline in major label interest, but there's little doubt that as the number of poor quality recordings multiplied, major record label interest in the band decreased.

Let's be clear, these albums characterise the group at specific points in its history and have a real value in describing the band's development through the first half of the 1970s. For example, the alternative *Space Ritual* set has a mix that leans more heavily on Turner's saxophone in place of the thundering bass-lines of the official release. It also contains complete recordings of 'Brainstorm' and 'Time We Left', both of which had been edited on the original double album. *Yuri Gagarin* features Robert Calvert performing two poems not found on any other recorded gigs: 'Wage War', a sinister, revolutionary counterpart to the 'Urban Guerrilla' single, taken from the short story collection *Steps* by Polish-American author Jerzy Kosinski, and his dynamic recital of 'In the Egg' by the German writer Günter Grass. The latter track, which conceptualises human life as being created in an embryonic shell with its purpose being to break through to the 'real world', seems to perfectly encapsulate the fantasy roleplay that absorbed Calvert.

But it's also true that some of these recordings, and their alternatively titled reissues, have dogged Hawkwind, allegedly producing little in the way of royalties. The implication from Langton is that the general decision to independently release archive material cost the band the renewal of their RCA contract and the chance to sign for another major label. "There were all sorts of things coming out, so we all got 'invited' to RCA's offices and told that if anymore emerged that would be the end [of any contract extension]. Unfortunately, it carried on. As a result, RCA refused to renew."

It's easy to see where the temptation for these archive releases came from. As a band that, by its fluidity and revolving line-ups, is very different from tour to tour (even from night to night) there's a very entrenched 'taping' culture amongst its fans. This led to the situation where bootleggers at 1980s record fairs could distribute an eclectic selection of live recordings, often badly duplicated, or truncated to fit on a C60 or C90 audio tape. Unlike The Grateful Dead, who Hawkwind have been regularly compared to in terms of the sheer volume of bootleg recordings, back in the day Hawkwind never openly embraced the concept of audience taping and at some points in recent years the band felt it in their best interests to make a public declaration of disapproval, though that philosophy has been very much loosened more recently. The Flicknife releases, and a set of live and demo tapes released by Dave Brock via mail-order under the collective title 'The Weird Tapes', could legitimately be seen in the context of sales conceded to bootleggers had Dave not opted to issue or licence historic material himself. Nonetheless, the resulting decision by RCA not to further their relationship with Hawkwind cut the band adrift, with no financial muscle supporting their records.

While some other options were explored, the Flicknife connection moved from being a useful outlet for archive material in the early 1980s to handling the band's studio recordings as the decade progressed. Flicknife had entered the scene by releasing previously unavailable tracks from Michael Moorcock, who Flicknife founder Marc 'Frenchy' Gloder had encountered at a London gig by former Adverts leader TV Smith. His success in releasing the single 'Dodgem Dude' had onward linked him to Robert Calvert for Calvert's 'Lord of the Hornets' 7" and his *Freq* album as well as Nik Turner for the terrific Inner City Unit LP *Punkadelic* and on to Dave Brock for various historic Hawkwind releases.

Sheer economics aside from the growing availability of archive records may well have come into play. The RCA albums weren't hugely successful, while the singles released from them, as usual, made little impact in the UK charts. The quality of the releases was patchy, *Church of Hawkwind* particularly, and even though there is some dynamic material spread around these records, as a whole they didn't really represent a cohesive idea for the band in the early years of the 1980s. "*Church of Hawkwind* saw the band slipping into an esoteric rut destined for oblivion," commented Dave Dickson, in *Kerrang!*. "*Choose Your Masques*, while not exactly 'commercial' has indications that their imaginative flair has been rekindled." That vaguely positive reporting on the final RCA album was tempered however with disapproval about a stodgy 'Silver Machine' re-recording that the LP included, supposedly as a '10th Anniversary' celebration of the original. "What on Earth possessed Brock to revamp this? Take a severe rap across the knuckles."

Kingsley Ward: "The [RCA] albums did well, but perhaps not well enough. The market had changed; in the 70s you could make a lot of money from album sales, but in the 80s it cost record companies a lot more to run bands so there wasn't as much money to be made." When I talked to Douglas Smith, for *Record Collector*, he summed it up: "RCA weren't really interested in renewing their deal. A lot of the labels had problems with so much bootlegged material and so many side releases, that there was not much point in investing in them. I had a big to-do with a label once that had a compilation coming out [many years after the RCA contract]. I put a public letter on the Internet telling all the fans that the material was being reproduced for the fifth or sixth time and became very heavy about it. The photos on the album didn't even reflect the people playing on it! *Onward Flies the Bird* – I was so angry about that one."

The thorny issue of archive material was not the only problem experienced between the band and RCA. A projected single release of 'Solitary Mind Games' was abandoned, with the record company refusing to release funds for its promotion. Instead, the single taken from *Choose Your Masques* was that totally unnecessary and rather unappealing studio version of 'Silver Machine'. "I think Dave had this notion that it might sell again," says Bainbridge. "In fact what it did was restart sales of the original version." Small wonder! The 'tenth anniversary' remake offered nothing new and sounded clunky alongside its illustrious predecessor, demonstrating that though the 1972 version might have been an unexpected jaunt into the mainstream, it had something magical about it as well. Totally misunderstanding the band, RCA then presented the idea that the follow-up single should be a cover of Bowie's 'Space Oddity'. Doesn't this indicate that RCA saw Hawkwind as little more than a novelty act?

These differences of approach left Hawkwind outside of the mainstream music business and reliant on independent companies for future releases. "It was quite a problem," said Langton. "As far as I'm concerned Hawkwind should have had a really good recording set-up, but unfortunately, with all the bullshit that had gone down, they didn't." Possible homes for the band were considered, "I think Virgin might have come into the context." However, the same increasing profile of the 'archive' releases that RCA balked at were there for all potential suitors to see and no major label could be found. "It's all like a little country club... word got around that Hawkwind were putting these things out, and presumably that's why nobody was interested, it's a hell of a shame."

By mid-1983 some of the musical differences that would dog the band through the following year were beginning to manifest themselves in public. Veteran fan Mike Holmes recounts a particular instance at that year's Stonehenge festival: "They did a mid-evening gig up at a pyramid tent right at the back of the Stonehenge fields, towards the army base at Devizes. Dave, Nik, and Huw were there, and I think Harvey was. I'm not sure who was on drums. It was a sunny summer evening. A couple of girls had been dancing nude at the front to the previous band. By the time Hawkwind came on everyone was sat on the grass and the whole scene was very mellow. Once Hawkwind took the stage, the folks at the front stood up and there was a bit of good-natured shouting from people sitting further back for them to sit down again. Nik and Dave took the part of the folks sitting and suggested everyone sit down before they got going. A few songs into the gig, during 'Uncle Sams on Mars', Nik went into his 'Get off my mummy Uncle Sam' and 'Uncle Sam's on heroin' rock circus act. A couple of comments between tracks suggested that Dave and Huw were getting irritated. Then Dave and Nik had an argument about what to play next. Dave started one song and Nik attempted to sing the lyrics of another. There followed a tussle between the two on stage! By that point, I'd become fed up of being dragged from mellow to irritated by the argument in the crowd, and the haphazard and unprofessional quality of the gig. So, I wandered off. After a long and eventful night, I was down in the stones watching the sun come up over the haze and could hear the band playing very well. I believe they'd moved to the main stage and were clearly playing a stonker of a gig."

"I was quite happy with the kind of pantomime aspect of [Turner's work]," says Bainbridge. "But it was a funny period. In hindsight, I don't feel Dave was happy. I think he would have liked everyone to have gone away, so he could have started over again." This may well be a telling perception as to the possible motivation for decisions made by Brock in re-channelling the direction and personnel in the following year.

With typical understatement, though he has no recollection of the onstage tussles at Stonehenge, Langton noted a "slight conflict in styles, not terrible but Nik is Nik, and Hawkwind is Hawkwind. Nik tends to run amok and take things over, and that as far as I'm concerned was the problem. I think everybody else felt the same." Turner's performances displayed an increasing domination over Hawkwind's stage personae. The image of shadowy figures merged into the relentless psychedelia of the lightshow and stage design was overtaken by Turner's charismatic, larger than life, antics. For the dedicated audience, a Hawkwind that was persistently satirised by its own frontman rather missed the point of the group itself. Turner delighted in his opportunities to endow his fellow musicians with verbal caricatures, "Pretty Boy Langton" attracted a particular amount of ribbing, whilst some Hawkwind standards were given punk-style overhauls that owed a lot to Turner's vocal style. Aside from this, Turner was dedicating songs to his favourite causes (The Motorcycle Action Group, Inner City Unit fans, and the striking miners) with such regularity that the rhythm of the shows became pantomime-like in their delivery.

"I sat down and had a conversation with Dave soon after the *Choose Your Masques* era, when Martin Griffin left," recalls Bainbridge. "Dave was quite interested in the notion of not having a drummer and just using a drum machine, going more electronic; just the two of us, with Huw on guitar. I said I didn't think it would work... and that was the worst decision I made. It might have been strange for a while, but pulled up something interesting."

In hindsight, that seems to encapsulate part of Dave Brock's motivation over the years. You can acknowledge the skill with which he's put together very different musicians and had them work together in an overall context, and that's a large part of his success. But there's another angle to that which is in his fascination with seeing how those different line-ups would work and being enthusiastic about pushing the structure of the band in different directions to achieve myriad different sounds while staying true to the idea of what the band is all about. I've already noted the idea that had Lemmy not been ejected from the band during the *Warrior...* era, then Brock was becoming interested in stripping the band down to a three-piece of just himself, Lemmy and a drummer (presumably Simon King at that point) and seeing how an abbreviated membership might work. Indeed, when that opportunity arose, with a different set of musicians, he steered the ship that away for a couple of years. So Harvey's recollections of a potential Hawkwind with a drum machine and the three 'core' members of the day ought perhaps to be seen in this context, another throw of the dice or turn of the cards to mix up the present and challenge what had gone before.

There also had always been this sort of interest within Hawkwind in pushing at the boundaries of music technology, and advances in recording techniques in the early 1980s accelerated those opportunities. "Technology was beginning to change rapidly, gadgets, electronic toys, were all getting quite remarkable and you could do things that you couldn't hitherto," considers Bainbridge, 'like harmonising your voice and making it sound like something else entirely. It just opened-up the notion of recording ideas, an array of different fields you could get involved with. If there is a new way of organising sound, then let's see how far we can take it."

**Dave Brock and Friends? Turner (L), Bainbridge (R)
(Oz Hardwick)**

A temporarily stripped-down line-up expressed their interest in contemporary electronic experimentation, whilst also exploring Brock's idea of a drummer-less band, by playing at the Electronica '83 festival in Milton Keynes (3rd September, 1983). Long-time Hawkwind enthusiast and photographer, Oz Hardwick, recalls the event as perhaps being "to the non-aficionado, a little bit po-faced. I bumped into Dave Brock at one of many one 'man and his gadgets workshops', and he greeted me with a shrug and a wry exclamation of 'Johnny Serious!'." Not so serious, though, was the approach of other members, who were billed as, alternatively, Uncle Nik and the ETs or Dave Brock & Friends. The latter title "prompted a cry of 'Dave Brock hasn't got any friends,' from Nik, who was in the audience," notes Hardwick.

In passing, Huw commented to Hardwick that it wasn't the sort of event for guitars. "Indeed, when the time came, Dave and Harvey took up places at their synths, with Nik in the middle by a clothes-rack from which hung sheets of scrap metal, oil cans and suchlike," but Huw didn't play at all. The set was a little under an hour, all improvised, with Nik coming up with some pretty tasteless – but funny – E.T. & small boys related lyrics, as well as his repeated mantra, 'It might get more exciting if we had a great big joint on stage.' All of this was delivered standing at attention (except when bashing the scrap metal) and in a deadpan voice." As for audience reaction, Oz concludes "I don't know what the chin-stroking electronic musos made of it." The next time that the band would play in a similar electronic format, Huw would join them.

It seems in retrospective an ill-defined and unfocused period despite the return of Nik Turner, with very little going on. They played only ten gigs during the whole of 1983, with a high-profile headlining appearance for a Motorcycle Action Group rally at Cricket St. Thomas and their final show of the year at Electronica being the only concerts of significant interest. There had always been a tradition of a UK winter tour, but with 1983 passing without any such outing for the band, and no serious vinyl output in evidence, the level of interest and commitment of even its most senior members seemed in doubt.

Hawkwind was not a fulltime occupation for any of its personnel during the early 1980s. Brock had spent time working on solo material, releasing a single, 'Social Alliance', on Flicknife in September 1983 and a much-loved, if rather demo-like, solo LP, *Earthed To The Ground*, in 1984. Langton pulled together his own outfit, the Lloyd-Langton Group and, under pressure from the availability of bootlegs of his band's shows, produced a live LP, *Outside the Law*, to be followed by several studio albums. Bainbridge had temporarily returned to his previous occupation, working as a supply teacher, while most extraordinarily, Turner was to become the Musical Director of Gerry Cottle's Circus!

"I got involved with Gerry through a girl called Katie, who was working for him at the time. She was somebody I'd met through a group of people called The Tibetan Ukrainian Mountain Troupe, who were a sort of circus group themselves. They'd developed out of a troupe put together by a couple of London-based clowns, who worked the free festivals and travelled together in old buses, like a sort of mobile commune. Katie mentioned to Gerry Cottle that she knew me, and Gerry was very interested, so I went along to meet him and discovered that he knew about my Hawkwind background and was quite impressed with that. Gerry had pitched his circus on Clapham Common for the Christmas season, so I went over before the first date for a couple of rehearsals and started to find the whole thing very interesting. Actually, Dave came to the show one evening; it must have been one of the times I was on good terms with him, or that he was on good terms with me."

The move to an independent label, with its limited financial firepower, meant a lack of promotional support and a reliance on existing recordings. In addition to the continuing *Friends and Relations* collections, *Zones* arrived: a compilation of previously unreleased archive tracks. A recording of Keith Hale's 'Dangerous Visions' and that curious mash-up of live track with Moorcock's narration glued-on, 'Running Through the Back Brain' are the better selections. But it's Dave's solo LP, wistfully noted as being "recorded at home in Devon whilst waiting for Hawkwind to get going again," that is the release post-RCA during this period that cuts the mustard and stands the test of time. It doesn't drift too far away from sounding like it could be the proto-demos for an unrecorded Hawkwind album, but at the same time it has points of difference to stand it aside from that notion, and a genuine charm.

**Nik joins the circus
(Oz Hardwick)**

In some ways, having what had become an ingrained distaste for the organised record industry, Brock was more comfortable dealing with an independent label, as he told Alan Moore in that interview for *Sounds*. "I think we're happy with the personal touch. You can get on the phone and get straight through… with RCA there's no contact with people. You'll have a guy on the case for a couple of weeks and then it'll just evaporate." However, without a major label channelling their energies, funding studio time, and scheduling new LPs, Hawkwind became rudderless, relying on the release of live material to maintain a degree of income.

13

An Era Ends, A New Chronicle Begins

**Friends Reunited, Part One: Brock and Lemmy, 1984
(Dave Brock Collection)**

During November 1983, there were efforts to mirror the concept of the Space Ritual with a new presentation, 'The Earth Ritual', with some formative planning taking place at Brock's Devon home. The ensuing album and tour was intended to be a reverse image of the original production, involving Celtic mythology, ley-lines and what might best be described as 'inner-space'. It would have been a chance for former band members to have some musical input, as Calvert was interested in working with Hawkwind again, and there was also a plan for Lemmy to appear.

Turner claims that he invited Barney Bubbles to assist with the production of the planned album. Turner's view was that, "He was doing it for me. I'm not being egotistical about it; we were good friends and if I gave it my seal of approval then he was happy." Barney had not worked with Hawkwind since he felt his work to have been compromised in the financially pragmatic restructuring of the Hawklords tour. He had enjoyed success in working with the maverick independent label, Stiff Records, and subsequently Jake Riviera's Radar Records, including the first half dozen sleeves for Elvis Costello & the Attractions. For a short time, Barney experimented in music video direction, including the classic

171

promo of 'Ghost Town' for the Specials and both 'Clubland' and 'New Lace Sleeves' for Costello. Barney had also collaborated, in early 1980, with Turner on a concept album, *Ersatz*, as The Imperial Pompadours. It absolutely wasn't an album that suggested his many and mercurial talents extended into producing a headline album for a major rock band at a particularly critical point in their history.

Ersatz is, for the main part, frankly unlistenable. A collection of cover-versions comprises the first side, whilst the second is an impenetrable reading of *Mein Kampf* set to backing music. Steve Pond, a former ICU member, details this on his website: "[Barney] chose all the cover versions, recorded them on a cheap cassette and only let the band hear the songs once." The band made notes as they listened and had to reassemble the tracks from whatever they'd gleaned.

Turner: "Barney produced the rock 'n' roll side and I produced the other side, about Adolf Hitler, which Barney had devised and which we co-wrote. It's a very strange record. Barney had all these ideas and said 'what shall we do with it?'" Turner suggested that they took a band, mostly members of ICU, down to his home in Wales, set up the equipment and then interchanged the instruments. "Barney played bass, I played bass and synthesiser, somebody had a go on the saxophone and we recorded about two hours of material which we used as the backing tapes for the 'Krankschaft Cabaret' side, Insolence Across the Nation. I worked in the studio with Barney on 'Fungus Amongst Us', 'Moo Go Gai Pan', 'Fu Manchu'; it was really brilliant because he did it in a very graphic way. He didn't have conventional ideas about how music should be produced. It was very minimalist and the placement of the instruments was very bizarre."

Phil Reeves: "Bob Calvert sang 'Brand New Cadillac' at the Imperial Pompadours' first session. He also did a great version of 'I'm a King Bee'; his throat bleeding at the end, such was the ferocity of his vocal." All sounds like great fun for an afternoon's diversion, or even an interesting artistic endeavour. You just wouldn't want to listen to the results.

"Nik, Bob and I converged at Brock's house," recalls Reeves, "Lemmy didn't arrive at all. It was late autumn [sometime around 11th or 12th November 1983] and it was cold. We were planning on staying five or six days as Nik and I had a few new pieces that we were hoping to demo. Bob had some poetry but no songs." Amongst Turner and Reeves' collection was a rough number called 'Stonehenge, Who Knows?' "Bob Calvert tried a few lyrics [for this song] but nothing gelled." With hindsight Reeves reflects this to be "a good thing, as I consider the later lyric to this probably to be Turner's *meisterwerk*." It eventually appeared on ICU's *Presidents Tapes* LP. The attempt to demo the 'Earth Ritual' project was a total misfire, however, Reeves recalling that "Dave wasn't even there most of the time, and when he was it was only to drive his new mini-digger."

Barney had recently returned from Australia and was extremely depressed about the rights and condition of the indigenous Aboriginal population. He also had a fixation about the Cold War, but his manic-depressive state had been fuelled over the previous three years by the deaths of his mother and father, from which

172

he never recovered. There is some confusion as to the final parting of the ways between Hawkwind and Barney Bubbles. Turner recalls that, during the demo sessions, "Dave came in and said, 'Barney's phoned up… I told him I didn't want him to come down here… he hasn't any money… I don't want him to produce the record.' I said, 'Why didn't you get him to speak to me? I'd have paid his train fare.'"

Phil Reeves has a different recollection of the events: "Nik and I would head out in the early hours looking for a telephone box. Nik would make long and expensive calls to Barney back in London where Barney was designing the stage sets for the 1984 tour. Barney was feeling very vulnerable."

Dead Fred – Amsterdam Melkweg 31/7/84
(Oz Hardwick)

Any plans that might have been developing around the 'Earth Ritual' concept that might have involved Barney Bubbles were fated to come to nought for the most tragic of reasons. On the 14th November 1983, the date of his late parents' wedding anniversary, Barney committed suicide. Will Birch, in his history of the British Pub Rock scene, *No Sleep 'Till Canvey Island*, describes Barney as "posthumously recognised as one of the most important graphic artists of his time." He went on to praise "a fine exhibition of Barney's work," staged in London during 2001.

In his seminal work, Birch clearly describes Bubbles as having been in a "three-year depression" leading up to his death. And so, all told, the event had something of a terrible inevitability to it, the genius artist who never quite received the recognition from the wider creative world that was his due during his lifetime, whose humility caused him to refrain from signing his own paintings. In a moving tribute letter to Barney, written for *Hawkfan* in January 1984, in which he characterised himself as Barney's "little brother," Turner paid tribute to the artistic genius he described as "too sensitive for the hard world of rock & roll."

"Punk graphics," wrote Turner, "Dada had nothing on you. Expressionism, eat your heart out Pablo Picasso." Turner summed up Barney Bubbles as being "a true artist – a seeker of truth. You always said, 'Does this way have a heart? If so, let's fucking do it!' I know all you ever wanted to do was paint."

With the news of Barney's passing, the 'Earth Ritual' demo sessions were ended, Reeves recalling how, "Nik, Bob and I packed up and left as quickly as possible."

That failure to pull together a full album for the pending spring 1984 tour left a void, partially filled by Flicknife issuing a 12" EP, *The Earth Ritual Preview*, with a rather hurried feel to it and not really giving any clue as to how the overarching concept that had been started on might have developed had circumstances and fate proved kinder.

It did contain two tracks that would stand the test of time within the Hawkwind setlist; the Lloyd-Langtons contributed Marion's Arthurian fantasy, 'Dragons & Fables', destined to become a much-loved part of the Hawkwind set, while 'Night of the Hawks' was a strident call to the faithful clearly inspired by the free festival culture and credited to Dave Brock, though some of the lyrics were provided by long-time fan Julian Bishop, who recalled that "It was written as a Hawkwind anthem, for everybody to sing along with! A reflection of the festival scenes… people looking like peacocks in their bright colours," and which hailed from as far back as 1977. Those tracks would indeed prosper over the years, despite the *Earth Ritual Preview* versions of them being curiously flat and muted affairs, though David Tibet, in Sounds, at least hailed 'Night of the Hawks' as "a crushing war song… [which] should be bought by everyone who has ever slagged off the 'Lords, including me." There was also 'Green Finned Demon', which had also aired on Brock's solo LP the previous year; again a number that received more justice in its interpretation by a future line-up.

It's just a very muddled release. Time has not warmed to it and it's almost a forgotten part of the catalogue in some ways. The three songs on the EP (there was an instrumental, 'Dream Dancers', included but it was an inconsequential filler), gave the impression of a record for expediency rather than creative intent and it's difficult to understand what the configuration of the band even was at that point. Without a full-time drummer, John Clark – an associate of Langton's side project - and the band's drum roadie Rob Heaton, later a member of New Model Army, were drafted in. There was a suggestion that Clark should join Hawkwind, though this was not met internally with any enthusiasm. Of more potential excitement was the appearance on bass and backing vocals of Lemmy on 'Night of the Hawks'.

"Bob was living down in Devon at the time; we'd gone into Jeff Hocking's studio in Bideford and recorded 'Night of the Hawks' and had already started writing stuff for the Earth Ritual, which is where 'Green Finned Demon' came from," recalls Brock. But with all this talk of returning members, Harvey Bainbridge at least was beginning to feel side-lined. "I remember going over to do some recording sessions at Dave's, some with Nik. But I knew other people were coming and going as well. Nik and Fred were staying in Dave's coach house. I did some recording with Jeff Hocking, but he didn't tape it. I remember feeling very angry and didn't take much notice after that. I knew Lemmy was coming to put stuff on, though I didn't know Bob was, and didn't bump into him." It all has the aura of groping around for direction, not knowing whether to look to the past or push on into the future.

I asked Frenchy Gloder about this time, several years after this book's original edition, while researching the history of Flicknife Records that became a feature for *Record Collector*. "Lemmy was a friend from the punk days and I just asked him as a favour because in my mind if Lemmy did it then the others would just follow, though he'd stated many times that he wouldn't record with Hawkwind again. He was supposed to do a track for the *Hawklords – Friends & Relations* album that we did in 2011 but he couldn't do it in the end, but I'm eternally grateful for him doing 'Night of the Hawks' because that created a big, big, wave. We were supposed to be doing an album, *The Earth Ritual*, which was going to be the follow up to *Space Ritual* with a gatefold… but some people who were in Hawkwind, such as Harvey, weren't on the A-side [of the ensuing EP] and so weren't going to be on the radio. Harvey was mightily pissed off, being their bass player at the time. And Harvey was the one who said that if it wasn't for Flicknife, RCA would have taken Hawkwind more seriously. I love Harvey, he's a great friend, but I don't know why he would say that."

Calvert wasn't involved in the spring tour, though it had been planned to build the shows around appearances by former band members. This left a gap in the structure of the shows which was once again largely filled by Turner's theatrical antics. Dave Anderson played three gigs, having remained on friendly terms with Turner, and having been contacted a few years previously by Brock that led to the *Space Ritual Volume 2* set. "Dave invited me to go and visit him," recalls Anderson. "He wanted to talk to me about all the [archive] tapes he'd got; he didn't know what to do with them. I suggested that he set-up a little label and release them; that led on to me licensing stuff from him and Nik."

**Dave Anderson & Huw Lloyd-Langton
Dunstable Queensway Hall 8/3/84
(Oz Hardwick)**

Anderson, appearing with Hawkwind for the first time since 1971, was stunned by the advances in infrastructure that the band commanded. "The last time I'd been on the road with Hawkwind was in the back of a transit van. I got a phone call asking me to play – I didn't even know where my bass was - turned up at the first gig to find three articulated trucks, an American mobile home, chefs... I thought 'It wasn't like this when I was on the road with them!' They had this brilliant backdrop of a hill, a couple of hawks on either side. Halfway through, the ultraviolet lights came on and the whole thing turned into the inside of a spaceship. It blew my mind."

At the band's two-night stopover at the Hammersmith Odeon, there were guest appearances by Lemmy and Moorcock. There had been some interest shown by Moorcock in contributing lyrics to the aborted *Earth Ritual* album, though "Bob called me and asked me not to go on with it, since it was his concept. I continued with my principle not to interfere with Bob's career and immediately dropped any work on *Earth Ritual.*" Moorcock had assisted with some of Calvert's earlier solo work ("I thoroughly enjoyed playing and doing background vocals on *Lucky Leif*"), but his great regret was "that we could no longer work together."

The tour included a fleeting appearance for 'Green Finned Demon', dropped after the opening night and not played live again until 1993. 'Dragons & Fables' and 'Night of the Hawks' fared much better, the first remaining in the set until 1988 and the latter a regular inclusion on subsequent tours, but there wasn't much to show for the overall misfire of 'Earth Ritual' and it essentially seems that post-*Choose Your Masques* there hadn't been any substantial development. For the tour, they freshened things up by adopting one of Turner's ICU songs, 'Watching the Grass Grow' and casting the net way back into the past for 'Born to Go' and 'Paradox', though neither made a particularly successful transition to the punk-toned style of the mid-80s.

Into that void of new material, Turner's theatrics became ever more pronounced. American fan, Roger Neville-Neil, following the first half of the tour ("about as close as I've come to running off to join a travelling circus") provided the inspiration for one of Turner's most explicitly political sequences. "I went to Soho and bought an American flag," he recalls. "Nik had joked that as I was American I should carry one with me. So I became Uncle Sam, lurking in the audience. Hawkwind would start playing 'Uncle Sams on Mars' and Nik would suddenly spot me in the audience. 'I see you out there, Uncle Sam.' He'd take the flag from me and march around with it on stage." The song involved a long and rambling diatribe on the evils of the USA and ended with Turner wiping his rear on the flag. "He got a bit carried away and apologised after the show. I laughed and said I loved it... so the flag became one of Nik's props for the tour."

Reviewing for *Sounds*, David Tibet noted that "Their espousal of the anarchistic 'Stop the City' protest... was another reminder of just how close Hawkwind have always been in sentiment to groups like Crass and Conflict."

Following on from the Earth Ritual tour, there were two idiosyncratic gigs that saw Calvert returning for guest appearances; the last occasions that he would appear with Hawkwind.

On 22nd April, Calvert joined Brock, Langton and Bainbridge for an impromptu hour of music at the Easter Science Fiction Convention (SeaCon). It was a musically loose affair, akin to the earlier Sonic Assassins gigs or the Electronica '83 performance, Bob arriving with his wasp synthesiser and reading from a recently published lyric book. "We played in this really small room, doing this weird electronic thing. I've got a tape of it, quite awful," notes Brock. "I think it was an extension of the ideas Dave had a few years earlier, when he was talking about trying to go electronic," considers Bainbridge. "I thought it worked okay; doing Hawkwind songs, but in a totally ad-hoc way."

Oz Hardwick recalls "an over-zealous security official who, clearly not knowing who he was, confiscated Bob's radio cassette on the way in. Calvert was going to use some shortwave signals, apparently." In contrast to the Electronica gig, "Huw had decided this time that a guitar-synth would be appropriate," which Hardwick felt, "gave proceedings a much harder edge. Twenty years on, it still stands out as an amazing set, very powerful, pulsing and purposeful." Hardwick photographed the show, capturing the atmosphere and style of the show for posterity.

Bob Calvert, Ramsgate Marina Park 28/5/84
(Oz Hardwick)

The following month, at a 'Battle of the Bands' in Ramsgate (28th May), Calvert joined the full Hawkwind line-up, again playing his Wasp but contributing less to the vocals. "It was a great, loose, sprawling set, focusing on the special alchemy that occurred with Dave, Bob and Nik at the front of the band," comments Hardwick. It seems a reflection of Calvert's ambivalence to Hawkwind that his approach to these two appearances were so different. Foursquare at the front, contributing his electronic improvisations and his masterful vocal deliveries at SeaCon, but treating the Ramsgate show as simply an opportunity to catch up on old friendships. Perhaps, with his fading public profile and with Turner dominating presentation in the bigger Ramsgate show, he felt intimidated, his pronounced fear of rejection heightened by the possible comparisons with former glories.

The creative shortcomings of the post-RCA Hawkwind of 1983 and the Earth Ritual shows of spring 1984 seem to have been exacerbated by an attempt to recapture past successes. The reinstatement of Turner, who appeared to have a free and increasingly uncontrollable hand in setting the visual and theatrical direction, had become a blind alley. With very little new material generated, and the adaptations of old numbers taking them further away from their original concepts than ever, there was a sharpened sense of a need for either closure or renewal. Had a reintroduction of Bob Calvert occurred, then almost certainly it would have reenergised the situation. In his solo work, he was still demonstrating the sharp, incisive overview of modern scientific perils that had been such a key element of the Charisma period; and that would likely have countered the excesses of Turner, pushing Nik's flamboyancy out to the fringes. But the whole 'Earth Ritual' project looks now to have been a final attempt to revisit glory years.

Before 'Earth Ritual', Hawkwind was a band that could be seen as having continuity back to its origins in Ladbroke Grove. Aside from the group's founder members, as replacements arrived they tended (Ginger Baker's convenient recruitment aside) to be pulled from the same Notting Hill fraternity that the band itself had sprung from. Adrian Shaw, Simon House, Tim Blake were all regular faces around the *Frendz* magazine, Clearwater Productions, All Saints Hall scene. Paul Rudolph had been associated through his membership of The Pink Fairies. Musicians such as Harvey Bainbridge and Martin Griffin were the exceptions to this, but they arrived out of Brock's Devon-based associations and originally as a side project to the main event, being drawn into the line-up because of the Hawklords situation. After 'Earth Ritual', the musicians who came into the band were drawn from the free festivals, or were those who could claim influence from Hawkwind; it's as though the membership began to regenerate itself from its own legacy as people came into the band because of their love of what had been done before. The great thing about that was that it brought in people who felt passionate about the idea of Hawkwind, who wanted to add to the legend, and that had the effect of renewing and revitalising it in a way that the 'Earth Ritual' singularly failed to do.

That year's Stonehenge Festival, the final drawing together of the faithful before it collapsed from internal and external pressures, not least that of the antipathy of the Thatcher government, saw Brock conducting his own Prime Ministerial reshuffle of his available pool of musicians, with Bainbridge reassigned to keyboards, and a young bass player, Alan Davey, recruited in his place. Davey had written to Brock, putting himself forward as a potential replacement for Bainbridge, and then met with Dave at the Ipswich Gaumont on the Earth Ritual tour (9th March). This led to an exploratory session between Brock and Davey at Brock's home studio and the result was a trial at the free festival for a musician who would become one of Hawkwind's longest serving members. "It was a blood transfusion," comments Brock wryly.

Recent Hawkwind tours had met with a good deal of dissatisfaction from their own fandom, and that manifested itself in the music press. One letter in *Sounds* wondered why Brock and Langton were allowing Turner to take the band down a punk route. Davey was another Hawkwind fan unhappy with the sound that the contemporary version was generating. "After I saw Hawkwind in 1983, I wrote to Dave and told him it was completely the wrong direction. What he needed to do was to mix *Warrior on the Edge of Time* - that sound - with the technology of *Church of Hawkwind*, which was one of the best albums. At the time, there was nothing like it around."

The new boy: Alan Davey
(Oz Hardwick)

Davey, only twenty years old and working his way into a band of seasoned veterans, was undaunted. "It was really because what I thought Hawkwind should be doing and what Dave thought [were the same]. He just didn't have anybody around him at the time that could see it. When I sent him a tape, and we talked on the phone, it must have given him some sort of boost."

He'd first encountered Hawkwind aged twelve, when his brother played him *Quark Strangeness & Charm*. In it, he found a synergy with the tele-fantasy programmes which he enjoyed. "All the old sci-fi stuff, Gerry Anderson's *UFO*, *Star Trek*... they all used these weird sound effects, like the stuff done by the BBC Radiophonic Workshop. When I heard 'Spirit of the Age' it sounded like all that stuff and that's what drew me into Hawkwind, I wasn't into any music at the time."

The addition of Davey on bass and the moving of Bainbridge to keyboards was an occasion when, though his judgement proved sound, and the decision beneficial both to the band's creativity and longevity, Brock demonstrated an inability to impart difficult news to his associates. For Davey, the way Bainbridge accepted him into the camp revealed the man's character. "He bought me some hash cake and we went off together and had a chat. He was a real gentleman that day, and I will always respect him for it."

Langton saw the change as being of artistic value, redeveloping "the enthusiasm within the whole situation. Alan had always been a complete Hawkwind freak and Danny [Thompson, a friend of Davey's who filled in on drums at Stonehenge] was another fan and they played their hearts out." However, Huw was critical of the way these musicians were installed in the Hawkwind camp. "As far as I know, Alan hassled Dave concerning the next time a bass player was needed: he was the man. But it was a little bit sad when it happened. It was the last official Stonehenge, and Harvey had rung me that morning and said, 'Are you going?' I said I thought so… Harvey said he didn't know what was going on, he'd been told he should just bring his keyboards, as there would be a few bass players there. Harvey was confused by it, and so was I because nobody had spoken to me. We turned up there and low-and-behold, Alan and Danny were there… but there weren't any other bass players."

Nik Turner, Jenny Chapman, Alan Davey
Stonehenge 1984 (Oz Hardwick)

"Alan stuck to my side like glue all weekend, saying, 'I'm really sorry.' Huw was wandering around saying, 'It's absolutely disgusting,' and Clive [Deamer], who Danny replaced, didn't actually turn up," notes Bainbridge. "I told Dave I thought that was it. Dave said, 'Oh, we want you to play synthesisers,' and I said, 'Well, I'm not a keyboard player' and left it at that." Bainbridge's departure was more from wounded pride than anything else and he returned as the band's fulltime keyboard player for the autumn 1984 UK tour.

The fact that the two members who had the most influence in rebuilding Hawkwind out of the ashes of the Hawklords concept had no idea that this change was imminent is surprising. From the playing of Brock, Davey and Thompson it was clear that this new rhythm section had been rehearsing together. Their contribution to the sound was very tight compared to that of an extremely below par Langton and a disheartened Bainbridge. "I can't play the piano, but I kind of know my way around the theory side well enough, and I do enjoy playing synthesisers and making interesting noises. In hindsight, it turned out a decent move, though I would have preferred to have stayed playing bass." But Langton saw this reorganisation as good for Bainbridge. "Harvey's far too intelligent to be a bass player. It suited him much better to be a keyboard player. He has all these really good ideas ..."

Not surprisingly, Turner is particularly critical of Brock's recruitment of Alan Davey, and of Dave's motives for doing so. "[Davey] joined the band as a fan, because he could play like Lemmy. Well, at the time there was already a bass player in the band." Bainbridge had shouldered a fair amount of negativity about his bass playing, despite occupying the position for six years. Turner saw such criticism as unfair. "Harvey was in Sonic Assassins, then in the Hawklords, so I think Harvey's quite a good bass player. He's not Stanley Clarke or Charlie Mingus, but it's all horses for courses."

"Originally, the band to me was very much a communal thing," says Turner. "That faded away as people left, or were coerced into leaving, or manipulated out, myself included, to the point where Dave was the only original member. When Alan Davey joined the band, only Dave had a say in it. People were in the band at Dave's behest, until he didn't want them anymore and they left."

Hawkwind performed three times during the 1984 Stonehenge Festival. The full band played on the 20th June, a set similar in content to the Earth Ritual tour but also including 'Brainbox Pollution' (the B-side to 'Urban Guerrilla' in 1973). They also played a more improvised set the following morning without Huw and finally a loose arrangement of both Hawkwind and non-Hawkwind numbers on 22nd June. The last set, in the 'Tibetan Tent' as 'Snorkwind' and minus Bainbridge, was meant to be Hawkwind playing a collection of songs by 'Jenny Chapman and friends', though it effectively turned into a third Hawkwind set, including 'Brainstorm', 'Master of the Universe' and 'The Right Stuff'. It was a low-key end to a successful festival for the band, though for the organisers the antipathy towards the annual running of Stonehenge from the Thatcher government was reaching fever-pitch.

At the beginning of 1985, work began on an ambitious studio album, *The Chronicle of the Black Sword*, and tour focused around Michael Moorcock's 'Elric of Melnibone' fantasy novels.

182

Before the project's completion, Turner was sacked for a second time, widening the rift between himself and Brock and having a significant impact that remains to this day. "I'd set up a management deal for the band with a guy called Jim White, as I had with Tony Howard… and a similar thing happened, a sort of manipulative gesture," says Turner. "We'd been rehearsing for the *Black Sword*. I'd read all of Mike Moorcock's books. Dave said he found them boring and couldn't be bothered to read them, Huw also said he couldn't be bothered to read them. I'd written songs that were relevant to them. I hadn't spent much time in the rehearsal rooms working out the three-chord music; I'd spent my time reading and writing."

Alan Davey: "We were rehearsing the Black Sword songs at Rockfield. Nik was doing some of the vocals, it sounded all right, but in the background, there was this thing going on to oust him, so he never made it on to the tour. He did write some lyrics, but they didn't get used."

"When there was a meeting called I didn't think anything of it, I didn't attend, thinking I didn't need to, until I received a phone call telling me I'd been sacked from the band! I couldn't understand why…" Turner claims to have visited the remaining members while they were rehearsing for the Black Sword tour: "I was passing by, on my way to London and said, 'Well, what's the problem? Why have you sacked me?' Dave said, 'It's not me! It's everybody else!'" Conflicting views came from the rest of the band. "Alan Davey said, 'Well, my mates don't think you're what Hawkwind is all about!'" Bemused by this assertion, Turner claims he then spoke to Langton, who, he says, told him, "I think you're trying to turn us into a punk band."

"So, Alan's view was based on what his friends said, and Huw's was probably because he is a Jehovah's Witness and didn't like the fact that I was such an exhibitionist," comments Turner, with a smile. "I never had a problem with Huw, and got on very well with him, so I was quite perplexed!" Turner traces any disagreements with Langton over the theatrical elements of Turner's performances to the autumn 1984 shows. Turner's antics had become ever more outrageous, opening the shows by emerging, centre stage, from a coffin, playing his saxophone to 'Ghost Dance'. "I had this idea of generating phoney mass hysteria. I went to Oxfam and bought about twenty suits, for a quid each, that all fitted me and I slashed the seams with a razor blade. They looked like suits, but if you pulled them the arm would fall off. Before the encore I'd put on one of these suits, then during the encore I'd go down into the audience and somebody would pull my sleeve, and it would fall off. Then they'd get the idea and someone would pull the other sleeve, then my trouser leg and that would all fall off, my jacket would fall in half and they'd go off with these bits of souvenir. But in some cases, I wouldn't have anything on underneath. Huw was quite flabbergasted."

Langton: "Nik has so many different talents, and ways of going about things. Sometimes he's a smooth jazz man, but at that point with Hawkwind he was just sailing onto the stage with his roller-skates and a horn sticking out of his head, and that's just Nik." Huw didn't feel that was what Hawkwind was about, "and other people in the band didn't either." And that's the rub of it; since Nik's return to the band it had ever more become the 'Nik Turner Show' in many eyes, and where the theatrical presence of Robert Calvert in the latter part of the 70s had added to the narrative of Hawkwind shows, the flamboyancy of Nik Turner had a completely different effect, side-lining the overall show in favour of a single focal point. It simply wasn't working.

During the writing of what became *The Chronicle of the Black Sword*, there was on the of band's rare television performances, on the Channel 4 programme *ECT* (26th April, 1985), playing 'The Right Stuff' and 'Angels of Death'. Though the 'Silver Machine' clip had played on *Top of the Pops* back in the day, and there had been the appearance on Marc Bolan's show, Hawkwind appearances on British television screens had been few and far between, with the only other opportunity, being an aborted booking on Chris Tarrant's late-night ITV show *OTT*, an 'adult' version of anarchic kids Saturday programme *Tiswas*. Despite being moved off the top billing of *ECT* due to the last-minute booking of the American band, Warrior, this latest television appearance managed to capture at least some of the atmosphere of a genuine Hawkwind gig. Playing in a redundant power station ("like a disused hanger in *Red Dwarf*," recalls Bainbridge), the band commenced with the double-headed Hawkwind logo emblazoned across the screen. Brock's distinctive grinding guitar chords were joined by Davey's rolling bass and then an electric lead guitar count-in from Langton to cue Bainbridge and drummer Clive Deamer. At the end of 'The Right Stuff', Brock wryly advised the audience, "We like smoking the right stuff, you know!"

"I thought it would be a good idea if they made me up like an old crone," says Bainbridge. "If I had to sit behind keyboards, I could merge into the background. I went up to makeup and said, 'Make me all gnarled so that I look like part of the background'. So two girls got to work, and then I got dragged down to a photo shoot. When I looked in the mirror I was horrified! They made me into this gloriously good-looking woman! We had the photos taken, and I was trying to hide at the back but the rest of them kept pushing me to the front. After the session, I told Dave I didn't want the photos to come out; then we did the *Friday Rock Show* [for BBC Radio 1] and they used the photo on the contents page of the *Radio Times*."

By the time the band were out on the road again, some of the material that would comprise *The Chronicle of the Black Sword* had made it into the live set on a work-in-progress basis. Bainbridge's instrumental 'Shade Gate', 'Sleep of 1,000 Tears' and an early version of Brock's 'Song of the Swords' were played on a short UK tour that spring. Also introduced, slightly outside the Elric theme, but tied to Moorcock's 'Eternal Champion' characters via his Jerry Cornelius stories, was 'Needle Gun'. Included on the *Black Sword* album as a Brock solo credit, the lyrics were provided by Roger Neville-Neil, who describes them "written on the USS Fox for a dare. I was reading one of the Jerry Cornelius books when a crew member challenged me to write a lyric while he watched me do it." Though

Neville-Neil toyed with the idea of sending the result to Lemmy, it was put to him that it would make a great Hawkwind song. "I suggested that the chorus should be rewritten, I thought Dave could come up with something catchier than I'd thrown on the page in haste. He did a great job, the result being a fun sing-along type song." Widely held to be an anti-heroin song, the lack of a credit for the lyricist was "due to the subject matter. I didn't want to end up blacklisted by the government."

Bob, Huw, Dave. SeaCon 1984
(Oz Hardwick)

The largest operation ever mounted by the Wiltshire Police Constabulary prevented the 1985 Stonehenge Free Festival from taking place. On 1st June, the mass buses and vans of the 'Peace Convoy', travelling from Savernake Forest, were blockaded five miles away from the stones and trapped in fields and narrow country lanes. Witnesses contend that the convoy attempted to negotiate a departure from Wiltshire and an abandonment of the festival. The police were clearly in no mood to countenance either. The objective became apparent; nothing less than the systematic destruction of the convoy's vehicles, possessions and way of life.

After a day of stalemate, what became known as 'The Battle of the Beanfield' started; estimates of between 700 and 1600 police rampaged through the convoy, destroying whatever they could. Nick Davies, of *The Guardian*, wrote "There was glass breaking, people screaming, black smoke towering out of burning caravans and everywhere there seemed to be people being bashed and flattened... men, women and children." Reporting for ITN News, Kim Sabido described "some of the most brutal police treatment of people that I've witnessed in my entire career as a journalist."

Kris Tait recalls being told how, "They came in at teatime and shot all the dogs. Then deliberately sent the parents to different prisons throughout the country, and put their children into Social Services." It had been made clear for many months running up to the Solstice that the traditional free festival wasn't going to be permitted to go ahead, so Hawkwind weren't planning on their annual appearance, but their response was a gut reaction to support the people who had made up much of their audience for so long. "We launched a fund," says Kris, "because we were doing a few dates around the time. We did a collection and sent it down to get all the vehicles out of the pound. Vehicles that were completely roadworthy, that people were living in, were getting confiscated. The police were after any vehicles that weren't taxed or roadworthy, and people were saying 'well, mine is roadworthy' [makes sound of breaking glass] 'It isn't now!'... Then piling up kids' toys and setting fire to them."

Hawkwind, along with Here & Now and Ozric Tentacles, joined those elements of the convoy able to regroup, and played to around three thousand people on White Horse Hill, at Westbury, as Brock recalls: "It poured with rain and we nearly got electrocuted. But it got seedy there as well, somebody's bus got burnt, it was like the end of the festivals. Things had got so big and corruption had crept in. There were a lot of people who were involved with us, who would try and speak with the police and amiably try to keep relations together. But it was like outlaws, and you can't have outlaws, in a sense, in any country."

"They'd erected this makeshift stage, with a tarpaulin hooked up between a couple of buses and a generator," adds Bainbridge. "I remember standing in pools, with the rain dripping through the tarpaulin and wondering when it was we were going to get blown up!" He viewed the whole relocated festival as "a kind of siege. It was right down in Ministry of Defence country, so you had helicopters flying around... the police had set up roadblocks at the bottom of the hill. You could leave but you couldn't come back up."

"I had to go and call Danny [Thompson], tell him where it was," recalls Davey. "I drove off the site, down to a telephone box. I was in it for about twenty seconds before being pulled out by two policemen and told to leave... I wasn't sure if I'd get back into the site afterwards." Just as at the previous Stonehenge, Thompson drummed for Hawkwind. Unlike 1984, the recruitment was on a full-time basis, and he remained in the band until mid-1988.

"We had a young music journalist with us," says Bainbridge, "who had never seen anything like it, the running battles and then having to chug off down the hill to be besieged by the police and the army. Surprisingly, it wasn't scary, it was just a question of how far were they prepared to go. If there wasn't anything illegal happening in terms of revolution, there was nothing much they could do about it."

Aside from the chaotic performance at Westbury, where the current members were joined, or gate-crashed, by Nik Turner, depending on who tells the story, the only other Hawkwind appearances before the autumn's *Black Sword* shows were the session for the Friday Rock Show, an anti-heroin concert at Crystal Palace (24th August) and a 'Live Aid' festival in Norwich on 31st August. At Crystal Palace, the band were joined by Lemmy for 'Brainstorm'. Though he noted Alan Davey as "the perfect replacement for Lemmy," Derek Oliver, reviewing the gig, enthused that "the man-in-black dutifully provided extra metallic weight with his customary and unique bass technique." Less customary was the bizarre appearance of 'Forces' Sweetheart' Dame Vera Lynn as headliner for the Crystal Palace show. Brock recalls having to line up on stage with his family and the other acts (including Spear of Destiny and Doctor and the Medics) to be photographed with the World War II icon. As one website reviewer recalled: "virtually all Dame Vera Lynn saw of the crowd was their backs as they made a pretty swift exit following Hawkwind. 'We'll Meet Again', Vera? Unlikely."

Huw, Lemmy & Alan. Crystal Palace 24/8/85
(Dame Vera not pictured)
(P!KN!K)

The Chronicle of the Black Sword, Hawkwind's only full-length studio album for Flicknife, did extremely good business in the UK Independent chart, but merely grazed the mainstream Top 75. The LP demonstrated how far Hawkwind had come from their dalliance with the industrial rock music of the RCA era. Though leaning in places in the direction of a softened heavy metal, it also revealed a mellower, more ambient tone that reflected Davey's insistence that a fusion of the driving *Warrior on the Edge of Time* and the electronic experimentalism found in *Church of Hawkwind* could create a new musical agenda for the band.

Arguably the finest Hawkwind LP of the 1980s, *The Chronicle of the Black Sword* found favour with the music press. David Tibet, critiquing the record in comparison to Killing Joke's Night Time album, noted 'Horn of Destiny' was, "as good as anything Jaz and the boys are producing at Joke Mansion." In *Kerrang!,* Derek Oliver was moved to say that 'Song of the Swords' was "on a par with anything on the *Levitation* album" and 'The Demise' was "the prize-winning sound of urban spiritualism in operation." But Oliver saved his most incisive commentary for the method that the band were employing to push the envelope on their musical techniques. "Hawkwind's carefully cultivated enigma works by the creation of illusion through the sharp contrast of the traditional ('spiralling oscillators') with the future present ('modern' production techniques, 'fashionable' ethics)."

"Hawkwind might be a cultural institution," wrote one journalist, "but their noise is so perfectly realised and empathetic they defy the unwritten rules of consumption. They are their own fashion and style."

"I thought the concept translated very well," comments Bainbridge. "The live show did a good job of putting over the story. We took the show to the World Science Fiction Convention in Brighton [28th August, 1987] and some photographs appeared in the *Mail on Sunday*. The colour photo of the stage set was tremendous and must have been a really exciting thing to watch. It ran the danger of being a bit Spinal Tap-ish but it avoided that trap. It set an interesting mood and atmosphere."

From the *Space Ritual* era came Tony Crerar to play the character of Elric ("Tony was a terrific mime artist," says Bainbridge), whilst Kris Tait appeared as the tragic love interest, Zarozinia. As the story unfolded, Danny Thompson would emerge from behind his drum-kit to play the villain of the piece, Theleb Kaama, though the part was also played at times by friend of the band Tim Pollard. It's Pollard who appears on the opening sequence of the ensuing video, menacingly drawing his sword across his throat; he was later rewarded for his efforts on the tour by being presented with the Stormbringer stage prop, a wooden sword painted black with ultraviolet 'runes' written on it. "Danny would have been happier as an actor… if he pushed himself in that direction he'd be as happy as Larry, the perfect character for it. He's got the presence, six-foot-six. We were the funniest rhythm section in rock music at the time, drummer six-foot-six", bass player five-foot-four"!" says Davey.

**Elric meets his maker. Mike Moorcock and Tony Crerar
Hammersmith Odeon, December 1985
(P!KN!K)**

"The whole thing was structured quite well, it looked a lot more complicated to perform than it was to plan," Davey adds. "All the books had been read by the band, so it was easy to pick moments out and deal with them. We sat down, went through the books, decided on the significant parts and concentrated on them; otherwise we'd have got hopelessly bogged down and ended up with a ten-hour show that would have bored everybody. Tony Crerar choreographed all the dances routines. He was great, a real professional. He came down for a week before the tour and worked it all out. Without Tony's involvement, I don't think it would have looked so good."

Michael Moorcock, his imposing figure incongruously clad in full dinner jacket and white scarf, appeared at the Hammersmith Odeon (3rd & 4th December, 1985) to elucidate the proceedings with newly written linking material, whilst Bainbridge provided the story's narration throughout the tour. "I wore a tuxedo for the occasion, since I was just about to go on board the QE2 for a voyage to the US," says Moorcock. "I told the audience I was their waiter for the night. I distributed a bunch of Elric books, throwing them into the audience and was shocked when people tore them to bits trying to get them!"

"On the outside, Michael likes to give the impression that he's quite soft but underneath he's grim and determined," suggests Bainbridge. "I certainly don't think he takes things like Hawkwind too seriously. He was never disparaging, he enjoyed being there and we all enjoyed his company. He's a rock-and-roller at heart, but all his energies lie in being a 'proper' novelist, the music's just fun."

"My problem with the *Black Sword* album was that I'd worked out some elaborate stuff with Nik Turner, including costumes. We had decided it would be an entirely new stage production, using no old Hawkwind numbers," comments Moorcock. "We had been disappointed before when Dave had originally decided to do a new show and had then fallen back on old standards. However, Nik was again squeezed out of the band. He came to me and said it had all been done behind his back." Moorcock notes that he took this "with a pinch of salt," but that he considered "Nik was a friend I had more in common with than Dave. I felt Nik was the 'spirit' of Hawkwind, even though I understood he could be irritating." The result was that "I decided quietly that I would do the gigs I had agreed to do, but no more."

**Black Sword Stage – Autumn/Winter 1985
(Oz Hardwick)**

The Black Sword tour was followed up with the 2-LP *Live Chronicles* the following year on Douglas Smith's GWR label, recorded at the Hammersmith Odeon. There was also a video of the highlights, particularly interesting in capturing some of Moorcock's narration from the show. Doug Smith recalled to me, for *Record Collector*, that "*Live Chronicles* was the first thing we put out on GWR. They'd asked me if I'd get involved in management again and I said no, I wasn't interested. I was working principally as a label, so I said I'd guide them and release their records. GWR had a whole lot of stuff: King Kurt, Anti-Nowhere League..."

"As far as I've heard from the horse's mouth," Langton considered, "the fans seem to think the live album is the better of the two." The *Live Chronicles* set, was a better reflection of the Black Sword concept, since the extra space enabled the full range of material from the show to be included and, if you place the music side-by-side with its studio compatriot, there is a sense that it has more zip, more verve, and that the studio version sounds softer and over-produced in comparison. Though the album didn't feature Moorcock's on the night narration, due to a long-term disagreement between Moorcock and Smith, his recitals were reinstated on a subsequent CD release by Rob Godwin's Griffin label, and in the UK when that portion of the catalogue re-emerged on Cherry Red's 'Atomhenge' imprint.

Langton's contributions to the stage show are highlights of *Live Chronicles*. 'Sea King' appeared on the studio LP minus one verse, but his two other major contributions to the show, 'Moonglum' and 'Dreaming City', were not included at all. Ironically, aside from 'Needle Gun', these last two songs would be the most enduring live picks from the Elric tour. 'Dreaming City' continued to be played for most of the following year, whilst the crowd-pleasing 'Moonglum' stayed in the setlist for the remainder of Langton's second tenure in Hawkwind and was revisited in his third stint with the band in 2001. Marion Lloyd-Langton: "I was working at Chappell's Music in Bond Street at the time and wrote the lyrics during my lunch hour! The character reminded me of Huw in some respects... fiercely loyal to his friends."

"The trouble with studio stuff is that some people will steam in, determined to get their own material down, but I'm not that way inclined, I don't fight for it," explained Langton. "Harvey would play a couple of synthesiser 'joining' pieces and they'd get named as tracks for publishing rights!" It's such a shame, really. Songs such as the ones written for the Elric tour, as well as overlooked Langton numbers such as 'Got Your Number' (recorded for a 1985 BBC Friday Rock Show session) and terrific 'Mark of Cain', played on the autumn 1984 tour, languished as temporary inclusions in the live set without being committed to vinyl from studio sessions. They number among the great 'lost' Hawkwind songs.

14

Agents of Chaos Get Back To Their Roots

**Hawkwind in unusually settled formation, 1988
Thompson, Brock, Lloyd-Langton, Davey, Bainbridge
(Roger Neville-Neil)**

The Black Sword concept having reached its natural conclusion, the band settled into a period where the line-up remained unusually constant but without new projects to develop, the music stagnated. "It was all becoming a bit controlled, in my opinion," says Bainbridge. "Dave was kind of reining it in and you just salvaged what you could. Rehearsing was a big financial drain. That was the difference between being financed by a major company and just living off record sales." Bainbridge notes the other discrepancy between members in that "when you had a variety of personnel, who have come in at different times, they'd not really got the financial weight that Dave had from being around all those years."

There was the occasional high-profile festival performance, including a headline appearance at the 1986 Reading Festival. Reading had been cancelled in 1984 and not revived the following year. On its return, the event made a transition out of its traditional domination by heavy metal bands, with Killing Joke and The Mission appearing. Alongside them were the new wave of British psychedelic bands such as Doctor & The Medics, and Zodiac Mindwarp & The Love

Reaction, both having something of a stylistic nod in the direction of Hawkwind. "That was a big gig for us, and quite a welcome one," says Bainbridge. "Lemmy came and played on that one [for the 'Silver Machine' encore], and things like that helped finance the band, kept the whole thing going."

Davey: "Lemmy was coming on, and I'd said before the gig, 'let's do something with the basses, smash them together. Imagine that through the great PA.' I wasn't sure whether he was into it, but the first thing he did was wander up and started sliding the basses together. It sounded like somebody was dragging corrugated iron across a concrete floor at about a hundred thousand watts! Lemmy's amp was next to Huw, Lemmy being loud Huw began pulling Lemmy's plug out of the amp. In the end Lemmy gave up, didn't even play on half of it. Some people say that I've copied Lemmy, but I played like that right from the word go, before I knew he played like that. When I first got a bass guitar, I didn't know what I was supposed to do with it, so I started strumming it, playing lead on it. It dawned on me one day that was what he was doing, but I just played it wrong." Once Davey had discovered this parallel between what he'd taught himself to do, and what Lemmy had been doing in Hawkwind, he revelled in it, "but it was a mad coincidence."

The following year, there were a couple of other major gigs, in the 'Super Tent' at Finsbury Park at the first Acid Daze Festival (28th August, 1987) and again for the second in Leeds on 12th December. At Finsbury, where Lemmy once again made a guest appearance, the bill was again filled-out with contemporary British psychedelia: Doctor & The Medics, Ozric Tentacles, Pop Will Eat Itself (who had covered 'Orgone Accumulator' on vinyl) and Gaye Bikers On Acid. Naz Nomad & The Nightmares, Dave Vanian's spin-off from The Damned, were also on the bill. At Leeds, Robert Calvert appeared with his band The Starfighters.

Brock: "We hadn't seen each other for a while, but we shook hands and started discussing the Earth Ritual again." Davey notes that one of his great regrets was "not playing with Bob Calvert; or with Simon King. It looked like Bob might join us again, but it never happened."

Instead, the Black Sword line-up cut a second studio album, on GWR Records, *The Xenon Codex*. "We were thinking about *Ledge of Darkness*," recalls Davey, referring to a long-harboured plan to complete Michael Butterworth's trilogy. "But we got this phone call saying that as there was a tour coming in five weeks, we had to do a new album, press it, do all the artwork… and we couldn't get *Ledge of Darkness* together in that time, we just had to use whatever songs we had hanging around."

Guy Bidmead was drafted to produce the album, an unlikely choice who had previously engineered albums for more mainstream heavy metal bands such as Motörhead and Whitesnake. "We couldn't understand it," comments Brock, "he didn't actually do anything, just sat in a chair." Bainbridge agrees with this assessment of Bidmead's contribution. "I gave him this weird thing called 'E.M.C.', which was this attempt to do trance music, although it didn't work out unfortunately. [Bidmead] didn't know what to do with it, so I just said, 'I'll do it then.' He made Dave's songs quite pokey and commercial, 'Heads' and 'Wastelands of Sleep' sounded pretty smart."

Once again, Brock looked outside the band for lyrical contributions, choosing two further pieces by Roger Neville-Neil. For the album opener, he selected 'The War I Survived', a lyric that Roger had "based on Kurt Vonnegut's novel, *Slaughterhouse Five*. I was thinking back to the days when Calvert would select a book for inspiration. I was consciously trying to write something that might sound inspired by Calvert. I listened to his music a lot, getting into his words and wit." The second Neville-Neil lyric was 'Heads', which had the working title 'Spare Parts'. "I had joined the Oxford University Speculative Fiction Group, which is where I first heard about Alcor Life Extension Foundation, a cryogenics company in California where you can arrange to have yourself frozen for the future. Only one catch – you had to die first! It sounded like a good idea for a Hawkwind song… what would it be like to be frozen alive? What would be your last thoughts as you drifted off into oblivion?" Hawkwind introduced 'Heads' into their set during 1987, the first time Roger heard the completed song. "I purposely worked-in the necromancy reference ('Necromancy lives forever/Preserved within a jar') as a joke to get the gossip-types jumping to conclusions. It was great, Dave repeating that line, building it up. One of those conspiracy know-it-all types turned to me and proudly smiled. 'I knew he was into witchcraft!' I cracked up laughing."

'Sword of the East', with its references to the 'blood of the past' seems a spiritual successor to 'Assassins of Allah', and indeed Davey drew on his deep interest in things Arabian to produce a song "about the troubles of the Middle East, all arguing with each other even though they believe in the same thing. The Arabic scale was the first I learned when I got a bass. Ever since I was a kid, I loved the imagery." And if that sounds a bit on the profound and heavy side of things, there was the madcap 'Good Evening', which closed proceedings. "It seemed like we all went mad, plugged in and hit the record button; 'Good Evening' was the result. Dave put all the weird noises on the end."

Bainbridge felt his contributions were once again increasingly marginalised by this time. "I reckon I was living a bit more on the outskirts of what was going on. Possibly I wasn't enjoying it anymore. It seemed a bit of a closed shop with Alan and Dave rehearsing between themselves and everybody else having to figure out what it was they were working on. But if you don't have your own material worked out and ready to go, it becomes the 'one-man-band' scenario." Bainbridge did have one instrumental masterpiece to bring to the recording sessions, 'Lost Chronicles', a strident, uplifting, keyboard and guitar arrangement that Hawkwind had been playing live since the Chaos tour of 1986.

"It was written for Huw to play a long guitar solo over," says Bainbridge. "I had this chord sequence, all very nice and pretty, and said, 'Huw, the sequence goes around and around, and each time it goes around we build it again. We just have to decide how many times you want to go.'" The music starts with

194

Bainbridge playing a slow and studied progression over a synthesiser wash and a quirky, recurring off-key oscillation. The composition builds gradually, the bass and drums coming in early, meandering around like a travelogue film score, as the musicians await the arrival of the maestro. Langton appears mid-track and throws in a glorious guitar line that weaves spellbindingly through the remainder of the piece until he reaches a natural peak and takes his leave on the penultimate cycle. "Just 'take it away, Huw, off you go', which he was simply brilliant at doing." With Langton's own writing contribution to the LP being an understated acoustic number, 'Tides', it sounds in retrospect as though 'Lost Chronicles' is two old-hands showing the younger upstarts, Davey and Thompson, just what they could do.

Danny Thompson on the drums
(Ron Wright)

Through the summers of the latter part of the 80s, the band continued to support the myriad free festivals that still dotted the summer landscape despite the problems that the ending of the Stonehenge festival had caused. The remaining festivals may have generally been smaller, and prone in many counties to heavy policing, but they were still happening on a regular basis. The continued presence of Hawkwind members, particularly Brock and Bainbridge, mean that there was a cross-fertilisation between the band that had straddled the scene across the 70s and 80s and those newer converts who were coming together in bands that possessed a fusion of anarcho-punk, psychedelic and spacerock. When members of Tubilah Dog, who would go on to Hawkwind support slots, notably on the *Xenon Codex* tour of 1988, staged the Rollright Stones Festival, in 1987, Brock and Bainbridge were there. Their guitarist Jerry Richards recalled how "Steve Mills, Tubilah Dog's singer, had bumped into Dave, who'd said, 'Liked what you were doing, I'm in a blue van over there, come and give us a shout in the morning.' We went and had a chat with them and I hit it off with Dave, there was a mutual respect. I think I reminded Dave of himself when he was my age, going for it, having loads of energy and wanting to get about and do things. I suspect it reminded him of how his band used to be when he was going out and trying to get it all together."

This 'new generation' of festivalgoers seem to have intrigued Dave and Harvey to the point where they decided, as Jerry puts it, to get involved. "Of course, we were quite happy to have Dave Brock and Harvey Bainbridge come and play with us! Getting immersed in all this Hawk-lore and finding out about it from the grassroots up, was quite a thrill. All of this turned itself into Hawkdog or the Agents of Chaos, whatever we wanted to call ourselves on any occasion. In doing all of that, it drew people back to the band because it almost seemed to those travellers and festivalgoers we knew, that Hawkwind had... not abandoned the scene... but maybe a dereliction of duty, if I can call it that [laughs]. In their minds, in the travellers' minds, the people who were going to free festivals back then, Hawkwind had become another entity and moved into a stratospheric world with their big tours and their sort of semi-detachedness from the festival scene. Hooking up with us wide-eyed, amphetamine-fuelled, eager kids, I think, reinvigorated them. If you're doing something that people like, then people will find you, and a scene develops. That's what Hawkwind did back then; the scene came to find them, which is fantastic. I think Dave wanted to reconnect with a grassroots audience and not have the pressure of having to do the massive rock shows."

In that finding that interconnection, Brock and Bainbridge could create a situation where their attendance at festivals could be a little more relaxed and perhaps found them more enjoyable for that. Principally as Hawkdog, though also sometimes as Dave Brock & The Agents Of Chaos, Brock and Bainbridge combined with members of Tubilah Dog in sort of Sonic Assassins for the 80s, a festival band that was adaptable and able to slot-in in a quieter manner than the presence of Hawkwind might deliver, and that worked for all parties, really. Jerry Richards: "We [previously] found Hawkwind to be this monolithic beast that had become, I hesitate to use the word 'corporate', but they'd become this behemoth and a lot of us were simply wondering, 'Where are the Hawks at these festivals we're playing at? The Ozrics are here, The Levellers are here...' When I started getting involved with free festivals, what was important was going out playing, meeting people, having a nice time... some of the gigs we went to, we were content to make a festival happen by taking our sound system and our lightshow, putting that up, we didn't even play."

Festival Life
Bridget Wishart (far left) and Richard Chadwick (far right)
(Chris Abell, from Collection of Bridget Wishart)

Also active on the free festival scene were singer Bridget Wishart and Richard Chadwick, a self-taught drummer and former art school student. Together with guitarist Steve Bemand they formed The Demented Stoats. Chadwick, who originally became enthusiastic about music through "the concept of punk – the idea that you could just do it yourself," had "an interest in Hawkwind when I was still at school. Then I saw them at festivals, it was a sort of soundtrack of what was going on." Chadwick's girlfriend, Sophie, recalls that, "Richard used to get into Glastonbury for years before he joined the band, by turning up at the gate with his kit and telling security he was the drummer from Hawkwind."

"We were influenced by spacerock: Hawkwind and Here & Now," says Bridget, "and punk, Nina Hagen in particular, and we were very noisy!" Bridget described the free festivals as the start of her adult education. "I met all kinds of people from the weird and wacky to the vile and violent… and I had all kinds of adventures, mainly wild and wonderful! Hawkwind were an integral part of the scene, they were 'The Festival Band', and they could be relied on to draw a crowd and play for free. It wasn't a proper festival if Hawkwind didn't play," Their influence permeated throughout the scene as Claire Grainger, bassist with all-girl punk band the Hippy Slags, who soon numbered Bridget Wishart among their ranks, confirmed. "Hawkwind always seemed to appeal to the young boys, I think. They'd go off on their two-hour jams… though with the punk thing, people wanted a bit livelier stuff. But we're surprised, listening to our music, how much we were influenced by Hawkwind whether we like it or not!"

Though Chadwick notes that Hawkwind were "able to keep themselves relevant, in a sort of underground, youth culture, mind's eye," he concedes their ubiquitous appearances were not held in universal affection. "I joined a punk band called Smartpils. We thought everything that had gone before was boring and old." Though he'd been a fan of Hawkwind, the typically revisionist punk view meant that by the 80s "we used to think Hawkwind were a bit of a joke really, 'God, those old buggers are still at it!' The Hippy Slags used to play along with us; they wrote a song about the Stonehenge festival. I suggested they should write about what Stonehenge was like, this fantastic stellar configuration but also the funny side of it from our point of view as young people going there. Punk rockers dyeing their hair green and seeing people you only saw once a year. They constructed their chorus like 'Silver Machine', except it would go '…Oh no! Not Hawkwind again!' Later they supported Hawkwind a few times…"

Despite this, Chadwick found a lot in the mythos of Hawkwind to identify with. "You can look at imagery of the band lolling around on farm machinery at Rockfield on a nice sunny day… it's proposing some sort of lifestyle that goes beyond making music. The thing about punk was that part of its energy came from the fuel of the burning rock icons that had gone before. What upheld Hawkwind during that era was that they went and played the free festivals, which were important to me because they cemented all those ideas. It was a lifestyle; you could live like this, an alternative way of surviving. You felt it was still relevant even though 'they don't play punk rock, do they!' an ideology that got mixed into, or was part of, that free festival culture." Chadwick lived in "a place in Bath, that was well-known on the travelling scene as somewhere that people would call into on their way to Stonehenge; we had a hundred people through in a week at one point." This was at the time that he was playing regularly on the festival circuit: "We'd just wait for somebody to come by with a bus and take us and all our equipment!" Still passionate for the community sensibility of the free festival scene, he enthused about "being at Stonehenge when Crass played there, hugely popular, attracting lots of young people. But a bunch of bikers didn't like them, and decided to make war on the punks. There were terrible battles going on, people being pulled out of their tents and attacked – but we were there and didn't see any of it!"

Hawkwind were in the familiar position of being 'between drummers'. Thompson had played his last show during the spring (probably at London's Town & Country Club on 30th May, 1988), bringing closure to one of the most long-lived Hawkwind incarnations. "Danny was having personal problems… he was married, and I didn't even know it… and I was his best friend," notes Davey. A temporary replacement, Mick Kirton, appeared for some late summer gigs, but the band were also aware of Chadwick, who's drumming was reminiscent of the fast, busy, swinging style of Simon King. This made him a potential good-fit in a rhythm section already looking back to the driving basslines of Lemmy. "I had Harvey tapping on my shoulder at the Wick Festival (1st June 1988) going 'Here, can you play for Hawkwind?' though I was going to be knackered – Smartpils

198

were playing their last gig – and then later 'Don't bother, we're not going to play.'"

"Adrian, my housemate at the time, organised '88 Aktivator' on the family farm in Tewkesbury," recalls Wishart. "It was memorable for being Rich's first gig with the Hawks. I was there with the Hippy Slags and we played earlier the same day." This was probably the 14th August 1988, and one of the summer's 'HawkDog' shows, for which Chadwick was simply sitting-in. There was a coda to the event that had parallels with the experiences many festivalgoers were now encountering. "Afterwards some people refused to move on… they and their dogs caused a lot of problems, cost lots of cash, and local attitudes changed towards such events, which meant no more free festivals there." [See *Festivaliazed: Music, Politics, and Alternative Culture* for more Aktivator stories].

By the time Chadwick officially auditioned for the band, he was part of an acoustic group, Childe Roland, who "sounded a lot like Tyrannosaurus Rex." At the Clyro Court festival (1st October) Richard "bumped into Dave, Alan and Huw; I asked Dave what was going on and he said, 'We need a drummer'. I said, 'I'm a drummer!' Dave said, 'What the band needs really is a pulse.' I said, 'I am a pulse!'" A few subsequent phone calls resulted in an opportunity for Chadwick to play with the band at rehearsals in Bournemouth, where Davey was living at the time. "We played away for an hour or so, just making up stuff on the spot. But what they wanted to know was if I could play in time with a click-track. I borrowed a drum machine from a mate, put it through the PA in our practice room at home - a bit like *The Young Ones*: that 'Motörhead in the kitchen effect' - and played along with it, I was getting eighty-percent success rate. Fundamentally it's that discipline of playing along with a metronome; with the use of electronics, where you can sequence basslines, rhythms or any part of the music you need to be able to stay in time with it."

"Richard wasn't keen to play along with midi pulses or clock pulses, but he was amenable to it, and capable of doing it. He was able to work with it, either by pushing it or being behind it, which some drummers find it hard to do," explains Bainbridge. "Danny worked with having a pulse in his ear throughout the Black Sword tour, but he found it disconcerting, Richard found it easier to cope with."

It was important that the band made the right choice to fill the vacant drummer's stool, since it was becoming widely recognised that the current format of the band had become stale. Brock's longest serving collaborators, Langton and Bainbridge, were becoming tired of the musical constrictions and it was clear that the whole concept needed redefining once again for the forthcoming decade. Indeed, though he accepted the job when it was offered, Chadwick was not particularly keen on the direction of the group. "I was for long instrumentals with lots of improvisations, really creating moods… I thought that was what Hawkwind were really good at." Richard felt he could help resolve this by bringing in "dynamics – because in the bands I'd been in before, the way we wrote songs was to jam." This writing method harked back to the early days of

Hawkwind and its Krautrock influences in the way that Chadwick describes it: "The way we made jamming interesting was in playing one note, a simple theme but in variations, just loud and quiet and that's what changed when I joined Hawkwind. Things got stretched-out again."

It wasn't just that he could bring something to the band through his drumming, and through that contribute to reenergising them. It was that Chadwick recognised and joined up what the band was all about, pulling together the strands of psychedelia and punk, and its relevance to the whole free festival vibe and for all those reasons being one of the key recruitments to the band for many years. And, a Marvel Comics fanatic, he bought into the sci-fi imagery of the band. "The initial idea that space was terrifying and cold and not a pleasant place to be, one that forced introspection – that the only place that was worth going was inside your mind…"

Chadwick became a full-time member from the winter 1988 tour onwards. The shows were in support of a benefit album *The Travellers' Aid Trust* compiled from the current crop of festival bands, including Hawkwind, Tubilah Dog and the Hippy Slags. The sought-after "pulse" increased the tempo and gave the set added energy. However, it would be well into the next year before wholesale changes created an environment in which Chadwick and Davey sparked together into the most powerful Hawkwind rhythm section since the days of Simon King and Lemmy. Asked if he subscribed to the view that Davey's development as a bass player was enhanced by the addition of Chadwick at the back of the band, Bainbridge's only comment is "Absolutely!"

15

A Farewell to Bob Calvert

Bob Calvert in thoughtful mode
(Roger Neville-Neil)

When Hawkwind reassembled for their first gig of 1989, it was for a tribute performance to one of its key visionaries. Robert Calvert died from a massive heart attack on 14th August of the previous year. Ironically, in reporting his death, the music press suggested that he had been on the brink of returning to the band.

Calvert's 1980s studio output articulated his concerns. The decline of the British industrial base, the moral issues surrounding advances in modern science and the vile apartheid of pre-90s South Africa all featured heavily in his lyrics. Freed from the constraints of the Hawkwind format, Calvert produced a greater range and depth of material than any of his former bandmates. *Hype – The Songs of Tom Mahler* (1981), Calvert's first solo LP since *Lucky Leif and the Longships* was released in conjunction with his maiden novel. It is a self-deprecating slice of rock star analysis. On the first track, 'Over My Head', Calvert references a myriad of contemporary icons and issues which are promptly debunked. 'I heard her say something clever 'bout inflation/and the Ayatollah's rule/It went over my head'.

Asked about the 'Fritz Lang movie where the hero loses his soul' his natural reaction was that he didn't find it too groovy, he was 'more into rock 'n' roll'.

Contrasted with Calvert's other solo work, the record is a bright, humorous and poppy selection of songs. Although some pieces appear underworked, others are amongst his best compositions. 'Hanging Out on the Sea Front' is an astonishing contrast of light and dark, influenced by his days in Margate. 'The Greenfly and the Rose' is probably Calvert's most haunting creation, whilst the Marvel Comics-esque 'Lord of the Hornets' would become something of a signature tune for him. If *Hype* is now somewhat neglected compared to Calvert's other works, it welcomes a revisit.

In the accompanying novel, Bob second guessed the reliance on manufactured pop that would be omnipresent in the years to come. Tom Mahler, an innocent caught in the financial wheels of the music industry, is 'hyped' into stardom and literally sacrificed by this own management in the cause of record sales. Issued in the UK by New English Library, the book boasted that it reflected the experience of Calvert who had "been there and back again." Bob described the book containing as "stuff I picked up hanging around record companies."

At one time, there was a possibility that *Hype* would become a stage musical. Steve Swindells explains: "Bob and Jill had this amazing ground floor maisonette in an old Victorian house near Ladbroke Grove. [It belonged to Mike Moorcock]. I used to go and hangout with them. [Bob had] written songs to go with the book, and he asked me if I'd try singing some. Bob had this brainwave, to turn it into a musical, and said, 'I want you to star in it'. He had an actress, who worked a lot with Steven Berkoff, all these proper actors who were very snooty to me. We had a week of rehearsals, and then I got double pneumonia; soon after that the production fell apart. I moved out of the area, and we lost touch."

Calvert's next work revisited the mixture of song and dialogue that made *Captain Lockheed* successful. *Freq* (1984), recorded using only synthesiser and drum machine, was set against the framework of the Miners' Strike. Calvert's anger at the direction and policies of the Thatcher government were reflected in a mixture of music interspersed with news recordings from the picket lines. His anxiety over the disaffection of the British working classes is given full vent. 'Ned Ludd has Japanese eyes!' he asserts on the opening track, whilst elsewhere he spends his days '…in dreams, so far from the machines'. In 'Acid Rain', Calvert revisits his obsession with cloning and genetics where, he claimed, 'heredity is chosen/by anyone who wanks'.

Freq had appeared on the Flicknife label, Calvert's idiosyncratic talent slotting in well with the label's other maverick and leftfield musicians. "With Bob Calvert, and Nico, and Nikki Sudden, Glen Matlock, we worked with people who had real talent," says Frenchy Gloder. "They're different, they've got something… Bob Calvert was not only a good musician but a great raconteur; he could tell you a story like nobody else could tell you a story. The album we did with Bob Calvert… you could not have a better document of the Miners' Strike than that album. You had interviews with the miners and in the original album you had notes on what happened when he did the interviews, like we often had to leg it because they didn't get the fact that we were supporting the strikes. They probably thought we were these two freaks interviewing them… for what? We had to explain it was for an album and that this was Bob Calvert and then people knew, because Hawkwind was still a significant name and 'Silver Machine' was still on most jukeboxes. So Freq wasn't only musically relevant, it was a piece of the time and socially very important."

"I actually made *Freq* in a computer studio, where they had microphones that had to be plugged into the desk to get their voltage," Calvert said in the fanzine *Warriors on the Edge of Time*. His final album was a return to a full band (including Dave Anderson, whose label Demi-Monde released it), 1986's *Test Tube Conceived*. As with *Hype*, *Test Tube Conceived* linked into other outlets for Calvert's writing: a play, about two geneticists whose experiments go wrong, *Test Tube Baby of Mine* has subsequently been performed on stage in London (directed by character actor Paul Jerricho) and New York.

Calvert had moved on from examining the perilous state of British industry and into a love/hate affair with the advances in modern science and the people who drive them forward. "I'm not opposed to scientific progress. What I'm opposed to is the possible misuse of scientific progress," he asserted, suggesting that developments in genetics overshadowed nuclear war as the major threat to humanity.

He sought other creative outlets. Along with Peter Pavli (linked to Hawkwind via The Deep Fix) he worked on a musical, *The Kid from Silicon Gulch*. With Jill Riches (later Jill Calvert), they appeared at the London Theatrespace during April and May 1981. This three-hander revue featured Calvert as a Raymond Chandler style detective, Brad Spark. The premise was that Spark investigated a conspiracy by the world's computers who planned to kill their owners. He would, of course, outwit the computers, solve the case, get the girl and make the cop (Pavli) look incompetent. This was hardly an original plotline, though Pavli remembers it as "funny, with some good songs," and that "the audience loved it, even though it was often shambolic."

Sharing an interest in the Futurists, the Italian art movement, Pavli had written the music for a series of Calvert demos that were posthumously released as *Revenge*. They worked together again on the songs for *The Kid from Silicon Gulch*. "We spent several weeks composing the music using mainly guitar, drum machine and synth, recording on to a Revox machine in a friend's front room." When it came to the show's week-long run in London, the songs were sung live to a tape backing, and the three performers doubled-up as the voices of various computers.

The revue had limited success. Pavli recalls the audience as consisting of "on the whole, Hawkwind fans," a frustration to Calvert, who "wanted to be taken more seriously, reach different audiences." There was a suggestion of taking the show to the 1981 Edinburgh Festival though nothing came of this. Pavli describes working with Calvert as "fun, most of the time," but he was another collaborator who found himself enduring Bob's notorious mood swings.

"Working with Bob was often fraught, he could go haywire at the drop of a hat, and would have to be placated until he calmed down." Musically, they had cooperated well but after the revue shows Pavli simply "had enough of Bob's tantrums," and drifted away.

In June 1981, Calvert appeared at the Arts Theatre, Leicester Square in a series of shows billed as 'Krankshaft presents Quark Strangeness & Charm – Five Evenings with Robert Calvert from Hawkwind'. Late the same year, Calvert started working again with Nik Turner. When Inner City Unit secured a Thursday residency at the Marquee, Bob was invited to appear as the opening act. Dead Fred recalls how "the first week he used a tape-recorded backing, not very dynamic. Second, third and fourth week [ICU] backed him but on swapped instruments. I was usually the drummer. We wore Maggie [Thatcher] and Ronnie [Reagan] masks for the whole set so as not to be recognised. The result was excellent."

By 1985 Turner had finished his second stint in Hawkwind and was playing in a regrouped ICU. A special gig at a London's Dingwalls, with Calvert guesting had been mooted. ICU guitarist Steve Pond recalls "at the next rehearsals Bob turned up with his Wasp synth in an old lady-style shopping bag and was full of enthusiasm for playing live again." ICU rehearsed some of Calvert's compositions. "The dynamic between Nik and Bob was great, just like old school friends at a reunion," says Pond. "There was a fantastic vibe in the room, Nik and Bob trading vocals and generally having a blast." The gig went ahead on 21st March, with the band playing a set lasting over three hours. Despite the initial intention that this would be a one-off show, when an invitation to play an anti-heroin benefit gig in Liverpool came, Calvert was again asked to play.

The results were less satisfactory than the Dingwalls performance, with Pond getting his first glimpse of 'Mad Bob'. "He spent the whole day getting more and more hyper. Just before we went on they had an escapologist on stage… an escapologist who couldn't escape. The ten-minute slot stretched to forty, Bob prowling the edge of stage getting angrier and angrier." The band finally got on stage and ran through a few songs only to have "Bob let rip with the first of several violent anti-Thatcher tirades, bashing the stage and being generally militant." Steve Pond goes on to note the gig as occurring on 11th May 1985, the day of the tragedy at Bradford City Football Club, where 56 people died when a small fire at the Valley Parade stadium was flamed by high winds and engulfed the wooden grandstand. "It was at this time that news started trickling in of the disaster which had happened that afternoon… a strange day."

ICU started their next tour the following month, and though Calvert had confirmed he would play some of the gigs (and was advertised for them) he didn't turn up. Pond attributes this to Calvert being busy writing and "a reliance on public transport." A report in *Sounds*, attributed Calvert's departure to somebody having stolen a favourite hat. There was no substance in this, a story that Pond in his role as ICU press officer circulated, "as a gag."

Friends Reunited Part Two: Bob Calvert and Nik Turner
Inner City Unit: Dingwalls 21/3/85
(P!KN!K)

Calvert's prestige received a substantial boost the following year, when he was asked to perform at London's Queen Elizabeth Hall. Needing only a small backing band, he recruited Dead Fred and Steve Pond, who had been performing as the Maximum Effect, since ICU had again split. They decided not to engage a drummer, as the material suited machines, Reeves and Pond arranging all the tunes for piano, guitar and synth. "We posted cassettes of the results to Bob, who rehearsed at home, then he sent back demos of songs he was working on and we arranged them too." Live rehearsals commenced two days before the show. Mary Cason, who had worked with ICU as their sleeve designer, was drafted in on additional synth; the result was that "the solo Bob songs were sounding good [though] the Hawkwind material suffered from not having a human rhythm section," concludes Pond.

The concert was considered a success, though Reeves is critical. "The venue did not lend itself to amplified music. Throughout the whole event there was a feeling of instability and unease. This may have been due to the pressure of playing such a high-profile shrine to the arts, and also the presence of the press." However, there was a lot of good-natured banter between stage and audience and the songs sounded crisp and fresh. Backstage was a large gathering of old friends in a relaxed and friendly atmosphere. Throughout the hall, Pond felt there was "a lot of love [towards Calvert] that night!"

The songs performed on the night were roughly fifty-fifty solo material and Hawkwind numbers, though a posthumously released LP of the show, to benefit Calvert's family, contained no Hawkwind songs, avoiding dissipation of royalties. With its strong trawl through Calvert's solo work, including a heartfelt statement on his native South Africa, 'Working down a Diamond Mine', it captures an artist enjoying a creative peak and was simply a testament to a writer and musician who never properly received the renown that his talents should have brought him.

Following the accomplishment of the QEH performance, the band decided that it would be a good idea to tour a similar set. Consequently, eleven dates were organised. Reception was mixed, with sold-out houses in London and Manchester contrasting with virtually empty rooms in Carlisle (where a 600-capacity venue sold only 50 tickets) and Middlesbrough. Reeves' view is that the togetherness and ability of the band improved upon the original QEH show. "The subsequent recording at the Stars and Stripes, Carlisle is far better."

The daily drudge of a band on tour soon became exacerbated by Calvert's hyper-activity and Pond recalls "cordial relationships started to break down, the reality of organising the shows [with no roadies], driving, humping the gear and looking after Bob were getting to all of us." Calvert in his manic state existed on no more than two hours sleep a night, lecturing his musicians on anything and everything. Sometimes he was full of schoolboy mischief, on other occasions he could be filled with destructive complaining. Despite the brevity of the tour, the last date couldn't come quickly enough for the rest of the band. They played a final show at the Hammersmith Clarendon and went their separate ways.

Would he have been a Hawk again? Bob reflects on past works.
Clarendon, 18/12/85
(P!KN!K)

Reeves was later contacted by Calvert with a view to collaborating on his next studio album: "The planned line-up was Bob, Steve Pond, Mick Stupp [a former ICU drummer], Mary Cason and myself, plus guests." The project failed to get past the planning stage. Instead, a new backing band, The Starfighters, was put together to play dates in 1987. Some live shows were recorded from the audience. A gig at Bogey's, Cardiff from January 1988 has the band essentially following the musical arrangements put together by Pond and Reeves, but lacking the banter that made Calvert's earlier shows feel so intimate.

Steve Bagley once spent an afternoon in Margate interviewing Calvert, arriving at Bob's residential address anticipating it to be that of his management's offices. He saw Calvert play his last gig, at Oxford Street's 100 Club, a week before his death. "Bob was so hyped up that night that it was difficult to get any sense out of him, he was really manic. I guess that this was an indicator of the massive heart attack that was only days away."

The obituaries in the music press rounded up Calvert's former bandmates for their final dedications. "Blow your bloody bugle till I get there," was the typically brash comment from Lemmy, who has since considered Calvert "quite talented but he wasn't as brilliant as people make out now." "Goodbye, old friend. I'll keep the 'Spirit of the Age' going," said Brock.

It has been claimed by those keen to draw some parallel between the continuing success of Hawkwind and the figure of Calvert, working away on the fringes and creating some of his most complex work neglected and forgotten by the music industry that Calvert died in poverty. Pond thinks this is overstated "[It's] too harsh a word… he brought up a kid, he had a shed in the garden to write in… but yes, he was poor."

In *Freq*, his incisive survey of the decline of Britain's industrial heritage, 'All the Machines Are Quiet' sees Calvert complaining 'All we're asking is a living wage'. This is something that rankled with him; he wrote to Hawkwind historian Trevor Hughes that "I have no desire to become a capitalist but I think I deserve to earn at least the average working wage for the work I do." Coupled with Calvert's genuine fear of rejection, there was a thread in his thinking that led Bob to become obsessive about a lack of financial recognition. Pond views that being "as much through principal as need."

Would he have re-joined Hawkwind, as the music press suggested? Pond thinks not, though "maybe, just maybe if they offered him enough money?" Bagley, who maintained a contact with Bob through the last years of his life, agrees. "I do remember [regarding a possible anniversary reunion show] that Bob was keen to be involved. [But] he definitely did not say anything about re-joining Hawkwind on a more permanent basis."

Robert Calvert's legacy is a diverse assortment of material. A collection of his poems, *Centigrade 232* was published by Quasar Books in 1978, later followed by a second volume, *The Earth Ritual*. His poetry provoked a thoughtful analysis by Steve Sneyd: *Gnawing Medusa's Flesh: The Science Fiction Poetry of Robert Calvert*. Lacking a record deal at the end of his life, Calvert self-released a collection of demos, *The Cellar Tapes*, which contained both unfinished new material and demos for songs from *Test Tube Conceived*. Most of these were posthumously collected onto CD as *Blueprints from the Cellar*. Also worthy of note is the album *Die Losung*. Described as 'Amon Düül with special guest Robert Calvert' it features, amongst others Dave Anderson, Amon Düül's John Weinzierl, Tony McPhee of The Groundhogs, and Joie Hinton and Ed Wynne of Ozric Tentacles (who once described the result as "a horrible album, with only a couple of moments").

Calvert never realised his full and unique potential. John Weinzierl talked of Calvert's ability to "[take] the remotest subject… and paint it in the most astounding, colourful way." Brian Tawn astutely praised Calvert's talent for seeing "ordinary things from new angles." But it's clear that Calvert's manic depressive nature prevented his collaborators from fully exploiting group projects and so, perhaps, we should look to him first and foremost, as Sneyd does, in that most solitary of occupations, as a writer. Calvert told an interviewer for *NME*, "I won't be a star until I'm over 40. Which is cool; neither was [George Bernard] Shaw." Bob Calvert was 43 when that heart attack drew a final line under a frustratingly incomplete career.

The Calvert tribute show proved to be the last gig of Langton's second stint in Hawkwind. Though Richard Chadwick had undoubtedly brought a new spark to the band, it was still clear that another creative impasse had been reached. Little of *The Xenon Codex* was particularly successful in the live shows, with only 'Heads' staying in the setlist beyond the album's promotional tour. Brock, Davey and Chadwick were increasingly interested in returning to a more electronic, psychedelic sound. Within this context, there might be less room for Langton's guitar, which had been mixed down on *The Xenon Codex* but which successive sound engineers in the live environment had allowed to dominate the music. "A professional musician should know where to stop and give people space," notes Bainbridge, "but a lot of the time Huw would say, 'well, I stopped but nothing else was happening – so I started again!'"

Though he appeared on all of Hawkwind's studio output throughout the decade, and rarely missed live appearances, Langton had ceased to be a member of the band's legal partnership from the mid-80s onwards. His contract and dealings with the group were that of a session musician, employed for studio work and tours and he increasingly focused on his own band, which had existed since the early 1980s. There may have been some difficulties within Hawkwind at the time, with different members focusing on developing the music towards their own ideas of what a Hawkwind line-up should sound, and there was a continued support for the free festival scene that not all members followed as enthusiastically as others. Davey had responded to a question about Langton's membership given his different approach to the festivals, saying that Huw fitted-in and that "he wouldn't be in the band if he didn't," which may certainly have been true even though it sounded somewhat harsh coming from a much newer recruit. But in hindsight Langton became keen to distance himself from that period, preferring to see it simply in terms of the not uncommon frustrations that evolve within any long-running arrangement.

"I was on the motorway with my own band and Dave rang up and said Hawkwind were doing a tribute to Bob Calvert and if I wanted to come down I could, but if I didn't want to I didn't have to. There was a very strange feeling in the dressing room. The gig was fine, but it turned out to be the end of our association at the time." Langton recalls that Tubilah Dog guitarist Jerry Richards was "hanging around" and gives an impression that he felt he might have been in the process of being eased out in favour of Richards (though Richards didn't become a member until much later). The overall feeling from Langton is that things had come to a natural end. "Everything felt really strained. I finished off my tour and then got a ring from Dick Taylor asking if I could do a few gigs in Europe with The Pretty Things, which I did and totally enjoyed. When I got back I had a meeting with Doug Smith and said, 'I'm out' and that was it."

Mr Bainbridge in thoughtful mode
(Ron Wright)

With Langton's departure, and contact re-established with Simon House, who had made a guest appearance at the Calvert Tribute show, there was a straight swap of guitar for violin to fill the perceived gap in the sound. This was demonstrated during a short mini-tour and at several festivals over the summer of 1989. These shows are remembered for the change in texture brought by House, and for the earliest appearances with Hawkwind by Bridget Wishart, providing vocals for a new song, 'Back in the Box'. "I thought Simon brought a lot back to it, at the beginning," considers Davey. "It was very apparent, the difference between what Huw was then, and what Simon was… you suddenly had a lead player who was on the ball. 'This was what Huw used to do, and now its back, but with a violin.' Every four or five years the band would go through a cycle; it was probably a bit overdue."

Did Dave Brock feel the same way? Of his two longest-serving associates, Huw Lloyd-Langton had departed and Harvey Bainbridge was feeling marginalised as the younger musicians that Brock had gathered around him made their presence felt. Two songs from this era that are credited to Dave Brock, 'Treadmill' and 'Damage of Life', are curious in this respect, both having a world-weary feel to them, a personal tone, probably more so than in any other songs with his by-line on them. He'd cut a cover of 'Motherless Children' a few years before and dedicated it to 'SPB' in memory of his wife, Sylvia, who had very sadly died in 1983, but he'd never been a songwriter or musician who'd otherwise revealed himself through his work to any great degree. It's hard to get to the real person behind Dave Brock, almost deliberately so, maybe. But these songs were melancholic in their words and in their phrasing, and, in that way, they are so different from his overall body of work that you'd have to believe that they tell us something. The notion in 'Treadmill' of having lived long and become old, the idea in 'Damage of Life' that he'd 'tried so many different ways/and watched each one of them decay', which sounds so definitively like a reflection on the ever-changing line-ups, and a rumination on his own quest to put together disparate musicians and find something in what they could achieve together under the Hawkwind banner. Could this indeed have taken a greater toll than he'd care to have let on?

16

Back to America

Chadwick, Bainbridge, House, Brock, Davey
Wolverhampton Civic Hall, 16/12/89
(Keith Kniveton)

Despite successful appearances in the UK, Simon House was not persuaded to travel to America when Hawkwind embarked on their first US tour since 1978. The core band of Brock, Bainbridge, Davey and Chadwick performed as a quartet, starting with a gig across the border in Toronto on the 24th September 1989 before moving onto Washington two nights later.

"We had to start all over again," says Brock. "Small clubs, working back up the ladder." It was a strategic plan to re-establish the band in America. "We had in our bank account a reasonable amount of money which we invested: two tour buses, a lightshow. Costs were really high and we didn't get paid a lot of money, $1500 a show, and we had fifteen people." Rebuilding Hawkwind's reputation stateside would require a series of tours, each building upon the previous one. They'd not been there in over ten years, and even then their previous stateside tour had been a lower-key affair than the big headline tours and major venues of the mid-70s. "We knew we'd lose money on the first tour, second tour we'd break even, third tour we'd start making money. Like any business you have to put your own money in."

There was no doubt that a market for Hawkwind's brand of spacerock existed in the USA, and that a need to see the band live was at its core. "Every gig we did was like a science fiction convention," recalls Chadwick, "A lot of 'experts' in one room, fascinated by the same thing. They're all visionaries and there is a certain kind of soundtrack that goes along with their vision – all psychedelic sub-culture type characters. The road crew were all ardent Grateful Dead fans." In a microcosm, this represented the appeal Hawkwind has for Chadwick: "A wonderful thing, because all those people got together, which is what I always thought Hawkwind was; allowing people to get together with a community sensibility, a thing going around Hawkwind, a lifestyle, not just the music; Bob Calvert's vision of ray-guns at dawn!"

This sense of collective between the band and the audience is reflected in the way that American Hawkwind fans describe the group's USA tours. Doug Pearson recollects the 1989 dates as "mind-blowing, since I never expected to see Hawkwind, and also because live Hawkwind circa '89 were light years beyond their last few studio albums. The only comparable band I'd seen was The Butthole Surfers. No one else had that kind of brain damaging potential!" Another enthusiast laments the lack of previous US Hawkwind shows during the 1980s and goes on to comment that "we had little warning the band were coming back. I saw an advertisement for the Lounge Ax show about four days before!" True to Chadwick's concept of Hawkwind, "We stood in line from before noon for the evening show, and made a lot of new friends among the other Hawkwind fanatics."

At the Chicago Lounge Ax (1st October), Hawkwind were supported by Friends of Betty, a band whose leader Glynnis Johnson, later posthumously immortalised in the song by The Smashing Pumpkins which bears her name, was described as "a Hawkwind fanatic, beside herself with excitement to be performing on the same stage as Brock and company." The venue was actually a small bar with stage, "we all pressed in and sweated it out. It was a great show, even if there wasn't enough room for the lights." Other shows had better capacity, the Phantasy Theatre in Cleveland being noted as having "a very large audience, maybe a thousand," by Keith Henderson.

"I was walking down a street in San Francisco and looked up at the marquee at a venue called the Stone, and there was Hawkwind playing," comments Jello Biafra. "I thought, I wonder what this will sound like this far after the fact – I'll go in. It was amazing. Having Richard Chadwick and Alan Davey in there was a major plus to get the pile-driving power back in gear, it rekindled in me how much these songs and this music really meant to me, and where would I be without it. The crowd was about ten times larger than 1978 and I thought 'where did these people come from?' mostly young people."

Although the compactness of some the venues allowed for only moderate use of Hawkwind's lightshow, in halls that had room for the full projection the effect was dazzling. Alien vistas, ringed planets, gas giants, crab nebulae and, for 'Wind of Change', an ice planet made up some of the solar landscapes. "I was used to Hawkwind's big lightshows from back home," notes one British fan who saw the band at the Palace, Los Angeles, "so was disappointed to see that they seemed to have very little in the way of anything showy, just a few strobes. Halfway through the second song the place filled with dry ice then they switched on all the strobes AT THE SAME TIME. The place went nuts; the effect was awesome. The strobes were actually high, very long and on top of all the amps which, when filtered through the dry ice, was mesmerising."

"We got incredibly good receptions," recalls Davey. "American audiences were louder, more enthusiastic [than in the UK], but that was probably down to not having seen Hawkwind for about fifteen years." For Alan, there was a thrill in being in America, playing rock 'n' roll. "I kept saying to Dave 'I'm really here, aren't I? I'm really here!'"

"In Toronto some guy came running over to me, I thought, 'What's going on?' It turned out he was a fan who had some home-grown weed. I'd never had American grass, though Dave warned me it would be stronger than I was used to. Wandered on stage, got my keyboard going, and stood there for about twenty seconds, thinking there was something missing. I thought I'd better tune my bass… and it was still in the dressing-room! Got back to the dressing-room and it was locked, finally found the tour manager in the audience watching the rest of them start. I did that three times on that tour; never had grass like it!"

The tour was an opportunity for Bainbridge to demonstrate his keyboard skills without his musicianship being overwhelmed by lead instrumentation, whether guitar or violin. "[There was] a gap that someone had to jump into. I had to start playing synthesisers up front, rather than just putting an atmosphere around the sides." This was most atmospherically demonstrated with the return of 'Wind of Change', played with a heavy keyboard emphasis, much as it was during the mid-70s. This inclusion aside, the set basically followed that summer's shows, opening with 'Magnu' and then moving on to the segued 'Down Through the Night' and 'Treadmill' and two verses of "Time We Left" sandwiching "Heads" as their middle-eight. 'Assassins of Allah' ("about oil and hashish" was Brock's introduction, or sometimes, "smoking dope and dealing in oil"), 'Assault & Battery/Golden Void', 'Back in the Box', 'Brainstorm', 'Dream Worker' and 'Damnation Alley' generally rounded out the show though 'Needle Gun' and 'Ejection' variously appeared as encores. It was a set moulded around pieces that could be pushed and expanded, that were perfect for this latest incarnation to use as templates for a psychedelic wall-of-sound that twisted away from the punk rock heavy metal of the 80s and delved back into the band's early years with the intention of giving that era a contemporary make-over. In that sense, it was a perfectly judged assemblage, leaning heavily on 70s Hawkwind without pandering to the traditional conservatism of rock audiences: no 'Silver Machine', no 'Master of the Universe'. "We get some new ones, some old ones we haven't played in a while, try them out and see if they work," said Brock, interviewed for a fan-made documentary of the tour (*Hawkwind – On Tour*, Horizon Films 1990) that showed the band live and in sound-check. He'd done that before over the years, of course, but where 'Paradox' had seemed out of place in the early 80s band, something such as 'Wind of Change' for this line-up absolutely let them loose in a new direction.

"I thought as a four-piece band we were actually very good on the 1989 tour," says Bainbridge. "Richard was the perfect drummer for what Hawkwind is all about, simple, straightforward, subtle, yet he could punch forward as well."

Interviewed by 'Annie' for *Hawkwind – On Tour*, Bainbridge talked about the difficulties that a performer could experience. "It's very difficult when you do a tour to leave this whole energy... when you come off the stage you're pumped up. You could go and fight a war. After doing that night, after night, it's very difficult to leave all that behind; life is dull and boring. To combat that, people go heavily into booze or drugs... or lunatic behaviour. The alter-ego that you are on stage is not your normal self, it's something hyped up. If you can't leave that behind when you are not working, then you're kind of lumbered." It sounded just as world-weary and tired as Brock had done on 'Treadmill' and 'Damage of Life', and Bainbridge concedes that may have been part of his outlook on Hawkwind at the time. "Probably it was, and too many drugs and constant partying... maybe not constantly but it feels as if you have been, even though you're working at the same time. It was Bob Calvert that pointed this out, just by watching him, because he would get wound-up as a tour went on, get more excitable. All the characters he was thinking about with his lyrics, he was turning into. The adrenaline buzz is constantly running and re-running, the gaps between become insignificant."

Chadwick, thoughtful and articulate, understands this dilemma: "The real excitement for musicians is playing live in front of an audience and people going 'Yeah! We Love It!' It's that appreciation of everything going right, where we feel were on the crest of a wave and making music is effortless. It's such a draw it'll bring you back time and again despite repeated failures; to get that fantastic feeling where everything is just right."

Following the tour, Davey, Chadwick and Bainbridge were caught up in the San Francisco earthquake of 1989. Davey: "The plan was to take a couple of weeks off, hire a car and drive off into the desert. I woke-up in the morning, with this horrible feeling. Really irritable; I just wanted to get out of the place. I went down to the harbour and all the sea-lions had gone. Everybody wanted to go shopping in the city centre, but I was so bad-tempered and said no. Harvey suggested we at least drive over all the bridges, and then we'd go towards Santa Cruz where there was a radio station that wanted an interview. We drove over Golden Gate, and then across a bridge that within ten or fifteen minutes was flattened by the earthquake. I thought, 'What's the road doing?' It was like driving on a sea of concrete. After the initial thing, it was enjoyable, feeling the power of what the Earth could do!"

Three weeks later, Davey was in another earthquake. "I was in the studio, in Wales, with [engineer] Paul Cobbold, just the two of us working on something, and there was this huge rumble... later-on, we discovered it was another quake!"

Richard Chadwick
(Collection of Dave Brock)

Arriving at Rockfield to work on their first album of the new decade, *Space Bandits*, the band now had both Wishart and Chadwick included in the ranks. Both admit to having had some difficulties in attaining the standards of the more experienced members. The record, the first engineered for the band by Paul Cobbold, was a chance to reinvigorate the Hawkwind sound on vinyl in the same way they had successfully managed to do live. The mixture of driving bass, cathedral-like keyboards and a warm and full violin sound had already crystallised in a live show recorded for the British television series *Bedrock*. This late-night compilation programme showcased major, but arguably neglected, acts. Aside from Hawkwind, also captured were fellow 1970s survivors as diverse as Buzzcocks and Caravan.

For the filming, Hawkwind were joined by Bridget Wishart's mixture of guest vocals and performance art. At the time, Bridget was still employed as a schoolteacher, specialising in ceramic sculpture. She recalls having to "persuade the headmaster that needing time off work to rehearse for the gig was a valid career move!" Although it wasn't the usual career step, he was supportive and

216

Bridget remembers the school as being "quite proud when I left to join the band," which was because of a strong performance on the programme. They were also joined by dancer Julie Murray, who had already appeared with Hawkwind at the Brixton Academy. In addition, regular lightshow man, Pogle, provided the visuals whilst Kris Tait and Wango Reilly threatened the very fabric of the studio with their fire-breathing act. Recorded on 21st January, 1990 the distilling of Hawkwind on film was considered by the members as visually far from a satisfactory affair, though it's immensely watchable and a great capture of the band at a transitional point in time, successfully re-defining the concept for the forthcoming decade.

Bridget thought the result "a bit unreal and lacking the true atmosphere of a Hawkwind gig." This was partly due to the requirements of the film crew ("neither the band nor their fans were too happy about their demands"), but the main problem was the studio's plan to record the show with heavy lighting, anathema to a band used to playing on a darkened stage to accommodate both the mood of the music and the power of the visuals.

"The rest were really nervous," says Richard, "so I got nervous as well… 'Everybody's nervous. Why?' … and then I realised, because we had to play as though it was bright daylight. I pointed out that Hawkwind had been filmed before in low lighting and it didn't affect the validity of the footage. But they had to do it that way. It was disappointing because the lightshow wasn't there to back us up. At the time [lighting designer] Pogle was working closely with us and was very tightly choreographed in with what we were playing and it would have been a stunning thing to see." The filming of Hawkwind in low-lighting, might have been atmospheric when done on the 1984 tour, as seen on the *Night of the Hawks* video, but it comes a mighty poor second to *Bedrock* film, which suffers little from the higher lighting and which is a damn good recording.

One of the more striking elements of the TV show saw Bridget being tied to a pole and wrapped in bandages like an Egyptian Mummy. "When you think about it," comments Chadwick, "to actually do that onstage in front of a load of people and be totally at the mercy of whoever is manipulating you whilst you're wrapped up like a Mummy…."

"The night before, when we'd been in the bar for a while, I asked Dave's roadie if he'd carry me off stage in a silage bag at the end of 'Back in the Box'," Bridget remembers. "He seemed to like the idea, but next day I could see he was nervous and he probably wished he had never agreed. But he performed his role admirably and didn't drop me once! "The first lyrics I wrote for Hawkwind were the ones I sang on 'Back in the Box'. I turned up at Dave's one sunny afternoon and wrote them on the back of an envelope. The first run through I thought was great but the engineer wasn't recording, so I sang them again and that's the take on the CD [*Palace Springs*]."

The *Space Bandits* album was the only other major contribution to the Hawkwind archive produced by the line-up who had appeared on the Bedrock show, though a subsequent mix of live cuts and studio material, *Palace Springs*, has credits for both Bridget Wishart and Simon House. "For me, it was a complete nightmare," reveals Chadwick, "I'd been a punk drummer, playing live all over the place; I'd done quite a lot of Hawkwind gigs. Went into the studios, set up the drums in this amazing place and started working on this song, 'Images'. At the point we recorded it, it lasted about twelve or fourteen minutes, really long and very fast and I thought everything was fine. But playing along with the click track, I realised I was hopelessly inaccurate. It was accurate in feel, but it was inaccurate in a recording, where you need everything the best you can get it." The solution was for Chadwick to "learn how to programme drumming, very quickly. Paul Cobbold had set up his Atari with the keyboards triggering the drum sounds. I'd never even realised you could make drum sounds out of a keyboard. Paul was tapping the snare, going, 'is that a good snare... do you think it's a bit loud?' Meanwhile Alan was turning down the monitor that was generating the sound, so I was getting closer and closer to the keyboard, just trying to hear... that's how alien it was to me at the time!" But Chadwick soon developed a passion for this method and links it back to some of the music he'd been interested in previously. "Hawkwind had been using drum machines almost since they were invented, it wasn't new to them. Dave loves that electronic sound, and I liked bands like Sigue Sigue Sputnik, and ambient bands like Tangerine Dream. I loved that electronic pulsing that goes on and on, an important part of the music."

'Images' is a sprawling mixture of Siouxsie and the Banshees-style romantic Goth coupled with mournful violin and liberally peppered with a classic Hawkwind middle-eight jamming. The lyrics were derived from a song Bridget had written whilst a member of a band called Next Year's Big Thing. For Hawkwind, she "rewrote them, adapting and adding to them to suit the song. The chorus was new, as were the spoken words."

"It was such a long, complicated piece that we laid the bass down first, because I have a good memory for music, to give everybody else a foundation to work on," says Davey. "Dave wrote the most of the music and I did the some of the middle bit. Bridget is fairly complicated, deep and arty, and I think she said [the lyrics were] about herself." When it came to the vocals, Bridget remembers the band saying they'd stay to watch her record. "Paul kicked them out, thankfully, but even so after singing the song through for the first time, I lost my voice. Paul was very calming and it soon came back. Then followed five hours of exacting recording, with double, sometimes triple tracking. I can still remember the buzz of listening to the finished song on the speakers in the studio. I've never heard it sound like that since; it's always a bit thin on CD. But it was very satisfying to hold the finished product and feel a sense of accomplishment. The first time I heard 'Images' on Radio 1, I was really chuffed." She professes dissatisfaction with the album's 'weedy' sound, and that's a view widely, though not universally, shared.

"I look back on it now and think it's a breath of fresh air," comments Chadwick. "When you listen to the albums that came before it, there's a lot of new vitality and tempo. Like 'Images', a monster fast track with all the typical

Hawkwind ingredients of the 90s: a big, elongated middle-eight section, changing moods and colours as you go through the track. I thought it was inventive."

Davey felt his song, 'Wings', had suffered from being "a bit sweetified; it needed to be menacing and dark, it's that sort of subject. I was after 'keyboard darkness' but I didn't know how to do that at the time." Davey was moved to write the song having seen coverage of the "Exxon-Valdez disaster – shocking images of birds covered in oil," and the album notes that a tenth of the royalties for this song would be donated to the Royal Society for the Protection of Birds [RSPB]. Though visually it had a big impact as a live performance on the ensuing tour, he's spot-on that it doesn't deliver quite the tone and texture that it demands on the album. Fast forward to his album, by-lined as being by Alan Davey's Eclectic Devils and titled *Live at SRS 2011*, to hear Davey and collaborators nail this one.

Space Bandits is an album all about the new blood that had arrived in Hawkwind over the previous few years. Bainbridge, contributing a number entitled 'TV Suicide' to what became his last full studio album, felt himself more outside of the band's main thrust than ever before. "I recorded 'TV Suicide' all by myself. I went to a studio with Paul Cobbold for a couple of days. Alan and Dave did their bits and when they'd finished I went in and did mine. There wasn't much communication going on. That can work okay, but I guess that the thing had split up into minute factions. I was neither positive nor negative, just waiting to see how it would all pan out, as the line-up was once-again changing constantly."

But it's also a record of two halves really, to adapt a metaphor, and because of that it isn't a totally satisfying listen. The opening salvo, Images, absolutely sets the album up and tells you, like *Astounding Sounds...* and *Levitation* before it, that things have changed again in Hawkwind land and so it's every bit as startling as 'Reefer Madness' and 'Levitation' were as gambits and when it moves into the atmospheric tribalism of 'Black Elk Speaks' with its authentic spoken-word Native American mysticism, using tapes of John Neihardt from back in the 1930s reciting the words of Nicholas Black Elk, it seems to demonstrate a band finding its way again. But after that, Davey's 'Wings' doesn't properly express itself and once past an exciting, but done better before and after, 'Out of the Shadows', described by Chadwick as "an anarchist's manifesto' and using the words of a different song by American fan Doug Buckley and a riff written by Brock and Davey during a soundcheck at Shank Hall, Milwaukee on the US tour, the album fizzles out without delivering fully on its early promise. There's Bainbridge's 'TV Suicide' wherein he asserts 'everything I need is on my TV', though he claimed not to own one, a very plodding and forgettable 'Ship of Dreams' and an experimental Davey track, 'Realms'. "All there is in 'Realms' is my vocal and bass guitar and a good tab of acid. I did it one night, and when I got up next morning and played it back, there was this great film soundtrack music. But I've never worked out how I did it... there's a big reverb backwards section..."

"The first half has the plausibility of the original version of *Flash Gordon*," wrote Roy Wilkinson (source unknown). "By side two they've acquired the hi-tech authenticity of, ooh, a really good episode of *Blake's Seven*." I'm hearing it the other way around quite frankly, but in the final analysis, it's a starting-point for a new era, but not a fully rounded mission statement. Better would be to come.

Before Hawkwind could get out on the road in support of *Space Bandits*, there was a graphic illustration of the decline in the community spirit of the festival scene. At Brighton, on 19th August 1990, a horrible moment of misunderstanding nearly ended in tragedy. "When we turned up at the site to play," recalls Bridget, "we were told there was only brew and hard drugs around… the atmosphere was pretty grim. Before the gig, a rumour went around that Dave was going to 'get it' while we were on." This may have been because of the increasingly hard line stance taken by Hawkwind and other noted Festival attendees, such as hippie 'spokesman-in-chief' Sid Rawle, against the use of heroin.

Though she was on the far side of the stage from Brock and unable to see exactly what transpired, Bridget's understanding was that "one or two blokes came on stage and approached Dave, apparently with the intention of 'egging' him, as it was around the time of his birthday. Dave thought he was being attacked and protected himself. The scuffle grew to include Alan and they disappeared off stage. I was oblivious to this and jamming with Harvey on the other side… it was only 15 or 20 minutes later and Dave hadn't taken over that I wondered what was happening."

When the rest of the band went to see what was going on, they found "a couple of men wearing motorbike helmets, wielding big chunks of wood and attacking Dave's bus… I could hear his dogs barking inside… I went on stage and asked people to come and help stop them. A lot came, but were scared to intervene. Alan had hidden in his van and although they had attacked it, he'd managed to remain unseen and they had eventually left it alone." There were police patrolling the perimeter of the site in a Land Rover, but "not surprisingly, they refused to get involved." If anything, it was a stark demonstration of just how badly the free festival movement had declined in recent years, under pressure from the Thatcher government and the subsequent John Major administration ("New Age Travellers? Not in this age! Not in any age!" Major had exclaimed), but also pressurised from within and damaged by a preponderance of heavy drugs and strong alcohol. In that respect, it was a bad accident waiting to happen.

As though for some form of catharsis, Kris Tait laid out the events, in a generalised way, in the form of a poem, later set to music. In it, she decries the collapsing festival culture which she always felt would be destroyed from the outside. At the end, she reflects on its demise being caused by 'our own kith and kin'.

"What was a happy festival scene, a wonderful thing, had become this sort of periphery of menacing people, wandering around robbing others," notes Brock. "It was the opposite of what festivals were supposed to be about. It should have been drawing people together, having a good time listening to music and selling their wares. But it ended up being foreboding, a decline and fall, like the

Roman Empire." He casts his mind back to where it all started. "Notting Hill Gate is the proof of it. In the late 60s and early 70s it was a great place of camaraderie with lots of free things going on, underground newspapers, everybody channelling their energies. Then it became corrupt, seedy. Bad drugs crept in and the whole thing turned sour."

There was a mass desertion of the scene by festival regulars after the events at Brighton. "Scouse, who had 'Wango Riley's Travelling Stage', which was the main stage that did the Travellers Field at Glastonbury, sold up and moved out," notes Kris Tait. "Gruff & Dee who had had a shop and café, went straight to Ireland and said 'forget it'. Lin, from Travellers' Aid Trust and Chaos Café, pulled out. That really was the end of the free festival scene." Brock adds: 'We had a meeting and said 'that's it'. It was a very unpleasant and worrying time."

**Alan Davey gets his Breakfast in America
(Bridget Wishart)**

In *Space Bandits* there may have been delivered one of the weaker Hawkwind studio albums, but it gave rise to a strong promotional tour, both in the UK and the USA during late 1990. Simon House had once again departed, but Bridget Wishart had stepped up to the role of front-person and embraced the showmanship of Calvert, with mime, costume and dance. "I had eleven costume changes on the Space Bandits tour," notes Wishart. "With each I assumed a different character. I had complete autonomy over these personae and I think most of the audience enjoyed my visual interpretations of the music. A lot of work went into each character, for example on the opening number I wore a radioactive protection suit and learnt semaphore. All the moves made with the UV flags were valid communications, usually something like 'Prepare for take-off.'"

"There were some hard-core fans quite distressed that there was a woman on-board," notes Bridget, "however, when I met them they were polite and on the whole kept their opinions to themselves." This wasn't the only problem Bridget experienced in the reactions of the male fans. "Throughout one gig there was a bloke at the front shouting at me... 'Bridget, give us your wig... give us your mask... give us your goggles'. I didn't give him anything as I needed it all for the rest of the tour. At the end, he shouted 'Bridget, give us a kiss!' I thought, 'fair enough', and bent down to give him a quick kiss, not thinking that he'd grab me and try for something a bit more passionate. Luckily I was sweaty and slippery and squirmed out of his grasp."

Though Hawkwind were still selling-out good-sized halls in the UK, their diminished profile stateside meant that they were booked into smaller venues at times, which proved difficult for Bridget. "Some of the gigs we played were quite small and the backstage areas weren't connected to the stage. This meant onstage costume changes. This made me feel a bit self-conscious and exposed at first, because as each costume came off, the 'mask' did too, exposing the real me until the next costume was on. I just pretended I wasn't there and it seemed to help."

"Bridget's artistic side was really good," says Davey. "All the costumes and the imagery was great but she once said to me she wanted to be to be more of a singer than doing that... but I thought that a girl singing lead vocals in Hawkwind wouldn't work."

"We toured the USA and Canada in The Grateful Dead's old greyhound bus," recalls Bridget. "It was painted on the outside with a flying horse and had a mad hippie driver who could drive, and drive, and drive, and through the most terrible weather. One night, driving up through the Rockies there was a blizzard and only the passenger windscreen wiper was working... Harvey sat there directing the driver from pole to pole for hour upon hour."

17

The Dave Brock Trio Construct an Electric Tepee

Biker festival; Bridget Wishart, Alan Davey
(Collection of Bridget Wishart)

This was the unthinkable: A Hawkwind tour without Dave Brock. Nevertheless, 1991 commenced with perhaps the most unexpected jaunt in the band's history. After so many years of being on the road, with often quite extensive itineraries and with a third US tour in as many years looming, he'd reached the conclusion that although there were European dates scheduled, driving around Europe in a bus for a month playing small clubs, held no appeal at that point.

"Dave didn't want to do it, but I needed the money, and Alan agreed with me, we reckoned we could do it," notes Harvey. "It was reasonably okay [without Brock], but it wasn't quite the same, obviously." Davey admits that he had a concern about the acceptability of a Hawkwind without Dave, but "we played so well that hardly anybody brought it up [though] a couple of people got passionately annoyed."

Beginning in Amsterdam on 12th March and taking in Germany, Greece, Italy and France before wrapping up in Belgium on 10th April after 24 dates, it was a gruelling schedule. "I think Dave decided not to come," comments Bridget, "as he needed a break from touring the same venues and seeing the same faces and doing the same things and living on a bus with lots of noisy, smelly people.

223

Eating food at weird times and trying to get enough sleep." Chadwick saw the whole environment as "this sort of myopic existence, inside a bus and the only people you tend to meet being those working on the production or fans who are really into it, so you get this distorted view."

Dave's temporary replacement was former Smartpils guitarist Steve Bemand. "Rich and I knew him well as we were all in The Demented Stoats and had lived in the same house. It meant that 'Silver Machine' could go into the set, as Dave wouldn't play it anymore," says Bridget. "A bloody good guitar player," adds Chadwick. "Already the jamming had been extending out the music, but without Dave to say 'right, that's it, let's come back and finish it', it was getting even longer. I was drumming away thinking 'this is going on for ages', but it was great fun!"

It does, though, hark back to Mike Moorcock's comment from earlier, of how the band "surged and subsided" at Dave Brock's touch and so despite these being good shows without the Hawklord-in-Chief at the helm, they also underlined how vital his all-seeing musical eye is. Television presenter Matthew Wright, of who's involvement in Hawkwind we'll come to a bit later, recalled watching a much later incarnation and describes exactly that sense of Dave's control over the ebb and flow of the band, compared to the clichéd notion of Hawkwind often being largely improvisational: "Dave is a band leader and he leads a properly tight band; they rehearse and rehearse, they all know exactly what they are doing. I watched 'Angels of Death' at the Isle of Wight, they were due to play 'x' numbers of bars of the main head-fuck riff and I could see as it was coming around, Niall [Hone] trying to catch Dave's eye and Dave shaking his head, "give it to me again," so we got another 'x' number of minutes of the riff and then I see Niall thinking it's time to get back, Dave shakes his head, "do it again," and you end up with eight minutes of this hypnotic, trippy, music that comes from being super disciplined and having a leader who is prepared to take a super disciplined band into fantastic new directions."

'Silver Machine' aside, there wasn't a great deal of variance from the Space Bandits tour, despite Davey's desire to play some of the more neglected Hawkwind classics. "The thing about rock standards is that music is a mood or a chemistry of sound made by people playing together. If you swap one musician for another, then the sound changes," says Chadwick. "What you had was one member gone and four others remaining who already had an established way of playing together. We had one other member coming in who was not a dominant character and would just fit in with what was going on; that's why there wasn't much change." Chadwick, Davey and Bemand already had experience of playing together, performing Hawkwind and Smartpils songs around the pubs of Bath and Bristol as 'Pilwind'.

"Hawkwind were going to play in Sarajevo," notes Chadwick. "When we stopped outside the venue, it was like a small village hall – and us in this big tour bus. All these soldiers were standing outside it, guarding the government buildings. It was obvious there was some unrest going on. We didn't play. We tried to persuade Harvey to do a solo gig…" It was only two weeks before civil war started to tear apart the former Yugoslavia. But being scrutinised by the army in Sarajevo wasn't the only indignity suffered by the band. "We always had to take our clothes off at borders, as they'd want to search us for drugs! Harvey particularly found it a gross indecency."

They next returned to the USA for the third consecutive year, but reduced to a three-piece of Brock, Davey and Chadwick. Personal matters had kept Bridget at home, whilst Bainbridge had reached the end of his mercurial, but immense, contribution to the cause.

"I didn't want to go to America straight away [after returning from Europe], we were going to have a couple of weeks before going, but Dave had pulled it all forward. As soon as we had got back, Dave informed everybody we were going the following week. I said that I wasn't going, that I had things to sort out," Bainbridge recalls. "Everything had fallen apart on me. I'd run off with this young girl to live in a truck, a beautiful girl, then that broke up and I went back to my wife. But that didn't work out and three years down the line we split up properly."

The USA tour was a curtailed affair, kicking off in New York on 9th May, 1991 (a month after the end of the European tour), finishing in Chicago on 23rd May. "We did all we could on the East Coast, but we didn't reach the West Coast, it was too expensive on a small budget," notes Davey.

"I had a phone call from Dave saying that they'd come back," says Bainbridge, indicating that the tour was truncated from the original plan. "Doug Smith was organising a couple of gigs, one in Glasgow. I remember saying, "Great, okay, see you in Glasgow. Then Alan phoned up and said we'd got to go and rehearse for a week, but I said I couldn't until I'd been paid some money. The story was that we weren't going to get any money until we were in Glasgow so I said, 'I'm sorry, I won't be rehearsing then', and left." Bainbridge professes one last parting piece of advice to Dave Brock; that he should "look after Richard."

On their return from America, the remaining trio were re-joined by Bridget for the planned summer gigs, including the Brixton Academy on 6th July where Hawkwind once again featured Tim Blake. There had been a plan for Tim to open for Hawkwind on some of their American dates, but it had fallen through: "In fact, we never met up in the States," Tim recalled for this book's first edition, before he'd returned full-time to the band. "But when I played at the Brixton Fridge, Hawkwind were on at the Academy the night before and a meeting and jam happened there and then. It was a very good Hawkwind indeed, the version I liked to play with the most, though Dave says I played a lot of bum notes!" It was a fortuitous opportunity to open one of the avenues of communication with past members that eventually resulted in the reunion show of October 2000.

Aside from that, there were some festival appearances, including a show at Mildenhall (3rd August) of which an audience recording reveals the line-up in a very contemporary drum 'n' bass mode, freshening up old numbers such as 'Needle Gun' and 'Night of the Hawks' and producing an almost perfect but sparse and stripped-down 'Snakedance'. However, the next show, a totally unsuitable sports hall in Exeter, on 31st August, with 60s star and would-be politician Screaming Lord Sutch opening, proved to be Bridget's final show with the band.

"A lot of my performances occurred halfway into songs," comments Wishart. "At Exeter I remember coming on in the middle of a song and the crowd cheering... I just knew my days were numbered. No way would the band be happy to hear cheering in the middle of a song! My popularity was not received well by some of the band and when Dave told me that I'd sung out of tune at Exeter I thought, here we go..."

"The official reason I was given by Alan and Richard for my leaving was that my singing was out of tune. Sometimes this was true. Hawkwind never practised harmonies and coming from singing lead in an all-girl punk band, I could have done with some. I was often singing a harmony line too low for my voice. Alan refused to sing the lower vocal in 'Wings' and this caused me much stress as I would nearly always lose the tune."

"I would have preferred it if Bridget had stuck to her performing; it looked really good," says Davey. "But in a live situation she had trouble pitching. With me and Dave singing, it was always on the button, which you've got to be. Punters aren't deaf anymore – like they used to be in the seventies – they notice it nowadays! When I'm on stage, I like to go off in another world sometimes but when things like that start happening, it drags you back, and you don't want that."

Chadwick, on the contrary, thought Bridget's contribution to Hawkwind very successful: "It brought in that sort of 'Dada-istic' showmanship that was missing. I think a lot of women in the audience could relate to it, because there was a lot of symbolism in her act for women. During 'Wings' she'd do this mime where she was this little figure with a shawl over her head, then she'd take the shawl off and make it into a soft little ball, really gently. Suddenly she'd get aggressive with it and appear to tear it to shreds. I thought stuff like that went quite far. No man could put over that image in the way she did."

The slim-line Hawkwind's first album, *Electric Tepee*, saw the band fully embracing the possibilities of computer technology. This was partly for aesthetics, but also on financial and logistical grounds. Electric Tepee was the first Hawkwind album fully recorded at Brock's home studio, a converted milking-shed on his Devonian farm that is a wonderful Aladdin's Cave of Hawkwind memorabilia, which gave the band the double-edged sword of unlimited recording time. "It didn't make any difference in terms of discipline, because we tend to work quite quickly," contests Chadwick. "We recorded *Space Bandits* at Rockfield Studios and that took days and days, so actually we were working faster by the time we did *Electric Tepee*."

Chadwick: "*Electric Tepee* was the album where I said, 'everyone else is using drum machines, look at all this dance music everyone is into. Nobody minds, let's just go for it'. With programming, a lot of people end up with generic sounding music; you could say that the last decade of dance music has been the easiest kind to make." His take on this was to turn the concept of computer-enhanced music on its head. "If I was going to take on drum programming I had to get it to sound like me, so instead of fitting around the confines of the machine, I needed it to sound like a real drummer performing, starting from bar one and going through the human sweat and endeavour of the song. I play on an electronic drum pad, with kick pedals and hi-hat pedals. I press 'Go' on the computer which starts it going into record mode and generates a click track which is the timing of the song, and everybody plays together. Their performance goes onto the tape, mine goes into the computer as notes played, in a long strip. Then I have to go in and edit this, because playing on a set of rubber pads is not the same as playing on a proper drum kit. When I've edited it all I get an exact reproduction of what I've played, with the bonus that any part that has drifted slightly out of time can be pushed back into time as midi notes."

By the time Electric Tepee was recorded, the three core members of Hawkwind had got to grips with redefining their approach in a way that made any possible alternative line-ups redundant. "Alan was getting really good at playing Wave Stations," says Chadwick. "Stacking up his synthesisers and getting huge soundscapes from them just by setting off these algorithms to produce constantly evolving sound patterns. On the other side you had Dave, who was getting really good at sampling and multi-track sequencing, with a big selection of instruments in a massive rack that could all be fired off by a sequencer, and also using his guitar as a synthesiser, which trigged all these sound modules using midi." This gave Hawkwind a new-found synergy with contemporary musical trends and led them to being referenced in the same breath as ambient aural sculptors The Orb and electro-house duo The Chemical Brothers. Once again it was that thing of pushing the boundaries of what made Hawkwind work, twisting the concept in another direction and making it relevant to what was being done in a wider context. "I was fascinated with dance music and stopped listening to rock altogether," says Chadwick. "Working in an electronic domain just seemed futuristic and different from everything we'd done before."

After the relatively truncated Space Bandits, the new album showed that Hawkwind still had a lot of inspiration for new material, although the result sounded in need of some judicious pruning. "We wanted to make a double album, to give the impression that there was so much of it, it couldn't be shelved aside, a positive outpouring," explains Chadwick. And it was an outpouring; at times, it reminds the listener just why the single vinyl LP's limitation was a positive thing, constraining the musician and demanding that each track justified its existence in a way that the more expansive possibilities of running time that the CD format was now offering, and in that respect, it set the scene for some other excesses in future Hawkwind studio albums. But when was it good, it was bloody good.

Some of the material had already received a public airing the previous winter, including an instrumental that, married up to the lyrics written so many years before as 'Mirror of Illusion', became 'Mask of the Morning' and a dense and dirty Chadwick/Davey song, 'LSD'. "I had the bass riff, but it needed a slightly unusual drumbeat to roll it along," recalls Davey. "Richard came up with the beat, and wrote the second part. I came up with the lyrics, on acid. It's life, sex and death, the whole existence."

And 'LSD', as the album's account opener, did a lot musically to explain where this new phase was going. "It's like a live number which has various subtle cues that each member plays to take the music into the next section of the song," says Chadwick. "It was difficult to recreate that in a studio environment. But with just the three of us playing, we could work out how to make this deep sound, which was based on listening to each other, playing along with each other... we got really good at doing that."

There was a hope that *Electric Tepee* would produce a successful single, the radio-friendly 'Right to Decide', much later revealed as partly drawn from a Brock song demoed around the time of *Choose Your Masques* and titled 'Radio Telepath', partly because of renewed interest in Hawkwind's music on the part of Radio One. The opportunity, as with 'Urban Guerrilla' all those years before, was lost in controversial circumstances. The two-verse song of the album was a revised version of the original cut, in which a third references a tragedy in 1991, when a Durham householder, Albert Dryden, became the first person to commit murder live on British television. Dryden had built a bungalow on land designated for agricultural use only. When confronted with council planning officer, Harry Collinson, serving a demolition order, Dryden produced an antique pistol and shot Collinson dead. Brock's additional lyrics had been a rage against the powers of local councils, despite this case being largely down to Dryden's intransigence over a prolonged period. The national press picked-up on Hawkwind's intended reference to this story, with the result that Brock "received a telephone call from Dryden's sister suggesting that we were 'just cashing in to make money'. I said, 'No! What we're trying to do is prove a point. You have the right to decide if you want to do these things, the council can't just say what they want to say and that's the end of it all'. After I'd had a talk with her, I took that offending verse out, but the song didn't make that much sense any more. It was withdrawn before release, but it could have changed everything for us." Brock has more than enough perspective on the machinations of the music business to be philosophical about this. "It would have earned us a lot of money, got us a record deal, but at the end of the day, it didn't. A little niche appears, a window, and if you don't jump through that window and take your chances, it's gone." Was he right in this assumption? Quite possibly; even shorn of its third verse, it's a smart, sharp radio-appealing number that is not only the highlight of the album, but is a 'proper' Hawkwind song; provocative in lyric and dynamic in delivery and is an acute demonstration of why the three-piece Hawkwind, with Davey's driving bass and Chadwick's swinging drums to the fore, worked so well.

Unnoticed by the media 'Death of War', a poem set to a strident military march, had potential for controversy as well. The track, credited to

Brock\Rowntree, was an angry rumination on the disconnection between soldiers and leaders in a conflict. The co-writing credit 'Rowntree' was for Mark Rowntree, a serial killer imprisoned for life in June 1976 after a week in which he murdered four people in an attempt to imitate his 'hero', the notorious 'Black Panther', Denis Neilson. Rowntree had been sending a few his poems to Brock, and to another musician, Edgar Broughton, and Dave had selected this one to set to music, though later reflecting on Rowntree's victims he'd distanced himself from the correspondence.

"I think *Electric Tepee* was the most daring album that Hawkwind have ever done," suggests Davey. "To go down to a three piece and put out a record as Hawkwind... because a three-piece Hawkwind doesn't sound right on paper, but we made as much noise as a six-piece band." Davey saw the reduction in the band's line-up as beneficial for the remaining musicians. "There was so much more space, we could experiment, do things we hadn't been able to do before. It gelled straight away; people seemed to like it, full gigs, *Electric Tepee* number one for a month in the *Kerrang!* charts."

From the drum 'n' bass crash of 'LSD', through its distillation of psychedelic wash 'Blue Shift' to the full-on 'Right to Decide', *Electric Tepee* was the freshest, most vibrant, statement of musical intent Hawkwind had produced for many years, even when we consider that sharper editing would have produced a more definitive album. The more traditionalists among the band's fandom considered the trio's follow-up, *It is the Business of the Future to be Dangerous*, the name taken from a quote from mathematician Alfred North Whitehead ["It is the business of the future to be dangerous, and it is among the merits of science that it equips the future for its duties"], to be less successful.

For many years, there had been a yearning for an instrumental Hawkwind album. By 1993 when this was almost realised by Brock, Davey and Chadwick's more experimental offering, their ground had been captured from within the free festival circuit, notably by Ozric Tentacles. When the Ozrics found themselves described in Guitar Magazine as producing a "bucolic blend of progressive rock, English rural psychedelia meshed with strands of world music," it might have easily been a critique of the expansive and forward looking nature of the Hawkwind trio's sound. As it was, Ozric Tentacles' *Jurassic Shift* album moved them temporarily from being a crustie fringe band to Top 40 album chart status in the same year that *It is the Business of the Future to be Dangerous* alienated Hawkwind's more conservative followers and pushed them further outside the mainstream.

"I remember reading one review that said 'track one, no guitar... track two, still no guitar... track three, still no lyrics'," muses Davey. Brock described it to the Glasgow Her-ald as "trance music... the sort of thing Can, Neu! and Kraftwerk started."

Reflecting on the more negative responses the album received, Chadwick still finds the CD "interesting to listen to because it's very psychedelic, very washy. Songs surface through this psychedelic noise and I like that; it's very interesting on that level." Arguably, though, the songs that emerge just feel somewhat misplaced

229

on the album and, texturally, they interrupt the flow, another Hawkwind album that left the whole sounding less than its magnificent parts. It creates a sensation of attempting to deconstruct the Hawkwind sound into its base thematic elements, and then rebuild them in an 'Ozrics' style, but doesn't quite have the balls to abandon traditional song structure. So, as the record develops and gets under the skin of the listener, the spell woven into the fabric of the early tracks is broken by the return to Earth of the quasi-reggae reworking of 'Letting in the Past' (based on 'Living in the Future', from *Church of Hawkwind*) and 'The Camera that Could Lie' ('Living on a Knife-edge' from *Sonic Attack*).

The first half of the record is a genius move from the trio, an instrumental suite of complexity and innovation that never strays from sounding like a Hawkwind record, but which still comes across as totally fresh and ambitious and pushing at the boundaries of what a Hawkwind album could be. It's sometimes abstract while still being carefully constructed, but it's always an exploration of both ambient and hard-driving spacerock. But in the days where expressions such as 'missed opportunity' are banded around Internet forums without due thought, this one does seem a genuine missed opportunity, as the three musicians balanced themselves on the brink of doing something totally radical but pulled each other back from the edge. It's a huge shame; the early tracks on the record are vibrant and dynamic and distilled into a standard LP would have created a classic album that was both relevant to what had been done before and a brave leap out of the box. But it's again that curse of the expanded run-time that affected the trio's previous offering, with things such as 'Letting in the Past' and a cover of 'Gimme Shelter', for example, requiring somewhere different in the Hawkwind canon to live, rather than being lodged out of place and out of context on what could have been a terrific instrumental suite.

Some track titles reflected the political tensions of its time: 'Space is their (Palestine)', which developed in the live set as a new bridge for 'Assassins of Allah', and the evocative two part 'Tibet is Not China', a world music chant that leads into a classic explosion of Hawk rhythms. "Where that one came from," says Chadwick, "was that Dave had got this sequence going with a kind of back-to-front click track and I was trying to play around it. Dave and Paul Cobbold were trying to help: 'can't you get this Richard – it's easy!' and I just lost my rag. 'I can play the fucking drums: look at this!' and went wild, all that mad toms working and stop/start, then just went into the end coda bit which was the actual part I was supposed to be playing. Unknown to me, Paul captured everything I'd got and just overdubbed on top of it. It's the thing with electronic music, something entirely irrelevant, when put in a certain context becomes a useful bit of music." Davey: "Can would do that, play all day and pick out ten minutes of it, a bit here and there would fit together."

When they appeared on the VH-1 satellite channel, Brock was asked by the show's presenter about the "Free Tibet" emblem on the CD's cover. This led to Brock inciting the audience to "throw red paint over the Chinese Embassy." The unexpected off-shoot, notes Chadwick, was that "they were really taken with

Dave as a character and did tentatively approach him with the idea of being one of their presenters because of his demeanour; he was really good on TV."

There are those who argue, just as it was mooted years before that *Church of Hawkwind* was a Dave Brock album, that the best way to interpret *It is the Business...* is to see it as a Richard Chadwick solo album because of the electronica dovetailing into trance elements that he must certainly have had a major hand in creating, and there's some merit to that outlook, even though Richard himself considers such a notion as "Bizarre! It's not the case at all!" But it's much more arguable that it's a Hawkwind album made two years too late. "I felt that Hawkwind weren't leading the way anymore," notes Davey, despite believing it to be a very strong record. "Hawkwind were always the innovators, *Electric Tepee* was like that, but on this one, other people had done it first."

Jurassic Shift took Ozric Tentacles and the crustie festival scene mainstream by reaching number eleven in the UK charts in May 1993. The Orb had already achieved number one status with *U.F.Orb* the previous June, whilst The Chemical Brothers enjoyed a string of albums that topped the charts through the second half of the 1990s. "We've done things and been noticed for them five years later," commented Brock in the Glasgow Herald. "We get sampled by other bands, big ones. I don't like name dropping, I don't have to." Despite the success of bands so obviously influenced by the legacy of Hawkwind and even though the *Independent on Sunday* newspaper noted that the rave audience had embraced "hoary old Hawkwind" such respect didn't translate into chart success. *It is the Business of the Future...* grazed the lower reaches of the charts. *Electric Tepee* achieved the heady heights of fifty-three.

Apart from their two substantial studio releases, the trio also contributed to a collection of CD singles, all comprising covers of The Rolling Stones classic, 'Gimme Shelter', in aid of charities supporting the homeless. The various artists who provided music for the CDs were broken down into generalised categories, leading Hawkwind to share a release with heavy metal bands Thunder and Little Angels. The Hawkwind version featured guest vocals by Page 3 icon Samantha Fox, providing a surprising duet with Richard Chadwick who claims to have been "tricked into singing on this." He explains: "We transposed [the song], dropped it a key or something. There was an initial sample from the original record and then in came our new arrangement. Normally Dave would do his vocals when we're not around, but this time he said, 'Ah, I'm having trouble getting the vocals on this'. So I said, 'Well, you can sing it like this...' and just sang the song, and Dave said 'Right! That's it then!'" The cause was another close to the band's heart. Interviewed on a promotional film for the EP, Chadwick noted how "the reason we're involved in this, is because it's vitally important that something is done... there shouldn't be people homeless in this country, there's no reason for it."

"We asked [Richard] to put it down on tape, as a guide... and of course he did it really well... and we had the vocals for that song without him realising," adds Davey.

Attempting to retain creative and financial control over the new material, Brock, Davey and Chadwick, along with manager Doug Smith and his partner Eve Carr, established a record label, The Emergency Broadcast System. Though the three members of Hawkwind were shareholders of the company, the day-to-day running was in the hands of Smith and Carr as the sole directors. "We returned to Douglas [on occasions] and he would take charge and sort things out; not as a manager, as a consultant," explains Brock. "Douglas thought it would be a good idea if we formed our own record label and put it out through a major, it worked quite well for a while."

Douglas Smith recalled how "The problem with EBS was that it was just three members of the band that owned the company: Richard, Alan and Dave, plus myself and my wife Eve. The deal was that they supplied the material and we supplied the work and whatever we made from it would be split five ways. There wasn't any increased value to us, it was equal to us getting a commission, but we ran the label and it was quite successful for a while, but the reality was that the highest sales was on the first one and that did about ten thousand copies. We cut vinyl releases on EBS because vinyl was still wanted, we could guarantee at least two to three thousand copies of each album. But again, it whittled down until with [live album] *Love in Space* we probably only sold about a thousand copies and we were doing digipack CD releases to compensate for that lack of the packaging that you got with the vinyl."

The first release was an album from the UK tour that promoted *It is the Business of the Future…*, the double-entendre *Business Trip*, recorded at Hastings Pier Pavilion on 27th November, 1993. "I'd rung-up my friend Simon Tepee," recalls Davey, "and somebody said 'he's away on a business trip', and I just thought what a brilliant title it would be for a live album. It's so obvious but it needed that phone call to get it." The recording demonstrated that however abstract and inventive the band had become in the studio, live they were still a power-house rock band with all the trimmings. The only clue to their reduced line-up was Brock's telling, 'Stop that tape – I heard it!' on the introduction to 'Right to Decide'.

Most telling, the 1993 dates revealed a band already moving away from the direction of their latest album and rediscovering a denser approach, as shown by the addition to the live set of Davey's 'Sputnik Stan'. This number, the first-time Davey had written a character-driven song (an orbital scrap dealer: Albert Steptoe marooned in an episode of *Red Dwarf*) had the pace and drive of the trio's first album rather than the Middle Eastern flavour of their second. "I saw this programme on the Discovery channel, about the problem of space junk: there is a phenomenal amount. Apparently within twenty years the odds of an astronaut on a spacewalk being hit by this stuff will be very high. I figured at some point they'd have to send a scrap merchant up there! It triggered this idea."

Other surprise inclusions were a reinvented version of 'Quark Strangeness & Charm' and the first appearance of 'Green Finned Demon' since it was scratched from the playlist in 1984. "Sometimes when we dug-up old songs, they didn't work if we did them as they were on the original album, because the chemistry just wasn't right," explains Davey. "We were trying to work-out how to do 'Quark' and we thought of halving the tempo, slowing down the verses but speeding up the chorus, and getting that piano sound. Sometimes you have to reinvent songs."

EBS also released what was effectively a third Brock/Davey/Chadwick Hawkwind album, *White Zone*, credited to the 'Psychedelic Warriors', a further extension of the ambient mood of *It is the Business of the Future...* "We had so much stuff left over, a lot of it really good, though no rock stuff. Douglas suggested we put it out under another name," Davey notes. "I think we were trying to slip it into a different market, but it didn't get pushed or advertised." In truth, it's a pretty inconsequential record, not much noticed at the time, not much cared for when it re-emerged as part of Cherry Red's catalogue reissues in more recent times. If we think of it as a Hawkwind album, then it vies for the title of most forgotten, if we pass on it as part of the main catalogue, then it holds scant interest as a side-project. When I interviewed him for *Record Collector*, Brock reflected it on it as "an offshoot, doing a sort of dance music and playing with loops and things. We've always tried to experiment and learn the latest technology but it's good to try lots of things. It's like painting, you might do loads and throw them away, but at least you're doing something. We did have some bits and pieces for a second Psychedelic Warriors album but they've never seen the light of day and technology has moved on." Chadwick's interest in dance music influenced much of the trio's studio output. However, to take the view expressed in *The Encyclopaedia of Popular Music* that Hawkwind became "totally dance music-orientated" and "started to copy rave ideas" ungenerously misreads this cross-fertilisation of pop-culture trends.

This synergy with the techno generation was recognised by Swordfish of ambient trance band Astralasia and their free festival counterparts, The Magic Mushroom Band. Interviewed by Toby White for the website *Phase 9*, Swordfish noted the influence of "psychedelic rock bass and early synthesisers... when the acid house thing kicked-off there was this technological breakthrough. It enabled the people making spaced-out music to move into a different genre using more electronics." David Gates, a member of "intelligent techno" DJ outfit Salt Tank, recognised his musical education as spanning "New Order, Steve Hillage, Robert Fripp and Brian Eno, Gong, Hawkwind, disco, reggae, punk…"

Gates: "We hit this wave around 1988 when everything changed in music and acid house happened, which was what it must have been like in the sixties and seventies. Astralasia had invited us to play at an all-night rave in Bracknell and it was great. When we did a second one, we wanted a whole new set of songs and decided to play around with some tracks by Hawkwind. I recently read an article which reviewed *In Search of Space* and it suggested this was the original trance record. It took us ages to learn not to put chords into our dance music. It's got to be that single repetitive beat. You look back at Hawkwind and it was pretty much what they did."

Having sent a tape of remixes to Brock, Gates received a call suggesting that Salt Tank play with Hawkwind at a gig at the Brixton Academy (15th August, 1992). "We did a day's rehearsal in Devon, and before we knew it we were on stage." At this show, the trio played inside three individual tepees, Gates recalling that "The cables for their instruments weren't long enough for them to move outside... almost comical. But I could see really clearly that they knew something interesting was going on." Gates sees a synergy between "the whole counterculture of the original rave scene... and the free festivals, the same kind of people," and a crossover between "psychedelic rock and trance."

"I think, to this day, Hawkwind kind of stuck where they were and didn't move on into that next phase," Swordfish told me a few years back. "They embraced it a bit, maybe for commercial reasons or perhaps spiritual reasons but perhaps it was a bit alien because it involved dance beats and they had a different kind of mantra."

Astralasia arranged four versions of 'Spirit of the Age', released as Solstice Remixes in July 1993. Their 'dance' re-mix of 'Uncle Sams on Mars' was included on the 'Quark Strangeness & Charm' CD single. Gates compiled an ambient Hawkwind remix CD, *Future Reconstruction – Ritual of the Solstice*, for which Salt Tank provided 'Master of the Universe'. "For the purists, the unthinkable has happened," wrote Phil Brook on the Farfield Records website. "Modern 'electronic' bands have been allowed to unleash computers and sequencers to reconstruct ten of Hawkwind's songs."

In essence Brook had described the chasm between rock fans and dance culture, the former with their stuck-in-the-past "it doesn't sound like Hawkwind" view, and the latter happy to position their remixes far away from the source material to create a more modern vibe. Richard Chadwick summed up it when describing the concept behind *Electric Tepee*: "You can sum [it] up as a kind of tribal enclosure within which a lot of modern things are going on. It's that paradox, looking like something old but containing something very new. Barbarians with technology, basically."

The free festival scene finally collapsed from internal and external pressures. It had become overloaded with an influx of younger people whose aspirations were as different from the peace-and-love generation that had created it, as they were from the DIY punk ethic that helped sustain it. The travelling community that had defined the anti-establishment ethos were giving way on the organised festival scene to the increasingly corporate Glastonbury and Knebworth weekend crowds.

The rave scene defined its own identity based on new drugs. If the drugs consumed could be described as governing the user's worldview, then there was little room for one set of people smoking dope and another set favouring the new brand of stimulants (such as the dance-till-dawn Ecstasy) to share a common set of values. The rave scene was also more financially self-interested, charging people to attend, anathema to the seasoned free festival revellers.

At the same time, there was the continued pressure on the travelling community's way of life from the Conservative Government. It had been made increasingly difficult for the sort of congregations that characterised the festival scene to come together. For a group of people whose vehicles were their homes, the repercussions of flouting the laws were too heavy: the threat of having their bus confiscated or their children made wards of court. Many of the travellers' sites had become contaminated with heroin abuse, creating a situation where the very people who were needed to get the free festivals together were, by the nature of the drugs they were taking, unable to get anything together.

"As the age of the travellers and revellers grew younger, the drugs harder, and the ideals changed, anyone who valued their health, sanity and property moved abroad or gave up travelling," notes Bridget Wishart. "Not everyone gave up straight away and it wasn't always all bad."

The Criminal Justice Act of 1991 sounded the death-knoll for the whole culture. The Act allowed police to remove any gathering of two or more people whom they believed to be trespassing on a piece of land for the 'purpose of residing there'. Furthermore, it enabled police to act against any gathering that caused damage to a piece of land. It has been noted that a court could define this damage as being caused by someone walking across it. The effect was to create an environment where, in the words of the Chief Constable of Greater Manchester, David Wilmot, what was achieved was to "criminalise anyone who has a travelling way of life and lives in a caravan."

It is possible to see a parallel between this destruction of the rootless way of life of the travellers and the imagery employed by Hawkwind, visually and musically, of the Native American peoples. The use of the Neihardt recitals from the Lakota Sioux spiritualism of Black Elk on the *Space Bandits* track 'Black Elk Speaks', the cover artwork of the trio's studio albums and of the single 'Quark Strangeness & Charm' from *The Business Trip*, suggested an identification of the plight of one people with the historical near extermination of another.

"There was a romantic fascination with the ideology," concedes Chadwick of this comparison, "nomad people under threat from 'blue coats'. It was unfolding before you; Chiefs of Police decommissioning the Peace Convoy, all that sort of stuff. The Plains Nomad people were suffering the same sort of thing, either they were on reservations and part of society or they were moving around, outside of society and people would be trying to push them in. But that's an entirely romantic view, though you can see how people might think that."

Romantic notion or acutely observed parallel, the Brock, Davey and Chadwick era presented a version of the band that leaned heavily on the tribal nature of the band's following.

18

A Tree is Planted and Alien Abductions Abound

**Three become four; Ron Tree centre-stage
(Dave Brock Collection)**

The 'Dave Brock Trio' played their final show in Köln (13th November 1994). "We'd been out working a lot; a couple of European tours and quite a few other things," says Chadwick, "but the writing was going into a bit of a lull. We weren't coming up with as much stuff as we should have."

Ron Tree observed how, "Hawkwind were running out of ideas as a three-piece. They'd been good, but it was getting a bit stale." He wrote to Brock, saying that "I could be a singer for you! I'm crazy enough!" and received a call suggesting that he met with them to "give it a go." The result was that "I went down, sung 'Death Trap' and apparently, that was it. I was in. I didn't know it [at the time] but later they asked if I wanted to go to America."

Prior to joining Hawkwind, Tree played bass in Plato Jacuzzi before moving on to Captain Jesus & the Sunray Dream (who supported Hawkwind in the early 90s). "Between that I was in a band called Bastard, then 2000DS and went around Europe, but it was too violent and mental, so I left. Came back and made up a band called Sewer Suckers. Then I made a robot and played a few gigs with it." Though Tree was joining an unusually stable Hawkwind line-up he found it "quite relaxing to slip into, like putting your hand in a glove. It was easy." Recognising that the trio had reached a creative impasse, Tree's goals as their new frontman were clear: "I wanted to revitalise the lyrical content of the band, the imagination, to take steps forward in psychedelic music, add a bit of attitude and raw power." The difficult aspect was working with one of his heroes. "I had a lot of respect for Dave Brock and suddenly I'm playing in a band with him. It took a year just to get over that!" Tree noted that "Dave was the boss," but found that "anything goes, as long as it was a reasonable idea."

Tree's first performance with Hawkwind was on their spring 1995 tour of North America, opening in Toronto (4th April). His addition led the setlist back towards the Calvert-era songs with '25 Years' making a surprise reappearance alongside 'Death Trap', 'Urban Guerrilla' and 'Ejection'. Like Davey before him, Tree saw to it that reintroduced 'old' songs came complete with early lyric structures. On its rare appearances, 'Silver Machine' regained a line in which it 'turns everything green', dropped for the original single version, though retained by Calvert through to the Hawklords era. It was also an opportunity to try-out some work-in-progress tracks for the project that later became the *Alien 4* album: 'Are You Losing Your Mind', 'Alien (I am)' and 'Vega'.

Scott Heller, who interviewed the band during the tour, observed at New York's Limelight (9th April) that "Hawkwind had this insane new frontman who had apparently eaten a ton of drugs that people were more than willing to give him and was out of his mind!" The show itself proved a biting disappointment to Heller: "The band was really tired and only played for seventy minutes. The lightshow was totally lame. When the band was coming out they had this woman who was dancing to techno music and making erotic moves inside this cage that was hanging from the ceiling. Alan Davey was particularly amused by it!"

Interviewed by Heller, Chadwick enthused about the new lease of life that the addition of Ron Tree brought to Hawkwind. "He really helps us out; fills up the spaces in the middle… revitalised and invigorated us all." He certainly did bring something to the party. Unpredictable, energetic and intelligent with bucket loads of charisma on the one hand, on the other as a performer he sometimes lacked a self-editor so that his performances could be commanding and quite riveting, or they could be indulgent, incoherent and full of foul language. In that sense, listen to any recording of the band with Ron Tree at the front and you'll be waiting to hear exactly which version would have turned-up on that occasion. When he's brilliant – and this applies now as it did then – he's *absolutely* brilliant, but there's unpredictability at the core of his work that makes it a rollercoaster ride.

Although Hawkwind twice returned to the USA to build on the investment of the 1989 tour, it had not turned out to be the fresh start in America that Brock anticipated and this would develop further as the 90s progressed, widening the chasm between himself and Nik Turner. During February and March 1994, Turner fanned the flames of the antipathy that would increasingly characterise his relationship with Brock by touring America as 'Nik Turner's

Hawkwind'. Brock saw the move as a deliberate attempt to capitalise on his own hard work in re-establishing the Hawkwind name: "We had good bookings for our next tour. We had a record label behind us, but Nik scotched it. Doug Smith went bananas and got an injunction against Turner." The court prevented any promoter from booking Turner as 'Hawkwind', with the eventual result that 'Nik Turner's Space Ritual' appeared instead. "I was originally going to call the band Nik Turner's Hawkwind, but we got all this legal bullshit," says Turner. Claiming innocence, Turner notes that he "just thought I could call it Nik Turner's Hawkwind as different from Hawkwind... I didn't really know that Hawkwind were successful in America at that time. They were a name that people knew, and I wanted to use that name because I felt I'd been instrumental in creating the success of the band... I felt I had a right."

The case allegedly had potential ramifications for the group in its ability to deal successfully with promoters in the USA, who might subsequently associate the name Hawkwind with the legal problems they had encountered. In the future, it would come to represent a battle, both legal and conceptual, for Hawkwind's identity and ethos. "We invested £56,000 over the three tours... three years of hard work down the drain..." states Brock, "and we had the same thing in Europe..."

Turner pleads to having scheduled the dates in complete ignorance of Hawkwind's attempts to develop their American audience: "The tours came about from a guy called Tommy Grenas, who is actually from Belfast, a great fan of Inner City Unit. He used to live in a squat in London, and ICU used to gig at the Hope & Anchor in Islington; I think he squatted the Hope & Anchor eventually!"

"During punk," says Grenas, "Hawkwind and Bob Calvert seemed to fit into the anarcho-metal groove perfectly. I was deeply affected by them, under magical influences and adolescent urban shamanism. I moved to Los Angeles in 1984 and began to do music [and] was surprised at how many young folk had no idea of what or who Hawkwind were. Some did, like Jello Biafra, but the up-and-coming underground didn't." Grenas became involved with Cleopatra Records. "They approached me about doing a new version of the Sphynx album [*Xitintoday*]," says Turner, "which Tommy was very interested in, and he became a co-producer on it along with the guitarist Helios Creed. I was amenable to that, I sent recordings of the original flute music, re-read all of the lyrics and they produced the album."

Having been such an admirer of Turner's work, Grenas then contacted him regarding Nik travelling to the USA and playing with two bands Grenas had formed: Farflung and Pressurehed. "It seemed the time was right," asserts Grenas. "Hawkwind were becoming a rising myth, due to friends spreading the gospel and a slew of hip, cheap, good quality compilations coming out. A few conversations with Nik and a plan was set to put a band and a tour together. The group would basically be Pressurehed and Farflung, with Helios Creed and ex-Hawks Del Dettmar, Simon House, Alan Powell and Nik. After the first rehearsal, we knew a pysch destroyer had been built and was ready to slip out of dock!"

238

This tour was extremely successful: "It was close to a sell-out," recalls Grenas. "People were packing in to see a show of at least two hours of relentless space drone. I remember many notable nights, especially the show in Seattle when Mudhoney, members of Pearl Jam and Nirvana showed up to offer praise… and this was when Seattle grunge was at its highest."

Scott Telles, whose band ST37 was formed from a desire to fuse "The spacerock of Hawkwind and the SF-punk energy of Chrome" feels that "The 'Nikwind' shows were very important for the US spacerock scene, because the tour brought a diverse group of influences together. The fact that [members of] Pressurehed and Farflung were the backup band showed that the American scene had become 'world class'. The addition of Helios Creed united the late-70s punk scene with the spacerock renaissance and validated the whole progression of influences." For Telles, it was not only the performance of Hawkwind's early 70s back-catalogue that appealed, but that the set also "included some Pressurehed numbers and some Helios/Chrome songs which put them on the same plateau with the Hawkwind stuff and they held their own! Then the fact that Nik started working in the studio with this assemblage really put the stamp of legitimacy on the whole thing." And in terms of raising the bar for the members of Pressurehed and Farflung, there was the significant addition of Jello Biafra, and Psychic TV's Genesis P. Orridge, on some of the 1994 dates.

Grenas: "Dave Brock and Hawkwind had been over, performing new material and the usual stunning live sets with a young and vibrant band, but there was a feeling of want for the heavier, theatrical, wall-of-sound of the old days. Dave was doing what Hawkwind was meant to be about… the future. But people still needed to know the past." What was pleasing for Grenas was the profile of the audience the shows attracted: "younger and eager than I expected; to this day anyone who had seen the tour offers compliments and excitement about being there. We toured Japan soon afterward [in 1996], which was awesome, and Europe, which was okay but nowhere near as high of an impact as America. The following year another tour was made but by then it was winding down a bit."

Without the baggage of a full group and stage equipment to transport, and relying on local musicians for support, Turner was thought to have been able to price himself at the same level that Hawkwind had been earning on their profile-establishing 1989 visit. His sets were built around the Hawkwind crowd pleasers that Brock was, ironically, beginning to remove from his shows. Turner also raided his own back catalogue for songs rarely played live: 'Kadu Flyer', 'You Shouldn't Do That', 'D-Rider' and 'Dying Seas'. Even Brock considered that "[Turner's ensemble] wasn't a bad sounding band."

"Working with Nik was a special time for us. I look back on it with pride as a rite of passage, a strange education deserving of an honorary 'space cadet' badge," comments Grenas. "With Nik the audience almost becomes the band, that's the magic of early Hawkwind, the charm of what it is about. Like his Can counterpart, Damo Suzuki, Nik believes Hawkwind is a family of anyone who has ever listened to the band as well as those who have performed. I know there is some edginess between Dave and Nik, but Hawkwind is Hawkwind, the space tribe, the vibrations are the same and the intent of all performers is the same... to blow your mind!"

**Hawkwind dancers reach new heights, Alien tour 1995
(Collection of Dave Brock)**

With Ron Tree on board, work was completed on *Alien 4*, a concept album probably partly inspired by the conspiracy theory paranoia of the then high-profile

240

and successful TV series, *The X-Files*. "Dave had this idea about UFOs and extra-terrestrials as a musical theme – alien abductions," relates Chadwick. "This led to the song 'Alien (I am)', a sequencer-driven tune with us playing bass and drum parts around it."

Alien 4 starts with a spoken-word passage, 'Abduction', invoking the contemporary mythology of otherworldly visitations and the apparently widespread belief amongst Americans that humans are regularly taken aboard alien spacecraft and subjected to experimentation. It goes on to borrow from the archetypes of the new breed, the post Little-Green-Men, post Bug-Eyed-Monster view of alien visitors. 'Large black eyes… reptilian and insectile facial qualities…' describe one facet, but there are also 'the little ones that are so blissful'. What really horrifies the narrator, though are the ugly ones who are like 'larvae inside the leather-faced skin of a hard, dark scary machine'. It's as though Tree has opened his creative account with Hawkwind by declaiming the contents of his most deep-seated nightmares. "I was doing stuff about aliens, because I know they exist, there is no doubt. Anybody who doesn't [believe in aliens] is a fool, a total fool." This 'fool' reserves comment!

Tree found the finished record something of a disappointment, which he partly attributes to coming into the band midway through their work on the album. "There was quite a lot done," concedes Chadwick, "or at least we knew how it went, so some tracks are more Ron-driven than others. He just glued himself on top of it."

"I could only do so much on the album, in a creative way," adds Tree. "The music wasn't written by me, so I'm singing Karaoke over Hawkwind music. I didn't think some of the riffs were that good, like 'Xenomorph'; I thought they should move away from that style and do more like 'Blue Skin', which was Dave's. I had to make the best of what was there."

Chadwick has different reasons for finding fault with the result: "The record sounds to me disjointed in terms of getting the idea across, and ended up being a collection of songs roughly tied in with the theme. It didn't have that really good integral narrative that makes it a story with a beginning, middle, and an end – or at least a new index of possibilities at the end."

From the supporting tour came a live CD and video, *Love in Space*, by far a better fusion of the conspiracy politics and grand Space Opera than the studio CD. "I think the tour was probably a bit more cohesive," Chadwick reflects. 'It would have been nice to have made it a bit more 'High-Art' than it came out as, but as a stage show it was very successful. We had some terrific dancers, who were interested in mime. The part with the alien abduction and the whole idea of a secret agenda with government people knowing what is going on and not letting any information out came out well in this beautiful mime sequence. It really broadened out the whole idea that there's something going on here that not everyone knows about, but there is something going on and that it's worth keeping your eyes and ears open."

Things were once again in that seemingly endless cycle of flux and change. Having joined-up with Brock and Bainbridge as part of 'Hawkdog' in the late 80s, Jerry Richards had come back into the band's orbit with a lead guitar guest-spot on a version of 'Death Trap' for the *Alien 4* album, a BBC Radio session cut on 27th July 1995 and a few festival dates that summer. "I got invited to go and play in Greece and did one of those Rock 'N' Blues festivals over here, one of those biker festivals and then I got sort of 'laid-off' from the band for a little while, and I think that was down to concerns that Alan Davey had about the direction he thought the band ought to go in."

Though the four-piece line-up continued for the remainder of 1995, and through most of the following year, there was an opening up of musical differences that were exposed by Jerry's return to the band that August. "I don't know whether there was some confusion or a breakdown in communication between Dave and Alan at that point in terms of the direction of the band, because that was kind of the beginning of winding-up the EBS label. Doug Smith was becoming involved with some other acts, most notably Chumbawamba and while he wasn't strictly 'managing' the Chumbies, they did need his help, and Douglas was, and is, a brilliant manager. He was at the top of his game at that point and he right stepped in to help Chumba… which meant he couldn't fully concentrate, in my view anyway, on Hawkwind. The band wasn't in free fall at that time, but it did find itself in a more precarious situation. Some of my role when I was invited in, as Alan Davey was about to step away, was to bring a bit of business acumen in, a bit of tour management."

After twelve years, Alan Davey left Hawkwind having played his last gig at the Rodon Club in Athens on 9th November 1996. The development of Davey's own band, Bedouin, was partly a factor in his departure as, he's suggested, was a supposed reluctance of Brock to reintroduce 'old' Hawkwind numbers into the live set. But there's little doubt that the recruiting of Jerry Richards ran contrary to how Alan perceived the Hawkwind sound should be created. Having himself come in with a particularly apt vision of how the band should regenerate itself after a period of stagnancy, that idea of meshing the sounds of *Warrior on the Edge of Time* with the then more contemporary experimentalism of *Church of Hawkwind*, he'd had hit upon the right formula for the mix of musicians around the membership at that time and arguably rescued the band from a creative impasse. But what had happened more recently was that the revolving doors had once again allowed through people with fresh ideas and in the combination of Chadwick, Tree and now Jerry Richards there was a free festival mentality that had a shared outlook informed by a potent mix of anarcho-punk and psychedelia that was coming from a very different angle from the one Alan Davey had.

"Jerry's not a Hawkwind musician," Alan asserted in the first edition of this book, though he's since worked amicably again with Jerry Richards. "After playing with Dave, Huw… Jerry had nothing to offer Hawkwind as far as I could see." Accepting that's a view that comes from one particular way of hearing what the Hawkwind sound should consist of, we'll come back to that, because Jerry

Richards is a highly intelligent and creative individual with a massive work ethic, who brought the self-reliance and 'make it happen' philosophy of the free festivals first to Hawkwind and then to various spin-off projects, culminating in a re-imagination of the Hawklords concept that has delivered forward-thinking albums and impressive live shows. And though it is possible, when reading interviews with Alan Davey, to gain the impression that negative comments made of fellow musicians are off-hand, perhaps thoughtless, this would be to misunderstand the candour with which he is prepared to discuss other people's, and his own, contribution to Hawkwind. It's arguable that second only to Brock, Alan Davey was, and still is, passionate about Hawkwind, joined-up with a deep concern that the band's audience are given something of value. "We played at the Warrina Stadium, in Peterborough, and I took about two hundred mushrooms, just to see what it would be like. I'd never usually do anything like that, you have to be together, because people pay money and you don't want to go on and mess it up. But this time, all I could see was the dry-ice and I couldn't hear anything. All of a sudden, there was a tugging at my trousers… Dave had crawled under the smoke on his hands and knees! I'd started 'Assault & Battery' when the rest were playing something else. I thought I played a right mess of a gig." One Internet commentator succinctly summed-up Davey's importance to Hawkwind when suggesting that if Alan were cut down the middle, he would have 'Hawkwind' written through him like a stick of seaside rock.

Brock: "It was very difficult for Alan, because he felt like he wanted to do his own thing. To be his own man and run his own band, which he did; but it's hard, it's a fucking headache. When you run a band, you've got to put a lot of your own money up-front for advertising and so on, and as people get older in life they're not going to be big stars. Alan really is a very good musician; his big spacey keyboard stuff was really fantastic, he had a style, which lots of people strive to achieve, but he'd actually got to that point. But off he went doing his copy of Motörhead, which is a shame, but there you are. He thought it was a big mistake getting Jerry in the band."

As for Jerry's take on the situation, he's phlegmatic about the changes that needed to be rung. "I think Alan's view of the band is rooted in that early 70s, hard-edged approach, which is fine in itself, but fashions and attitudes change and you can find yourself on the roadside waiting for things to come around again, waiting for reality to catch back up with you. Dave was very open-minded to the sort of influences that Ron and I brought into the band. They weren't the sort of themes and approach that he'd have naturally chosen. You could say there were always punky elements within Hawkwind and the *25 Years On* album has always been seen as Hawkwind's answer to the punk scene… I'm not sure that's necessarily true, they were just in the right place at the right time. The big advantage the band had at that time was Calvert's input which elevated all of them to a level they couldn't achieve on their own, but then it's very difficult to match that man's insight, he's probably regarded as a genius because of his illness, very much like Spike Milligan. But Dave was very accommodating with what Ron and

I brought into the band, and more accommodating than I would have expected, because you always have preconceptions of what is expected of you. You've got to push the boundaries."

The loss of Davey didn't leave Hawkwind without a bass player, since that was Tree's favoured position. "I suggested that I play bass, unless we could get somebody as good as Alan. I'd rather play bass than sing. We considered Dibs from Krel [who had supported Hawkwind on the *Electric Tepee* tour] but that came to nothing." Despite this, Tree's preference would still have been for Davey to have remained with the band. "We begged him to come back." Although the change gave Tree a much harder task to perform, since he also retained most of the vocal duties, he was happy with the final situation as "I could put more creative work in, because I could write tunes."

Jerry Richards
(Rik & Val Richardson)

It was well into 1997 before the latest realignment would make their first live appearance, at a benefit show in Blackheath, London on 7th June, featuring a guest appearance by Huw Lloyd-Langton. Meanwhile, Chadwick, Tree and Richards had decamped to Dave's recording studio to work on a new album, *Distant Horizons*, a record that at the time seemed a disappointingly weak affair both for the fans and the band themselves: "I weren't impressed with it," states Tree. "Dave himself thought it sounded demo-ish. I didn't think he put music on it that was his best; I thought he took the easy way out. A couple of things were interesting, could have been good." There is a belief that *Distant Horizons* suffered from being released before it was finished due to management pressure.

"I both enjoyed and endured the process of making that album," says Jerry. "It wasn't made under the best conditions: difficult battle conditions I would say. We weren't best served by the cuts that ended up on the official album release, which weren't the ones that the band had chosen. There was an element of technical nonsense that got in the way of what we'd imagined that album was going to be. I don't think that was necessarily down to the band, or the mastering plant, or the record company, it was just a lot of copies and crossover and things are going to go astray, and once the damn thing is out there, the cat is out of the bag and that's it."

Tree: "Doug Smith told us it had to be done by a certain date. Tracks were mixed when I wasn't there and then it was put on the shelf for a month. So we could have had another a month to work on it." Given that the band had worked on the album for the first half of 1997, it is difficult to see anything that could have been done to salvage *Distant Horizons*. Tree effectively concedes this when asked what might have been different if the album had been properly finished: "It might have been mixed better, a bit tidier. Sorry, but mine are the better, stronger songs; it's obvious when you listen to it!"

Dave certainly doesn't disagree with this." It was one of those rushed things where Douglas wanted us to get an album together; we didn't have enough material and I had to use some of my solo things and it wasn't particularly wonderful. It could have been really good but it had to be gotten together quickly and that was it. We called it the 'tombstone' album because Douglas did [the tombstone cover] on his computer in paint shop."

Distant Horizons contained some flashes of inspiration but what it appeared to lack was any sort of cohesive game plan for presenting the band, post-Davey. Without his driving bass-lines, the Hawkwind package sounded thin, and although this might have created an opportunity for the band to experiment with new moods, as with the recordings immediately after Langton's departure in 1989, there is a feeling of nature abhorring a vacuum but not having anything substantial to fill it with. The title track, a native rhythmic chant set to a techno beat that sits up and blasts off into a classic Brock chord progression is the highlight of the record, though it had originally been planned for a second Psychedelic Warriors CD. There are some moods pieces that in a way are like ambient wallpaper, even though in and of themselves most are quite pleasing. Falling uniformly into this category are some very good pieces: 'Waimea Canyon Drive', 'Clouded Vision', and 'Kauai', though not the gutless instrumental version of 'Love in Space' which was far removed from the powerful and atmospheric song of the Alien... tour. Tree followed up his stated intent of adding raw power to the band's material by contributing 'Phetamine Street' and 'Reptoid Vision', both heavy thrash songs, cyberpunk SF contrasts to Calvert's sci-fi imagery, but lacking finesse. On paper, the input from Jerry Richards amounted to a couple of predominantly instrumental numbers, 'Wheels' and 'Alchemy'. The view of

Chadwick is that to dismiss Jerry's involvement in so meagre a way is to not appreciate the commitment that Richards made to Hawkwind during a period of immense practical and emotional difficulty for the band. "His amazing contribution to Hawkwind was in just keeping us going when we would have collapsed, because Jerry has this fantastic capacity for work. He'll stick at something when other people would have given up. He spent many hours frantically programming stuff for *Distant Horizons*, staying up all night getting things together."

In some ways, *Distant Horizons* was *Astounding Sounds, Amazing Music* for the 1990s, a twist away from what had been done before, shocking its listeners in its radical overhaul of what the band were doing. And, like *ASAM* before it, it seemed a democratic record, with writing credit opportunities shared around the band and a genuine meshing of different ideas and textures, even though there is no amount of time that could pass which could rehabilitate it in quite the manner to which *Astounding Sounds* has improved its legacy with age.

"I did notice, when Cherry Red were kind enough to send me the updated copy, that it has a couple of extra tracks on it which were recorded around about the same time," notes Jerry Richards. "I don't think they were part of the *Distant Horizons* sessions per se, but they were recorded around about the same time. Dave's obviously given a couple of extra numbers to stick on the re-release. I do notice, with regret, that my name is absent from the credits on both, because Ron and I wrote those. In retrospect, those two songs ('Morpheus' and 'Archaic') are the two best tracks on the re-release, yet they never made it on to the original. Now, here we are in 2014 talking about an album from 1997 and in retrospect, with this glorious hindsight we've got now, listening to these two numbers, you would say 'Wow, this is fantastic, listen to this playing,' it's very psychedelic: crawling, screaming acid rock from this crazy old band called Hawkwind, and it's the new direction that Ron and I, and Richard to a large extent, were keen to push. I think the sessions were very successful in doing that. If you go back to *ASAM*, it's full of different flavours. You've got 'The Aubergine That Ate Rangoon' coupled with the madness of 'Steppenwolf' and those two things couldn't be more different in musical approach, subject matter, all that kind of thing. *Distant Horizons* is a bit like that, except that it's a little more experimental and out of the groove. Sometimes you've got to be brave and try things out. You're not trying to dismiss what your supporters have got to say about it, because they've got their own particular things that they want to hear from their favourite band, which is great, but by the same token as people who want to produce music and keep standards up you've got to confound their expectations on occasion and think outside the box."

Arriving just in time for the promotional tour in the autumn of 1997 and largely ignored by the music press, *Distant Horizons* was the first Hawkwind album to be critically picked-over by the scribes of the Internet generation. Circulating on the BOC-L mailing list were downbeat viewpoints: "the whole album sounds to me like an outtake recording of Hawkwind practising tracks in the studio," mused Jill Strobridge. On the same discussion group, John Majka considered the release to be "very tired, very half-done… it definitely does not rock, neither is it mellow…"

Following the recording of *Distant Horizons*, Hawkwind again travelled to the US for a handful of dates and an appearance at the inaugural 'Strange Daze' festival in Sherman, NY on 31st August. The plan was to temporarily resolve the dilemma regarding bass duties by including Lemmy on these dates, and the shows were advertised as such. Naturally this generated excitement amongst US fans and a corresponding disappointment when the appearance of the legend himself firstly turned out to be for the festival show only, and then failed to happen altogether, reportedly due to illness. The Strange Daze festival organised by US spacerock enthusiast Jim Lascko was a notable success, however, both for Hawkwind and the whole spacerock scene. Lascko had for a long time held a desire to assist in some way in the re-establishment of Hawkwind stateside, which he felt had not been as successful as anticipated. "Unfortunately [Hawkwind] had ended up losing a bit of money on the 1989 tour and that made them wary of mounting any further big tours in the US. Hawkwind appeared to bring a little less with them on every subsequent tour." Together with some friends and colleagues, Lascko began "harbouring dreams of helping out Hawkwind by offering to do their sound on a future USA tour."

Before this could progress, Lascko's band of willing and knowledgeable volunteers fell apart. "Even though one may sometimes glimpse the correct path, it's another thing to faithfully tread it. Death, doubt and discouragement – eventually they all come like uninvited guests into your home." When the opportunity arose to work with Hawkwind, on the USA tour of 1995, the best that Lascko could offer the band was to promote and work on "the show at the Cleveland Agora Theatre, where they had an in-house PA system we could use." In fact, this wasn't the only chance for Lascko to assist with the tour: "I helped Doug Smith arrange a few other things… It was a great time and I ended up with the mailing list we had gathered from the tour." From this, Jim could send out his first 'Strange Trips' newsletter, named after Brock's *Strange Trips and Pipedreams* solo album, to 2,000 US-based fans. "I began to think of the different things we could do to promote spacerock in the US during the long periods when Hawkwind wasn't there. From this, other shows sprang forth, and the natural culmination of this activity was in creating Strange Daze '97.

Amongst the bands playing was ST37. Scott Telles re-members it being "fabulous" and is particularly enthusiastic about Hawkwind's set: "It was spellbinding. Beautiful." During the gig, Hawkwind were joined onstage, for the first time since the Calvert tribute show, by Nik Turner. "The audience was in awe," says Telles, "many were ecstatic and almost weepy when Nik joined Dave onstage. Dave made some humorous comments about how old and feeble Nik was [Turner had broken his leg in a motorcycle accident the week prior] and Nik good naturedly bantered back." Telles thought the highlight of the set to be "an achingly beautiful 'Love in Space'."

If the audience had been misty-eyed about the reunion of Turner and Brock (Lascko cites this as "paving the way for a future Hawkwind reunion"), Brock himself was cautious about agreeing. "Ron and Jerry had never played with Nik, so I told them 'Look, Nik will play over everything we do'. They said 'no, no, he won't do a thing like that, surely'. So I said, 'Listen, he will saxophone across everything that goes on'. That's why I don't like working with Nik." Straight after the set came one of those moments that showed the gulf between Brock's professionalism and Turner's more ad-hoc 'man of the people' styling. "We did an encore," says Brock, "but Nik would not leave the stage, then he started lampooning the band 'oh they won't come on, they're boring... I'll play my saxophone'... and he did that for half an hour." Of course, what is quite legitimately one man's unprofessional style is another's idea of giving the audience something extra. Chuck Johnson's online review of the festival noted that: "At the first sign of the crowd's disappointment at not getting a second encore, Turner appeared centre stage wearing his sax. He broke into one of those little ditties that he does and the crowd starting cheering." Johnson records the additional material as including a ten-minute rendition of 'Master of the Universe'. In fact, this had been a technique Nik employed at least as far back as his ICU days, and maintains today, of carrying on when fellow musicians have finished; a part of his act.

While the Strange Daze show was generally viewed as a triumph for Hawkwind (Johnson noted the band as having a "great new sound that pumps more energy" and anticipated that "their new album is looking really good, based on the live show"), the pending major tour of the UK was beset by cancellations and rumours of poor ticket sales. Alan Davey saw the band on the autumn tour, at Poole Arts Centre (3rd October 1997) and was unimpressed: "I left after four numbers. I couldn't believe it. It was terrible, just going through the motions with no one taking the lead. Sometimes I would get a flash of inspiration and just take control of the band, same as Dave would. That is what Hawkwind's all about. At Poole, they might just as well have put a record on and mimed to it."

Hawkwind were joined by Brock's 'Agents of Chaos' bandmate Crum on keyboards and by 'Space Reggae' toaster Captain Rizz, the latter providing walk-on, walk-off guest appearances with Hawkwind throughout the next few years to widespread dismay amongst the more vocal and traditionalist fans. The idea of having someone 'spouting' on an ad-lib basis had, of course, started with Calvert in the band's early years and continued with Bainbridge through the 1980s, but in fairness to some of the traditionalists who baulk at any deviation from the standard format, some of the contributions that Rizz provided were little short of embarrassing (witness his outbursts on 'Your Fantasy' and particularly the ill-conceived 'Hawkwind in Your Area' on this tour). It was an extension of the cod-reggae theme that Brock had used earlier in the decade and which hadn't been particularly appreciated back then either, a strange addition to the mix.

(I must add to the bits above, which are from the original edition. I never saw Rizz with the band back then, but, though I still don't care for those tracks, I saw him with Dave Brock, assorted Hawks, and associates at a charity afternoon in Weston-Super-Mare in the summer of 2015 and was mightily struck by what stage presence he has. Dave Brock: "Rizz is a great character, a good musician. We were doing this big festival in a park in northern Spain, we went over with three buses, two campervans and a truck. When we went into the VIP lounge, where you could watch the bands, with an exclusive restaurant. We walked in there and the manager was, 'Mr Brock! What a great honour it is to see you here! Champagne!' We had our dinner and champagne, and after that we had to do interviews. But there was an air strike and none of the other [main] bands turned up. They were expecting all these big stars, but there was only Hawkwind... and Captain Rizz! We're all sat down at a table with these journalists... 'Would you like to ask questions of the band?' ... and there's this shuffling around and silences, and nobody had a fucking clue who we were. Rizz just stood up and did this spectacular rap, and they all stood up and applauded! All these big stars weren't there because of the air strike, and we'd travelled across the Pyrenes in our old buses!").

What Hawkwind had in this latest period of redefinition was a desperately disappointed following, an album that at the time was viewed as a seemingly nondescript studio recording, and the departure of the person who most represented the continuity of Hawkwind's style and musical ethos. All these factors were serious issues that the band had to confront to ensure its long-term viability. But while the loss of other key members over the years had, in retrospect, contributed to the bands longevity, everything now seemed piece-meal, fragmented and lacking in a proper mission statement for the future.

19

A Trip Down Under, And a Difficult Reunion

1998 began with the promise of European dates, a new studio album and a second Strange Daze festival to head-line. By the end of the year, none of these had fully materialised, and a Dave Brock-led Hawkwind had failed to perform a single gig within a calendar year for the first time in its history. It signposted a fallow period stretching into most of 1999, but it would lead into their first tour 'Down Under' and onwards to a high-profile reunion gig at London's Brixton Academy.

The year started badly with shows in Belgium, Holland and Germany cancelled with 'money problems' cited as the reason. If the embarrassment of having to cancel gigs wasn't bad enough, 1998 would be most notable for the failure of two members of Hawkwind to appear at Strange Daze II. On 12th August, Dave Brock and Ron Tree were refused entrance into the USA from Canada. Ron had gained admission to the country for two previous Hawkwind tours: "I got into America twice because [customs] didn't look at the computer. Third time they did, and I couldn't get in." With Tree unceremoniously bundled onto a plane and sent back to England, Brock was left at Niagara trying to organise a visa for himself to travel onwards to the festival site at Garrettsville. Four days were spent going to the US embassy in Toronto, with Brock's friends in the UK sitting outside sorting offices at 4.00am because officials claimed they had sent the relevant visa and a courier service on stand-by to deliver the documentation. It never arrived. The two remaining band members, Chadwick and Richards, were joined by Steve Haynes and Steve Taylor (members of a Hawkwind tribute band, Sun Machine) for the performance. As with the 1997 festival, Captain Rizz guested and this one-off line-up has since been dubbed 'Strangewind'.

"That was a very fraught time," recalls Chadwick. "We travel to America via Canada. [Customs] search all of us, and they wouldn't let Ron through. We didn't know about Dave, as he wasn't travelling with us. We get to the festival [to find that Dave has been refused entrance to America]. Me, Rizz and Jerry are walking around, and we know where Dave is, and that he's trying very hard to get across the border. We're wondering what the hell to do. People are going 'Yeah! You're going to play soon, you're the reason we're here... we've travelled from Texas to see you!' We latched onto these two people who were friends of Jim Lascko and got them in to help us play. We had a practice in a tent, with loads of people wondering what we were doing in there. Come the gig time, no Dave, no Ron, we had to get on and just do something based on the afternoon's plan – threw out the set we planned to do. We did keep in a version of 'Space is Deep' which we'd worked out with Rizz, but the keyboard player's mushrooms had kicked in and he was playing the wrong thing all over it."

Scott Telles: "They were real troopers for pulling it off, and everyone really respected that and appreciated it... a pretty good set considering the circumstances... highlight was probably 'Starfire Mountain Dreaming'."

A short statement on the non-appearance of Brock and Tree was made at the commencement of the show ("we are the ones who are left") but Brock was fuming: "I asked for a mobile to link up with the PA so that I could explain to all," he later posted to the BOC-L mailing list. "Nobody seemed to want to do this." He spent the evening of the concert in a hotel room, waiting for a phone link to address the fans: "I was going to sing a number down the phone... no call came." He blamed his visa problem on being "busted in 1974. The US seems to regard me as some dangerous character about to corrupt people." On his return to the UK, Brock was "inundated with e-mails from people who had been told that it was our own fault and that we had not been bothered to get the visas together. The passports had been at the US embassy since June. The embassy would not do anything until the paperwork at the US side had been completed by the promoter." Brock had been given a lesson on the new power of the Internet to distribute rumour and misunderstanding: "You can imagine how it felt to come home to all of this."

He increasingly appeared to view his role in Hawkwind as a mentor to the younger musicians he had surrounded himself with. "I act like a teacher, a bit. You get some young guys in the band and you have to try and exercise a bit of control. They are like apprentices," he said in one interview. Some of the more inexperienced personnel who have served in the band over the years described this approach as more of a 'sink or swim' style, that Dave identified talent and creativity but expected people to step up and deliver for themselves. Nevertheless, he consistently demonstrated an ability to challenge younger musicians to achieve standards above the level they had been performing at before their Hawkwind association. "Someone with that breadth of experience has something to teach," concludes Chadwick. "His way of doing it is to put people in a situation and see if they come up with anything."

Keith Kniveton, a synthesiser specialist and a "fan since 'Silver Machine'," visited Brock during this period. "I remember going over a couple of times and everybody was working on new material, something called The Mars Project." Kniveton describes himself as being inspired by Hawkwind "completely, in a musical sense." Like Davey and Tree before him, he'd sent some tapes to Brock, which Dave liked, and the result was an appearance with the band at a private party near Honiton in August 1999. "Richard and Ron were always keen on the idea of analogue synth sounds streaming in when nothing much else seemed to be happening," he recalls. In this respect, Kniveton's occasional stage appearances can be seen as an extension of the roles previously filled by Dik-Mik and Del Dettmar. "Dave and Richard are reliant on sequencers a lot of the time, and I wanted to add that kind of random element to the sound again. The swoosh that comes out of nowhere, the guitar sound that suddenly shimmers from the opposite speaker." Brock, Chadwick, Tree and Richards played a further private party in Cornwall during August of 1999, the week of a solar eclipse that brought the Duchy to an effective standstill. Their main appearance, on August 11th, featured one new song, 'Aniseed' (aka 'Anna Seed'), and Tree reading the anti-capitalist tirade 'Wage War'. The rest of the set was principally a reprise of the numbers played on the 1997 winter tour.

The Mars Project (an ambient/electronic venture) never materialised into anything more than a handful of treatments. Chadwick: "We were doing a lot of work in the studio, synchronising our tape recorders to the computer and getting all sorts of effects going… music that was to be The Mars Project." "It was an idea of Dave's," recalled Tree. "We were also working on the 'Death Generator' [Ledge of Darkness], I wrote three songs for that. Then Dave went, 'Oh, we're going to do Mars now'. It's like 'what the fuck are we going to do – make your mind up!'" With a lack of clear direction, it appears that frustrations built up. "You'd get something done and then [Brock] would move the goalposts. The Mars thing never happened. In the end, I stopped taking notice of ideas Dave had for albums, because at the last moment he'd change the name, or whatever!" Tree concluded.

"Things were very tough financially at that point," concedes Jerry. "Dave had decided to sort of give it a slight rest; I think he wanted a little time away from it because it was a massive responsibility. He'd often said to me, 'the thing about Hawkwind, it's a monster. While it's dormant, it's OK, but when you crank it up it's a big machine and when it's out on the road or has set its mind to a project, it becomes unwieldy and unstoppable and nobody really is in control of it, it takes on a mind of its own.' I could see that after all that time, I mean 35 years back then, you'd want a little bit of time off."

Any other band may have thrown in the towel and gone their separate ways at such a low point. Brock, however, was still dedicated to the group as a full-time occupation, telling this writer, during a Q&A Internet session at the time, "I am on Hawkwind duty every week and over the past few years I have financed rehearsals etc. We are not dead, only sleeping!" For all the criticism that Brock has endured from former members over the years, it says something about him that he could rely on his current line-up to support his longer-term view that, while he needed a something of a rest from the band, he was still "concentrating on getting more music together."

Chadwick: "We survived by hand to mouth; it was very difficult, just keeping our heads above water. Time is more important and valuable than money, so bearing that in mind we could handle periods where things weren't going so well. At least we had the time to devote to doing what we loved. If any one of us ended up doing a regular job it would have sacrificed that creativity." The only new material to surface during 1998 was an American release, *In Your Area*. Aside from a few tracks recorded live the previous autumn in Belgium, it featured a reworking of the Calvert poem 'First Landing on Medusa', and 'Hippy', a Richards/Chadwick/Tree composition that would be featured live the following year. For fans waiting for an upturn following *Distant Horizons*, this wasn't it.

Aside from a blast through the Calvert number 'Aerospace-Age Inferno' the live material was weak, whilst the new studio tracks, 'Hippy' aside, were very much in the vein of the much-maligned previous offering. Ron Tree saw it as just "an album so we could have a few quid. We didn't get paid a right lot!" It was a release for practical purposes and not a pointer forward to the 21st Century.

In a more general sense, a much-needed profile boost during the summer of 1999 arrived with the release of an EMI three-disc compilation CD, *Epocheclipse*, which featured tracks from every era of the band's history. With the EMI publicity-machine able to generate some serious attention in the British press, there was a chance for traditionally hostile music journalists to re-evaluate the band's contribution over the previous thirty years. "The Hawks have been subject to more ridicule than perhaps any other band in rock history," wrote Dave Simpson of the Guardian. The review acknowledged their new-found 'mentor' status to groups such as Kula Shaker (who had covered 'Hurry on Sundown'), Primal Scream ('Motörhead' was included on their Exterminator album) and Bill Drummond and Jimmy Cauty of the KLF, who had remixed 'Silver Machine' for the anniversary project. "Hawkwind epitomise that quality lacking in many a credible rock band: adventure," wrote Simpson, describing a sound that "took a combination of turbo-charged riffs, squawking sax and barmy synth effects so far out they demand NASA investigation." The *NME* was moved to describe Hawkwind, on the strength of *Epocheclipse*, as "Several men on drugs, quite possibly playing in your garden now. Hell of a band." Noting the anthology as being "a worthy document of that long, strange, trip," the reviewer divided the band's career into two halves (both seventies entrenched), either "a whiffy collective more often than not wholly incapacitated by Mandrax" or "powerful, repetitive and sinister."

Taking the same approach, that pre-1980 everything was wonderful, and thereafter nothing was worthy of note, *The Sunday Times* delineated Hawkwind's back-catalogue as peaking with "'Psychedelic Warlords' and 'Assault & Battery'… lost trance classics" whereas "Post-1979 every-thing's largely awful," though it went on to praise 'Right to Decide' as "an irrepressible and strangely successful drum 'n' bass pop song" and exhorted its readership that "even buying the single album would go some way towards the apology that Hawkwind deserve."

Brock had been espousing his ambitious plans for the 1999 autumn tour, resurrecting Ledge of Darkness. "What we're probably going to do," he told the Music Street Journal, "is get all the old members to actually come and do a few numbers per night over the period of the tour. It could be a continuing saga." It appears he had great deal of enthusiasm for this project. "Ron Tree has ten oscillators all linked up… the Death Generator. They warp the senses in your head. Done the right way it could be very hypnotic." But he conceded that it was "a lot to get together," and the omens of the previous eighteen months were not good.

Kniveton: "Ron Tree's audio generator was called the Psyclone and was custom built for him by Steve Smyth, an old friend of the band. It had oscillators, some filters, amplifiers and a patch-board. He had various controllers added, one of which was a light-sensitive Theremin. 'It's very good if you shine it on your teeth', I recall Ron saying."

The Ledge of Darkness tour would have been a parody of the band. In the end, despite Kris Tait reporting to the BOC-L list that she and Dave had contacted Lemmy's manager and foresaw an autumn tour with their former bass player and their two-time lead guitarist Lloyd-Langton, the plans came to nothing. Instead, a short mini-tour was pulled together, advertised with an emphasis towards three musicians: Brock, Nik Turner and Simon House. Harvey Bainbridge appeared as support act and guest keyboard player for the main set, with Turner and House appearing separately until they both played on the final date at Croydon's Fairfield Hall. "I thought I was going to do all of the gigs," Turner told Santtu Laakso for *Aural Innovations*, "Then it turns out they want me to do two."

At the St. Austell Cornwall Coliseum, Kniveton, who also assisted Bainbridge during the opening set, joined the band again. "Harvey was a real gentleman; he asked me to guest with him and shook my hand afterwards. 'That was really beautiful, thank you'." Turner, ever the unofficial star of the show, made an entrance through the audience playing his sax to the opening of 'Motorway City', in a spiky alien costume. "Nik wore just his alien suit, which had no backside. Ron and Dave were frequently pointing at his bare arse and laughing," says Kniveton. The show whilst very dynamic for the first part, wandered badly in the second and degenerated during the encore into a series of verbal exchanges between Turner and Tree, with a bizarre onstage debate over whose mother could make the best Yorkshire Puddings, giving some members of the audience an unwelcome reminder of the pantomime tone of the Turner-fronted gigs of 1983-84! Despite this, Kniveton noted no bad feeling behind the scenes. "[Turner and Tree] got on quite well backstage." In fact, it seems that all previous unhappiness between the band and Turner had been put aside: "Nik seemed genuinely glad to be 'back on stage with the lads'."

Turner may have reported that the shows were "all very well accepted by people. Packed houses," but the fact was that only the smaller venues (in particular Wavendon Stables in Milton Keynes) could report successful ticket sales. Croydon was "a third full" according to one member of the audience, or "a third empty" as described by the band. Cornwall was much worse, though accentuated by the size of the venue. It appeared that the success of *Epocheclipse* wasn't being reflected in ticket sales, despite the gigs being promoted as a mini-reunion. Tree, an engagingly honest and open personality, had mixed feelings about these shows, which came at a particularly bad time for him. "I was having a lot of problems with opiate addiction and I tried to come off, using the tour to keep my mind focused. It didn't work very well. Some of the gigs were atrocious, some of the gigs were blinding." He freely concedes he was "up, down, all over the shop. I was withdrawing a lot, taking Valium to sleep and speed to do the gigs, which I didn't normally do." At each show, he let forth a rant about heroin abuse:

"This band is anti-heroin, but we're not against people who are fucked up on it." Without the audience understanding the context, there was much speculation as to the motive. He'd later say that it was "because I fucking hate it. I nearly lost my life, my kids, yeah?" He goes on to ponder the effect of his addiction. "Probably some of that is to do with why I'm not in Hawkwind now." While Tree struggled with drug use during his time in Hawkwind, he was generous in acknowledging the support of his bandmates. "It must have been difficult for Dave and the rest of them. Richard and Jerry helped me, and Dave did – he showed sympathy. He's alright; he's been alright to me."

So many observers have drawn a comparison between Tree and Robert Calvert that it is almost a cliché to revisit this analogy. The telling parallel is to look at both characters as having their undoubted creative talents mirrored by a dark side. Calvert had his manic, hyperactive personality, although he is noted by many of his colleagues as not being a drug user. Tree had his issues with drugs but his extraordinary abilities and contribution to the band, and his general likeableness, had the other members supporting him during (and, in some cases, after) his membership of Hawkwind. Other comparisons of presentation and vocal delivery are not welcomed by Tree who, rightly, prefers to stress his own artistic strengths. He does profess an admiration for Calvert's work ("an obvious genius"), and Tree's own vocal delivery made the reintroduction of Calvert numbers into the setlist a natural development: 'Robot' on the Alien 4 tour, 'High Rise' for the 1999 mini-tour. "I sang them in the style they were written. They suited my voice and they hadn't been sung for ages." Although some songs were given a very Calvert-esque interpretation ('Spirit of the Age' at the Hawkestra reunion concert the following year followed the coda from Calvert's delivery on the 1978 USA tour), Tree was determined to remain his own man: "It's just me singing, it's got a bit of a Calvert sound but I'm not putting that on. Dave thought it great that I sounded like Calvert and I was told to sing Calvert songs. I did say, 'I'm not Bob Calvert, I don't want to be in his shoes'. I can mimic, I can act, but I haven't been acting to be Bob Calvert." There is a sense of frustration in Tree's words. "Someone said I sound like Syd Barrett, Johnny Rotten and Robert Calvert put together. I don't want to be anybody else but myself, right?"

The much-anticipated trip Down Under was pulled together early in 2000. Hawkwind were unable to take Ron Tree, "not allowed in… drug conviction… don't get busted!" and turned to Alan Davey for bass duties. Davey was unavailable, having previously booked studio-time for his band, Bedouin. Finally, Steve Taylor (from the 'Strangewind' ensemble that filled-in at Strange Daze '98) was recruited on a temporary basis. Simon House and Harvey Bainbridge also returned for the tour. The original plan was to play a few shows in North Island and then to spend the final ten days in South Island with some tentative gigs set up. However, Kris Tait had been receiving e-mails from a promoter in Australia, Neil Price, who wanted the band to perform there as well.

When Hawkwind arrived in New Zealand it became clear that, despite the enthusiasm of the organisers, the logistics left a good deal to be desired. The band had to start almost from scratch, booking advertising, road crew and PA equipment. "I enjoyed myself [in New Zealand]," said Brock afterwards, "but I did not enjoy having to set up my own gear before we played and take it down again afterwards. More organisation would have been appreciated… I am not the manager of this band!" And indeed, it appears not to have been a particularly happy tour despite the opportunity of travel that it offered, with reports of a general lack of discipline within the touring line-up leading to Brock at one gig firing the entire band before recanting in advance of that evening's show. ("Yes, we were all sacked and then reinstated within half an hour so that he had a band to do the gig that night!" Jerry confirms). Chadwick, though describing the set-up of the tour as "fabulously messy," approved of the New Zealand lifestyle: "a busy, thriving social scene. We stayed on the edge of town with some people who'd let the whole area grow back to bush. Wonderful!"

For the first date of the trip, on 4th February, around 200 fans turned up at the intimate Waihi Beach Hotel, with a contributor to BOC-L describing the audience as coming from far afield. The same correspondent noted Steve Taylor admitting to "some nerves before the concert as this was his first live gig with the band," but that he "had a smile on his face" by the end. The audience doubled for the second gig, at the Auckland Power Station, where the venue size permitted the use of the full lightshow and a display of fire-breathing by Kris Tait. A show in Wellington was less successful, with a 500-capacity venue attracting no more than a tenth of its potential ticket sales. An enthusiastic reviewer describing the contributions of the band members: "Brock anchoring the rest with his ceaseless tinkering and arresting voice, Chadwick rolling all over the drum kit, around which the violin and keyboards kept the continual maelstrom afloat." The second-leg trip to South Island was anticipated to be expensive and given the financial risk it was decided that the more prudent approach was to take the proposed Australian dates if they could be fitted around the band's plane tickets and contractual commitments and that proved a highly successful add-on to the tour. Hawkwind played five gigs (prior to returning to New Zealand for some final dates), including a sell-out show at Sydney's Metro concert hall, and one at an enormous techno-based festival in the Australian bush. The Metro concert brought back memories of the band's heyday. "It was just like 1981 in England again!" says Kris, "We got taken care of so nicely…"

That extended to an appearance on the Australian TV show *Studio 22*. Very different to any of the band's previous television performances, with the musicians crammed into a circular stage and the audience seated for almost 360 degrees around them, it turned into a fabulous recording. The thirty-minute programme opened with 'Silver Machine' (performed last on the day of recording) and featured 'Love in Space', 'Arrival in Utopia' and 'Free Fall', interspersed with an interview with Brock and Bainbridge. The responses to the questions posed showed their different perspectives on Hawkwind's musical influences. Bainbridge attempted to draw a comparison with the American West Coast music and ethos of The Grateful Dead, which Brock dismissed entirely out of hand. Brock's long-time friend, fantasy artist Peter Pracownik worked and travelled with the Grateful Dead in 1994: "When I met Jerry Garcia, I mentioned Hawkwind to him. He said, 'Yup! They were experimenting, like us... a great rock band'."

"Harvey was in a really bad mood," recalls Chadwick. "We were playing one song where he had to verbalise what to him were really meaningful comments, but he was glowering across the stage yelling into his microphones. I thought, this is falling on deaf ears, whatever it is." Bainbridge would note this as being a dilemma faced by the improviser. "This is why people write songs, because it's captured then. At the same time, it's wonderful, if you're brave enough, to make it up as you go along."

"Neil Price really blagged the show for us," says Kris. "The station wasn't very keen... didn't know much about us. They said, 'Look we need a studio audience, about a hundred people, so you'd better do some publicity'. Apparently within four hours of announcing that Hawkwind were going to be on, they'd had more people apply [for tickets] than in the history of the programme!"

Huw Lloyd-Langton and Alan Davey
(Oz Hardwick)

For nearly three years, the on/off saga of the potential Hawkwind reunion concert had rumbled along. When the show finally took place, it could hardly be anything other than an anti-climax. That 'Hawkestra' failed to live up to higher expectations could be attributed to many factors. That it would end in bitterness but still kick-start the band into the 21st Century was the unpredictable side-effect.

"With the idea of the Hawkestra being ongoing," says Brock, "Doug Smith told us not to do any gigs for a whole year, to create some interest." This goes some way to ex-plaining the relative inactivity of Hawkwind from the beginning of 1998, even if it was a strange way for a band with the most 'tribal' of audiences to maintain its profile. The lack of live appearances generated a growing sense that Brock's commitment and enthusiasm for Hawkwind had finally ebbed away, and that the reunion show was not one that he had any great wish to see materialise. Brock refutes this: "It was a good idea. Doug Smith came up with this wonderful notion of getting all the ex-members together to do a show. One year went down the drain because Lemmy was touring and couldn't do it. The next year we were stopped from doing it – Lemmy was doing a show the prior night and the agents wouldn't let us go on the night after because they were frightened we would take the audience away." The idea of a major reunion without Lemmy was pretty much inconceivable, and so arrangements had to be made to mount the show when he was available to perform. "We were in France when all this was going on," recalls Brock, "on a camp site. I had to go down and collect faxes from the local shop that would say 'You must get in contact with Lemmy immediately'. It was jolly exciting because [the show] could have been fantastic."

There were a few small Hawkwind-related gigs that prefigured the reunion. Alan Davey, Danny Thompson and Huw Lloyd-Langton revived 'Snorkwind', which they used as a by-line in the 1980s, as an opening act for some of Davey's Bedouin shows. At the Potter Butt Pub (Bath, 18th December 1999) Chadwick, Tree and Richards performed a set as 'Whirlwind' with Bridget Wishart guesting. These shows were a bonus for the dedicated Hawkwind audience, as were gigs billed as 'The Original Hawkwind Reunion Band,' led by Nik Turner. With the timing of the full-blown get-together regularly pushed back, it might be thought that Turner's gatherings were in some way a 'hurry-up' for the full reunion. However, like the difference in views between Turner and Brock over Nik's motivations for his American tours, there was a widening rift developing between the two over the direction and format of what became the Hawkestra. In Turner's view, the band he pulled together came from an interest in playing again with some early Hawkwind members: "Thomas Crimble lives just down the road, and I'd been speaking to him about getting a band together featuring him, myself and Terry Ollis, maybe Huw, and possibly Mick Slattery. That was more like a revival of the Isle of Wight band, nothing to do with the Hawkestra." Turner's use of the Hawkwind name should have been prohibited by Brock's earlier acquisition of the trademark. However, there were the inevitable listings errors in the events sections of newspapers, even The Times listing the second 'Reunion Band' show (at a festival in Ystalyfera, Wales 21st July 2000) as simply being an appearance by 'Hawkwind'.

Brock however was still intent on his Ledge of Darkness project and wanted a major gig with as many past band members as possible. This would be followed by a tour, featuring different guest members at each gig. "It was a monster to get together," reflects Brock. "Alan, Richard and me worked really hard... it was a task and half!" But this wouldn't reach fruition and a more traditional reunion show based on a one-off performance with multiple past members taking to the stage at differing points of the evening was decided upon. Rehearsals commenced early in September 2000, with the core band joined at Brock's farm by Davey, Blake, Swindells and House. Swindells, who was considering a return to Hawkwind, characterises Tim Blake as "a fascinating, eccentric character, he's from a super-rich family and lives in a windmill in France." Swindells also held an affection for Ron Tree. "I made sure we had some quality time by having lunch every day in the beach café [at the nearby coastal village of Beer]. Ron was so broke, I had to pay for his lunch and buy him drinks in the evening at the hotel. But he's a lovely bloke, so I didn't mind."

Ron Tree
(Steve Swindells)

Concerned that Dik-Mik and Del Dettmar might be out of practice, Brock invited Keith Kniveton to play. As it turned out on the night, a technical problem meant that neither Dik-Mik nor Dettmar appeared in the 'front of house' mix anyway. Kniveton observes that "one of Dave's main bones of contention afterwards was that his crew spent about six weeks getting it together, while the rest just did one week, or less, at a rehearsal room in London." At the London rehearsals, tensions rose. Terry Ollis was rumoured to have stormed out because Chadwick and Danny Thompson were handling all the drumming. Alan Powell and Martin Griffin had to wait for a percussion set to be brought in on the last day before they could jam with the band. Kniveton again: "Alan Powell came across as a really nice guy. He seemed rather bewildered by the whole event. Martin just wanted to play!" Lemmy rehearsed for two afternoons. One version of events had a roadie appearing with Lemmy's gear, a second roadie handling the set-up and a third arriving with the man himself and proceeding to get out the bass and tune it. Other musicians present were pre-equipped with earplugs, ready for when Lemmy played. Channel Four television sent a film crew along, as Hawkwind were to feature in a programme on progressive rock bands for the broadcaster's Top Ten series, interviewing Brock, Turner and Lemmy.

**Alan Powell and Richard Chadwick, Hawkestra rehearsals
(Steve Swindells)**

"My perspective was that it was a great idea and some-thing that the fans would love," says Turner. "But it was a bit problematic. I thought it should be done in a democratic way but Dave tried to control the whole thing. Dave was the one who decided which songs were played and who performed where…" That's hardly surprising; Hawkestra was a major endeavour needing massive amounts of coordination, strategy, inevitable ego-managing and massaging and could never be all things to all people. That notion of it being run as some sort of democracy is unrealistic in the extreme but it succinctly delineates where battle lines would be drawn.

The Hawkestra finally took to the stage at the Brixton Academy on 21st October 2000. The name, as well as being a play on Moorcock's concept of the 'Hawkwind Orchestra', and considering Brock and Turner's love of jazz, may have been a nod in the direction of Sun Ra and his band Solar Arkestra. Sun Ra traversed a similar experimental path, experimenting with first the electronic piano and then the Moog synthesiser. Claiming to hail from the planet Saturn (though actually Birmingham, Alabama), Sun Ra released some 600 albums; music that he described as "dealing with the dark things of the cosmos" and giving performances that included dancers and film-images. "They want me to play the furthest out things… wild, crazy Sun Ra stuff. They don't call it avant-garde; they say it's beyond that." Given Brock and Turner's musical backgrounds this most underground of jazz musicians must rank as one of the more neglected influences on Hawkwind.

There were some significant absentees on the night. Michael Moorcock refused to take part in anything that Douglas Smith was involved in, citing problems that stretched back as far as the *Live Chronicles* album. "I knew about Hawkestra as Rich told me it was happening," says Bridget Wishart, "but I wasn't officially invited until very near the date. By then I was going on holiday." Simon King, who had long-since sold his last drum kit and retired from the music scene, in Turner's words "didn't want to know about it."

Adrian Shaw had accepted an offer to play: "I was told when and where the rehearsals were scheduled for and waited to hear which songs I needed to brush up on. When I didn't hear anything, I phoned Brock up and he was very odd and evasive. I just didn't like the vibe and so told him to forget it." (Dave Brock: "Simon House told Douglas Smith that if Adrian played, he wouldn't have anything to do with Hawkestra. If I was evasive, it was because it was Douglas's responsibility, and that was it, really. People get their bees in their bonnets, and you can get painted with something that's nothing to do with you. I liked Adrian and he's a good musician, but I only saw him once after the US tour in '78, and that was walking through Chinatown. I did see him once more than that, we were doing a gig in Germany, and Adrian had said, 'Hello, Dave. It's really nice to see you again,' and we were sitting chatting in the dressing room. But then our roadie came in and said to him, 'If you don't take your fucking gear off the stage I'm going to throw the whole fucking lot off!' I said, 'Excuse me…' and left the room and I 've never seen him again after that! I think he was playing with Bevis Frond then. I used to get on alright with Adrian, and he was a very good bass player.").

Swindells: "The first time I'd ever sung live to an audience was at the Brixton Academy. I did the *Old Grey Whistle Test* for the *Fresh Blood* album but that was recorded." For the Hawkestra, the plan was for both Swindells and Brock to sing on 'Shot Down in the Night'. "I'd be doing the low octaves, Dave the high and playing guitar. I was freaked-out when I realised Dave wasn't singing, and I had to do the high bit. Ron was singing harmonies, but not the octaves. I think Dave broke a string, but maybe he walked off deliberately – I don't know. But when the chorus came around and the whole audience started singing it was fantastic. When Lemmy came on there was a huge roar and the energy lifted. But the highlight was 'Spirit of the Age', a seminal version. I loved the floaty, spacey keyboards, and the way it just powers up. Dave's chuga-chuga guitar was fantastic."

Steve Swindells, Hawkestra rehearsals
(Steve Swindells)

Chadwick: "I was surprised when I heard a tape of the gig. I thought it went badly, but some parts of it sounded quite magical. But there was Dave and Lemmy, and neither of them could hear the other, their playing was a bit staggered; I'd play a little fill to try and show where the end of a phrase was, but that didn't work. In the end, I'd just play a pulsing rhythm and let them work it... eventually they'd transmogrify together!" In truth, it was a messy, ill-defined concert, not quite at car crash level and realistically probably as good as it was going to be without a whole load of additional money thrown at more extensive rehearsals. Towards the of the show, Page 3 girl and pop-singer Samantha Fox was brought on, having 'qualified' as a Hawk by dint of her duet with Chadwick on the charity 'Gimme Shelter' single, and sang on 'Master of the Universe' to derision from some of the musicians and much of the audience.

Powell: "The Hawkestra thing was a complete pile of shit... a fucking mess. What was Sam Fox doing there? I was standing at the side of the stage with

creative egos involved made this an always unlikely proposition. Tree's assessment of the concept is pretty much on the button. The promotion of a 'reunion' implies a need to 'reunite' and that has overtones of artistic redundancy even if in the context of celebrating the past. So, despite the band having been regularly joined over the years by past members for particular shows or guest appearances, the Hawkestra was simply one of those great in principle, bad in realisation moments. Perhaps in some way it did celebrate the past but for Brock, always seeking out the next path, the latest regeneration, you must wonder what it offered and it's hard not to conclude that as fine a trip into nostalgia as it seemed, it could only be a moment in time and not a pointer to the future.

20

Happier Reunions, And Unwelcome Ones

Hawkwind 2001
(House, Davey, Blake, Langton, Brock, Chadwick, Kniveton)
Melvyn Vincent

If the reunion show achieved anything it was to open, at least for the moment, the bank of available past members, resting some old grievances even while it opened new ones. However, with the freedom to pick-and-choose from some of the cream of former Hawks (House, Blake, Langton) and a new-found impetus in the workings of the band, not every current member could come away satisfied. A cull was inevitable.

Davey returned to the ranks following the Hawkestra. "I always knew I would," he conceded. The artistically dubious reunion show was followed up with a special Christmas gig at London's Astoria with guests Blake and Bainbridge, later released on CD as Yule Ritual. An acoustic set from Huw Lloyd-Langton was well-received, and though he didn't perform with Hawkwind, the seeds were sown for guest appearances on a mini-tour the following spring. There was also a live telephone link-up with Michael Moorcock in Texas, one of two such instances before Moorcock decided to take no further part in Hawkwind. "I felt that it was appropriate that I should do my last work invisibly," he says. The result of the

Astoria gig was to give the audience a show of the quality they should have received at Hawkestra. One reviewer afterwards noted that the final nail had been driven into the coffin for Nik Turner's appearances with Hawkwind, and it certainly proved to be the case.

The gradual re-assimilation of Langton culminated with him playing a full set with the band at Donington on 22nd June, which included 'Rocky Paths' and the ever crowd pleasing 'Moonglum'. If his singing was weaker than it had been during the 1980s, he had lost none of his exceptional ability as a guitarist. There was a suggestion that Brock wanted to incorporate Huw and Jerry Richards as duelling lead guitarists ("not with a leading bass as well!" comments Davey) but Richards saw the writing on the wall. This was not his style of playing and he had no enthusiasm for the idea. "Jerry knew he was going; it was sad," says Ron Tree. "I could feel his heart bleeding. I had to watch it – my friend."

"At rehearsals for Donington, Jerry looked particularly uneasy and you kind of got the impression he was being phased out," comments Kniveton. Perhaps circumstances conspired against him more than anything. In a group where musical presence has always had as much importance as musical dexterity, the lack of prominence in the 'wall of sound' of his Stratocaster contributed to his relative anonymity in the mix. At one point, there was an attempt to solve this, by Brock lending his rarely used Les Paul Gold Top, perhaps to bring Jerry's sound into line with the 1980s prominence of Langton's own Les Paul; Richards preferred the sound of his own guitar. Thinking back also to some of the better tracks from the Distant Horizons era it's also possible to consider that new style the band had been developing, that screaming mix of anarcho-punk and modern psychedelia, which could have been hugely successful, was strangled by the partial hiatus that the band had taken in advance of the Hawkestra show; that it needed proper exploration and development that simply wasn't forthcoming. In any case, with the benefit of hindsight, and with his highly developed and wide-ranging skill sets, the role that Richards had in Hawkwind wasn't necessarily the right one. Since leaving he's proved himself quite like Dave Brock in one way, that of a band leader, and though that specific skill meant that he brought something to the party beyond what seemed at the time to be a minor entry in the band's history, it was a talent without an ultimate outlet in that circumstance. However, it's a set of tools that he'd go on to make formidable use of in the reimagined version of The Hawklords several years later.

"I felt that there was unfinished business and there were aspects to the musical direction which could have been made more of had I stuck around a little longer," he concedes. "But I think I was kind of relieved to leave the band in some ways; disappointed by the manner of my departure which I thought was grossly unfair and was manipulated by people who had agendas outside of the best direction for the band. Other people were used as pawns to eject both Ron and myself and were unwittingly drawn into the whole equation. The best thing I can say is that I had the best of times and the worst of times. The best times were fantastic, and they probably weren't ever on stage with the band, they were down on the farm or out on the road, or finding oneself on the other side of the planet in some of the worst conditions, with no money, and yet being with people with whom you were having a great time. Those days will not come again, but you had a great time while you were there doing that. The worst times were putting up with some of the Machiavellian aspects of being in a band, which every band has to put up with; it's the same in any organisation."

It's also a period from which he gained knowledge and perspective. "It's never as black and white as people might imagine. It's always that little shade of grey somewhere down the line. Dave doesn't wear a black hat, or a white one, he wears a grey one that changes colour, just the same as Nik does. They're people from a time that is long gone now, a business that has changed beyond all recognition from when they started. They learned from their predecessors, Dave will tell you he learned so much from Dick Taylor; I learned a lot from Dave Brock. For many years Karmen and I were visitors to the farm: festivals, gigs, Christmas and New Year and they were wonderful times with Dave and Kris, partying to all hours, getting up to all sorts of no good and genuinely having a fantastic time doing it. But everything has its time and you can't expect everything to last forever."

In the end, though, the return of Alan Davey tipped the scales against the very same musicians whose arrival had moved the band away from Davey's heavy psychedelic rock and into their own free festival punk vibe, and so it was inevitable that one person's return – and to be fair, the partial return of Huw Lloyd-Langton – squeezed out both Jerry Richards and Ron Tree. For Tree believed he had received assurances from Alan Davey that his membership was 'sorted', even though he'd identified that he was required to sing less often and didn't understand why. "I still went along with it; it was still fun. But two weeks later [from the departure of Jerry Richards] and Ding-Dong! It was my turn." Plans were being made for the next tour and the band was gearing up for rehearsals. Waiting at home, Tree expected to be collected by Chadwick for the drive over to Brock's studio. "He didn't pick me up and I thought, maybe he's fashionably late and it's going to be tomorrow. So he didn't come tomorrow, he didn't come tomorrow night." When Chadwick did arrive, it wasn't with good news. Tree's services were not required on the tour. Brock's intent was to use Langton and Tim Blake to play a set of 80s material, and his feeling was that this didn't suit Tree's vocal style. There was a notion that Ron should utilise the Robot he'd constructed and appear at a small number of gigs, a sort of special feature. Tree thought this had been agreed, but never received a call asking him to rehearse and so believes this was suggested merely to placate him.

He's candid about his departure. It rankles with him ("I was pissed off," he states at one point), yet it hasn't descended into destructive rancour. "I'm not saying it was Dave's fault. It was probably a lot to do with my own fault; my drug addiction didn't help." He speculates about other reasons for his removal, other people's possible involvement, but comes over as genuinely concerned about how his colleagues perceived him and is at pains to accept a share of the blame. "I do believe Dave never meant to hurt me. What it was, he didn't know quite how to tell me."

The band's website claimed that neither member had been sacked, but that 'we'll know more of their plans when they get back in touch'. This was at least partly correct in Tree's case: "I rang [Brock] a bit later. He said, 'What are you doing?' I said I was getting Bastard back together. He said, 'Let us know how things are going', but I never did. That's not his fault."

Meanwhile, Turner was playing strongly on his vision of Hawkwind as the free-for-all collective that he considered the earliest incarnations to be, though there's little real evidence that it was, asserting that any musician who ever played in Hawkwind should have the right to perform under that name. "Shortly after Donington," says Kniveton, "came Nik's invite to 'all Hawkwind crew past or present' to do the Greasy Truckers Gig [a regenerated version of the original concept, featuring a version of the Hawkestra]. Dave's view was that if Jerry and Ron did the gig they wouldn't be welcome in Hawkwind. Huw was going to play but was talked out of it and sided with Dave." This is at odds with Tree's assertion that he was asked to do some dates on the autumn tour, but clearly battle lines were developing and no musician could expect to have a foot in both camps.

Turner was not particularly surprised that Langton had opted for the Brock side of the divide. "People have to make a living, and if somebody offers you a gig in a band, it's a gig. That is why I went back to Hawkwind; you get paid." Though Langton played at a few Turner's 'Hawkwind reunion' shows prior to the Greasy Truckers, he was becoming increasingly "worried about it. I put all the years [of Hawkwind membership] together of all us, including Nik, and all those years added up didn't amount to the years Dave had spent keeping the band going. So, if anybody deserves the title [to Hawkwind], Dave does." From his longstanding relationship with both Brock and Turner, Langton was well-placed to understand the love-hate, off-on nature of their dealings. "It's all down to old-time commitments to each other and the band – I think they must be related!" Despite the way in which Turner has characterised Brock's domination of Hawkwind as being business-like, Huw put a different spin on this. "Dave is quite tough, but I wouldn't say he was that business-like a person. He's had to be, even though he's not that way inclined." Langton, who was always affable and laid-back about his own varied musical career, considered the way Brock had channelled his own energies through Hawkwind: "I've been in God knows how many bands over the years and music is my life's work, but Hawkwind has been Dave's life's work. He's put everything into it, and that's the difference between him and Nik."

Jerry Richards: "Nik has never found himself in the position of running the band at the very highest echelons of the business. He was an important wheel within the functioning unit but Nik was not responsible for the projection of the band within the business or maintaining a professional standard as such. And I don't mean that disrespectfully because Nik's ideas as such are the same as my ideas, coming from the free festivals, everything should be a carnival, like a Travelling Medicine Show…"

The culling at its end, the band played a headline show at the Canterbury Festival, Mount Ephraim Gardens, on 18th August. It was a triumph. As Brock intended, it was largely a showcase of 80s material. Except for the 'Space is their Palestine' insert for 'Assassins of Allah', the newest number played was 'Solitary Mind Games', a song nearly twenty years old. The element of unpredictability with the reintroduction of long-unheard numbers that had sparked from Hawkestra, and the Astoria, shows continued. The opening number was an unexpected run through 'The Fifth Second of Forever', with 'Dust of Time' and the title track itself also appearing from 1980's *Levitation* album. Assisted by Kniveton, the line-up that would tour the UK that coming autumn (Brock, Davey, Chadwick, Langton and House) laid down a quality marker that superseded any of the already well-received performances since the Hawkestra. "Hawkwind at their very best" captioned one newspaper article. As a bonus, Brock's long-held admiration for the presence and style of Arthur Brown was rewarded with Brown joining the band to sing on 'Silver Machine'.

Soon after Langton had left the band for the second time, Brock commented on the musical freedom the departure had allowed. Brock felt that although Langton was a "wonderful lead guitarist" he tended to not give his fellow musicians a break. What was so remarkable about the joint playing of Langton and Simon House – two lead instruments where only one could be expected to fit – was in listening to two maestro musicians giving each other space to excel in, even if backstage the two locked horns on who exactly should have been playing at which points. Brock had taken the opportunities of his bank of contributors, gelled together the most unlikely of combinations and seen it work. Once again, this was a clear demonstration of the talent that Brock possessed that has most to do with the longevity and constant renewal of Hawkwind. As an arranger of talent, as somebody who could harness the geniuses of others, as a person who could bring together and fuse into his vision disparate creative parts, he has few rock 'n' roll equals.

They toured again in the autumn of 2001, following a one-off show at the Royal Festival Hall. The plan was to feature Tim Blake as part of the band for the early part of the tour, with Blake also providing an opening support slot, then to have Kniveton take-over for the remainder. The cost of incorporating Blake into the tour proved prohibitive and the plan was abandoned in favour of additional road-crew resources, with the opening set split on a date-by-date basis between House and Langton (Bedouin played a few pre-scheduled shows on the tour).

Despite Blake's non-appearance they opened their set each night with 'Lighthouse', with Brock taking the singing duties. This developed from a rather abbreviated rendition on the first show (Swindon, 3rd November) and expanded as the tour progressed. 'Levitation', 'Hurry on Sundown' and 'Spiral Galaxy' had already become setlist regulars through the summer. They were joined by Davey's dark, prowling take on 'The Watcher', Langton's 'Moonglum', and 'Brainbox Pollution', another great 'lost' Hawkwind song, a fusion of 'Johnny B. Goode' rock 'n' roll chops with stoned-out lyrics.

Overwhelmingly favourable audience reactions aside, it was another tour not without its problems. "The drama started after the Hitchin gig when the bus driver had a heart-attack," says Kniveton of his first date on the schedule. "Poole was a bloody awful venue, but Salisbury was much better all around – the promoter was on the case, he had been out leaflet dropping and the hall was packed," while a sparsely attended Torquay was, "the worst gigging experience I've ever had. I had very little help setting up my gear and when I finally did get everything working I was told I had to shift because a metal safety curtain had to be test-ed." There was a storming set at Walthamstow still to come, though Kniveton had left the line-up by that point, but the cohesive sound that characterised the middle part of tour was falling apart due to an illness that beset Huw. What appeared to simply be a winter virus at its outset ("To-night we've got Flu Lloyd-Langton," quipped Davey at Walthamstow) turned into Legionnaire's Disease. "Huw is really very poorly," observed one reviewer of the final date in Dublin. Though he recovered for the band's Christmas show at the Kentish Town Forum (20th December) the effects of this major illness meant that his contribution to Hawkwind diminished throughout the following year.

House, Langton, Chadwick, Davey, Brock
Kevin Sommers

Through 2001, the fresh collaboration between Brock, Davey and Chadwick, as well as the past members they could now call upon, gave them new impetus, and it seemed as though the following year would consolidate the band's renewed appeal. However, that year saw more turmoil due to the continuation of the reunion band that Turner had assembled before the Hawkestra show. What had started out as the 'Original Hawkwind Reunion Band' had transformed, via

271

'2001, A Space Rock Odyssey' into the infamous 'xHawkwind'. If the original band name had been somewhat dubious in its use of the Hawkwind trademark, the new title was a single character of an innocent copyeditor's adjustment away from the real thing.

The problem rumbled through the Devon courts for much of the summer, causing new material and live gigs to take a backseat, even though an album with Langton and House had been commenced upon. In many ways, it is not an unfamiliar story. Past members of a successful group (particularly members as integral to the band's original identity as Turner was undeniably to Hawkwind's) feeling some degree of ownership and challenging for the right to trade on the name is a regular occurrence. As the demand for nostalgia grows ever greater, this situation will evermore continue to plague long-established bands and in some ways, as the interest in those bands shifts from the back-catalogue to being able to revisit them for a good night out and a trawl through the classics, it's pretty inevitable.

You can equate that with Hawkwind in the sense that there is a wide audience out there who probably haven't bought an album in years, who might spot a poster for a show and fancy their own nostalgic trip through 'Silver Machine' and 'Master of the Universe'. But there's an element that differs the band from others still playing on the truncated music circuit. The Damned, for example, play many shows year-on-year, but look at their 'new' output and it stretches from 2001's *Grave Disorder* to 2008's *So, Who's Paranoid*, with nothing in between and nothing since. They're happy to play the standards; the crowd is delighted to hear them, and you could probably write the setlist on a napkin before heading to the gig, and find that you were largely right. There are many other examples. But though there has been gaps in the Hawkwind output, and though it's really not possible to argue that everything they've done has been real top-drawer stuff to rank easily alongside *Space Ritual*, or *Quark...*, or the ever intriguing first LP, what's been done, through the shifting, changing, line-ups is to further a body of work and build upon past endeavours. You can only really see that there is one band, one constantly evolving identity, and so when the case was eventually settled in the favour of Brock's continuing lineage and custody, that had to be the correct decision, and the fairest evaluation of contribution and influence. It wasn't an outcome that satisfied all observers, and Turner was not without his supporters, but many of those possessed a misty-eyed, rose-tinted view of the band. "Nik is stuck in the old days... but Hawkwind of the 70s wouldn't have lasted five minutes in the 1980s, it would have collapsed and died," said Davey. "It is Dave's foresight to make changes [that kept it going]."

Turner: "I didn't go out as 'Nik Turner's Hawkwind'. I went out as xHawkwind because the band was all ex-members of Hawkwind. Even though Brock had trademarked the name I didn't see an infringement of the trademark." Turner claimed that to some degree he'd dug his heels in as a matter of principle. "I thought I had this right, and it took some time for me to realise that I didn't." Unpleasant as the legal proceedings most certainly were, perhaps the most hurt that the entire episode inflicted was in Turner's use of a letter from Michael Moorcock to sup-port his case. "Nik told me Dave was suing him and trying to get him to stop performing as X-Hawkwind [sic], which I thought was a reasonable name in the circumstances, and would I write him a letter he could use if the lawsuit took place." Moorcock believed he had "written a letter specifically to stop the lawsuit, but when Nik put it on his website and everyone started writing to me about it… I felt I'd had enough." Though Moorcock's tendency is to "be loyal to my friends," and he has previously noted in this context having more affinity towards Turner than Brock, he felt "betrayed by Nik [and] regretted writing the letter. If I could have reconciled them I would have," Moorcock noted regretfully, though, as a result, "I still can't see [Dave and I] working together again."

Turner's band continues, originally under the unwieldy name SpaceRitual.net, now refined down to simply Space Ritual. Initially it included Mick Slattery, Dave Anderson, Thomas Crimble and Terry Ollis, though Anderson later stood down and was replaced for while by Jerry Richards, while most recently Mick Slattery retired from active duty. It's fair to say that they recaptured some of the sprawling improvisation and excitement of the early Hawkwind, originally playing a nostalgia set dominated by 'Master of the Universe', 'Brainstorm', 'Born to Go' and other 'old favourites'. By 2007, before Anderson departed the ranks, they'd got themselves organised with new material, and resurrected some other numbers, and released *Otherworld* on Cherry Red's subsidiary Esoteric Recordings, a very decent album, that seemed to echo Hawkwind's 'PXR5' on its title track. Back then, Brock had written how 'three of the crew who were with us then did not survive', often thought of as a reference to the upheavals post-*Astounding Sounds* and referring to Turner, Alan Powell and Paul Rudolph. Now, Turner's lyrics turned that on its head, as the seven members of Space Ritual (they'd managed to bring Del Dettmar temporarily on-board) recorded the saga of how 'Still only seven breezed back from the otherworld', and it's not hard to draw these two songs together and see 'Otherworld' as a very belated response to 'PXR5'. But it's generally good, solid stuff, with several numbers including 'Otherworld', 'Sonic Savages' and the jaunty and appealing 'Time Crime', written about Turner's meeting with Timothy Leary in his prison cell back in the days of Hawkwind's original American forays, all making it into Space Ritual's live set and giving them a validation beyond the simply nostalgic. That said, they've not produced any new material since then, and their concerts have been become fewer in number in recent times, with most of the Hawkwind-related members having drifted away.

At the same time, Dave Brock and Kris Tait were refining their vision of the band as being an extended family of musicians and followers, rethinking and updating the ideas of community that had spawned the band in the first place. They conceptualised those ideas under the 'Hawkfest' banner, sometimes an outdoor weekend festival, sometimes more recently an 'outdoors festival indoors', private parties that have been a chance for the longest serving devotees to revisit the roots of Hawkwind, and for the new audience to experience a little of the atmosphere of the original festival scene.

"It all rises again," Brock reflects, with the collapse of the festival scene a decade previous in mind. "It does fall, but there are people who want things to be exciting and good again. Consequently, somebody will resurrect it. On the Friday night [of the 2003 Hawkfest] Kris and I walked around arm-in-arm and we thought 'well, we've succeeded'. We had about a thousand people there, all the things we wanted, stuff for the kids, loads of wonderful cafes, everybody having a marvellous time. We felt we'd done something to be really proud of. This is what it was like twenty years ago, before it all went bad." At one Hawkfest, Dave and Kris were married, sharing the event with the assembled fans.

Alan and Dave, with Arthur Brown
(Oz Hardwick)

Those early Hawkfest events coincided with what seemed to be something of a scaling back in the band's touring commitments, though when they did take to the road their abbreviated tours had something special to offer each time so that focused each appearance as an event distinct of itself. Arthur Brown followed-up his appearance at Canterbury with a further guest slot, at a very welcome high-profile gig opening for Motörhead at Wembley. On a short tour in December 2002, also featuring Blake and Langton (who was unable to attend the last couple of gigs through illness), Brown's stage presence and vocal abilities brought a new air of theatrics to Hawkwind's show. Dressed as Claude Rains in *The Invisible Man* and reciting "Sonic Attack", out of the spotlight, using a miner's lamp to read by, or wearing a neo-lit boiler suit for 'Aerospaceage Inferno'. It was, as one Internet writer commented: "like he has always been a band member… pure essence of classic Hawkwind." At the same time, Hawkwind embraced Brown's material in something of a tribute to the way Brown's unique brand of performance art had influenced them over the years. From Brown's *Kingdom Come* phase, they played 'Time Captives' and from *The Crazy World of Arthur Brown*, 'Time/Confusion'.

Touring again with Hawkwind in the spring of 2003, this time with Simon House but without Langton or Blake, Brown reflected Calvert's delivery of 'Steppenwolf', complete with gothic frock-coat and top hat but also hinted at fresh concepts, particularly resplendent in Phoebus mask for a new song, 'Sunray'. "Arthur's contribution was great," commented Richard. "He's incredibly talented, very funny… he's a well-established solo musician, known for his legendary performances. He's playing with us because it's fun. It's not a serious endeavour to raise world consciousness or something, it's just fun. I've never played with any singer with that phenomenal range of ferocity and power… it's wonderful to play with somebody like that." And Alan considered how, "For his age, he's as energetic as any teenager! And he's always good fun to work with, nice to be around, it was a pleasure to work with him… and we got on well with our humour, our dirty jokes!"

Though it wasn't to be a long-lasting relationship, the connection to Arthur Brown validated a whole set of ideas and opportunities that the band had long harboured and progressed, and which took them right back to that time-worn but still relevant idea of the audio-visual thing, the idea that they'd declared on first setting out on their spacerock journey all those years ago.

21

The Dave Brock Trio, Revisited

Tim Blake and Dave Brock
(Kevin Sommers)

"At the Hawkestra, Lemmy asked me how I'd stuck with Dave Brock so long," recalled Davey during his second stint with the band. "I guess there must have been something between them in the past. But Dave's fine to get on with, that's why we've worked together for twenty years; he's a good friend. We sit in the studio, in front of a computer screen for hours, days, together, producing stuff. With the computer skills I've learned, and Dave's experience, it's a good combination." During his time away from Hawkwind, they'd maintained a regular contact: "We'd been out in the world together, having all these marvellous adventures. After all of that, you just don't stop being friends." When they subsequently did stop being friends it was a pretty permanent looking situation, however.

Without underestimating the input of Tree and Richards, and the irregular contributions of Langton, House and Blake, Hawkwind had essentially been Brock, Davey and Chadwick for the last sixteen years. During the second phase of the 'Trio', post-Hawkestra, Chadwick noted that he'd "got involved in music in the first place because I just loved the idea of doing things with people, that whole team spirit of producing something, utter quicksilver stuff. Me, Dave and Alan are really good at playing together, we can just tell what each other's going to do... a kind of synchronicity that is wonderful." And they did work well together, producing music that while not to the liking of every die-hard fan, had added records of lasting value to the canon back in the early 1990s. Once again they'd renewed the band by coming back together after the reunion show and playing alongside others in an expanded format that relied on the three of them to essentially be the heart of the band, its pulse and its driving force.

Through 2002 and 2003, assisted by various former members, they worked on the first major Hawkwind studio album since *Distant Horizons*. "Alan and Dave love recording, far more than I do," commented Chadwick at the time. "For me, it's just a load of sequencing work to do, but they love the production side of things. We've got a new computer system and have spent a year learning how to use it, a real learning curve for non-computer literate people. Alan has discovered a love for this way of working that he didn't know he had, so it's opened up new creative doors for him."

"People go to University to study-up on this," said Davey. "I first used it when I did my Bedouin studio album and found what you could do with it was quite fascinating." In terms of technology, it was an even bigger step for the band than they had made in embracing midi at the start of the 90s. "We'd always had these great ideas, but no way of achieving them, but now the possibilities are there." He'd use them for that album, *Take Me To Your Leader*, and make much more use of them within a few years for his own albums and his work with other musicians, particularly in the Hawkwind-influenced but contemporary and dynamic Pre-Med, getting involved with their debut album *Medication Time*. "Danny Faulkner, who's a friend of mine, wrote all the songs and brought them down and I could hear the potential, but there was no arrangement in them and the mixing was poor. To his horror I started chopping them up and swapping them around on the computer and the poor guy had a cold sweat going on but I put some bass on and played some keyboards, produced it for him and it got nice reviews everywhere." It was something that came out of that learning curve with Hawkwind, experience gained on what was to become their first album of the 21st Century. "We did it all on a digital programme. It was quite daunting, took a year to master [using] it, and another to learn more that I didn't know was in there! But as opposed to using tape we found that we could cut anything we liked and try out anything and start messing about, which allowed us to do stuff that we hadn't done before."

Take Me To Your Leader, was essentially a Dave Brock Trio album, with additional contributors glued-on. Arthur Brown appeared on three tracks, Simon House also contributed to three, while Lene Lovich, who'd made her name in the late 70s on Stiff Records with the memorably quirky 'Lucky Number' appeared on a couple and played with the band at a handful of shows, notably at the now lamented London Astoria at the interchange between Oxford Street and

Tottenham Court Road, while the jazz musician Jez Hugget provided saxophone and flute, and played with the Hawks on and off.

The new album revisited their most enduring theme, of the many and varied threats to humanity. "The concept is about how badly things are going in the world, and why," noted Davey. "There is so much that is wrong; we needed to make an album about it. There's always another threat coming over the horizon, but when you look back at the stuff that Bob Calvert was writing about, his words are still relevant."

Some of the material for *Take Me To Your Leader* was introduced into Hawkwind's live shows in early 2003, notably 'Angela Android', featuring Chadwick's first lead vocal on a Hawkwind track since 'Gimme Shelter', and 'Sunray', a collaboration between Alan Davey and Arthur Brown.

"'Angela Android', written by Richard, is all about a robotic sex doll," explained Davey. "There's so much sex on the Internet now, romance is going down the drain. Apparently, in Japan a third of all young men don't go out anymore, just sit in front of their computers. It's a big problem." The title track looked at the flipside of this scenario, "people going out and getting drunk, women getting pregnant and not even knowing who the father is. A lot of people don't seem to be aware that these things are destroying our society." A balance is achieved by the wonderful 'Sunray', which "is about Sarah [Davey's then girlfriend, now wife] … a sunray in my life. I told Arthur all about her, and he came up with the lyrics. He went for a walk from my place to Dave's, which was three or four miles, and I got down there later and met him and he said 'Hey, how do these sound?' and sung it over the top! 'Pretty good!' I kept saying, 'That's got to be the single', and Paul Cobbold agreed, it was the catchiest one on the album. But it's like 'Wings'. That would have been a good single but instead 'Images' got put out which wasn't catchy or commercial… a great rock number, but it isn't a single." Another Chadwick contribution was 'Digital Nation', according to Davey, "about going-off into the fantasy world of game-playing." 'Cyberspace' meanwhile was the first Simon House composition for Hawkwind since 'Forge of Vulcan'.

Arthur Brown delivered a spoken piece, 'Letter to Robert', that Davey described in advance of the release as being "very controversial; bits are very funny, but other parts are going to really shock people." As a contrast, there was also 'Out Here We Are', one of Davey's now traditional mellow, keyboard-wash tracks, also featuring Hugget. "It goes into a bass-picking chord structure. We got Jez to play sax, but the result is half sax, and half trumpet. We made the trumpet sound by treating the sax via the computer programme."

Take Me To Your Leader had an unusually long gestation period. Davey: "We had to discover how to use the programme as we went along, just experimenting. It's a bit like treading on eggshells, not being sure what the software is going to do, but gaining the confidence to press buttons. We'd get something recorded and mixed, but then we'd learn something new and need to back-track and improve what we already had. Every time we thought we'd got there, we learned how to make it better."

"When we've finished a track, we like to give it a rating. We'll say, 'this track's an A-side, this one is a B-side', Brock told me before it hit the shelves. "It's how we judge our work. This time we've got an album that's all A-sides, really very strong material." Alan, however, reflects on the album differently and in doing so, it reveals his mindset towards the band at that point in time, looking back and considering that the constant process of trying to rework and improve their material as they learned more about the computer software that was helping them make the album eventually led to the music becoming overworked.

"I don't think much of it [in hindsight], to be honest. I didn't feel from the others that they were putting their all into it, and I was. That was kind of how it was at the end, for me. I was trying to put my all into it and others seemed to be happy to cruise along and not accelerate at all. Tracks like 'Out Here We Are', I worked on that totally on my own, and I think that one sticks out as a major track on it. 'Sunray' was another, what I did with my tracks was take them home and work on them in my own studio. I should be mixing and producing my own tracks, in the same way Dave would do his. It all just seemed a bit lack-lustre to me and I got very frustrated: 'Come on, we need to come out with a rock album', we've done the keyboard pulse tracks, been there, time to go back to doing something that rocks. The fans liked what we did with the synths, but not all the time, but there was no way [the others] were going to budge from it. We just drifted apart that way."

I visited the band for interviews for the first edition of this book while work was ongoing for *Take Me To Your Leader*. The first time I met Dave and Kris, we'd had lunch at a local pub, in lovely warm spring sunshine, conducting the initial interview for the project, largely focused on Dave's early career. Afterwards, I was thrilled to be invited back to the farm, to see where the band rehearsed and recorded, and to meet Alan Davey and Richard Chadwick. I sat at their kitchen table and Kris talked about a request they'd had for Dave to appear on a radio show with a presenter who'd claimed – and they were sceptical about this – to be a Hawkwind fan of longstanding. Should they take up this one, they wondered? "Well," I said, "It's all publicity, isn't it?" The radio presenter in question was Matthew Wright, now known for his long-running TV series, *The Wright Stuff*, who has since become a firm friend of the band.

"It was a Saturday morning show on LBC Radio," Matthew recalls. "The producer was very new to radio and didn't really know what she was doing, and I'd got a bit frustrated because in radio the producer does a lot of background work for you, so you can just rock up and sound like you know everything off the cuff. They make everything easy; she struggled but she came up with one brilliant idea which was to get Matthew off her back she'd fill the show with people Matthew would like to interview. She'd rather cunningly extracted stories of my life, down the pub after the Saturday sessions, and Hawkwind came up, and Gong, and over the year and a half I did the show Daevid Allen came on, and Dave Brock. Dave Brock was the pinnacle of it all, really. I mean, Hawkwind have had big periods, less big periods, but they are internationally renowned still to this day. To have the main man turn up on your relatively small beer radio show was an honour. The first thing I thought when he came through the door: 'Fucking hell! It's Dave Brock.'"

That claim to be a fan of longstanding was totally true. "At school there was one guy who was the least likeliest bloke to get into spacerock; he was the cross-country champion for the school, he ran for Surrey, he was a nice bloke... and he obviously had very advanced musical tastes because he was listening to *Warrior on the Edge of Time* at, what, ten, eleven. So, I was hearing it then but didn't quite get the bug, but then picked up the *Masters of the Universe* compilation on cassette, with it going round and round, and me getting hooked in, without realising what I was getting hooked into. Then eventually I committed myself, shall we say, to a path of internal experimentation and started to get a grip on what Hawkwind were all about, and they started to get a proper grip on me. On my 21st birthday Hawkwind were playing a venue right in the middle of Exeter and a mate of mine who I knew from university smuggled a note back stage, would they read out a dedication to Matthew Wright, it's his 21st birthday. And, fucking hell, Dave Brock did it! That was the first time I got close to spaceship Hawkwind [laughs]. But here I am on my radio show and it's the first time I've come face-to-face with him. I was just blown away, met Kris, and they were both charming. Sat down and did the interview and Dave is as revealing as Dave can be, knocking back the trickier questions and trying not to sound too bored with the ones he's answered a million times before. In between we're playing Hawkwind tracks and talking about albums; I think we had *Hall of the Mountain Grill* on and I'm singing along to 'You'd Better Believe It' and he says, 'You know it better than I do!'. Went through a few more lyrics and he was, 'you really do know it better than I do...'. Literally the next line was, 'do you fancy doing a gig with us?'."

That gig would be at the London Astoria for the band's Christmas gig of 2004. For most of the year the band had settled into its early 90s trio configuration, since Simon House had once again departed, as had Arthur Brown, who'd continued to make appearances with the group until the summer of 2003. But a new texture to the sound was starting to be added by the recruitment of Jason Stuart on keyboards, who'd previously played with Captain Rizz and was bringing in a totally new dimension with jazz-led piano sounds that turned things around on a sixpence again and offered another new index of possibilities.

"That was always going to happen," Alan recalls. "Jason lived in Honiton, where Dave and I did as well, and he was such a nice chap to have around and have a laugh with. As soon as we thought about looking for another keyboard player it all went straight to Jason, really. I knew him a few years before Dave and Kris did, because he used to live in London and I'd go and see a friend there and he was always around. There's nothing bad to be said about that guy, nothing at all."

"Jason was in Captain Rizz's band, years and years ago," says Dave, "so our paths crossed quite often. We asked him quite a few times if he'd like to come and have a jam with us but he was always too shy, believe it or not! He was an over-the-top character, but quite shy within himself. But we eventually persuaded him to come and play here, and it was wonderful, such a good keyboard player, and a nice character. He had a good style of playing, which suited him well. I used to see him twitching sometimes, when he'd hit the odd bum note… I'd look over and see his eye twitching, 'Oh, you heard it!' Jason played at my mum's funeral, 'When the Saints go Marching In', on the organ, in church, jazzed it up a bit!"

What Jason Stuart brought to the band invigorated the captain of the ship, as Matthew Wright, who got to know Jason well, describes: "Jason and Dave really clicked. Dave needs people to write with, he's generated his best work when he writes with someone, Turner stuff, Calvert stuff, he's always liked to have a writing partner. I think that with Jason he found someone who was extremely gifted musically, a great improviser on keyboards and if you are a musician's musician, as Dave is, you want someone who is fantastic on the keyboards. So, they were having a wonderful time writing stuff together, and they had a wonderful, warm, relationship. Jason was one of my favourite people that I ever met, he never took life too seriously, always had a smile on his face, and if you can imagine that life on the road can get very emotional and difficult, touring can be tough and when tensions are at their highest and everyone is wired and paranoid you had this bugged-eyed and balding lunatic, Jason, in front of you, who never took anything very seriously and was a good diffuser of tensions within the band and a fantastic laugh."

At the same time, crew member Mr. Dibs was enjoying a promotion to the stage first posited way back in 1996 when Alan had departed for the first time. At this point it wasn't a full-blown thing, and not for the bass role that he'd been suggested for originally but wandering on as a reciter of poetry. It was, though, an ad-hoc continuation of an embryonic start that had been made during encores back on the *Distant Horizon* tour. Jonathan 'Dibs' Darbyshire had been a fan of the band since his teenage years, though without realising it to begin with, since he'd acquired a cassette tape of the Hawklords album, *25 Years On*, that had no sleeve or label to identify it. "I was Joy Division, Tubeway Army, The Stranglers at the time," he recalls, "and I just thought it was contemporary to all that dystopian punk that I was listening to. It was another year before I heard *In Search of Space* and realised what I'd been listening to. It didn't change me from a punk to a hippie, but got me into that lifestyle and finding out about free festivals. I went around the festival scene, usual sort of fanboy stuff getting autographs, always turning up, but I guess the proper association started just around the turn of '89, '90, when Krel had been formed and we started sending Dave tapes. The first one we'd sent was called *Send In The Clones*, which was a jokey reference to his line in Kris's book [*This Is Hawkwind, Do Not Panic*] that what he needed was five clones of himself. He saw the humour in that and invited us to do some dates on a mini-tour called 'The Five Days of Christmas' and that was how we got to know him. Krel were at the punky end of spacerock; we started off doing Hawkwind songs in our own way, but we quickly got our own material together."

By the time Krel had been invited onto the Electric Tepee tour, Dibs had become a traveller on the festival scene, buying in wholeheartedly to that part of the Hawkwind ethos. "I spent a few years going to the Stonehenge festivals, wasn't at the Beanfield but was trying to get there, got caught in a roadblock and tried to get to Savernake Forest. It was wanting to do music, which isn't a regular income, so how was I going to afford my own home? Well, I could afford to buy a bus. I lived in Hulme, in squat world, just behind the Crescent, for a while, which was where a lot of the Northern Peace Convoy would winter up, because you could find a flat and electric and get a new vehicle or do your old one up and it was quite a good community. That was where I got my first bus from, because a guy there was upgrading to a bigger one. I was delivering pizzas to raise money for it! It was good money and raised enough for the things I was doing."

For the *Electric Tepee* tour, "[Krel] travelled in my old bus which I'd converted, the benches folded out into bunks and we had a fold-down thing in the cab, and we managed to fit the whole band in it, seven of us with the guy who was our roadie, and two dancers. It was unheard of then not to have to buy on to a tour, and to get paid, but we got a support fee and were well looked after, even a little rider, which was brilliant. We missed one gig on the tour when my bus overheated, that was Preston, got halfway there and the timing had gone one, could smell this smell and the whole manifold and exhaust was cherry red so we had to wait for it to cool down and made it to Preston just as they were clearing out, but they'd saved us food and beer! We knew then that we were getting to be a part of the family. I left Krel and got my own band, Spacehead, together, and that ended up getting some support slots as well, not full tours because by then they were picking bands from local areas, so you'd get local support, or bands that Dave liked, or some of the band liked. It was the same again, I sent a tape, Dave phoned up… we started talking about cricket and found a mutual thing to natter about there. He said, 'Oh, we've got this label, Emergency Broadcast System, send it down and you could put an album out, which was amazing. I sat there for a good hour afterwards going, 'I've just been asked to go on Dave Brock's record label. Whoo!'"

Dibs was well-placed to observe the way the band had developed, twisted and changed, across the 1990s, from the trio of the early 90s through to the punk psychedelia of the decade's latter years. "The power trio, for want of a better expression, worked really well but it was very technical with a lot of midi stuff going on that was always going wrong. But it seems to go in peaks and troughs, and that was a peak time for them. It was building up, but then Alan left and it changed again. That's part of the joy of Hawkwind, you never know what you'll get year by year. I'd written about the bass job a few times, and I'd heard there was a bit of disgruntle going on so as soon as I heard Alan had left I did write, but Ron was a good bass player and he was there at the time. There were a few occasions where I could have joined the band and that was the first, but I got a lovely letter from Richard explaining that had they not already decided that Ron was going to do it, that I could have had the job. But instead of interrupting the flow of the band at the time they gave it to Ron, who is a very good bass player."

Instead Dibs started to become a regular presence on the road crew, recognisable to fans because of his previous stage appearances in support slots and because of his imposing figure. "I really liked that line-up [with Ron and Jerry], possibly because that was the first tour I worked on the crew. I'd gone up to Whitby 'DracFest' to see them [27th September, 1997], and got backstage the day after, when they were still there. They had a tour bus, and Captain Rizz's bus, 'The Rizz Bus', was there as well. Richard poked his head out and said, 'Hey, Dave! Dibs can drive a bus!' I got roped in, 'Go and pick up this bus from London for us and meet us at Worthing Assembly Hall.' Trundled back to Buxton, found someone to look after the dog for three weeks, went to London and it was another hippie bus for the crew and it ended up with me, Crum, Captain Rizz, and the drum tech travelling in that. I found myself at Worthing humping gear, selling merchandise, driving the bus, and quickly learned that Hawkwind was a multi-role combat team, as I described it halfway through that tour. It was manic. If you're on the crew you've got to know a few jobs so that you are not just a bass tech or a drum roadie. On one tour, I was setting up Alan Davey, Huwey, and Simon House. Coming up from being in a support band to being on the crew was amazing. And I got a guest spot, doing the 'Cockpit Check' from *Captain Lockheed*; there was one soundcheck where I was setting up Ron's bass and ended up playing the song and Ron was, 'Dave! Dibs can play that for the rest of the tour.' Wow! Bloody hell! And I had about six gigs on the tour where I was doing the encore."

Once Alan had returned, Dibs was assigned as his bass tech, among his many roles within the crew. "We got on really well; he was happy to be back. I was happy to still be in the crew and see another incarnation from the side-lines. The work dynamic changed, because of being Alan's guy for a while, but the multi-role thing kicked in when Huw and Simon came back. The writing went back to being Dave, Alan and Richard but then there's always been a 'core' to the band, Richard's just been the solid one, the glue."

Matthew Wright's involvement with the band continued to grow, giving the opportunity for a boost in profile for Hawkwind at a time when the band was indeed starting to gain renewed interest from the music press with interviews and features that were more respectful or enthusiastic than had been the case in some past times. Things seemed on an upward trajectory, as evidenced by full houses at venues such as The Astoria, where on 19th December 2004, the band were joined by Wright on 'Spirit of the Age'.

"I've been asked on stage with Hawkwind, and I'm immediately going to say 'yes'. Dave asked what do I want to do, what's my favourite ever track, and I said 'Spirit of the Age'. 'Oh, that's a hard one. Alright, turn up in the afternoon and we'll have a rehearsal and you can sing it in the evening'. And that's what happened. Met Dibs in the passage way down the side of the Astoria – it's all gone now of course – and he says 'OK, up you go', and within five minutes of going through the door I'm singing 'Spirit of the Age' at the rehearsal. It's all a bit iffy, I wouldn't ever describe myself as singer but I know the words and it's decided that Dibs or Jason Stuart will give me some sort of cue to start singing because it's quite difficult to gauge which part of the song the lyrical part starts. On the night, Dibsy gave me a bloody great shove which is just what I needed, as I'd no idea of when to start to sing! It was a performance of two halves, the first absolute terror and I suppose a curious and increasing sense of euphoria as the seconds turned into the minutes. In the second half, the euphoria got the better of me and I possibly had two or three of the greatest minutes of my life, it was fantastic. At that moment, I felt I'd been welcomed into the Hawkwind family, and that's still how I feel all these years down the line."

Matthew is self-effacing about his abilities as a singer, but for a song that in recent years had lost something of the tone of Bob Calvert's delivery back in the 70s – or indeed Dave's reciting of it on *Live Seventy Nine* – and become an incongruous singalong number, he gave it some much needed attack and so though the next surprise would be an opportunity to cut a studio version, he threw himself into that with due gusto as well. "After the Astoria there was a party which I went along to, and Kris was saying 'You should do a studio version'. Well, there's part of me that thinks I'm a rock god because I did two minutes that I liked at the Astoria, and the other part is still sensible enough to think 'you are what you are, you're not a singer in Hawkwind,' but I duly went down the farm not long afterwards. The recording was almost as lo-fi as the concert, one minute I'm in the kitchen drinking tea, the next Dave says, 'shall we go and record it?' and I'm in the cowshed with all the psychedelic recording equipment and Dave's sitting in front of me nodding in the cues and going for it. I don't like the vocal I did on it, I wasn't in the groove, and I think if I'd warmed up I could have done a better job. I hadn't heard the version of me doing it live until the single had been released, and I thought the second half of me doing it live didn't sound too bad. Maybe there's a better version of it in me, but I don't think anyone is going to hear it!"

That lo-fi approach was then to manifest itself in a video that made classic *Doctor Who* look positively *Star Wars* in its rendition! "Kris said, 'We're going to make a video'. OK, I'll go along with it, so we had to go up to Granada Studios because her brother worked there, and she'd worked there in the past, and we could get access to a studio and cameras, for free, over a very limited period, one weekend. Turn up and Dibs and Jason are on the tour bus, so I go and join them for a chat and it's as you imagine a tour bus to be, quite a state inside and there's a mound of old laundry for which the mind boggles what kind of filth one might find in it, but we're chatting, and I see that the laundry moved. I'm thinking its rats or something, then out of the bottom of the pile comes this extraordinary hair, and there was Huw Lloyd-Langton! Huw Lloyd-Langton *emerged* from below a pile of dirty laundry! He wasn't doing any music at the time, and he wasn't in the video, he was just *on the bus*, and specifically, under a pile of laundry! Then I get called in to do my bit, and again in true Hawkwind style... I mean, for someone who has been working in television for a few years I'm expecting a plan of how the video was going to be made. Get in there, and Alan Davey had a mask, Dave had a mask, everyone had a mask but I didn't, but I had a lab coat so that was great and it was, 'well, what are we going to do, then?' There was about enough ideas for the first twenty-five seconds and then we'd wing it! [Matthew roars with delighted laughter] Wing it! There's three minutes of instrumental! So, in a cold, empty studio with no atmosphere to it whatsoever – and stone cold sober – I thought the only thing was to give it my all and dance around like a mad thing, which is what I did. Even if I cringe with embarrassment every time I see the video, it's not that bad, seeing the budget it was made on!"

This, then, was the reinvigorated Hawkwind in the early years of the 21st century, the core 'trio' working together, with Jason Stuart adding keyboard flourishes to the dynamics of the sound, an album that, while it wasn't a classic in the catalogue, had added new material to the setlist and a useful relationship built with a noted media figure. Dark days lay ahead.

22

A Personal Tragedy

**Alan and Dave, with Arthur Brown
(Oz Hardwick)**

Alan Davey's return to the band wasn't to last, ending in acrimonious circumstances that are so murky that neither side of the divide could even today agree on exactly when he'd departed from the line-up. They'd muddled on through 2005 and the following year, playing UK dates and some European festivals, principally as a four-piece, with a setlist drawing from *Take Me to Your Leader* and on some old standards, and with neglected tracks such as 'Upside Down', 'Psychedelic Warlords', and 'Brainbox Pollution' being revisited. At the same time, Davey was working on a solo-album, *Human on the Outside*, and seeing some of his own earlier work being issued by Voiceprint. I spoke to him during the spring of 2007, interviewing him for *Bass Guitar* magazine in the UK, and for the US-based spacerock website *Aural Innovations*, and he was still talking about Hawkwind in the present tense, even though the band hadn't played any shows so far that year.

"If I've got something that I think would be good in Hawkwind I'll take it down and play it to Dave," he said when we talked for *Aural Innovations*. "If it gets rejected it becomes a solo work; some of those ideas became the *Captured Rotation* solo album. I thought tracks like 'Ancient Light' and 'The Call' would be really good Hawkwind numbers, but for some reason they didn't make it there, so I started working on them by myself." That's no different than Dave Brock would say about his own solo album tracks at times, that he'd written songs for Hawkwind that other members then hadn't liked and which ended up being used for his own records. Alan was, though, talking enthusiastically about his own work, and a revisiting of his pre-Hawkwind band, Gunslinger, with whom he then played a few live shows and issued a new studio album of their early songs, *Earthquake in E Minor*.

For *Bass Guitar* we'd talked generally about Hawkwind, though the focus was more on Alan as a distinctive musician. I'd asked him if he'd ever fancied the idea of swapping instruments with Dave, as Paul Rudolph had done back in the mid-70s. "No. The bass is a bigger sounding instrument and when you strum bass chords with a naturally distorting amplifier... I've played Dave's guitar during soundchecks, it doesn't make my flares flap like the bass does!" On whether he preferred following original basslines on Hawkwind songs, or inventing his own, he'd said that, "The riff after the chorus on 'Psi Power', for instance, is a very distinctive part of the song so I copy things like that. But my lines on 'Assassins of Allah' are new. I slipped in a few Egyptian-style scale runs. Generally, I'll improvise. If you haven't got your own thing, you haven't got anything!" There wasn't any hint that his time with Hawkwind had already passed, even though he seemed weary of talking about the band and more energised with his own multiple projects.

Within the band, however, the idea that he'd jump ship at any moment was gaining traction during 2006, leading to his relationship with his bass tech, Dibs, deteriorating. "Everything was good; the *Take Me to Your Leader* tour was quite successful but then it was in another dip. Alan was getting unsettled, a bit disgruntled, culminating in him leaving in December 2006," says Dibs. "He spent that tour telling everyone he was off, said goodbye to everyone at the after show party and I noticed that he took everything with him, nothing of his went back to the farm, and that, to me, was a big tell because he never took everything back to his house, just the stuff he needed to do his home recording. He walked off that bus in December 2006 and that was it. He'll have his own take on that. That tour I was kind of on 'Orange Alert', the rumblings were there about him leaving."

Alan does indeed have his own take on what happened that December, a mini-tour culminating in that show at the Astoria. "I think we'd done about six gigs in a row at that time [it was five gigs, from 14th – 20th December with two days off], and we always *used* to have a hotel room. A lot of musicians will say this, at the end of the night you need your own space and somewhere to get some sleep, so you can operate. On stage I was running the whole show, counting in, when Dave wanted to use the computer onstage I had to keep an eye on how many bars had gone past, so I had to keep myself together. But we did this tour and there were no hotels and we were all on this bus. After the gig, drinking is going on, on the bus, until five o'clock, but by one o'clock I'm done because I've given it my all on stage which tires you out physically and mentally. I need my sleep! I've got a lot of pride in what I do, but I'm not getting to sleep until 5am and then waking up at 8am because they're all snoring, so I'm getting three hours sleep and by then I'm pissed-off and angry with everyone. The bus is parked in the middle of nowhere, you can't get off because it's locked, the toilet is overflowing... by the end of the dates I was crabby because it was a slog. I might have said a couple of things at Dave, a bit angry at him. He'll say it's up to me to get a hotel room, but isn't that a band expense like it's been for the last twenty years? I didn't say that I was leaving the band. I might have said something along the lines of being sick and tired of the band, but you can always talk about these things later and try to solve these problems. But people will understand that things can get said in the heat of the moment. Everyone's been there."

Dibs is not the only person to have recalled Alan announcing his departure at the Astoria show (December 20th, 2006), though when I did some bits of publicity for Alan during 2007, for his *Human On The Outside* album, and later for the terrific *Eclectic Devils* record, which he'd recorded with the assistance of, among others, Simon House, he was at pains to note a specific June 2007 end-date for his membership, "Dave and Richard were wondering why he hadn't got in touch," says Dibs, which casts some doubt on the finality of Davey's departure that night at the Astoria. "I got asked down to the farm, started rehearsing, and he turned up one day, around June and just before Dave and Kris's wedding, which was going to be at Hawkfest. He came in, had a mooch around and there was a bit of an atmosphere. I'd been doing the odd bits of poetry and vocals, did 'Lord of Light' once; there was one gig where the support band hadn't turned up, but I had my bass with me and the drum tech and Keith [Barton] the guitar tech could all play and that was the beginning of T.O.S.H. [Technicians of Spaceship Hawkwind]. Alan was a bit suspicious – 'why have you got that bass with you?' – but I'd been practicing because I'd been asked to do so, in case he jumped mid-tour."

The band hadn't played live for the first six months of 2007, and there were no new albums on the horizon. They'd always rehearsed to a weekly schedule, getting together at Dave's farm on a Tuesday, Wednesday and Thursday, but Alan had made no appearances there during the first half of the year. Alan Davey: "When it got close to Hawkfest, I'd sent Dave a text now and then to say 'when do you want to get together and rehearse?' It had all gone very quiet, nothing happening, though I knew Hawkfest was coming up. This went on for a couple of weeks with no replies and I thought I'd better go down and see what was happening, and they were rehearsing with Dibsy on bass and hadn't even told me. My roadie is using my bass gear to replace me!" He took what remaining equipment he had at the milking shed and that marked the end of Alan Davey's second stint in Hawkwind. "The thing is about Hawkwind – Lemmy and I talked it about several times – we both loved being in Hawkwind so much and put so much in, that when you get cold-shouldered it hurts."

**Dibs in *Sonic Attack* T-Shirt and Sonic Attack Mode
(Oz Hardwick)**

"Alan is a great musician, he's good at doing his keyboard stuff, good at a lot of stuff, and could have been a well-known musician in his own right because he has the creativity," Dave told me, "But he would have these freak-outs at times. Back in the 90s there was an instance where some albums had turned-up and his name had been missed off a credit somewhere. Just a mistake, Douglas had been doing the artwork and a credit got missed, it wasn't deliberate. But Alan took it personally, 'Look at this, they've missed my name off on purpose!' And the next thing me and Richard knew, he'd thrown them across the studio, like Frisbees, and was jumping up and down on them! It was like Basil Fawlty, in *Fawlty Towers*, when he's thrashing his car with a branch because it won't go! We were watching him, from the outside, through the window!"

As for that night in London and subsequent contacts, Dave recalls how, "At the Astoria, Alan was telling everyone he was leaving, that he wanted to go fishing and to make his own music. There *were* hotels on that tour, but not every night. Then in the January my mum died, and my dad was heartbroken, it was unexpected and only two days after my dad's 100th birthday, and they'd been together over seventy years. We moved in with him the day my mum died; he was deaf and almost blind so we were sleeping on the floor of their living room, becoming his full-time carers, we were all he had. He died seven months later, and we'd remained his carers throughout that time, driving over to his cottage three times a day. A stressful and very sad time. Alan knows all of this. Richard and I went up to his cottage that January to discuss things, and we were in touch by text; it was clear to us all that he'd left the band for good."

"When he left I wasn't the first choice," says Dibs. "Because I live so far away, they'd tried a friend of Richard's but he didn't know the songs as well, though it was convenient because he lived close by, but I said I didn't mind travelling. I'd looked at moving to Devon but it's so expensive and I've got a good situation up here so it would be a big thing to up sticks and end up back in bedsit land. I mean, Jason was living in a tiny flat above a shop in Honiton. I've been there, done that in my student days, I'm away from that. Even getting another bus, park-ups you can't get them, you are constantly being moved on. So, I commute!"

Dibs would make his first appearance as a full member of the band at the 2007 Hawkfest, which took place at Castle Donington, where Dave Brock and Kris Tait married, with the assembled Hawkfans as their guests. "The first gig I did, it was Dave and Kris's wedding," says Dibs. "So it was even more massive than just being my first proper Hawkwind gig. And I was stepping into those shoes. [Alan] was a well-loved character in the band and a good player, and it was another drastic change. I got a lot of detractors and a lot of flak, and it was hard work, to get asked [to join] by Dave, but to have the fans going, 'he's rubbish.' I'm not, I'm just not Alan and it's taken a few years to get to the attitude where I'm not bothered by it and I'm well accepted now. I still get the odd bit but I don't rise to it. I used to get into massive arguments online, some people being extremely nasty, but I spoke to Matthew Wright about it and he'd said that it comes with the territory. In the Internet age, you get to see a lot of it, whereas before it would be discussed post-gig in the pub and it would be a drunken argument that wouldn't go anywhere, whereas now it becomes public. But it was nice to be accepted into the band by Dave and Rich, and by Jason."

If that suggests there is still a rawness somewhere deep inside someone who'd spent his life waiting for the moment to be called to the ranks, then perhaps that's the disappointment of having some elements of the audience unfairly and unreasonably rejecting his elevation to the band. "Alan had been there another five years or so, and was established and had made his mark. The person who thinks I should be in Hawkwind is Dave, and that is good enough for me! I'd had an argument at one show when I was crewing. 'I'm off.' And Dave came running after me: 'Calm down, you work for Hawkwind, not for one particular person. Go and have your dinner.'"

I don't think that Alan's decision to announce his departure, if indeed he did, rather than make his unhappiness generally known without intent of leaving, at the Astoria the previous year was as much a line in the sand as those (Dibs, Matthew Wright, Dave and Kris) who'd heard it might have thought. I think he was unhappy, that he fully intended to make the break again, but I don't believe it was truly set in stone until that encounter in the milking shed the following June. Whatever the truth, Alan Davey never played with the band again after that

December night. He'd go on to release a wide selection of his own material, in his distinctive styles. Aside from those solo albums already mentioned, there's been a sequence of demo collections, a marvellous concept album revisit for his character, Sputnik Stan, a terrific live album from the Sonic Rock Solstice Festival, an Arabic-themed album, *Djinn*, with Bridget Wishart… it goes on.

"I was being held back by Hawkwind," he now reflects, "because I was putting forward all these great songs that got ignored because they were rockier stuff, like 'Angel Down' [later, on Davey's *Eclectic Devils* album] which people think, why the fuck wasn't that on a Hawkwind album! When I left I just exploded with ideas I'd had from the past, new ideas… just exploded with a load of good records."

No argument – once again his departure left a significant hole in the band. And while the following quote from Dave Brock does not specifically refer to Alan's leaving, though the wounds of Alan's comments subsequently are still quite raw, it is apposite. "Each person was a real character within their own right. It could get fucking annoying, because you'd be on the road touring, but the camaraderie, the friendship within a band, this is what a band is. You'd know each other better than wives would. Conversations, confiding, everything that used to go on. It moulds people together and it's upsetting when people go sometimes and friendship goes down the drain. Different people that you were friends with turn around and slag you off. For fuck's sake… don't they remember all these wonderful experiences and the good times?" In any event, much worse was to follow.

A blog post from the band on 8th September, 2008, titled 'Jason Stuart', read simply: "We are very sorry to have to let you know that our keyboard player Jason Stuart is seriously ill. On Friday, he was rushed into hospital with an aneurysm which unfortunately lodged in his brain and caused a haemorrhage. The doctors have been trying to save his life ever since. His condition is very serious indeed. Please send positive thoughts and prayers. We will update you on his condition as soon as we have more news." That update was not long in coming and confirmed the worst possible news. "This is one of the most difficult things we have ever had to announce, but we have to tell you that unfortunately Jason lost his fight for life today."

I never met Jason, but I've talked to Dave Brock about him on a couple of instances, and Dave does not talk about him without both enthusing about Jason Stuart's skills as a musician, nor without choking up about the loss of him as a person. Matthew Wright: "The last weekend I spent with Jason was a balmy August weekend at the Levellers' festival, Beautiful Days, and he was like a naughty imp taking me here, there, and everywhere, because it was local territory for him in Devon and it seemed he knew everyone who was there. I became a little partner to him in God knows what psychedelic crimes, on and on. Even though the band had a room for him in the buildings connected to the festival,

Jason said, 'I need a lie down, I'm going to go that tent.' I said, 'is that your tent?' 'No!' Off he went, got in somebody else's tent, went to sleep!"

It's story with a coda that Kris Brock relates: "The next day, Matthew and Jason are wandering around, and this big skinhead bloke, massive bloke, comes rushing up to Jason. 'I've been looking all around for you! You were the one asleep in my tent last night! Weren't you?' and Jason is all how sorry he was… and the bloke goes, 'Here you are… you left your car keys!'"

He comes across as someone with a true zest for life, mischievous, and a bit of a man for the ladies. "We played at this large club in New York, run by the Polish mafia," recalls Dave, of a little US mini-tour from June, 2007. "Jason, unbeknownst to us, got off with the owner's girlfriend. We'd done our set and were in the dressing room having drinks, and Jason said he was going to pop out and have a wander around. Off he went, and somehow he'd managed to chat her up. We're sitting around and he comes back, 'I think we ought to go now. I think we ought to leave really quickly.' Why? 'We should leave… Look, I've been threatened by the club owner.' We rushed out to the car and all these bouncers are there waving their arms! Dibs was driving, got lost in the one-way system and we came back round again and they were in the middle of the road stopping cars. Fucking hell… just because Jason got off with the owner's girlfriend!"

"At the time [of his death], he was madly in love," Matthew remembers. "He'd met a girl; he'd been in a long-term relationship that had ended and now he'd met this other girl and was crazy about her. They were going to move down to Beer, move in together, and two weeks later I got a call and he was dead. It's still hard to take in. The love that people had for him was reflected in his funeral which was one of the most touching services I've ever been to; I was next to Dave Brock at the service and by way of confirming everything I've said about Jason, Dave looked like he was broken in two that day. He was absolutely grief-stricken."

Jason appeared with the band between albums, so there's not a studio album that encapsulates his contribution, though naturally numerous live recordings circulate, including the album *Knights of Space*, recorded at the Astoria on the 2007 Hawkwind Christmas show, and there are many clips on YouTube that represent his keyboard skills. He did enter the Hawk-orbit in time to appear on a couple of tracks on *Take Me to Your Leader*, 'Greenback Massacre' and 'To Love A Machine', and his memory has been kept alive on subsequent releases. When the next incarnation released *Blood of the Earth*, the standard version included the bonus track 'Starshine', credited to Brock/Stuart and sounding for all the world as though the two of them were having a delightfully creative afternoon in the milking shed, free from cares and experimenting with luscious and spacey jazz-infused spacerock. His archive recordings appeared on the following record, *Onward*, on a version of 'Right to Decide' and playing some lovely plonky piano on 'Aerospaceage Inferno', and on an instrumental jam, 'The Flowering of the Rose'. And, releasing an album described as being 'those magic moments one tries to achieve' and noted as being recorded over a period of five years, 2007 to 2012, he's represented on 'A Lover's Whim' from Dave Brock's solo album *Looking for Love in the Lost Land of Dreams.*

In practical terms, Jason's loss meant another evolution in the Hawkwind sound. "Jason dying changed the direction of the band again," Dibs reflects. "We were going in one direction with Jason and the way he played, very jazzy which of course Dave is very into and we were getting almost a Doors feel to the stuff, there's a middle eight to 'Damnation Alley' where Jason's playing is very 'Riders on the Storm' and we loved it. Tim [Blake] was just coming back into the fold as well, so you'd get the thing where it changes and Tim becomes a bit more prominent, and Niall [Hone] came in, on guitar at first."

"Jason was a big loss," says Dave, "when Alan Davey left, Jason blossomed, he was writing some fantastic stuff. Jason and me, we used to sit around at my place and we used to play loads of weird old jazz stuff together, but then he died [before we could properly record these things], so that you've got just the odd little bits here and there, little snippets as it were."

We'll step away from the changes within the band for a moment, because 2008 also saw the Hawkwind back catalogue from 1976's *Astounding Sounds Amazing Music* to 1997's *Distant Horizons* acquired and gradually restored to print by Cherry Red Records, via the Atomhenge imprint run by Mark and Vicky Powell. This gives us the right point in our narrative here to reflect on the differing fates of the catalogue, from those early records maintained in print by EMI, who also started to embark on an expansion of their Hawkwind interests and who owned rights from *Hawkwind* through to *Hall of the Mountain Grill*, to the more problematic rights to *Warrior on the Edge of Time*, and onto the catalogue as bought-out by Cherry Red.

Over the last ten years, there's been a re-evaluation across the music press of the legacy of Hawkwind. I'd like to think the original edition of this book played a modest part, and combined with the higher profile of Carol Clerk's *The Saga of Hawkwind*, published by Omnibus Books and revised and updated again during Carol's lifetime, the presence of heavily researched hardback biographies may have contributed to this fresh appraisal. At the same time, the interest of the glossy music monthlies was being re-awakened. *Classic Rock* ran a substantial extract from Carol's book and has continued to cover the band more substantially than before, while *Record Collector* has had two Hawkwind-related covers in recent times alongside much greater coverage of the band throughout their pages. *Mojo*, with Phil Alexander, a confessed Hawkwind fan, at the helm has picked up on the band again, and newer publications, including *Prog*, *Vive Le Rock* and *Shindig!* have run features, interviews and myriad reviews. It's fair to say that a sea-change in how the band has been viewed has swept through the music press.

The most important driver on this re-evaluation must have been, however, the bringing of the back catalogue back into print. Of course, the EMI portion of the catalogue has been well serviced by the rights owner across their interest in those titles: *Hawkwind, In Search of Space, Doremi Faso Latido, Space Ritual,* and *Hall of the Mountain Grill*. They've been constantly available and regularly reworked with re-masters and valued-added material, and appended to by the release of the 1974 live album, *The 1999 Party*, and a collection of BBC recordings, including the legendary *In Concert* set, under the title *Hawkwind at the BBC*. Most excitingly a 3-CD compilation entitled *Parallel Universe* set alongside a judicious collection of the best of the United Artists albums some intriguing 'alternate' takes and demo studio versions contemporary to those selections. This made available a studio cut of 'It's So Easy', a proto-version of 'Wind of Change' recorded before Simon House joined, an 'in-development' rendition of 'You Know You're Only Dreaming' and the little known 'Take What You Can'.

I talked to Nigel Reeve, who has done so much to maintain EMI's interest in Hawkwind about these releases, particularly the *Parallel Universe* set. "I'd gone so far with Hawkwind that it seemed there was very little else I could do. Then, a couple of years ago, I came back to it, had a look again at the tapes and thought, 'Hang on a minute, there's some stuff here that doesn't seem to add up.' Some of them were absolute revelations to me... I did a little bit of research online to see what the fans knew, and of course I know the catalogue well myself, but there were things there that nobody knew about and I couldn't understand how this stuff had never made it out. It just seems to be that whatever happened, these tapes stayed in our vaults over the years and kind of got forgotten about until I started delving a little bit deeper and, bingo, these tracks came to light."

In Nigel's view, "You can hear how the band was developing. 'You Know You're Only Dreaming' is very much along the lines of 'Mirror of Illusion' or 'Hurry on Sundown'; there were bits and pieces that were coming in from the live show, but the live show of the time was pretty much just the rest of the first album. You can hear there are ideas coming along there, but perhaps the band weren't quite ready to go down that route and it took until a little bit later, until *In Search of Space*, when they finally did. It's interesting that 'Kiss of the Velvet Whip' appears around the time of *In Search of Space*, a more formed version than the earlier one and you can hear that it's something they wanted to do but it took them that time to get it right. 'Wind of Change' is listed on the multi-track as being 'Rock Around the Clock' so I'm playing the tapes wondering, 'What's this? Is it really 'Rock Around the Clock?' No, it's this alternate version of 'Wind of Change'. It's clearly early in the sessions, elements of that early version were taken [for the final cut], but it stands on its own, it's very powerful and that justifies putting it out."

As to whether this was the final drawing of material from EMI's vaults, Nigel was pretty much convinced that it would prove to be so. "We do have other things but unfortunately things like the *Hall of the Mountain Grill* tracks are noted as being 'live' but that's just the basic track with overdubs done later. On the Space Ritual tour, Sunderland was recorded before they made it to Brixton but there's a fault on the recording and whatever you do in the mixing you're just not going to be able to retrieve it. That's the problem, there are live multi-tracks and I've been through them all but it's very difficult to piece them all together and they are just not good enough recordings or performances, certainly nothing better than what is already available."

But while one company was achieving the final evaluation of its Hawkwind vaults, another was achieving what others had failed to bring to fruition, in acquiring the rights to the remaining 'key' catalogue items – for the moment, sans *Warrior on the Edge of Time*, though we'll come to that – and that company was Cherry Red, in conjunction with Mark and Vicky Powell, respected label managers and packagers.

To bring the remaining catalogue into one ownership (the deal was for a buy-out of the rights rather than a licencing of the albums) was a mammoth task that need negotiating the difficulties of multi-rights holders in the individual musicians who'd comprised the band on any album and the labels that had previously contracted those records. Attempts had been taken before to achieve this, but these records had remained stubbornly out of print, the Charisma LPs since the Virgin 'budget' CD releases of the 1980s, the RCA material since the demise of Hawkwind's EBS label, while others had had limited profile releases on smaller labels before disappearing from the record store racks.

The driver on the deal was inevitably Douglas Smith, possibly the only person who could visualise and bring together the disparate vested interests that would have to be reconciled to enable a wholesale realisation of the catalogue's value. At one point, there were contract talks with Sanctuary, but that label's own fiscal difficulties drove them into an acquisition by Universal which caused those talks to fail. But with Mark Powell working alongside Cherry Red's buying power, and a vision being developed for how these albums would be brought back into print with re-mastered music and unreleased material from the archives, a deal was struck in. "It took about a year of negotiations, as these things do, it's quite a mammoth catalogue, but it was signed off in July 2008," Mark Powell recalled to me, for *Record Collector*. "As soon as that happened it was a case of retrieving the tapes from the various sources. All the Charisma stuff was still with EMI at that point, they sent it over straight away, the RCA material was held by Kingsley Ward at Rockfield Studios, and that all came over, Doug Smith had much of the later stuff and Dave Brock himself had a lot of the masters. He sent over a courier with a lot of multi-track tapes."

Atomhenge commenced their association with Hawkwind not by releasing any of the newly acquired main catalogue items, but by issuing a new edition of Robert Calvert's industrial politics masterpiece, *Freq*, before following it up with two box sets of choice cuts from the Hawkwind catalogue, *Spirit of the Age*, described as 'Atomhenge to Earth Ritual' (1976–1984) and *The Dream Goes On*, covering the two Black Sword albums through to *Distant Horizons* (1985–1997). Such a fine job was done on the two box sets by Mark and Vicky and their Cherry Red colleagues that the releases were nominated in the prestigious *Mojo* Awards as 'Best Reissues' of the year.

The subsequent new editions of this part of the canon have been uniformly of high standard; not always containing valued-added material but

295

generally providing a handsome selection of alternate takes, previously unknown demo recordings and live tracks, and in doing so, Cherry Red and Atomhenge have made a substantial contribution to the process of seeing Hawkwind in a new light while respecting what had been achieved across the years. Originally the plan was that the acquired albums would be back in print across a period of eighteen months, "that's the schedule to be able to do it properly and give people a bit of financial breathing space," Mark Powell told me at the time. There wasn't a chronological release schedule, though quite properly early releases included the four Charisma albums. "The other point is that we've had e-mails from fans who find it difficult to get some of the later albums on CD. Albums like *Love in Space* are incredibly collectable and go for lots of money on eBay. A lot of people missed out on those for one reason or another at the time, and some are unfairly overlooked as well, so we decided to mix everything up rather than do them as chronological batches of albums."

As it happens, the releases have stretched themselves much further than the original envisaged eighteen months, joined by Atomhenge's edition of *Warrior on the Edge of Time*, matching the long-awaited reissue of the original album with a new remix by Porcupine Tree's Steven Wilson, the most notable progressive rock musician of his generation. "I only take on remix projects of albums that I genuinely have affection for and history with," Steven Wilson told me when I'd cheekily asked about this remix at the end of an interview for one of his own albums. "*Warrior on the Edge of Time* and *Hall of the Mountain Grill* were two of the first albums I ever heard that really turned me to 70s music. I mean, I was growing up in the 80s and it was only through a friend's record collection that I discovered bands like Hawkwind, Camel, Pink Floyd... those two albums totally blew me away, and still to this day the first five or six Hawkwind albums are very special to me. You need to listen to *Warrior* in its 5.1 sound, not because of what I did but you can imagine that psychedelic swirl of sound is pretty extraordinary in surround."

I'd asked Nigel Reeve about its non-appearance as part of the EMI portion of the catalogue, and he explained how he'd like to "clarify the point that it's not ours anymore, much as I'd love it to be, and that the tapes aren't missing [as often had been rumoured] because we have them. It was on a separate contract at the time, under licence to us, and then reverted to the band."

***

**Niall Hone
(Oz Hardwick)**

Here's the thing. Nobody ever replaces someone else in Hawkwind. Jason Stuart passed away, but with the band during his tenure having adjusted itself to Jason's jazz-orientated keyboards it was inevitably then going to move in a different direction again when that sound was no longer there. No thought of getting someone in the same vein, it doesn't work that way; just as when Huw left in 1989, Simon House returned to turn the sound on its head. Just as when Lemmy was fired and Paul Rudolph brought in a funkier style of playing. Just as Alan Davey's heavy spacerock became Jerry and Ron's screaming punk psychedelia. Never a replacement, always a change.

Niall Hone was another musician who'd been on and around the fringes of Hawkwind for many years prior to joining. Born in June 1968, when the band he'd eventually become a member of was yet to crystallise into that dense soundtrack of their eponymous debut, he came from what he describes as "an alternative household." His father, Mo, knew Dave Brock, "in their early teens, for a fleeting period," and the family home was full of guitars and LPs. "I can remember hearing all this strange music that my father would record on an old reel-to-reel thing, but it wasn't until I was about twelve that I snuck downstairs and put on a Jimi Hendrix record, *Are You Experienced*, and heard all this strange guitar playing that I thought was really odd and couldn't understand. But then six months later I did a similar thing, played a selection of vinyl and I was intrigued by the various tones. I asked my dad about this and he explained about Jimi

Hendrix and his changing of the style of guitar playing. I remember trying to replicate these sounds on my dad's semi-acoustic guitar by rubbing my front-door key up and down the fretboard. I got told off, because I blew one of the speakers on his new hi-fi by trying to get feedback!"

He portrays himself as having been "an alternative kid, not quite fitting into society." A teenager in the mid-80s, he'd tried the culture of the day, those big hairstyles, synth-pop noodlings and "crap clothes", coming to them via the immediate predecessors of those styles: "Madness and The Specials; Two-Tone." When Pink Floyd's *The Wall* appeared, in 1979 and then in film form in 1982, he became fascinated by their work. "I used to do a paper-round, listening to *The Wall* on repeat, on cassette. Then I went from discovering the great *Dark Side of the Moon*, to a friend loaning me a cassette of Rush. I couldn't stand the voice but I was mesmerised by the bass playing. I rummaged around in the cupboard under the stairs, where my dad kept old guitars and stuff, and found this early 60s Burns Tri-Sonic three-quarter length bass guitar, and spent the next two years learning Rush bass parts. Once I'd exhausted that catalogue I stumbled across Hawkwind and was overwhelmed by the *Space Ritual* album, which is a kind of common theme among Hawkwind fans, and started learning the bass licks from that."

Time went by, and Niall went to college to study computer science, having grown-up with computers from an early age, and then getting into computer games programming. It didn't last, though it would prove to be a springboard for later life. "I forgot about the computers because they were boring and not used for any creative purposes, just number crunching, and I'd started getting girlfriends. But I carried on playing guitar and bass, and for my eighteenth birthday I got a Westone guitar, which is what Dave uses though that is total coincidence, and started going to local parties where alternative bands would play in fields." Those bands included the crop of free festival favourites, such as Ozric Tentacles and Magic Mushroom Band, and Mandragora, who'd been formed in 1983 by Simon Williams and who took an influence from Hawkwind. (Sadly, though, not taking their name, as some think, from the Tom Baker *Doctor Who* serial 'The Masque of Mandragora'.).

"Simon from Mandragora kind of befriended me; he and his mates took under their wing as a seventeen-year-old. I dropped out of computer science because it dawned on me that I wanted to play bass guitar in these sorts of bands. A month later I got a phone-call from Simon saying there was a job going playing bass for Mandragora. They were based in Eastbourne, and I ended up playing bass and moving in with the band and we spent two or three years living together as a band and pissing off the neighbours with all night parties and things that I shouldn't have done at that age, and went gigging."

Through the free festival scene, Mandragora, like others of their ilk, became connected to Hawkwind, described by Simon Williams as "the chiefs of the scene. There was a lot of respect for Hawkwind because they were doing, and had been doing for years, that great thing of being at the festivals. I mean, some bands were seen as 'old duffers', bands like The Enid, but Hawkwind had a lot of respect." But the Hawkwind connection that advanced Mandragora's ambitions was with Dave Anderson, then establishing Foel Studio and playing the live circuit as a member of The Groundhogs.

"From going to see The Groundhogs and chatting to Dave Anderson, who had that iconic bass playing on 'Master of the Universe' and 'You Shouldn't Do That', we were invited to recorded at Foel Studio, when he was starting it up, I believe, second time around," Niall recalls. "He agreed to have us in the studio for seven days, for £400, which at that point, prior to hard-disc home recording, was really cheap. We got the pennies together, got in our truck and drove to Wales. We were there doing our first album, and the next band in were Ozric Tentacles doing their first album. We realised that Dave didn't have much equipment then, so he borrowed our echo unit, our guitar pedals and my wah-wah for the Ozric album, and later-on my wah-wah got pinched by My Bloody Valentine from his studio, but we came back with an album recorded in a week."

Through a connection of Simon's in Antwerp, Mandragora started playing in Europe, while also building themselves a following back in Britain on what was starting to become a burgeoning psychedelic and spacerock scene, playing in London at notable venues such as The Crypt and at Club Dog on the Seven Sisters, in North London. They'd also be regularly attendees at Hawkwind shows. "Through my dad's connection we managed to get a bit more involved and ended up supporting them in 1988. Dave Brock would ring up and say, 'Niall, you can do the southern tour dates,' which was Croydon Fairfield Halls and Folkestone and that area, and Tubilah Dog would do the middle ones. Then Dave rang my dad up and was playing a gig - Alan Davey didn't want to do free festivals at that point and Dave did – and we were asked did we want to do a couple of shows across the summer of what must have been 1988 [Mo on guitar, Niall on bass] and I found myself playing bass in a car park on the A303 near Stonehenge with car headlights as the lighting and one strobe! We did another one that was at the Kings Cross Fire Station, squatted by the likes of 2000DS and the guys who used to cut up cars for sculptures, Mutoid Waste Company, and those gigs were my introduction to playing with Dave Brock."

Hone cut three albums with Mandragora; aside from the Foel Studio recording, *Over The Moon*, they then made *Head First*, in Worthing at a studio run by Jon Harris, who was also a member of the Lloyd-Langton Group, and then *Earthdance*, at "a little studio in Shoreham. But, I fell out with Simon over fifty quid, at that point in my life a lot of cash. It wasn't Simon's fault, but tensions had been building and that was the final straw. Huw then asked me to play bass for him and I used to go over to Rottingdean [in Brighton and Hove] where he and Marion lived, and we rehearsed quite a lot and I learned his stuff. That never came to fruition for one reason and another, but I've some fond memories of hanging out with Huw, drinking and smoking and having a laugh."

A short stint on bass for Captain Sensible came to nothing; Niall drifted out of the spacerock scene, and, like a lot of his contemporaries, started getting to dance music as an alternative. "I started getting back into computers. I discovered they were an integral part of music with the advent of the Atari computer and hard-disc recording, and I just slipped out of rock 'n' roll and spacerock. I had about four years off from playing bass."

When he re-emerged, it was as part of his brother's jam-band, Tribe of Cro. "Because we were both bass players, I said I'd play guitar. Borrowed a guitar, dusted down my amp, and the Tribe of Cro was born. The drummer, Kevin, who was very young at the time, fourteen or fifteen, came from Belgium and his father was the manager, and he booked us a load of gigs on the continent and that led to me spending a lot of time bumming around Europe. A few years later I encountered Dave Brock again, and Dave asked if Tribe of Cro would like to support Hawkwind, so we did a similar thing to that which we did with Mandragora, supporting Hawkwind on southern gigs – Plymouth, Bournemouth, Worthing and later at Exeter a couple of years before I joined Hawkwind, where I met the wonderfully kind and polite, and a bit eccentric, Tim Blake!"

Tribe of Cro, like Mandragora before them, developed a musical friendship with Hawkwind, playing regularly at Hawkfests as well as opening for them on those southern gigs. "I was standing at a Hawkfest in 2007, chatting with Dave and Richard about life, the universe and everything, and we were talking about recording things, because I'd spent years working in studios recording bands and I'd ended up teaching music technology and so had access to free recording time and could borrow recording equipment in the summer holidays. I arranged with them that I'd go down to Dave's place, I guess two or three months before Jason died, with a car load of equipment, to record the band. I spent the best part of a week down there, partying and recording them. And then poor Jason died in September, and about a month later, when I was at the end of my tether with working in education, being fed with teaching music when all I wanted to do was make music myself, and looking for an escape, I got a phone call, sat in a pub in Littlehampton on a sunny autumn afternoon, and it was Dave saying 'there's an open door here, come and get involved.' Yes, please!"

Hone arrived with his car loaded with an array of instruments: guitars, computer, synthesisers… and embarked on a new regime of mid-week Hawkwind rehearsals, trying to establish what his part in the band would be. "On reflection, I don't think Dave knew what he wanted me to do. He graciously gave me the chance to be *me*. I'd played bass in Mandragora, but guitar in Tribe of Cro. I'm no guitarist like Huw was, but what I'm very good at, I think, is making what I call 'car crash guitar'. Heavy on the effects, simple on the melodies, but not a soloist in the traditional sense. I rocked up at the farm and played that car crash guitar with all these sonic devices, and that was my take on joining the band. Prior to my arrival, Dibs had taken on the role of running the computer from Alan but I'm very au-fait with computers and software and I kind of inherited the role of being the computer guy for the band. The very first tour I did, I took a full-blown PC with all this gadgetry running, and the difference was that I had the knowledge of how to improvise live with the computer onstage. Previously they'd used what Dave calls the 'red blob' system, where they had to wait for a visual cue before

300

they changed to a jam section, or a verse or chorus. When I came along, I could throw that out of the window and change the computer to fit the jamming. Out went the days of Alan Davey's computer systems, and I brought a different system, that goes back to the early 70s jamming stuff, bringing the ability to have the computer following the band rather than the band jamming around the computer."

Niall Hone played his first show as member of the band on 4th December 2008, setting into motion what is arguably the most settled Hawkwind line-up in the band's entire history, with the core settling down to be Brock, Chadwick, Tim Blake, who'd re-joined again on the band's Christmas tour the previous year, Dibs and Hone. That the core line-up had arranged itself into a stable cast of regulars didn't mean there wasn't a fluidity to who might appear at any show alongside the continuing members. Musicians such as Levellers violinist Jon Sevink made some guest appearances, Captain Rizz dropped in occasionally, but possibly the least expected return to the ranks was from Philip Reeves, Dead Fred, last seen with Hawkwind during the unloved Nik Turner Pantomime era of the early 1980s.

Fred had been doing some stuff with his old Inner City Unit friend, Steve Pond, in a new version of Calvert's backing-band, Krankschaft. They'd issued a live album of the Robert Calvert & The Maximum Effect gig from 3rd November 1986 at the Stars & Stripes, Carlisle, a show that had also received a release on the Voiceprint label, and then recorded *The Flame Red Superstar*, their take on thirteen Calvert songs. An excellent set of covers, its highlight was a piano version of 'The Greenfly and The Rose', though they did justice to Calvert's talent and memory across all the selections.

Krankschaft brought Fred back onto the Hawkwind radar, with Kris booking the duo to play at Hawkfests, including one on the Isle of Wight. A second trip down under, for a handful of dates in March 2011 almost saw him as a member, when visa difficulties experienced by Tim Blake may have made it necessary to rehearse a temporary replacement on keyboards. Kris Brock: "We got in touch when we were in Australia, saying 'Look, this might be a bit sudden…' because Tim had sent a message saying he might not be getting into the country, that they'd turned him away at the airport. 'Fred, can you get out here on a tourist visa, and do it?' And he'd sent us a message back, 'Bags ready!'. Then he didn't need to because Tim did get out just in the nick of time."

Fred was, though, in the line-up the following year, adding his own keyboards alongside Tim's, and playing violin on some numbers. "Fred was delighted," says Dave about another musician he clearly holds in affection. "He'd never visualised playing at some of the big festivals we've done. He never thought he'd be playing in Hawkwind again, playing those festivals. He's really good at blues piano… when there's a piano in a hotel, off he'd go playing a few good old blues and boogies. He'd entertain everybody, singing these old blues songs."

Though the old days of an album and a supporting winter tour each year is now a thing of the past, the regeneration of the archives has occurred alongside a continued push for new work, with the band's most settled line-up releasing *Blood of the Earth* in 2010, and following it up a couple of years later with a sprawling double LP, *Onward*, while the same year an abbreviated version of the membership – Brock, Chadwick and Hone under the name Hawkwind Light Orchestra – issued what is arguably the best of this sequence, *Stellar Variations*.

Of these three, *Blood of the Earth* is most like a standard Hawkwind album. *Stellar Variations*, perhaps because of the reduction of the line-up down to a temporary recording three-piece, a sort of heavier *White Zone* or more rock-infused *Church of Hawkwind*, experimental and pushing the boundaries, while the unfocused *Onward* is an example of more being less.

Brock described *Blood of the Earth* as being a concept album, though if it was the concept got buried somewhere along the line, and indeed in interviews Dave simply summed that concept up as being contained in the album's title. "It's the lava that comes out of the Earth." Explaining further on Prognaut.com, Dibs talked about it as dealing with "the four elements of the earth. Earth, wind, fire, and water. All of these elements influence and change the earth." It was a work of principally new songs, with the revisit of 'You'd Better Believe It' being explained as included by dint of it having "never been on a studio album, it was recorded live," although that 'live' cut way back on *Hall of the Mountain Grill* was essentially a bare-bones live recording with heavy studio overdubs. Of the other 'old' song included, 'Sweet Obsession' from Brock's *Earthed to the Ground* album, Dibs said "The modern vocal is different and brings the song up to date ... new loops and sounds bring more dimension and gives it a new vibe." He talked about the new line-up's approach to writing: "[we] jam some of the new ideas we have and record the ones we like. I get riffs in my head by hearing other sounds or music, or dreaming up something original."

It has some powerful moments, with 'Sentinel' and 'Prometheus' being particularly strong tracks, the former taking its name and imagery from the Arthur C. Clarke short story that became the film classic *2001: A Space Odyssey* and the other referencing the Greek Titan who brought fire from Mount Olympus. On stage, Dibs would cut quite the Promethean figure, imposing and bringing the word of Hawkwind to the masses – though off-stage he's amiable and approachable. "Sometimes we have two bass players playing together," said Dave. "Dibs plays very simple basslines. Niall is a wild bass player with interesting leads." Later, he'd reflect on how Niall's arrival in the band would cause Dib and Niall to initially lock horns on who should play what and where, just as Huw and Simon House would on the 2001 tour, a quite natural case of the creative tensions caused by musicians exploring each other's musical spaces. But Hone's playing would enable Dibs to assume much more of the frontman role, creating a focal point around which the musicians and the dancers, at that point the highly talented performance art duo of Laura McGee and Stef Elrick, could coalesce. "Brock does not only nurture talent, but also the rage he must once have felt to write such classics as 'Motorway City' and 'Urban Guerrilla', and in Mr Dibs he has done both," wrote *The Guardian*'s Ed Vulliamy, covering the events of the 2013 Hawkfest. "Scary to behold on stage, less so in the flesh."

"Niall started to play a bit more bass, we were doing it jointly, and then we both thought it would be good to do some of the songs with two basses," says Dibs. "'Angels of Death' with two basses, one at the bottom end and one at the top, really powerful. Of course, the detractors would say that we had to replace Alan with two bass players to get something as powerful. No! That's missing the point. We're doing something quite clever, because Niall plays it like a lead instrument at the top end and I'm covering the bottom end, and we only do it on a couple of songs to make it dynamic." As for becoming the band's frontman: "That's been a revelation. Some of the Calvert stuff is very difficult to sing and play, because Bob would come in slightly after the beat with his vocals for his style and delivery."

Niall saw that as, "down to Dave Brock's insight, using everyone to the best of their talents, giving everyone who joins the band a chance to influence the masterplan. I started out playing guitars and computers, live sequencing on stage, and I've since filled out a few different roles. Dave likes to make his own mind up, in a positive sense, as to what someone's best at in a Hawkwind role. I played guitar, then became the anchor-man bass player, because Dave saw some strengths in me, in my bass playing, because that's what I am rather than this car crash guitarist. While I'm an averagely competent yet wacky guitarist, I found playing the same lead guitar licks on a bass much more comfortable. The 'Angels of Death' live track on the second disc of *Blood of the Earth* is a good example. I slowly became a lead guitarist, playing a bass. Over time, Dave saw that Dibsy's strengths were his singing and his lyrical content and so, without me meaning to, I ended up playing most of the bass."

Continuing his own involvement with the band, Matthew Wright had a go at writing some lyrics for the album's title track, though as with his vocals previously, he's engagingly self-deprecating about the end results. "I thought I might be able to contribute lyrically, from an off-stage position, given that I had a relationship with Hawkwind, and what I've found is that it is much harder than it seems! I had a go at few things, and 'Blood of the Earth' was written as a sort of homage to Calvert, lyrical references to 'Hassan I Shaba' which I hope came through a little. I think the reason why I love *Quark...* and *Astounding Sounds...* as probably my favourite albums, though it changes weekly, is that when Calvert is writing lyrics they would stand on their own as high quality poetry. When you sit down to writing lyrics that's when you realise he was a genius, and you're not! I was honoured to be included and it just heightened my respect for Calvert."

The Daily Telegraph no less – surely the most incongruous place for a Hawkwind album review to materialise – rated the album with three stars. "Hawkwind sound enthused and remarkably tuneful, albeit with cosmic sci-fi lyrics ... fully intact." Though yearning for a 'real' rock album next time out, Scott

Heller, on the *Aural Innovations* website, described it as "nice, laid back, psychedelic."

"With our albums, you live with them so long you don't really listen to them afterwards," says Dibs. "I've only just listened to *Blood of the Earth* again, after a few years, and it stands up well. I've always said that Hawkwind are the most truly progressive band, because every album has been different, partly because there's usually a different line-up, but it's always been Hawkwind. But even with us, *Blood of the Earth* and *Onward* are completely different styles of albums even though it's pretty much the same line-up. Truly progressive in that term."

In exactly that way, the band saw *Onward* as being their titular intent, always going forward, but it was a muddled mission statement in that case, with a mixture of new songs recorded over an extended period, interspersed with what was starting to seem like an inevitable clutch of old songs, in this case 'Right to Decide', 'Aerospaceage Inferno', and 'Green Finned Demon', though the first two were included as bonus tracks because they were live cuts that included Jason Stuart's keyboards. It was another album that needed judicious pruning, not being strong enough to justify its running length and even before its release – looking back at interviews with the benefit of hindsight - it seemed that there was some disappointment in the ranks about its realisation.

"It's not a bad album," Brock suggested to the website Uberrock.co.uk, "it's quite an interesting one," sounding as though he was damning the result with faint praise, though Richard Chadwick was a little more effusive about it: "This album is about stuff that relates to us all, from weird electronic happenings to internal movements of one's guts. It's a soundtrack to the cosmos!"

I'd reviewed it for *Record Collector*, doubtfully asking "Onward flies the bird? Maybe…" and rating it with only two stars. "What [its eighteen tracks] suggest is that while the hawk might be flying over the forest, it's struggling to see the wood for the trees. There's a reliance on yet more reworks of past numbers and cut-up sound effects that don't add anything … we're left trying to pick out the bones of what could have been a very good record from amidst what's actually a bit of a sprawl."

"*Onward* is more of a photograph of all the stuff the band was up to at a certain point," reflects Niall, perhaps in doing so, offering a subconscious explanation for the sum being less than the parts. "There's a couple of brand new banging tracks, there's the mystery track, which is one of my favourites, a one-day jam that really came off well, other bits and pieces, but, in my head, it's a subconscious version of *Roadhawks*, not a 'best of', but the 'best bits' of all the stuff the band was working on at the same time."

Arguably the best release of the time, however, is from the abbreviated line-up, Hawkwind Light Orchestra, and its *Stellar Variations* album. This one is an experimental, muscular, dynamic, tightly-focussed album, with provocative lyrics on tracks such as 'It's All Lies', a proper Hawkwind number that pushes at social and political ideas and challenges its listeners to think for themselves. 'Forget about religion/Down with The Pope!'.

It came out of what Richard Chadwick describes as "the tyranny of distance." That meant Dibs being based in Derbyshire and Tim Blake living in his windmill in France, whereas Richard and, at the time, Niall, were more local to Dave and his recording set-up, and, naturally, that meant that there were times when just the three of them were ensconced in the milking shed, with its abundance of rehearsal and recording time.

"Richard is very good, and very dedicated," says Dave, of the bands second-longest serving member, a weekly fixture at the milking shed rehearsals. "He practises a lot, a very dedicated man. A great musician, with a great musical ear." Being in Hawkwind means something to him beyond simply being in a band and making music. Dave: "It's the lifestyle and the family. It *is* a family."

"I'm based in Sussex, my roots are there and I tend to gravitate back there," says Niall. "But I spent three or four years living in Seaton and during that time Richard would travel each week to Dave's and so would I, because I was only ten miles away from HQ. We started to do a bank of stuff together and there became two projects that started without any specific intentions [to be separate]. *Onward* was being developed, and then we had all this other stuff that was full and complete, because of the hours the three of us put into it, that didn't fit with the Hawkwind stuff and didn't need more people. What I liked about it was that it was very cohesive as a piece of music, an album, and Dave said, 'Why don't we put it out as something different,' because it wasn't Hawkwind in the true sense, it only had three people out of five on it. It couldn't *be* Hawkwind, so it came out as a side-project because we were proud of it. I enjoy listening to the entire record, the whole journey, which I think is very true to the Hawkwind ethos. I'm not necessarily talking about the personnel involved, but the dynamics... if you look at *Onward* or *Blood of the Earth*, which are fabulous records, there are different tracks 'featuring' different people, so there's Tim Blake's track, or my 'Green Machine' track, but *Stellar Variations* harks back to the days of a bunch of guys in a room, partying on, and enjoying it, and it was just very fortunate that three band members who could cover the entire arrange of sounds required were in the same place for that amount of time and, I think, managed to collect some of the ethos dating back to earlier Hawkwind times."

23

No Stopping The Hawks

**Hawkwind October 2015
Pictured: Blake, Dibs, Brock, Chadwick, Hone
(Oz Hardwick)**

The *Onward* album, for all its faults, did still have that titular statement of intent, that this settled line-up should produce new work and push the band, well, onward into its fifth decade. Where it failed was in that mashing together some good new work with a slew of revisited standards; was it looking forward while glancing backward? Hard to tell. It's certainly true that Dave Brock reflected on it as being poorly mixed and was disappointed in the result, as indeed, Dibs later professed all the band to be.

Some of this was resolved with a release, *Spacehawks*, intended for the US market at a point at which it seemed possible there might have been another American tour to have product out in support of. As it happened, the tour didn't materialise despite a collection of dates and venues being announced, but *Spacehawks* did emerge, a sort of *Out & Intake* (an 80s Flicknife collection that did what it said on the tin), in the way it gathered live tracks and unused studio material, by the current band. Because this release had no agenda in moving the band forward, instead being a sort of 'catch up' for fans who'd not kept current, it was more accessible and appealing, containing a mix of live material and remixed studio output from recent records. "The production was lacking a bit on *Onward*," concedes Dibs, "which is why we remixed some of it for *Spacehawks*."

Before they'd move on to the next 'new' project, there would be a couple of significant revisits to the catalogue. Firstly, in support of *Warrior on the Edge of Time* appearing, finally, on CD as part of the Atomhenge reissues, they played a tour centred around that album, with some of its tracks – 'The Demented Man' and 'Dying Seas' for example – getting a live Hawkwind airing for the first time, and they then played a one-night only performance of the Space Ritual, in aid of various animal charities. "We reclaimed the Space Ritual back to Hawkwind," asserts Dibs. "Doing it once and proud like that was enough. In some ways, we could have done ten gigs and made a lot of money and I'm sure there were promoters who were champing at the bit to do that. The reason we did *Warrior*, was because it was a special reissue, it was a big occasion to do the *Warrior* thing. It would be dead easy for us to do the nostalgia thing and churn out a classic album [tour] a year, but we're looking forwards, always looking forwards."

Returning to these classics for the tour wasn't as straight-forward as it sounded, with tracks such as 'Spiral Galaxy 28948' being deceptive in their complexity. "There were lots of discussions about how we were going to do it," Niall told me for *Vive Le Rock*. "Dave had the very strong opinion that this is the band now, that was the band then, we're not going to do it note for note, so we spent a lot of time working the songs out. Dave, with his 45-year career, couldn't remember all the bits and pieces, so we had to work them out to start with, just jamming around with them for a period until they became comfortable. What happens, as a musician, is that you'll kind of forget the blueprint you've learned, which is the original song and its structure, and you interpret it in your own way with your fellow musicians around you."

But despite Brock talking in interviews of not having a fondness for *Warrior*, he came across as enthused by the accompanying storyline and presentation for the tour. "It's based on mysticism, traditional legend and old good British myth," he told the *Oxford Times*. "I've always been curious, and Hawkwind is about rock and roll mixed up with ancient legend and a bit of science fiction."

It was an opportunity for the established performance art duo of Stef and Laura to add their interpretations, very skilled mime and dance sequences that helped push the narrative along; they'd do the same for the one-off *Space Ritual* staging the following year. But at Falmouth Princess Pavilions on the *Warrior* tour, the audience would have been forgiven for thinking there was something different about the pairing. Stef didn't make it to the gig, leading Kris Brock to step in unannounced, and unidentified due to the use of mask and wig. "Even the band didn't know," says Dave. "I went into the dressing room during the afternoon and was quickly ushered out again because Kris had to do a very last minute rehearsal of Stef's moves!" [Authorial note here: I knew! I'd seen Kris very briefly before the show, a very quick 'hello' because she had to dash off to rehearse again, extracting a firm promise from your author not to tell anyone on the night! Very good she was, too!]

They opened the shows with a handful of standards, 'Master of Universe' and an extended 'Steppenwolf', where Dibs's developing frontman role came to the fore, and new songs such as 'The Hills Have Ears'. But the meat of the show was that run-through, in chronological order, of that classic album. Not slavishly copying it, despite maintaining the running order, but exploring it anew while being faithful to the original, doing justice to those tracks seldom heard, 'Opa-Loka' for instance, and with Fred coming into his own on 'Spiral Galaxy' with some lovely violin playing. And, for good measure, though the set-list clung to the LP, the encore generally included 'Motörhead', dedicated to Lemmy, whose declining health, played out in public, was causing concern.

The mounting of Space Ritual in aid of animal charities reflected, of course, part of the Hawkwind ethos that has been with the band since its very earliest days. There's been a mass of charitable organisations and causes that over the years have benefited from the band's support and willingness to play for them, whether that cause was the sort of counterculture politics of the 70s, or for animal welfare in the 80s with the band playing in aid of rhino conservation, for homegrown things such as for a CAT scanner at Treliske Hospital in Cornwall or the Air Ambulance in Devon, or recent things, such as the band's support for the environmental activists of the Sea Shepherd organisation.

"We got all these things together, and raised a lot of money for the charities," says Dave, "which is a good thing. You can't do it constantly, but it's a good thing to do what you can. The fans pick-up on these things, 'Yeah! Right on! We're behind you on that!' It's a great thing to do, like years ago when we were saving black rhinos in Africa, and bears in Asia. Look what's going on in the world! It is good if, when people are coming to our gigs, we can give them a leaflet, because they don't know what's going on, sometimes."

Sea Shepherd has been a key element of this in recent times. "Prior to Sea Shepherd, in the 70s, we used to do things with Greenpeace," says Dave. "In fact Kris and myself have been to the last resting place of Rainbow Warrior, down in New Zealand, an old Maori burial ground where they sunk the ship to make into part of a reef, off the coast. But with Sea Shepherd, we've been involved with them for about ten years now." This support included leafleting a series of gigs in Japan. (Kris Brock: "The Japanese didn't like us handing them out, so we took them back to the dressing room and got the band to sign them a few hundred and then we could give them out because they wouldn't refuse autographs.").

"We thought, this is what we want," says Dave. "People who are doing direct action, and by doing so putting their lives on the line. It's what they stand for; this is what pisses me off these days, all the trivialities of people on the Internet slagging things off with Facebook and stuff... why don't they channel their energies, if they want to be on the Internet, in going after things that need to be changed?" In the autumn of 2016, Kris and Dave were accorded the privilege of a tour of one of Sea Shepherd's vessels, the Ocean Warrior, in Amsterdam. 'Hawkwind are not only veterans in the rock world but are also long-time valued supporters of Sea Shepherd, constantly spreading the word about the organisation's campaigns to their extensive worldwide fan base,' noted the organisation. Dave: "It was a great honour to be invited to be shown around the ship and taken downstairs to the engine room, a fantastic tour." In these things, the spirit of the early years of Hawkwind still permeates to this day.

Concept albums and Hawkwind have been no strangers to each other, and there's a curious symmetry to them. 1975 with *Warrior on the Edge of Time*, though granted it failed to translate into a stage performance, 1985 with *The Chronicle of the Black Sword* and that brilliant supporting tour, and 1995 on the *Alien 4* shows. They'd started looking at a new concept around the end of 2014, a suggestion of Kris Brock's that they look at E. M. Forster's short story, The Machine Stops, written in 1907 but having a relevance to the computer dependency of today, with a populace driven underground and reliant on 'The Machine' for all their needs. Perfect Hawkwind territory.

It didn't appear in 2015 sadly, failing to add to that symmetry, though of course 2005 had already broken that perfect run. But when *The Machine Stops* did arrive, in the spring of 2016, it was almost universally hailed as a return not just 'to form' but to the glory days, with critics and fans falling over themselves to declare it the best album since, depending on who was commenting, *The Chronicle of the Black Sword*, or, indeed, *Warrior on the Edge of Time* itself.

Part of it was that it blasted out a purposeful collection of all new material. Part of it was that it had a conciseness that, say, *Onward*, lacked. And it was a good choice of subject matter, also recently used as musical inspiration by Pauline Murray, of 70s punk band Penetration, and by electronica legend John Foxx. It's a story that's been adapted many times over the years, from the BBC anthology series *Out of the Unknown* in the 60s, to being an influence on dystopian fiction by many writers and across multiple mediums, arguably including *Logan's Run*, *THX 1138*, and the Patrick Troughton *Doctor Who* serials 'The Krotons' and 'The Enemy of the World' among them.

Aside from that strong narrative, what *The Machine Stops*, released by Cherry Red rather than its Atomhenge sub-label, possessed was a proper collection of songs, largely Brock solo credits, and played by a revolving mixture of core members Dave, Richard, Niall and Dibs, though leaning mostly on the first three, perhaps because of their closer location to the milking shed for recordings, but also containing a charming curiosity, 'Hexagone', written and played by Dead Fred, making his first writing appearance on a Hawkwind album. Brock's songs though are good mid-tempo rockers, somewhat in the *Black Sword* vein perhaps, choppy numbers with lyrics that push the story along in a satisfying way. "The good thing about doing it here," Dave told me, sitting in the milking shed in advance of the band's Hawkeaster shows for 2016, "is that we can tinker around with it, change things; I've listened to things months later and thought 'that's not so good there... I can put this on it,' and it makes it more interesting."

Talking that day, it felt that *The Machine Stops* had come out of a particularly fertile period for him. I'd asked him about 'Treadmill' and 'Damage of Life', those songs from the end of the 80s which seemed to reflect a world weariness, but there was no such feeling about what was happening in Hawkwind today; instead he was energized, having only a few months previously put out a well-received solo album, *Brockworld*. If he was putting together a 'Best of' compilation, a single LP to sharply describe his legacy, what would be selected? "Probably 'Hurry On Sundown' when we had Dick Taylor [producing] and Huwey on guitar. I love Huwey's lead guitar on that first album, lovely lead guitarist. I'd have something off that album on it! I could pick a few interesting bits and pieces [laughs], but I couldn't really say what they are... there's a lot of it, hundreds and hundreds of tracks. Some are awful, you look back and you were pushed into doing albums you didn't want to do, and have to write stuff when you didn't have any ideas and so on." As reflected on 'Treadmill'? "But that's what you do, you carry on, you can't really stop. Recently I've been able to do it quite easily and come up with stuff constantly, I've got another half an album already, acoustic things and electric stuff. I just come in here and potter around with ideas, weird bits and pieces and off I go, with all the modern technology at my fingertips."

Reviewing *The Machine Stops* for *R2* magazine, Oz Hardwick asked, "Who'd have thought that, five decades on, Hawkwind could be producing some of their best works to date?" and noted that, "If someone told me 'Synchronized Blue' was an outtake from *Electric Tepee*, I'd not only believe them, but I'd also wonder why on Earth such a great track had been left off." In *Shindig!* Ashley Brooks declaimed a blend of "rock 'n' roll, new age and synth-psych in a most refreshing way," while online at Theartsdesk.com, Russ Coffey considered, "it sounds air-lifted from 1972," before going to say that some of it had, "a groove that may be more suited to sweat-soaked halls ... a communal trip for the like-minded."

They'd hoped that the tour was going to be another of the band's multi-faceted presentations, including new dancer Eloïse Curriè, a circus artist, aerialist, dancer and fire performer, whose contributions to the band in recent times, and following the departure of Laura and Stef, Dave is enormously enthusiastic about. "She's really good, very talented!" That didn't work out, due to a combination of winter bugs and other commitments, leaving the shows as stripped-down but rocking sets, propelling the narrative of the source story. "Eloïse is such a good performer, we hope she'll be with us again in the future."

Sweat-soaked halls it played to, some of the band's best houses in many a year, with a set predicated on the new material and only a few appropriate old numbers brought in to round out the content. "We've got 'Utopia' which fits in with the story line quite well," said Dave in advance of the tour. "'Orgone Accumulator' fits in wonderfully. And we've got 'Assault & Battery' and 'The

Watcher', so we've got some old songs in there, but they work wonderfully well with the new ones." Mostly though it was that drive to push the band forward that informed the set-list's structure, drawing on a wealth of new work. "A lot of bands tread water, and that's definitely what Hawkwind doesn't do," says Dibs. "Being on the crew was a good way to be involved, but I wanted to actually play it and help create new stuff. This album is incredible because the virtually the whole [live] set is new, and that's exciting."

Tim Blake had once again departed, having through choice not played on *The Machine Stops* album, and wanting to spend more time focussing on his own music, with the 40th Anniversary of his own Crystal Machine milestone arriving. And just before the tour, Fred had decided that, through bouts of ill-health from the rigours of touring in the recent past, that he no longer wanted to get out on the road again. Another of those Prime Ministerial reshuffles: Niall to synths covering some of the space created by Tim and Fred decamping, Dibs to cement his position as the band's frontman, and a young bass player, 'Hawkwind the Next Generation' perhaps, Haz Wheaton, coming in, not far into his twenties but playing with confidence and verve, recognisably in the style of Lemmy and regenerating Dave's guitar playing on stage. That gets him well-deserved praise not only from fans, but from one of his bass predecessors, Alan Davey. "Haz is a very decent bass player, you know? He really is one of the better bass players. He's definitely done something for the band."

He'd been around and about for a few years, attending gigs and then working on the crew, as Dibs had done before him. "I remember Haz waiting outside Bristol Academy, aged 14, in the pissing rain, waiting for us all to come out. Then having to sleep on the station because he'd missed his train waiting for us."

"It's the same thing as Dibs," says Haz, and jokes about him 'stalking the stalker', "I was crew for three years. I got into Hawkwind when I was about twelve… so about ten years ago! I didn't even see Hawkwind until April 2006, but the thing is they were still a great band then, not just a great band in the 70s, because so many people reference albums from the 70s, but *Xenon Codex* is a fantastic album, *Electric Tepee… Blood of the Earth* and that's only six years ago. I had the whole back catalogue to be influenced by. How eclectic that is: the electronic stuff of the 1990s, the heavy stuff of the 70s, the proto-punk stuff of the later 70s, it was all there to access, with the common theme that is Dave's guitar, which is the sound that makes all of it."

"Dave is very good at guiding things and making it a bit better," says Dibs. "Even though we've had the most stable line-up of Hawkwind that there has been, it has changed within its own dynamic. I had the idea of coming in with the electric cello which would make things different. What I realised is, that it's very hard after playing a guitar for so many years, to go without that shield. The first tour where I did much more singing and less playing, I was just holding on to the mic stand for fear of wandering about the stage, but the confidence has gone up now. The cello is very uncontrollable to keep in tune on stage, it's not meant for the loud rock band thing, but it gives me something to do when there's an instrumental. Dave has always encouraged the theatrics, so for the frontman thing he says you've got to be an actor, make a persona for yourself and act that part when you're on stage, so that it's a character that you're playing that isn't you. I think that's what Bob might have done, and no one is ever going to touch Bob Calvert for that frontman thing, that cleverness. Ron came close, but in sounding like him, with a completely different stage presence. I've got more confident as the detractors have decreased, because the doubts creep in. But that's another thing about Dave's cleverness, he'll see that and just give you a little nudge and suddenly you're off on another path."

Reflecting on the same thing, Niall sees it as "coming with Dave's steering of the ship. I'm concentrating on the synthesisers and the sequencing, to keep up with technology. Not to follow the trends of music, but the trends of music making; it currently falls to me to use what I'd consider to be cutting edge technologies, software and hardware, to make the band sound current, still. If I think about my writing for Hawkwind, the first thing I did was 'Green Machine', which is me playing lead guitar and playing synths [set-up] on my kitchen table. That follows on to some synths bits on *Onward*, and 'Lonely Moon' on *Spacehawks*, and then 'Harmonic Hall' on *The Machine Stops*, which again was done on my kitchen table, so it's an obvious choice, upon reflection, that my strongest input into the band has been my synthesis work."

It certainly feels as though *The Machine Stops* has set Hawkwind off on another path as well; when I interviewed the band in advance of the tour, Dave talked about it being something they'd feed off over the next 18 months, intending a live album, as with *Live Chronicles* and *Love in Space* before, consolidating the material and the concept in its development as a live set and then recording it to give it a facet beyond what had been done at the outset with the studio recordings. That's what it's all about in the end, a constantly evolving, changing, twisting and turning thing; perhaps that's why it means so much to its followers.

"Not knowing other bands they all must have similar things? Maybe not, I don't know," Brock reflects. Well, some do of course. The Levellers, New Model Army, and there are others, have an intensive, committed, tribal, fandom behind them. But Dave has done something unique, something very special indeed, across the decades with his band. "In a way it's quite a responsibility because people believe in what we're doing."

Afterword

The Captain.
(Oz Hardwick)

The 47th anniversary of that legendary Group X show at All Saints Hall recently arrived, with various Facebook users declaring it 'Hawkwind Day'. In the same month Dave Brock enjoyed his 75th birthday in the company of fans at Seaton Town Hall, scene of recent Easter-time Hawkfests, with the hall itself being declared as 'Brock Hall' in his honour. On his birthday, the previous year, he'd been performing with various Hawks and associates, as The Elves of Silbury Hill, at a charity afternoon in Weston-Super-Mare, where he was presented with a beautiful, one-off, and very moving hardbound book containing many fans' recollections of what his legacy has meant to them over the years. How fantastic that this musician, and so many others who've passed through the ranks, are still making music and delighting their followers with records that are warmly received by fans and in the music press.

Time moves always onwards though. The band has suffered tragedies, and has had to reflect on the passing of past members. In December 2012, Huw Lloyd-Langton lost a quiet and dignified battle against throat cancer at the age of only sixty-one. Earlier that year, one of his last public performances was alongside his great friend Dave Brock, in Sidmouth for an acoustic show in aid of the Devon Air Ambulance. Though ill-health had dogged him across several years, it came as a great shock to his fans, this writer included. I received the news by text from Frenchy Gloder after returning into central London following a nice lunchtime spent together chatting all things Flicknife and Hawkwind. Frenchy was clearly upset and shaken.

An iconic image of a wonderful musician.
Huw Lloyd-Langton, Ramsgate Marina, 1984
(Oz Hardwick)

Huw's legacy with Hawkwind is huge, and yet, like the man himself, understated. His playing on the eponymous first LP, that unique part of the catalogue, is a thing of joy, and I know that for Dave Brock, that album, and Huw's playing on it, is one of the things he's most proud of when he reflects on the achievements under the Hawkwind banner. "Huw was a wonderful lead guitarist with a style all of his own, he was an individual musician," he told me, reflecting the regard that he held this great musician in. Huw's return to the band for the *Levitation* album enlivened and refreshed the sound and he was a key

314

component of the group's sonic identity in the 80s. When he appeared on the 2001 tour it was a thrill for the audience, and even though it didn't herald a full-time resumption of membership, he continued to be in and around the band from there on, sometimes as a guest musician, sometimes as an acoustic support act, but always held in affection and respect.

His solo albums, usually under the Lloyd-Langton Group by-line and overlooked in comparison to his Hawkwind recordings, are an engaging catalogue that, as Brian Tawn once noted, rock on without getting heavy. The initial release under the LLG name, *Outside The Law*, is a rough and ready, bootleg quality, live recording, but its studio follow-up *Night Air* is a soft-rock triumph and all of his following LPs have much to recommend them, full of heart and feeling, as on 'For Whom The Bell Tolls' on *River Run* or 'Voices That Fade' from *Like An Arrow, Through The Heart*. At the same time, there are songs, such as 'Wars Are The Hobby There' that have a strong moral compass, and some delightfully delicate instrumental acoustic numbers that showcase his classical guitar skills, little gems scattered across his work.

Huw dipped in and out of Hawkwind over the years, filling-in occasionally after his original membership before re-joining in 1979 and staying with the band until the Robert Calvert memorial show of 1989, then reappearing many times afterwards. He clearly held an affection for the band that remained with him all his life. The same can be said of Lemmy who, having been dismissed in that notorious incident on the North America tour of 1975, constantly popped up as a live guest, even having Hawkwind as a support act on one major Wembley Motörhead show, and, of course, appearing on the 'Night of the Hawks' Flicknife EP. So much has been written about the great man that it's difficult to know what to add here, but as Frenchy Gloder noted in his own memoirs, despite transcending the band that brought him to prominence, Lemmy always continued to consider himself one of the Hawks, suggesting in interviews that had he not been sacked, he'd never have left.

Dave and Lemmy remained friends despite that hotel room sacking all those years ago. When Dave and Kris married at the 2007 Hawkfest, it was Lemmy who was intended to be the 'Best Man', announced on Motörhead's official website, but sadly not coming to fruition due to one of Lemmy's periods of ill-health. But that notion of them having an almost telepathic empathy during their time together in the band was the start of an enduring friendship built on shared experiences and respect for what each had achieved with their bands.

"It's taken me a long time to get over [Lemmy's passing]; still now when I think about it I get sad," says Alan Davey. "I've never grieved that long for anybody. But then, I wouldn't have what I've got now without him. His bass solo on 'Time We Left' grabbed my attention to a point where I went and got a bass. If he'd never done that, if I'd never heard that, what would I be doing now? I owe Lemmy everything. I would never have met my wife, Sarah, for instance, because we met at a Hawkwind gig, so that would never have happened! He taught me a lot, how to do things his way, how to set the amps... I've sat in his house with us playing basses together, 'how did you play that one, then?' And he'd pick up a bass and show me. Perhaps that's why I got the credit from him: Bass Assassin No. 2!"

His physical decline is well-documented; indeed, it was played-out in public in the last years of his life, particularly at the 2015 Glastonbury Festival but also at various gigs where mid-show he found himself unable to continue performing. For *Vive Le Rock* magazine, some months after Lemmy's death on 28th December 2015, I'd asked Dave about the difficulties of seeing an old friend in such circumstances. "In the end, when he was going on stage really ill and had to go off a few times, the fans didn't want to see that, in a way. I don't know what went on behind the scenes. I did speak to him a few times: 'time for the old pipe and slippers' ... 'bollocks!' He liked [guesting with Hawkwind] when we were at festivals. The best one was when we had some of Monster Magnet and Lemmy on; that was at a festival in Finland. There's a YouTube clip of that, quite a good one."

Alan too recalls that appearance in Finland as being very special, and reflects on the physical decline of a man who he held in such high esteem. "I went to a Wembley show a couple of years ago, went backstage to his dressing room and when I looked at him, and I hadn't seen him for four or five years, he looked all drawn and thin, and it was a difficult thing to see, to be honest. But he lived it full-throttle, a real rock musician, did it his own way and didn't pander to image and there's not many like that."

Coverage of Lemmy's death was substantial, as befitted a genuine rock music legend, and touched on his time with Hawkwind, with the BBC including a snippet of the classic 'Silver Machine' promotional film as part of their televised obituary. In their online reporting the BBC noted an interview Lemmy had given to *Classic Rock* where he'd considered the impact of joining Hawkwind. "In Hawkwind I became a good bass player. It was where I learned I was good at something." And they quoted a piece from a Finnish interview from back in 1988, on the longevity of Motörhead, though it might just as well have been his summing up of his own seemingly bulletproof constitution. "We're still here, because we should have died a long time ago but we didn't." Along with Keith Richards, he was the epitome of the great rock 'n' roll survivor and when cancer got hold of him very quickly you'd be forgiven for thinking that in the end Death had to get him, because rock 'n' roll never could.

Happier instances. Amongst the clutter and bric-a-brac, dogged-eared sci-fi paperbacks, photos, posters and memories that adorn Dave Brock's recording studio, the milking shed Aladdin's Cave, is a seriously heavy piece of metal that is the *Prog* magazine 'Lifetime Achievement Award', collected in September 2013. Presented by Matthew Wright, who described Dave as "a true god of rock, a man who represents the very essence of the underground and who, as a result, has never received the recognition he truly deserves," and who praised "his sharp ear for the unusual and intriguing chords," it was a genuine reflection of a life spent in the service of his musical vision. Dave accepted the award in his usual self-effacing way, highlighting the contributions of others and making special reference to the then recent losses of Huw Lloyd-Langton and John Harrison while hailing the younger generations of musicians he saw and heard as coming through.

That was a presentation that quite rightly recognised, as Matthew Wright noted, the Captain of the ship rather than its crew. It was for Dave's own achievements, his vision and his dedication. *Mojo* had already bestowed the band itself with their 'Maverick Award' back in 2010, putting them in company with previous winners such as The Fall and Manic Street Preachers, and presented by another long-time fan, Jarvis Cocker. "I think they are a bit like Halley's Comet in a way," pronounced Pulp's frontman and leader. "They're there travelling through the universe and just sometimes we can glimpse them here on Earth … they recorded, I think, the greatest live single of all time."

These awards are part of the overdue validation of Hawkwind's influence on the British music scene through the decades and across genres. It's not just by staying the course that they've defined their own genre while leading others to take inspiration from them into their own styles, whether that be psychedelic, heavy rock, punk, or even dance and trance. It's come from having someone at the helm whose deft hand on the tiller of the ship has steered it in many directions, seeking out new sounds and redefining what the band is about while staying true to its vision. Few bands have stepped outside of their remit, very few others have done so and stayed relevant across generations. What a fantastic achievement, now worthily honoured.

"Ultimately, don't forget, it's the wonderful Dave Brock's concept, Hawkwind," says Niall Hone. "You can pile as many ideas as you want into the band, but Dave will pick and choose the bits he wants. The choice of tracks, and the choice of elements within the tracks, stops with Dave. Dave has the overview. But he is very respectful of, and loyal to, other people's artistic abilities and I think he reflects that in the albums. I don't know where the original Dik-Mik and Del ideas came from in using the screaming oscillators but that is the thing that sets tracks such as 'Silver Machine' apart from all the other rock 'n' roll tracks of the time. I can remember being six or seven years old at Christmas time, at other people's parties, and my dad would be resident DJ and would always put 'Silver Machine' on. That pulsing, oscillating noise at the start was so recognisable to me as a kid. I was no different to any other kid at that age, so everyone must have thought, blimey… that's the weird band with the strange synths on! I don't know whose idea that was, but that must have been one of the genre defining moments of spacerock. Regardless of who started it, it was obviously Dave who turned around and went, '*That* is the sound. We need more of *that*. More oscillators, more echoes, vicar!' That is one of Dave's great gifts, he has this unwritten, overarching, concept of what the band, and what the genre, should sound like. A fabulous gift, coupled with hard work, but that is what I like about the guy, aside from his thousand other qualities! On a musical level, he's got a very strong direction. He won't suffer fools gladly, but he sticks to his guns through thick and thin, look at the Ginger Baker/Harvey Bainbridge argument. That's a testament to his loyalty, but also to his musical production ability to pick and choose, and guide the good spaceship forward."

That touches on one of the aspects that has made Hawkwind so interesting over the years, the continual throughput of members, whether they were coming, going or returning. Clearly this hasn't always happened by natural progression and certainly some former members feel they were in some way disappointed by their departure. Others have accepted their fate in a philosophical manner, while believing their line-up could have achieved more if given time to develop.

Nik Turner, even when accepting that the merry-go-round of contributors has kept Hawkwind fresh musically, is critical of the way this has been arrived at. "It might have been more interesting if it had been a natural progression rather than something Dave has engineered. I think a lot of people would have liked to have been more creative in Hawkwind but were held back by Dave. People have got ideas, but Dave does things his way."

There has been a more wide-ranging creative input to the band than Turner gives credit for. The music has never been about Brock alone; usually developing a distinctive sound for an era that could lead the listener to seeing the band as a revolving creative partnership, with Dave Brock always firmly at the helm. Brock and Calvert in the Charisma era for instance, Brock and Langton in the 1980s, with Davey into the 1990s, perhaps with Chadwick on the more techno-orientated material around *Distant Horizons*, though Richard's huge contribution to the band, I'd suggest, has been more talismanic than as a creative force in a writing sense. Adrian Shaw, who joined as that fantastic key part of the catalogue *Quark, Strangeness & Charm* was coming together, acknowledges that back then the band was open to all members contributing ideas. Ron Tree, nearly twenty years later, identified the same thing. So, I'd argue that it's always been a situation where the members of the day have an opportunity to add their bits to the direction of the band, even though it's clearly Brock's vision and guidance that's always been in the ascendancy.

"In a sense it is a co-operative but you've got to have a captain of the ship, otherwise it would never go anywhere," is how Brock would, quite rightly, sum-up the contrasting viewpoint to Turner's assertions. "Everyone who has ever been in this band has given their bits and pieces and made it interesting. Some people go off and do other things, or they don't like what's going on; that's just the way it is. Lots of people have gone on to do other things, been creative and famous, there's no big deal. Lemmy did good." There are lots of members who've used the experience of being part of the band to springboard to other things, though not many musicians have been bestowed with the curious fusion of iconic rock legend and national treasure status that Lemmy acquired. Some members had a notable career already, Ginger Baker and Arthur Brown in particular. Michael

318

Moorcock was a substantial figure in the SF world prior to Hawkwind – and he has become important literary figure. For Mike, Hawkwind was, I'm sure, and as Harvey Bainbridge suggests, something that was fun, an adjunct to his 'proper' work.

On 18th July, 2003 I sat in the summer sunshine with Nik Turner outside of his beloved 'Cadillac Ranch' in deepest Wales, looking out over the vast swathe of countryside, and had a great afternoon chatting for this book's original edition. "It's Dave's band," Nik conceded. "I finally realised that, having been sacked twice." From a man that had not only accepted but indeed revelled in the label of being 'the conscience of Hawkwind' it struck me then as a surprising admission. When did it stop being a collective and became one man's vision? "Maybe it always was, and one didn't realise. If I had thought it was Dave's band [at the outset] then I might have been happy to be in it for a while, but unhappy to not have an equal share in it." On many points throughout our afternoon together, Nik's responses came back to "because it is Dave's band."

Contrary to Nik's views, I was convinced then, that it would not have been possible for this band, with its revolving membership and shifting soundscapes, to exist more than thirty years without somebody being, in Brock's favourite expression, the "captain of the ship." I'm even more convinced of that a further ten years on. Nik, quite naturally, disagreed ("there are very many democratic sort of bands, where everybody has a say and there is complete creative freedom"), but when pressed as to how much influence, for example, Charlie Watts might have in the running of The Rolling Stones, he could only shrug. "It depends what people's choices are."

It's not unusual for bands to be dogged by disagreements that turn into rancour and deep-seated resentment that lingers for many years. Witness the aftermath of Paul Weller's break-up of the Jam. Tim Blake charts this in his experience playing with Gong and contrasts that with the historical schisms of Hawkwind: "There are a lot of similarities... but they're similarities inside any microcosm; similar histories develop, with, finally, similar outcomes! Both are groups that choose to show 'Tribal' or 'Family' values, though Hawkwind never lived as a community. Both groups have found it hard to pass from the state of collective to privately run organisations, without causing hurt and disbelief to certain members, both groups have found it hard to weather the storms of the music business sea."

Turner regularly returned to the theme of the creative freedom that he feels should be available in band set-ups. His willingness to become involved with a multitude of bands, many in the spacerock mould, others within the jazz scene, and with some of the key punk groups (The Stranglers, Sham 69) has given him a sort of "father figure" aura. "I went to the States in October 2002 with a band, they invited me to tour with them. I've done things with two or three bands in Finland and Norway, some tours in Sweden, things with a band in Germany. I just think it's nice for these guys to invite me to go and do a tour. Half the time I don't even need to rehearse with them, because they will do some of my songs which they've rehearsed off the record and I just turn up and play."

Aside from his numerous ad-hoc musical collaborations, and his own two groups (apart from Space Ritual, he has for many years played big band jazz with his Fantastic All-Stars combo), Turner pounds the beat as a busker: "I've got around to looking at it as just another gig, go down to Cardiff, set-up, play for three or four hours… make a couple of hundred quid!"

I've often had the impression that, musically, Nik has enjoyed a far more diverse life than Dave, but then I reflect how Brock has managed to fold-in so many of his music interests into the band that has been his life's work, seeking out those musicians who shared some of his own musical passions and adding their contributions to the mix. That's where the possibilities of Jason Stuart's tragically abbreviated involvement resonated so much with Dave's interests. But largely that's planned and structured, even if some of those contributions arrive through serendipity or circumstance. Early in my first interview with Nik, I'd suggested that his outlook is simply to get up in the morning with a "What's happening today?" mentality. He didn't disagree with this view. Dave, by contrast, has developed Hawkwind while still, and despite Turner's claims to the contrary, allowing the people around him their individual expression. Though the Brock canon now contains a string of enjoyable solo albums, the Hawkwind catalogue is his defining legacy.

I asked Matthew Wright for his take on this: "[Hawkwind] dates still sell out, the gigs are still really exciting, they're still really productive and I think it's almost as important for the band to know that there's still an audience that wants to hear from them and wants more material, not like a heritage act who jacked it in in 1969 and regenerated in 2014 and go around to squeeze a few quid out. Nik's bands, when I've seen them, have been under-rehearsed in comparison. This my Nik Turner thing: I've met Nik a few times, I've had Nik play at a mini free festival that I put on myself; he wasn't invited, he heard there was something going on, turned up and offered to play a set, for free, for the 150 or so souls that were left there down in Wales. He just heard there was a do happening and he was welcome to come along. He provided two and half hours of entertainment at no charge and was lovely and gorgeous to everybody at that event. That's my direct Nik Turner experience and I respect everything he did in his musical career back in the day. I think it's fair to say that Nik was more of your freeform and Dave was 'let's get this together.' You can start picking that up from 1972, '73; that sense is there. That's how they are musically, and I'd imagine that's slightly as they are as people, and if you've got someone who wants to play in a disciplined way, you rehearse lots of times, you become proficient at the songs and you're able to do interesting things. The other way is the Nik Turner way, you don't rehearse as much, you feel the vibe and you make it up on the night. Back in the 70s the audience might have even preferred the latter because that's the way things were. But for a modern audience I think it's completely the opposite way around and people expect to hear music played properly."

Turner's opinion is that Brock has done extremely well from his approach to running the band: "Look at what he's got, when he started out in a 'cold water' flat in Putney." But, Brock doesn't live the life of rock star with its substantial trappings. Instead, he's much more authentic, living in beautiful country surroundings in an old farmhouse that is far from being a rock star mansion, achieved by being sensible and respectful of what he's earned from his work, from the 'Silver Machine' royalties onwards, while having given his audience so much back in the value-added performances of his band. When you think about what the Hawkwind name means, it's still about that multi-media thing with the lightshows and the dancers, achieved on a budget, sometimes on a shoestring. When I first talked to Dave, he quite fairly was at pains to emphasise how much Hawkwind costs him personally, both financially and in terms of energy and commitment. "I give huge amounts of money and time to keep the whole thing going, because it's more than just a band to people. I go to a concert and I want everything to be perfect... I want to perform to the best of our ability." He opened up on this subject to an Internet questioner who asked about the way in which recording and touring with Hawkwind had affected his life: "It has caused a lot of problems. If you dedicate yourself to doing something for a long period of time, you suffer, there are penalties... people get very jealous with what you do for a living. It's hard work... not easy."

Despite his many gripes and complaints about the way in which he considers Brock has worked himself into the ownership of Hawkwind – and I don't buy into any idea other than it was always Dave's band, started alongside John Harrison and Mick Slattery, the founding members - Turner was still able to characterise him as, "A very nice guy, on one level: personable, sociable, obliging. Otherwise I'd never have got involved with him myself, you know? In the early days, I thought he was a really cool guy, we used to hang-out, I'd stay at his house, we'd take acid together..." When I rang Dave in the initial stages of writing this book and mentioned that I was meeting Turner for my first interview with him, Dave was very quick to tell me how much I'd enjoy talking to Nik, that he considered him a "very charming man."

All that arms-length good commentary on each other, albeit no doubt delivered through gritted teeth caused by the xHawkwind debacle, has long since evaporated. These days there's not a stage been built that's big enough for them both to share. The most skilled of diplomats would find it a thankless and unachievable task if assigned to bring them back together. It's public domain information that, at the time of writing, there is another legal minefield opened-up over Nik's use of the Hawkwind name in concerts played in North America, a case in front of the US courts that has dragged-on for an extended period and which, because it has not reached conclusion, this biographer is not willing or able to start describing for this book.

I absolutely stand by what I'd noted in this book's original edition, that the legal tussles have left not only a sour taste within the membership of the band, past and current, but also divided the fans. I can see that there will always be an element that identifies strongly with the original crew and outlook of spaceship Hawkwind and who see Turner's attempts to trade on the band's name as a legitimate reward for his early input. Let me say, I don't agree with the way that they see things, as much as I am a fan of Nik's work with the band, with Inner City Unit, and on his own albums, and as much as I've enjoyed meeting him and interviewing him on several occasions where he has been kind and generous with his time. On Dave's side, there is a following that has grown up with the band and come together in the new tribal way of the 21st Century, through the Internet and social media, initially via Yahoo forums and mail server newsgroups, and now via some wonderful Facebook groups. There, fans have continued to expand the family of Hawkwind, building on that dual sense of self-reliance and the need to be looking out for others that's wrapped up in the ethos of the band from its outset, right through to today. In that way, and for both sides of the divide, a Hawkwind show is a chance to rekindle and expand on old and new friendships as much as it is an opportunity to watch and listen to our favourite band.

Who'd have thought, all these years and decades on from their first Group X performances at the end of the 1960s that there would still be a resonance and these ideas. "It still retains the integrity of the original vision," says Richard Chadwick. "Making music that wasn't the same as everything else, that was more about rhythm and mood. And it still has that way of being lyrically provocative. Perhaps not to the same degree when you had really talented writers such as Calvert, but it still retains that on the edge, rebellious streak. Poking at society, saying 'what about this, what about that?'"

Perhaps that's the legacy thing that Dave Brock, self-deprecating about his core achievement of creating something that has stood the tests and challenges of time, finds so difficult to quantify and talk about. A vital component of the counterculture of the 70s that has maintained its relevance across the years, having influences on, and an input into, the music scene as that scene itself has developed, morphed, changed. Never fashion, never out of fashion, as they say, but heartening that successive scenes have sought out Hawkwind's music and found something embedded in it that they can further twist and develop in a proper validation of this great band.

About the Author:

Ian Abrahams is the author of *Hawkwind: Sonic Assassins*, *Strange Boat – Mike Scott & The Waterboys* and, with Bridget Wishart, *Festivalized: Music, Politics & The Alternative Culture*. He has also written for *Record Collector*, *R2*, *Shindig!*, *Vive Le Rock*, *The Guardian*, *The Independent* and others. He lives in his native Cornwall and has two retired greyhounds who've never been to a muddy festival, tied on the end of a string.

Connect with me:

twitter.com/Abrahams_Ian
facebook.com/ianabrahams.musicjournalist
space-rockreviews.blogspot.com
sonicassassins-book.blogspot.com